nobody's home

nobody's home

DREAMS AND REALITIES
IN A NEW SUBURB

LYN RICHARDS

OXFORD
UNIVERSITY PRESS

Melbourne
Oxford   Auckland   New York

The author and publisher are grateful to Mr Michael Leunig for allowing the use of the illustration on the front cover.

OXFORD UNIVERSITY PRESS AUSTRALIA

Oxford   New York   Toronto
Delhi   Bombay   Calcutta   Madras   Karachi
Petaling Jaya   Singapore   Hong Kong   Tokyo
Nairobi   Dar es Salaam   Cape Town
Melbourne   Auckland
and associated companies in
Berlin   Ibadan

HT
149
A8
R52
1990

National Library of Australia
Cataloguing-in-Publication data:

Richards, Lyn, 1944— .
    Nobody's home : dreams and realities in a new suburb.

    Bibliography.
    Includes index.
    ISBN 0 19 554761 6.

    1. Sociology, Urban—Australia.   2. Planned communities—
Australia.   3. Social surveys—Australia.   4. Home ownership—Social
aspects—Australia.   5. Family Social aspects—Australia.   6. Women
—Australia—Social conditions.   I. Title.

307.760994

Typeset by Setrite Typesetters, Hong Kong
Printed in Hong Kong by Condor Production Ltd.
Published by Oxford University Press,
253 Normanby Road, South Melbourne, Australia

Contents

Introduction

The Making of a Study

The title of this book was easy to find; when the research team was first interviewing in Green Views it kept recurring: 'You can't do interviews out here, nobody's home'. The observation was false of course (though the warning of problems with surveys was only too true). But it encapsulated the feelings about this modern estate, and it took on new meaning as new themes began to dominate the study about the private home and the 'family community' of home owners. The title contains the tangle of themes that emerged and which make it hard to summarize the contents of the book.

The book is a community study, but not as that term is normally understood. It is a study of the idea of community and the ways it meshes with ideas of family and home, their combined power to dominate behaviour, and people's ability to make sense of the contradictions they contain. Part I is about the setting—physical, social and ideological—of this smart new housing estate, geographically isolated, sold as a better area in a process of land development the residents rarely questioned; about their purchase decisions, their social maps and their dreams. It tackles the apparent homogeneity of the suburb, examining the dividers of life stage, life chances and gender. It explores the inequality and discrimination, and the power of ideology to mask both: 'anyone can belong', the migrants 'don't matter', so long as 'we're all in the same boat'.

It is a family study, but not of the *range* of family lives lived in Australia. Very deliberately the project set out to study the nuclear family where it was most clearly established, and most clearly changing—in home-owning suburbia. But this book does not report data on family task-sharing or family budgets or marital dynamics. It is about the idea of the Family, family goals and what is becoming of them, the privacy of family life and what it means. It is also a study of home ownership, not by original design but because people's accounts of family always involved ideas of the home. It tackles the task of untangling the linked ideas of family and home, and seeking the ways they work as explanations of social life. It explores those links through two themes identified in the critical litera- ture on family—the separation of private and public spheres and the unquestioning assumption that there are proper paths through adult life. It examines residents' accounts for evidence of how dominant, interconnected and powerful those linked ideas are in this setting, and whether they operate as ideology, where and how they are changing, how people negotiate with ideology and with what social results.

It is a network study; in Part II those social results are examined in patterns of friendship and loneliness. Data on kin links and local networks were crucial in that analysis. I argue that the study of networks makes sense only in the ideological context of those networks, and that people's webs of relation- ships must be seen as constantly changing processes, not static patterns. Network management is stressed, seen here as a way of negotiating with ideology and a result of such negotiation. The critique of suburbia is examined in this context. Who is isolated? Who wants community? The incompatibility of privacy and community is explored. Patterns of neighbouring are re- lated to the dividers of life stage, class, gender. Neighbouring is explored through people's behaviour and their words. What emerges is a two-faced picture of neighbours, in which a good neighbour is 'there when you need them but not in your pocket'. The data show an ideology of neighbouring linked into ideologies of family and home; people test and negotiate with those ideologies as their needs for support change.

It is also a women's study, in several senses. It is most obviously a study by women and its central themes are raised and debated in feminist writing. It is strongly influenced by women's writing on sociological methods.[1] It emphasizes the acitivities and ideas of women more than those of men for several reasons: they are often the stuff of suburban life, they are central to understanding the web of ideas of family, and they have been splendidly ignored in past community studies.[2] But it is a women's study of both women and men, as couples and as participants in the making and remaking of ideology. It emphasizes the variety of women's experiences rather than assuming they are the same. It takes the denunciations of dominant ideology in patriarchal society as questions, and the dichotomies of private and public world—hers and his, home and work, suburbia and urban life—as problems. The final chapters explore the sense and the contradictions in the assumptions about the family community: 'Your fault if you're lonely', fund-raising is not work. The book looks at women as creators and custodians of family goals and family privacy, exploring the gender differences in the apparently unpatterned ideologies. Her dream of the home is very different from his, her idea of community from his, there are different meanings for her and him of privacy, security, the need for neighbours and their danger.

The analysis stresses the ways the dividers of life stage, life chances and gender interact, and ends up arguing that the greatest of these is gender. It shows women as bound to the wheel of the life cycle, whose movement inevitably alters their opportunities, constraints and resources for network management. Picturing a women's sphere not in the private home, it questions assumptions built into feminist critiques, as well as in that most male of sociological preserves, community studies. In what sense is suburbia feminine? How alike are women's worlds, and how private? Do local friendships happen through the children? Is neighbouring always a residual relationship? The research project set out to hear women's words and see women's work in places where sociology has persistently not heard or seen them—on cake stalls and in playgroups as well as in the home. The study of women's lives was central to making sense of the contradictions of a self-styled 'family community' in which one of the most common comments is 'nobody's home'.

Somebody's data: The methods

This book is the result of many social processes: those by which the suburb I have called Green Views grew, those by which people negotiated with the ideologies it expressed, and those by which researchers and residents made data and constructed ways of seeing it. Its presentation is governed by the conviction that data are constructed in interaction between researchers and researched, and keep changing. Researchers can extract few unchanging objective 'truths' from a studied setting (and the available ones are generally uninteresting). Their task is to do their best to understand and keep on interpreting what is going on and the meanings people put on socially constructed reality.

That conviction sets several requirements of presentation that are often violated in sociological books and may make this one look a little odd. Researchers who participated in making the data are named here, and the processes of interpretation are documented in notes where that seems important. I avoid the term 'respondent' since it implies a one-way model of interviewing processes that is obviously false. I also avoid the distancing techniques of referring to myself as 'the researcher' or 'the author'. It seems to me important to note research processes in the context of a report, rather than relegate them to the reflections appearing in in-group show-and-tell papers years after. Research diaries and team discussions are quoted here as data, since that is what they are, and notes carry the story of shifting interpretation.

For a study that acquired such vast quantities of survey data this book relies very little on statistics. This is not from any lack of commitment to quantitative methods; indeed the study represents the belief that quantitative analysis is often essential. But it is the qualitative data that drives the analysis. During the five-year project there were several points at which the themes emerging as 'core categories' in the qualitative material at last made sense of puzzles in the survey data. I have attempted to tell how that happened rather than fudge the result as though I had always tidily hypothesized it.

The project was designed as a longitudinal community study for portraying current family life in suburbia. The emphasis was on the social context of the family rather than on internal dynamics; my previous work had convinced me that family values could not be studied in isolation from an understanding of the social setting.[3] People's accounts turned it into a study of ideology, and current critical writing on family and women turned it towards a study of ideological traps. But even after these major shifts I did not interpret the data then as I do now.

My first interpretation of the mounting data is indicated in a paper delivered at a conference on family change in 1979 and titled 'The impossible dream'.[4] It presented a modern tragedy of contradiction between still-dominant patriarchal ideology and the necessity of home ownership for family life. I think it important to stress that (for reasons I explore in chapter 7) I now see that interpretation as plainly wrong. It provides a good example of how a theme can take hold of the analysis if it is projected by favoured theory and not subjected to rigorous analytic procedures.[5] It is easy to explain that interpretation. It was happily consistent with feminist critiques of dominant family ideology in suburbia and socialist critiques of home ownership; critical rethinks of both those arguments have happened since. At this point we were in the survey of Stage 3 of the estate's development, dominated by the vulnerability of the younger and less resourced purchasers there. And Green Views too was at an early stage, the processes of women 'dropping out' of the workforce to have babies had only begun, and their complex responses to that experience were not yet evident. Moreover, the tragic-contradiction argument was popular and easy to present: it was not criticized at that conference or by the media giving it attention. Most crucially, we had no methodological answer to the challenges of exploring ideology; we were just beginning to confront the problems of our inability to do exacting analysis of the unstructured data.

So that first interpretation was challenged not by theory or by professional audiences but by people's accounts, aided by the development of methods for the rigorous analysis of them. The data were not just about a single dominant ideology and resultant homogeneity, rather about a number of ideological webs masking a variety of life chances and lives. And the data did not support a simple revelation of inevitable social problems and false consciousness; to take that interpretation would be to deny the evident contentment and achievement of many people, their evident agency in reworking and working within ideological constraints, the complexity of the problems they faced and their battles to find ways out.

In much of the analysis here I have explored forms of interplay between data in words and in statistics—qualitative and quantitative data. One result of this project was my becoming convinced that in many areas, and the exploration of ideology is certainly one, such interplay is methodologically required. That not only queries the traditional dichotomy of methods but also argues for the recording of at least some data in a variety of forms, precoding but then taping replies, for instance, so that patterns of responses can show dominance of ideas while thematic analysis explores multiple meanings in them. Quantitative methods can establish the extent and patterning of the acceptance of ideas and importantly whether they can be treated as sets. Such methods can also tap the accessibility of 'knowledge' by locating the order of answers and patterns in data: one way of finding instant answers taken off-the-peg, the social equivalent of the ready-made suit and the indicator of ideology at work.

Qualitative analysis allows the investigation of how ideas fit together in people's accounts and behaviour, the range of meanings put on them, the relationship between ideas and action, and the processes by which people remake ideology. I emphasize here discovery of recurring themes, phrases repeated unquestioningly, confusion of ideas, equation of apparently dissonant ones, clichés which people expect will call up a set of related ideas. Such recurring themes—I shall call them 'keywords'—access modular knowledge which I argue is a sign of ideology at work. They also appear, or are heard, after the schedule has been designed! Much of the analysis here is halted by inaccessibility of the required statistical data: this is particularly true of the search for ways people negotiate with traditional family ideology. And the quicksand becomes more treacherous, of course, as the qualitative analysis undermines the assumptions about meanings which informed the schedule wording and precoding. The variables I do have as indicators of meanings of home and traditional family ideas all proved to carry multiple, gendered and highly fluid meanings.

For the present study the unstructured data proved more reliable than the quantitative. One reason for the dubious status of much qualitative methodology is the apparently *ad hoc* analysis process and the persistent silence on the ways data were handled. This study was designed to rely heavily on unstructured data, but the early years were to be taken up by surveys to acquire base data. The unstructured records from the five-year project would build up from tapes of interviews, participant observation and researcher fieldnotes and diaries. Those records were to be typed, wherever possible, and techniques developed for coding them in an emerging index system during the first years of the project. The goal was to index sufficiently thoroughly to be able to retrieve systematically across the body of data, but to maintain an index system that was flexible enough to incorporate new insights emerging from the data and *in vivo* codes.[6] Clerically, I was developing a version of the cut-and-copy filling system reinvented by most qualitative researchers in the 1970s.

In the second year of the project it was evident that the ceilings to such methods had been reached. Restrictions on the size and number of records that could be handled, the complexity of the index system and detail of coding were obvious, and the ability to recognize and incorporate the new conceptual categories emerging from the data was hobbled. The result was a project for development of computer-assisted techniques for concept-based qualitative data analysis, techniques that, unlike most software available, built on what social scientists did rather than imposing what computer scientists would prefer them to do. The package of programs was designed for Nonnumerical Unstructured Data Indexing, Searching and Theorizing, from which goals it gets its name.[7] The NUDIST system offers the ability to construct complex indexes, accepts details of coding not possible by manual means, and searches text in ways that combine aspects of quantitative and qualitative analysis, which allow the researcher to build and explore grounded-theoretical structures from which the relevant text can be retrieved instantly.

Most reports of computer techniques for qualitative analysis share with vacuum-cleaner advertisements the ability to make a messy process suddenly elegant and instant.[8] Experience with NUDIST, on this and other projects, indicates that the new approach challenges at each stage. Effects on research design and indexing are crucial. A major frustration of this project was that years of data collection had been designed for the hard metal sides of a filing cabinet; research design to take advantage of the computer would be different in many ways. There is no need, for instance, to do surreptitious structuring of 'unstructured' data as a guard against chaos: the computer will receive text and coding of it in any order, then reorder, sift through and locate it as required. And there is no need to compromise the goals of grounded theory by narrowing enquiry to cupboard hypotheses in order to keep a research assistant.

Effects on indexing are dramatic. Creating a good index

structure is always difficult;[9] given such freedom it becomes a major challenge. Indexing is a process which must now be recognized as requiring training.[10] The researcher's instinct is to parsimony, restricting indexing to the fewest possible categories to save time, trouble, money and human relations. NUDIST seeks variety and intricacy of index categories. It also thrives on detail and complexity of coding that are of a different kind from those used in any manual sytem. The novelty is not just in being able to do *more* coding, with *more* categories, but in being able to code different ways and handle different units, to retrieve in search patterns that involve unlimited combinations of codings, to build on those and explore them further.

The many areas of sociology where this book can be placed warn about the numerous areas of literature it draws on. I have tried to lessen the weightiness of frequent references by use of clustered chapter notes, but am aware that this technique draws off the theoretical argument. I have where possible referred to literature reviews available elsewhere and to recent summaries.

The requirement that data be seen as 'somebody's' affects presentation in several ways. Since people's words are integral to the analysis they are incorporated in the text as often as presented in block quotation, and transcripts are verbatim. I have also attempted to weave through the book the experience of a few people whose stories link the themes, to give context and setting to their words rather than have them stand just as important quotes. Where central claims are made on the basis of recurrence of words or themes I have noted how often and where the themes do not occur: the cost of such 'quasi-statistics' is not only the annoyance of detail but the loss of the convenient conviction that a quote represents all the material. The gain is that analysis can be justified properly by unstructured data. All quoted words are from direct transcription of tapes or write-ins on schedules, or from research notes and diaries. Where words are deleted this is indicated with ellipses. All names used, except those of the researchers, are pseudonyms, as of course is 'Green Views'.

When survey data are reported it is in the context of the wording of questions (given in footnotes). It is my strong belief that the first response to any statistical data in social sciences should be to ask 'Who asked what of whom — and in what setting?'. The second should be to ask how the answer was recorded. If precodings or postcodings are used to achieve statistical patterns readers need to know what those codings are and whether they were invented a priori by the researcher or reflect the patterns of answers. If wording of answers is analysed, how were those words retrieved from the past?

Some further rules follow. When statistical significance is claimed it must be explicit what questions and what codings of answers achieved it, and since recodes ultimately can achieve statistical significance for anything, they must always be justified. Published working papers are available from the Department of Sociology, La Trobe University, and copies of the question-naires from me. Throughout this book I have used the convention of accepting a probability level of .05, and to avoid myriad notes I have referred to that level of significance as 'significant association' and to any level higher than .01 as 'very significant'.

The majority of survey data used in this book derives from a random sample of 80 per cent of available house lots in Stage 1 of the development in 1978, a few months after the first houses were occupied in the bare paddocks. A total of 617 lots were available, 318 of them occupied.[11] A 71 per cent response rate was achieved despite a high proportion of households where contact was very difficult (since nobody was home!). The refusal rate was 7 per cent. At each household a random selection was made to decide whether a man or woman was interviewed, and the equal proportions of women and men (even in specific life stages) remained in 1981. In that year those who had said they would be prepared to do a second interview were approached; 150 reinterviews were conducted. There are two other sources of survey data in the project. In 1979 a further survey was conducted of a random sample of the first homes occupied in Stage 3. During the five years of data collection an attempt was made to contact and interview all people leaving the estate; 35 semi-structured interviews were conducted and taped. All statistical analysis was done using SPSS.

Unless otherwise specified, 'the sample' refers to the Stage 1 reinterview sample of 150 people. A section of that interview was taped and transcribed from all interviews; and the whole interview taped when it was with one of the residents who had been active in the group processes (35 of this sample.) These tapes form a tiny fraction of the qualitative data available, but for many purposes the most precious, since they allow systematic analysis of the patterns of response across the sample and combinations of qualitative and quantitative methods. Three other major sources provided unstructured data. During the five years of data collection unstructured interviewing and participant observation produced tapes and notes that were transcribed. The survey of 'leavers' was totally taped. And in 1983 twenty very long semi-structured interviews with group leaders were taped and transcribed.

Acknowledgements

This book goes to press ten years after the first houses appeared in the paddocks at Green Views, so it has accrued ten years of debts. The obvious debt is to Jan Salmon, Project Coordinator from 1978 to 1983, and variously organizing secretary of women's groups in the estate, source of knowledge to student classes, friend to Green Views and to me. In the book, 'we' refers to our joint efforts. My analysis draws on Jan's administration of the surveys, her management of statistical data, her participation in almost all local groups during those five years, and her conduct of unstructured interviews. She made of the project much more than a five-year job and kept it alive during long periods when I was seriously ill and absent.

Many others have come and gone in the research team, and are named in earlier reports. The Project Committee in the early years included Herb Bisno, Don Edgar, Les Kilmartin, Sue Harvey; my thanks for their encouragement and ideas. Funding was provided by the Australian Research Grants Committee and La Trobe University School of Social Sciences. Less official was the contribution of students in my sociology classes, who criticized and test-drove my ideas. I want to thank especially the year of 1981, a good vintage for researchers. Much of the data is *theirs*. They participated in all stages of the reinterview project, conducted observation projects in several areas, made me see things differently. Many are named in this book, where I use their reports directly: all contributed. Thanks are due also to my graduate students over those years, and especially to Helen Marshall for accepting the challenge of making 'ideology' into a research tool; and her research insights into processes of negotiation with ideology. Other women colleagues offered insights and suppost—particular thanks to Kerreen Reiger, Janet Finch, and Jasmine Gazic.

Most obviously, I owe an enormous debt to the anonymous residents of Green Views. In the years of research we made every effort to minimize our impact on the estate, while making sure our presence was very openly acknowledged. We met a range of responses, from curiosity through to very warm friendships, but virtually never hostility or rejection. I cannot name those who offered the most time and interest and contributed their experiences and very personal insights, but I hope they will accept my gratitude and approve of my reporting. I hope they will continue to discuss my interpretations with me. Thanks are also due to 'outsiders' who talked or listened; local professionals, employees of developers, estate agents and state and local government politicians.

Debts to colleagues are many. As I worked through the data I was reminded constantly of my debt to Jean Martin. As supervisor of my first efforts with unstructured data, she taught me to listen and recall; as a rigorous researcher she contributed substantially to the strong tradition of qualitative data analysis in Australia and insisted on the need to integrate qualitative and quantitative methods. An inspiring colleague, she was the early source of fascination with networks as human constructs, women's lives as sociology, the significance of local relationships and the recognition that 'a man's not a neighbour'.

Several colleagues have read this book in part, and I thank Helen Marshall and Peter d'Abbs for comments on sections, David Morgan for reading the whole and still encouraging. David Hickman tested and challenged my ideas over years of co-supervision, and rigorously criticized large slabs of manuscript. Publishers' readers offered valuable advice. Barbara Matthews did final word-processing. Angela Gundert's elegant editing, and the attentions of Louise Sweetland and Yvonne White at Oxford University Press saw the book through a long publishing process. My thanks to them all.

I want to thank my own very non-nuclear family for splendid support and friendship during the long years of this project, for being there when needed in what really is a family community. To Naomi and Marshall, my thanks for accepting my version of motherhood and understanding my commitment to this project that has taken more than half their lives and much of my time.

Finally, my debt to NUDIST. Without it, of course, the Green Views project would have been wound up much sooner, as we reached the ceilings imposed by manual handling of unstructured records. But being able to go on, and go on questioning, is a risk wholly rewarded. Less rewarding were the costs of pioneering; as the development project, we paid a price in delays, flounderings. In all this, one of my debts is to Lynne Sherwood, the human, unfailingly skilled interface between academic goals and machine responses.

The book is dedicated to Tom Richards, as co-author of NUDIST, a cross-disciplinary research colleague prepared to take up the challenge of designing software that freed qualitative methods of constraints rather than creating new ones, and then to keep exploring new possibilities.

Notes

1. See for example H. Roberts (ed.), *Doing Feminist Research*, Routledge & Kegan Paul, London, 1981; M. Eichler, *Nonsexist Research Methods*, Allen & Unwin, London, 1988.

2. See F. Gale, 'Seeing women in the landscape: Alternative views of the world around us', in J. Goodnow & C. Pateman (eds), *Women, Social Science and Public Policy*, Allen & Unwin, Sydney, 1985.

3. That project, conducted for the Royal Commission on Human Relationships in 1975−6, led to the publication of my *Having Families*, Penguin, Ringwood, in 1978 (rev. edn 1985) and, with Jan Harper, whose project was conducted in the same years, of *Mothers and Working Mothers*, Penguin, Ringwood, in 1979 (rev. edn 1986). The Green Views project was launched before the second book was published.

4. L. Richards, 'The impossible dream', in D. Davis (ed.), *Living Together*, Centre for Continuing Education, Canberra, 1980.

5. For spirited discussion of these problems see M. Miles & M. Huberman, *Qualitative Data Analysis*, Sage, Beverley Hills, Calif., 1983. Such discussions are relatively recent; in retrospect I find it interesting that in the same year I gave an informal paper, in the context of the *Having Families* research, in Queensland, worrying about the excitement and power of thematic analysis and the ability of a theme to take hold of the data, 'so you see it everywhere rather as, when you're pregnant, the world becomes full of pregnant women'. My concern in that paper was to rethink the analysis in *Having Families* and the ways the ghost of the 'old' good mother dominated that analysis. Years later, in handling the Green Views data on family, it got me again—because the resilience of those old ideas had so impressed in the earlier study that I heard them first and took some time to realize they were in ideas of motherhood but not in ideas of family life (see chs 8−9).

6. Like most researchers I had developed my own techniques for manual coding and retrieval and suffered from the silence on techniques of data handling in this area. See L. Richards & T. Richards, 'Qualitative data analysis: Can computers do it?', *Australian and New Zealand Journal of Sociology*, vol. 23, 1987, pp. 23−25. My techniques were adapted from approaches derived in the first instance from the teaching and example of Jean Martin, and strongly influenced by the writings of B. Glaser & A. Strauss, especially *The Discovery of Grounded Theory*, Aldine Publishing Co., Chicago, 1965, more recently presented as a far more practical guide to a method of analysis in A. Strauss, *Qualitative Analysis for Social Scientists*, Cambridge University Press, London, 1987.

7. See Richards and Richards, *Australian and New Zealand Journal*

of Sociology, pp. 23–35; T. Richards and L. Richards, 'NUDIST: a system for qualitative data analysis', *ACS Bulletin*, October 1988, pp. 5–9; T. Richards & L. Richards, *User Manual for NUDIST: A Text Analysis Program for the Social Sciences*, 2nd edn, Replee, Melbourne, 1987.

8. For down-to-earth exceptions the columns of E. M. Gerson in *Qualitative Sociology* are recommended; see E. M. Gerson, 'Computing in qualitative sociology', *Qualitative Sociology*, vol. 7, 1985, pp. 1–2, and 'Where do we go from here?', *Qualitative Sociology*, vol. 9, 1985, pp. 208–14.

9. Miles & Huberman, *Qualitative Data Analysis*.

10. L. Richards & T. Richards, The impact of computer techniques on qualitative data analysis, Paper to the Social Science Research Conference, Brisbane, 1988.

11. See J. Salmon & L. Richards, The Green Views Project, Report to La Trobe University, Bundoora, Vic., 1980.

Part I

The Making of a Suburb

1

Package Dreams

A warm spring afternoon on the hill overlooking the first thousand houses of the shiny-clean new suburb. The gardens are green now, trees up to door-height, oddly juxtaposed to the few massive old eucalypts left from the farmland the subdivision acquired. Heaps of topsoil spill over the footpaths and the concrete cross-overs to driveways (notoriously not funded by the developer). Patterned uniformity of house type is broken by carefully varied designs; from up here the currently fashionable dark grey tiles predominate, a few red, no metal roofs. No overhead power lines, clear; pretty views to distant hills and equally distant city. We have been talking after a late lunch in the nearly-empty new pub in the new, very empty shopping centre, and now as the agenda runs out we notice the silence. Nothing moves: not a dog or a child or a car, not a person. 'It's like the scene from *On the Beach*—after the bomb', I write later in my diary: 'Perfect homes, neatly new, packages for families that aren't there'. We stay talking until the school bus arrives; at this stage we have seen three women moving around in two hours. Now there are cars coming in; a few going out. The bus loops the estate, figures dropping off it, fanning out to houses, disappearing. Some reappear to play in the sun, one group dashing up our hill with a wildly excited dog.

W: When we first moved in and there was nobody around, it was like living in bush. We were one of the first families to move in and it was just—no hassles, no people, no fuss, no noise and it was beautiful.

It has become suburbia, but ... I think Green Views is going to be a beautiful suburb when it is finished, and I do like no power lines.[1]

M: Our life, no, I don't think it changed. We've got the same pattern since we came here; we still go to work, back, do this, do that, a bit of social life. But more peaceful here, I like that ... First, we haven't got traffic through Green Views. Second, everybody—most of the people here—work all day, so when coming the night, it's just inside the house, and you don't see their nose.

W: I hated Green Views. We had no side fences and no neighbours, we were in here for seven weeks before next doors' moved in. There wasn't any houses over the road I could see—there was nothing in front of us ... Nobody in any of these houses at the back either side of the court. There was nobody. I could go out of a night time and not see a light, and I hated it ... Lonely, I suppose, very. And not knowing this area—like I didn't know this side of town at all ... He worked seven days a week at that stage.

Who came?

Drive past it now and Green Views looks like all stereotypes of modern housing estates. On the fringe of the suburbs, it bordered open farmland when the first residents moved in; newer estates now invade that green space. Undulating land was for sale in Stage 1; trees were left standing in at least some areas. Design emphasized courts and crescents, advertising stressed style of life, family community and country atmosphere. It looks as though it epitomizes a life-style: indeed one of the slogans with which it was sold includes 'a better way of life'. A high green fence surrounding the estate was from the start a symbol of Green Views and an issue for residents. To those who liked it, and those who did not, the Fence suggested both exclusiveness and a sense of belonging, a better way of life and a shared one.

But the people who came were not nearly so alike as their houses appeared, or as the developers, and many of the purchasers, would have liked. In 1978, using a random sample of lot numbers, we interviewed 220 of the first residents (equal numbers of women and men). Three years later we reinterviewed the 150 people still in Green Views and available.[2] From these and other surveys, and five years' interviewing and participation in the estate, we put together a picture of the residents and their values. It shows much less homogeneity than expected by the developers, the residents, or the researchers!

The picture was uniform in three crucial respects. First, the family ruled; virtually everyone in Green Views was married and either had or intended to have children.[3] The shire secretary described them simply as 'family people'. And this was one sort of family: though 88 respondents said they had responsibility for others outside their nuclear family, only four households contained others, in all cases a parent.[4] Secondly, home ownership dominated. Renting in Green Views was highly unusual and unpopular.[5] We interviewed several renters during the project, but there were none in the 1981 sample, and only 11 of the 150 had seriously considered *not* purchasing a home. All but five said it was very important to them to own their own home. Suggestions by social consultants and local interests during the development process that rental housing be included were apparently not seriously considered. They would certainly have been opposed by residents. 'At one stage we were scared when there were plans to put up cluster homes', a young man remarked, explaining, 'We don't really have people running round late at night, making lots of noises in your neighbourhood. We prefer to have family type of people around'.

But the uniformity of nuclear families in their 'own home' covered considerable differences. The obvious dividers were age and stage of family life.[6] This was a young population: in 1981, 40 per cent of our sample were still under 31; two-thirds under 36. Nearly half had been married less than five years. All of these but one couple either had or said they intended to have children, and by the reinterview most had started the process. Only 15 per cent of the reinterview sample were still childless (40 per cent had been in 1978). As fig. 1 shows, the largest category was new families with *only* pre-school children and almost exactly half had a pre-school child. But over a third were past the stages of toddlers in playgrounds. And just over a third, mostly the same people of course, had owned or been purchasing a home before the move.

Across these life stage patterns were overlaid differences in those factors—income, jobs and education—which indicate life chances. Nearly everyone had a mortgage. Only 5 per cent of the 1978 sample owned homes outright, while 13 per cent had two or more mortgages, and these were normally higher-cost

Fig. 1   Sample Characteristics

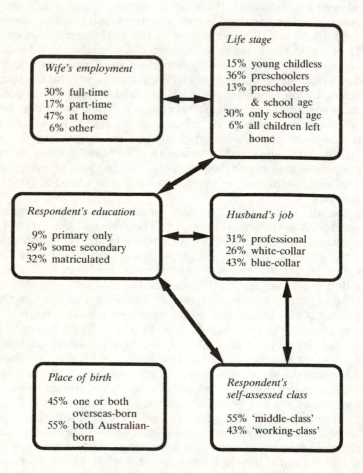

Reinterview 1981
n = 150
(Arrows indicate statistically significant association)

Wife's employment

30% full-time
17% part-time
47% at home
6% other

Life stage

15% young childless
36% preschoolers
13% preschoolers
& school age
30% only school age
6% all children left
home

Respondent's education

9% primary only
59% some secondary
32% matriculated

Husband's job

31% professional
26% white-collar
43% blue-collar

Place of birth

45% one or both
overseas-born
55% both Australian-
born

Respondent's self-assessed class

55% 'middle-class'
43% 'working-class'

finance.[7] Because it was much harder to finance land and house-building separately, all but 8 per cent had bought a 'house-land package', selecting one house style and land 'block' from a builder's range. The average cost of this in 1978 was $45 120 (the range being from $38 000 to $68 250)[8] and the average monthly instalment $281. These instalments were highest for those with teenage children: half of these had payments over $300, though none had second mortgages. For most people the houses represented the overwhelming commitment of family income. More than a quarter of the gross combined income of the household was going on housing in 24 per cent of cases and, we estimated, more than a quarter of *net* (after tax) income in 65 per cent of cases.[9]

The figures clearly demonstrate the vital importance of the second income.[10] Hers was always second, both in the sense that all women earned far less than their spouses and that the women's paid work was far more likely than the men's to be interrupted. In 1978, less than a third of the women were at home in our sample households; 88 per cent of women without children and 39 per cent of mothers were working full-time. Only 2 per cent of those without children, but 19 per cent of mothers, worked part-time. By 1981 the young ones were 'dropping out' of the workforce to have first babies, and in exactly half those houses there was a woman not in the paid workforce (though many of these were earning money for work they did at home).[11] Only 30 per cent of households had a woman in full-time employment.[12] In another 17 per cent she worked part-time; in more than half, then, she was 'home'. So it was not true that 'everybody works', except in the feminist recognition of the work of domestic labour—and *nobody* used the phrase in that sense. But the phrase recurred: 'Most parents are working here. They all work', said one of the women at home. 'I really can't put the way I feel about that'.

As the women 'dropped out', the difference between single and dual-income households became one of the major dividers in the estate. The transition to a single-income budget happened for most in the stage of maximum financial stress.[13] In 1981, over two-thirds said their level of financial commitment had increased, and a third said they had serious financial worries; 70 per cent of first-home owners said that. Second-home owners were much more likely to be dual-income households, and also more likely to have the home 'set up' with furnishings and consumer goods; less likely to have the symbolic sheets in the windows till drapes could be purchased; more likely to see the struggles of others. 'A lot of people—they can't afford it, but they get them in on a deposit, and they come and buy their home. I've noticed that, I've even seen people being evicted from their homes here because they can't afford it.'

For many, the other residents of Green Views were divided into those who could and those who couldn't. 'You can tell, there's quite a few houses that are up for sale and obviously have been let go. And obviously there's financial problems or other problems.' But however obvious, it was hard to document; not surprisingly, it proved impossible to get reliable data on the frequency of mortgage defaults.[14] People agreed that these were increasingly frequent as younger, more financially vulnerable couples were enticed to the estate. Certainly, as housing prices rose sharply in the Melbourne area in the first years of Green Views, more homes in the cheaper price ranges were built. 'When we moved here, you didn't get houses much smaller than what we lived in. But now that people are putting up their 11 square homes, and you can buy one on a $2000 deposit, it's getting ... young couples that move in and go broke and sell up and move on and let the next poor couple take over.' The implications were always about class, not just youth; as this man explained, 'Like, they're just little boxes that Jo Blow can afford.'

Some found they could not afford even a little box. We rang phone numbers on land for sale in 1978 and collected fading dreaming. A 34-year-old painter from Macedonia had come to Australia six years ago, and was renting in Westville[15] with his wife and two children. He saw Green Views when he was working on houses there and put a deposit on land on vendor's terms. Less than two years later he was unable to meet payments and had had the land on the market for four months without offers. 'Let time tell,' he said, 'I might buy out there again'.

A 25-year-old mother of three recalled: 'We took a drive. We had been close to buying so many times. When we saw Green Views, we sort of rushed into it. We liked it then; we'd go driving and look at the block'. They were renting now, after nine months in a caravan at her parents', 'getting nowhere'. But the land was on vendors' terms: 'That was the big killer.

We're supposed to pay off $13 000 by next year; we'd have to get a loan'. It had been on the market for five months with only four offers, and they had dropped the price. They would try to buy an 'established home': 'In this day it's too hard to build — you have to put in the carpets, drapes.' She reflected, 'I suppose I shouldn't have had kids. I really shouldn't say that. My brother-in-laws have got their own homes and they sort of look down their noses at you. They are Maltese, they go without everything to pay off their homes. I wouldn't. I like to have the heater on'.

Different paths

Those who made it were not alike. A range of life chances was indicated by the variety of both education and occupation. Of our 1981 respondents, a few had only primary education; the majority only some secondary; a third had matriculated (see fig. 1). Since the 1978 interview, forty-five men and twenty-five women had had further education or training. Men's occupations were also varied, with less than a third being in professional-technical work, and the largest category being unskilled.[16] It was not surprising that people saw differences in class, but unexpected that, asked to choose between 'class' labels, only 55 per cent said 'middle class', in this most middle-class-presented estate.[17] Self-assessed class was (of course) strongly associated with the husband's occupation, but not with the wife's. It was also strongly associated with the education of the person interviewed: women's education, but not their job, affected how they saw themselves.

That the indicators of life chances were connected is hardly surprising. But we were startled to find that both occupation and education were connected with life stage. Parents of older children more often tended to be in jobs classified as unskilled and to call themselves working class. Those most likely to call themselves working class were the parents of teenagers (61 per cent). But they were far less likely to say their neighbours were working class (39 per cent) — they *felt* different. Yet they were also more likely than the young couples to be in dual income households and second homes, so their household financial resources were greater. Green Views, it seemed, contained two class paths crossing.

Only a third of the young childless and parents of pre-schoolers called themselves working class, and about the same proportion said their neighbours were.[18] Those links were not simple; the associations of life stage with the husband's occupation and with self-assessed class are not statistically significant. Education, on the other hand, was very strongly associated with life stage: nearly half of those with no children or only pre-schoolers had matriculated, far fewer (15 per cent) of those with school-age children had, and only 29 per cent of those whose children had left. The few whose education had stopped at primary school all had children at or beyond school age. Education, in turn, was significantly associated with both self-assessed class and the husband's job.

Women's positions in paid work divided life stage groups more clearly than men's. The younger women were more likely to see employment as their normal way of life and more likely to be professionally trained. Few older women had maintained employment through family stages, but a quarter of those with pre-schoolers and over half of the childless had worked without interruption since marriage. While occupations of older women were clustered in those areas (clerical and sales) typically associated with women's employment, the young childless women included 14 of the 20 professionally employed, and 10 women now at home had been professionally employed in 1978.[19] Women leaving work in the estate's first three years had come, with one exception, from professional or white collar jobs, and most intended to return to work.[20] It was the unskilled women who stayed in their jobs, and they were older.

Even from such simple statistics it is evident that there was no single 'typical' resident. Rather, there seemed to be at least two typical couples: young people seeking a first home and older couples moving out to a second home. And the profile of buyers continued to change. A representative of the developers observed in 1977: 'We're continuing to get skilled tradesmen, they are the dominant mix, but it always seems to have been counter balanced. There is now slightly more emphasis on the labourers'. Three years later, he commented that those coming into the display strips were 'either very young, 18–19-year-olds to people in their middle twenties, guys who walk in with their Adidas suits which don't have any pockets; or people in their forties, in T-shirts and thongs'. Neither, the descriptions neatly implied, would have money.

Where did they come from?

Overwhelmingly, residents came from near suburbs. As the brochures insisted, and people kept repeating, the city centre was only 21 kilometres away. Draw an imaginary line from Green Views to the centre of Melbourne: 71 per cent of our 1978 sample came from the older and more industrial suburbs on or near that line; another 9 per cent were off it in directions indicating higher-status areas; 6 per cent from lower-status areas; and 12 per cent from country areas or interstate. Only 2 per cent came directly from overseas. Many did not look beyond an urban wedge familiar to them.[21] Several had picked this from childhood as the next stage out: 'It was just paddocks when we were kids and rode our bikes out here. Then we seen an estate and I said, "That's where I'm living", and that's where I did live'. A few older couples sought the desired environment within a broader range, in some cases covering all current new estates in the eastern suburbs! But the normal search procedure had been to explore all new housing in *their* wedge.

Like the Australian population generally, residents included a high proportion born overseas. In the 1978 sample, 22 per cent had been raised overseas and 37 per cent had at least one parent born overseas. The majority had been in Australia for over fifteen years, and they were spread across all occupation and income groups. Overseas-born respondents were most likely to be from the United Kingdom (38 per cent). A quarter were from Asian countries, but many of these had been educated in Australia. Italy and Greece were the next most common birthplaces. In 45 per cent of the households covered in our 1981 reinterview, either or both wife and husband was or were overseas-born, but their origins covered so wide a range of countries, and they differed on so many other factors that (like Australia's migrants generally) their common migrant status told little about their life chances or life-style, values or experience.[22]

Why Green Views?

Like the developers, we worked for a long time on the assumption that people were choosing Green Views primarily for the social and physical environment it offered—and we were wrong. Following critics of the effects of the suburban environment on women, we expected women and men to be seeking and seeing different features. We were wrong about that too. Most people, women and men, had come for the house. Just like suburbanites of two decades earlier in the United States, 'mainly they came "for a house and not a social environment"'.[23]

They restricted their search area by familiarity and vague ideas of acceptable or desirable setting, played off against much more specific ideas about where they could afford the house they wanted. Since the house was all-important, and the range of location constrained, sociologists' questions about choice of location often made little sense. Several different survey attempts to rank priorities produced 'hard' data that are easily reshaped! In 1981 we asked: 'Remembering back, what made you decide to move here?'. The answers were not consistent with what they had said in 1978. Over half said 'the house', a third gave it as the first answer. (And how many others did not bother to offer it at all because it was self-evident?) One woman answered in terms of location and atmosphere, but when asked the best thing about being in Green Views said: 'My house, my block of land. I love the house. I love the block of land, it is a large sized block in comparison to a lot of them and I enjoy it. But I could live in the middle of the Sahara Desert if I had a nice house and a nice block of land and I know I'd be happy'.

The 'environment' came into play after house and location were chosen. There were none who said they had come only because of advertisements for Green Views, but several had been impressed by the advertising. A woman laughed that they wished they had kept the newspaper supplements whose exciting promises had drawn them. Another described a typical search pattern:

W: Well we couldn't really go terribly high ... The land here was dearer than some of the places that I had seen but the area sort of compensated—we'd already got the idea that you would have to pay that little bit more or you would have to go to one of the other places [west] ... which was pretty crummy ... You sort of get the feeling that you're on the fringe of the suburban area here, but really it will be just another suburb ... it is not going to stay open forever but you will have quite a few years when it will still have this open look. Over the other side of the road is still paddocks; it will always be paddocks there most probably.

The paddocks were suburban housing within two years, but she had known 'places don't stay the same, unless you go in the bush where maybe you can afford a couple of acres'. Like most, she had got what she expected. This was not surprising, since the house was all-important. Asked in 1978 to rate a series of features by how important they had been in the decision to come to Green Views, 94 per cent rated 'owning our own home' as 'important' or 'very important'. They achieved, at least, beginning to own it. They had seen it, often, in display form. While many had complaints about structural detail, few were disappointed with the house. Their accounts of moving in were dominated by the word 'excited'.

But what about the setting—'country atmosphere', and a *better* way of life? While no other factor rivalled owning the home, over 80 per cent rated as important or very important 'quietness', 'layout', 'atmosphere', the 'style of the house', 'privacy of the area' and its being 'a better area'. So what mattered to most were first the house itself; secondly, aspects of 'atmosphere'—quiet, clean, 'country'; with practical convenience coming a poor third. Proximity to transport, job, relatives and friends were the reasons least likely to be rated important (see fig. 2).

With such unanimity, patterns are hard to find. Neither gender nor ethnic origin patterned these indicators of what was sought. But two indicators are associated with both life stage and life chances. The importance of owning your home was even greater for the younger and the more educated. (They are of course more likely to be buying a first home, the older couples more likely to take it for granted.) But having a home in a 'better area' was more important to the parents of older children and those with less education—perhaps because they are more likely to be staying. They also want quiet. The importance of a 'quiet area' rises with life stage from 65 per cent of the young childless to 90 per cent of those with school-age children (though those children might disagree with the goal). The quietness of Green Views was valued in comparison to previous locations: 'A better class of living', one mother described it. 'You can go to the city, you can go anywhere and when you come home, you can sit in that chair and think, oh

Fig. 2   Why Green Views?

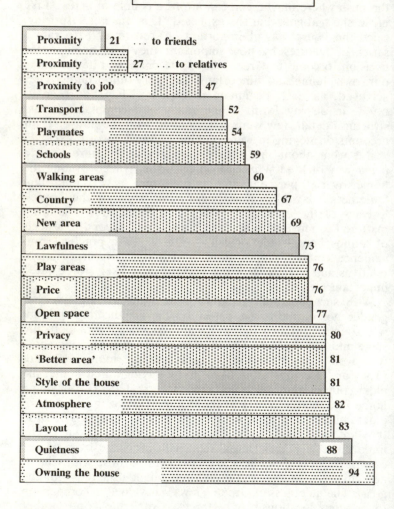

Percentage for whom these features
were important (1981 interview)
n=150

Proximity   21   ... to friends
Proximity   27   ... to relatives
Proximity to job   47
Transport   52
Playmates   54
Schools   59
Walking areas   60
Country   67
New area   69
Lawfulness   73
Play areas   76
Price   76
Open space   77
Privacy   80
'Better area'   81
Style of the house   81
Atmosphere   82
Layout   83
Quietness   88
Owning the house   94

by gee, it's good to be home. And there isn't any trams and buses, trams and trains and transports going past your door at 100 mph. It's just nice and it's quiet and that's what you need.' She laughed, remembering she always knew it would be so. 'I just saw that it was like a little haven away from the outside world when we turned into Green Views'.

Of the twenty such reasons offered, three others were associated with life stage. All were about children's needs (schools, availability of playmates and play areas).[24] None of these was associated with education, self-assessed class or occupation of the male. But self-assessed class was related to the importance of proximity of friends (only the 'middle class' cared at all), open space and lawfulness of the area (about which they cared far less). And to a husband's job were strongly related the importance of 'country atmosphere' and 'being a new area' (both were much less important to the professionals). A wife's occupation was related only to importance of layout (if she was in a blue-collar job in 1978 it meant much less) and of proximity to country (more important to white-collar and blue-collar women than professionally employed women or women at home).

So did the two 'typical' couples expect different things? The young were more likely to be looking for a house in a handy location; the older for quiet in a better area that was also new. Under the uniformity were younger couples just starting up and older families possibly moving up. And it was the younger, and more educated, who were likely to be moving on. But here, where the class paths crossed, there were common values. Looked at this way, Green Views was the temporary meeting of two streams of people, divided by stage of family and probably life chances but linked, for the moment at least, by goals of home ownership and environment—and by limited resources.

Who's satisfied?

Both streams had, overall, got what they expected, but was it what they wanted? In 1981 we asked people to rate Green Views *now* on the same list of features, and found that those ratings dealt them into four groups. One (51 people) was clearly satisfied; one equally clearly dissatisfied (41). The other two groups (each of 29 people) gave mixed ratings, one of them most critical of social aspects (lawfulness, privacy, space), the other of isolation (transport, proximity to job, kin and schools).[25]

Once again, attitudes varied with life stage and life chances. Each type had a different relationship to age and life stage. The young and the childless were clearly most satisfied: 38 per cent of the respondents under 30 were in the 'satisfied' group. The proportion in the satisfied group decreased at each older life stage, the proportion in the group concerned about isolation increased. Older couples were least represented in the group dissatisfied with social aspects; intriguingly this group was the one most clearly selecting first home owners over second. The young childless shared with parents of school-age children the highest proportions in the dissatisfied group.[26]

But it is important to stress the level of satisfaction. When older couples *were* satisfied their accounts glowed with it! One woman said her husband 'wouldn't be living any other way, now that we've settled. We've always said, you know, when Green Views first started, that it would be nice to have a house out there. But now we're here, he wouldn't change it for anything. Not even move out of the house. Give him a million dollars, I think he'd still stay here'.

Most came intending to stay and wanted to. Gender again showed no pattern: 33 husbands and 31 wives wished they had not moved here; 10 intended to move in the next three years and 25 might. Only 40 per cent would definitely buy in Green Views again. Yet 79 per cent said their expectations had proved right. Most of the 25 per cent who would definitely not buy here again had said in 1978 that they had got what they expected, or better. Life stage patterned those responses significantly. None of the young childless and only one parent of pre-schoolers said it was worse than they expected, but 12 of the 65 parents of school-age children said this. These older parents were also more likely to say it was better. The young ones most commonly had got just what they wanted.

It was likely not only that they sought different things, but that what they now saw was different. In 1981 we offered a series of descriptors[27] and asked people to ring those fitting Green Views. They were most likely to choose 'growing' (90 per cent), 'clean' (77 per cent) and 'young' (69 per cent). Only 18 per cent circled 'delinquency', 14 per cent 'social problems' and 7 per cent 'boring'. The patterns of responses clustered[28] in six different images of the estate. These spread across the life stage groups, but the familiar patterning by life stage recurred: each image was offered more often by those in one life stage.[29] And here at last we did find gender differences; but not the differences predicted in the suburban critique. Two, but only two, of these types were associated with gender. Far from indicating that they are isolated and dissatisfied, women were more likely to see community and friendliness.

There were two different versions of 'country atmosphere'. One was a 'country village' package that sparkled with the imagery of the advertisement, linking friendliness and well-planned community with cleanliness and greenery. It was least common, and mainly offered by young childless (those who were not home to enjoy the community). Two-thirds of these 'country villagers' were women. The second, greenery without community, was held most commonly by parents of teenagers. This image was the only one to feature 'prestige'—here linked to 'green' and 'growing'.

Then came versions of suburbia. The third and only completely unfavourable image offered the suburban stereotype: a place of social problems that was isolated, lonely, boring. It was produced by over a quarter in each life stage with children, and nearly two thirds of those seeing the estate this way were men. The fourth was of clean, green suburbia, albeit isolated: this was associated with the two youngest life stage groups. A fifth emphasized community over greenery, and included 'well-planned' and 'friendly'—popular with parents of pre-schoolers. They were also likely to offer the sixth image: more of a dormitory suburb, young suburbia, not isolated and boring, but not friendly either.

That satisfaction was always complicated is shown by the relationship of satisfaction to images. The satisfied were most likely to have the two first 'green' images of the estate, the dissatisfied to hold the suburban stereotype. But each of the images could be held by people with each of the very different types of satisfaction. Roughly, it seemed there were three ways of being satisfied: by achieving a quiet and green community; a quiet and green retreat; or by not being home much. But there were many ways of being disappointed.

Nor did satisfaction mean you were staying; indeed it appeared likely that the most dissatisfied were those most committed. Some had always planned to move. Of the 1981 sample,

36 had told us in 1978 that they would move within ten years, and now said they still planned to move. They were more likely, of course, to be the young ones. The majority (94) were staying and had always meant to.[30] That left 39 who had changed intentions: 19 in favour of staying; 20 who had now decided to leave. Satisfaction changed over the years. Of the 14 people who said the area was worse than they expected in 1978, only 4 were planning to leave three years later; 67 thought it was better than expected, and three years on 15 of those were leaving. Job movements, kin links and the pull of other areas shifted people out more often than disgruntlement.

Those who remained were likely to have moved out from lower status suburbs, likely to be older, likely to cling more to the image of country atmosphere, likely to be dual income families because they were likely to have older children. Of the two streams of people moving in, only one was clearly moving on—the younger and more educated. If such a process continued Green Views was certain to become more homogeneous, filling up by a sort of silting process as the stream moving out took the younger and more educated. Meanwhile, the different streams offered another sort of homogeneity: the common commitment to the house and contentment at its achievement.

M: It's still a great place to live. The scenery is round the place, like you're on the edge of the city, you can see nothing but hills at the moment. When people's gardens start growing, it'll block out a lot of the view, but that will be made up for by the niceness of it all anyway. It's well weighed out. It's catering for virtually everything that's going, there's football teams, junior football, junior cricket, yoga or whatever they call it, so everything's been planned. It was said to be planned, anyway ... We're proud to live here and we spend a lot of time maintaining our garden. I don't know whether it's made me a better person, but it's made me a better gardener! Before, when we were renting houses, all you tended to do was run around with a lawn mower every two months. Well now I cut a lawn every weekend, sort of thing. I suppose it's given me more pride in myself ... It would take quite a bit to shift us. Yeah, we identify with Green Views ... I came from the western suburbs, they didn't know Green Views, even though the slogan was on television and things like that. They knew of a place called Green Views, but they didn't know where it was. But now, when they say 'Where do you live?' I say 'Green Views', because my friends now are this side of town and they know where that is.

Notes

1. All direct quotations in this book are from transcripts of interviews or conversations either taped or written at the time. Speakers are identified by W (woman), M (man) and I (interviewer). All deletions from quotations are indicated by ellipses (. . .). Field notes are distinguished from interviews by indention on the left-hand side.

2. See introduction for details. It is important to note that the 1981 reinterview sample had lost 70 people from the first interview; it is possible that the dissatisfied were over-represented in those who left or refused a reinterview.

3. All but one of the reinterview sample were married at the time of interview; only three of the married respondents said they did not *expect* to have children, only one that they *intended* not to.

4. All four were still there three years later. The 1978 interview picked up one sibling staying temporarily.

5. In 1981 Jan Salmon made valiant efforts to find a house for the Richards family, then building 'further out', to rent on their return from overseas. Sadly, she was unsuccessful, so the only chance for one of us to live in the estate was lost.

6. Life stage is too often crudely coded in statistical studies; especially for women, it is the stage of children, not merely whether there are any, that matter. See Lyn Richards and Jan Salmon, 'There when you need them? Family life stage and social network', *La Trobe Working Papers in Sociology*, no. 68, 1984, La Trobe University, Bundoora, Vic. and A. Steuve & K. Gerson, 'Personal relations across the life-cycle', in C. S. Fischer *et al.*, *Networks and Places: Social Relations in the Urban Setting*, Free Press, New York, 1977, pp. 79–98. In Green Views it was necessary to distinguish in coding not only between families with pre-school and school-age children but between families with children in only one of those categories and those where there were both. In some contexts, this transitional category behaves more like those with only school-age children, in some contexts the constraints and opportunities of pre-schoolers seem to dominate. All life-stage analyses, unless otherwise noted, use five categories: young childless, parents of only pre-schoolers, parents of pre-school and school-age children, parents of only school-age children and 'empty nest' couples.

   The normal school entry age was in the fifth year, and I use the term 'pre-school' (or 'pre-school-age') to refer to all children too young to attend school (that is, normally under five). It was usual, though not compulsory, for a child to attend (in the fourth year) a year of kindergarten at 'the Preschool' (or 'the Kinder').

7. The Victorian average was 8 per cent at the 1976 Census. In our sample, banks and cooperatives, with the cheapest finance at 9–

11 per cent interest rates in 1978 and for periods up to thirty years, held the first mortgages of 64 per cent of residents, but others paid over 12 per cent, and second mortgages were normally by personal bank loan, shorter term and with higher interest. People who had made separate land purchases on vendor terms faced the most prohibitive interest rates and the threat of losing their investment if balance could not be paid in a few years; telephone interviews of people trying to sell land collected several cases where substantial losses were made.

8. The Melbourne average house and land price at this stage was $40200; it had doubled by 1986 and increased again by over a quarter by mid-1989. (Commonwealth of Australia, *Cost of Housing*, report of the Committee of Inquiry into Housing Costs, Australian Government Publishing Service, Canberra, 1978). For recent assessments of housing costs see T. Burke *et al.*, *A Roof Over Their Heads: Housing Issues and Families in Australia*, Australian Institute of Family Studies, Melbourne, 1984.

9. Average weekly gross income of households was $258, only 19 per cent earning more than $450.

10. For details, see *The Green Views Report*. The lower-priced packages in Stage 3, with economy builders, meant heavier burdens for those families because their finance was more expensive, on low-deposit loans. Only 3 per cent of families paid less than 25 per cent of gross income on housing. All had had to find deposits prior to purchase. *The Cost of Housing* report estimated that for 1976−77 a single-income family would on average take 12.6 years, a dual-income family 2.2 years, to save the average deposit for a new house-and-land package.

11. Three women in the sample did piecework at home; 20 others earned some money at home — 10 for child-care, the rest for ironing, clerical tasks and coaching.

12. In 1978, 56 per cent of these women had been full-time employed, only 11 per cent part-time.

13. See Bettina Cass, 'Housing and the family', *SWRC Reprints*, Social Welfare Research Centre, Kensington, Vic., 1980.

14. Official channels were of course not available, and those attempting home ownership at this stage were certainly facing increasing rates of disaster. A leading mortgage insurance company reported claims for 1978−79 twice the level of 1977−78, which doubled the previous figure (see Commonwealth of Australia, *Cost of Housing*, p. 49.) We attempted to obtain interviews in all homes advertised for resale, but while these 'Leaver' interviews proved valuable, they did not locate mortgage default sales, since previous owners had left prior to advertisement. It is one gap in the data sharply showing ethical dilemmas of social research; we always confessed deep relief when those attempts had been unsuccessful.

15. I have coined three pseudonyms for lower-status suburbs to the very symbolic west, commonly named in evaluations of Green Views. Westville was the near neighbour, Westburg a little further, with considerable public housing built during periods when this was very uniform and easily stigmatized. Far West was a more distant outer suburb notorious for both public housing and social problems.

16. These categories collapse professional/technical and administrative/ managerial to 'professional', clerical and sales to 'white-collar', and transport/communication, trades, process worker, labourer, personal/domestic to 'blue-collar'. Such categorizations are of course always crude, and this study includes no knowledge of the experience people had of their workplace or the significance of work in their lives—highly relevant to many of the questions considered, but excluded, like other regretted exclusions, as we attempted to cut the gruelling volume of questions in surveys.

17. Australians generally divide exactly between working and middle class in surveys asking people to put themselves in predefined categories. (In Britain, 95 per cent say middle class, in the United States 40 per cent.) L. F. Broom *et.al.*, 'Social stratification in Australia', in J. A. Jackson (ed.), *Social Stratification*, Cambridge University Press, Cambridge, 1968. What they *mean* is another question, and the subject of chapter 3. Our question, in the 1978 schedule, read: 'Most people say they either belong to the upper class, the middle class or the working class. If you had to make a choice, which would you call yourself?'.

18. The rest of the self-styled working class were made up of 46 per cent of parents of school-age children not yet in their teens, and four of the nine whose children had left home; most of these described their neighbours the same way.

19. Those who had left or were not available from the 1978 sample were more likely to be professionals—33 per cent of men had been in professional occupations at the first interview. Then 65 per cent were dual-income families; in 1981 50 per cent were. Twenty-three women had worked as professionals and fourteen were still doing so in 1978.

20. A sample survey in 1984 of women with an 18-month-old baby showed that virtually all were either in paid work or intended to return to it. P. McDonald, 'Families in the future: The pursuit of personal autonomy', *Family Matters*, no. 22, 1988, pp. 40–7.

21. This is recognized as the normal pattern of movement in Melbourne, as in similar cities: see L. Kilmartin *et al.*, *Social Theory and the Australian City*, Allen & Unwin, Sydney, 1985, pp. 152–4.

22. It is this indicator of ethnic mix, rather than merely the ethnic origin of the respondent, that proved most useful in investigating the effect on values and social interaction, and unless otherwise

indicated 'ethnicity' refers to whether respondent *or spouse* was overseas-born. That this indicator fails to distinguish people on most indices of values and behaviour does not of course mean that ethnic background did not affect anybody. The heterogeneity of ethnic origin and class and life stage of those born overseas guarantees that few simple effects of ethnicity will be shown— indeed it makes more remarkable those that do appear. Statistical investigation of the effects of particular geographical origins or combinations of class, life stage and ethnicity were confounded by small sample sizes.

23. H. Gans, *The Levittowners*, Vintage Books, New York, 1967, p. 37. The quotation is from S. D. Clark's earlier classic study, *The Suburban Society*, University of Toronto Press, Toronto, 1966, p. 110.

24. This is one body of data where the sensitivity of coding categories is indicated. Life stage in 1978 showed an association with three other variables: quietness and privacy (importance increased with life stage) and importance of walking areas (those who then had pre-schoolers stressed this). Open space was also associated with life stage in 1981 when we recoded to separate the parents of teenagers from those with younger children.

25. The groups were derived by cluster analysis of ratings on a 5-point scale of the following items: price of land or housing, atmosphere of the area, being close to relatives, friends, job, school, countryside, style of the house, being a better type of area, having playmates for children, layout, community open space, lawfulness, privacy, quietness, play areas for children, closeness to public transport, being a community-minded place, space between homes, friendliness.

26. Neither sex of respondent nor whether they were first or second home owners was associated statistically with these types of satisfaction.

27. The list was as follows: clean, young, isolated, green, well-planned, lonely, prestige, suburbia, country atmosphere, boring, social problems, friendly, small, big, unique, community, dilinquency, active, growing, established.

28. Cluster analysis produced six types, containing, in order of appearance, 21, 25, 32, 22, 33 respondents, with 16 not allocated.

29. In each case over 20 per cent of that life-stage group was dealt into that image, and others were spread across all life-stage groups.

30. The figures are not comparable to those from Newtown because we asked about immediate plans to move, but there too slightly less than a quarter planned to move (almost half within five years). See L. Bryson & F. Thompson, *An Australian Newtown*, Penguin, Ringwood, 1972. H. Gans in his classic study, *The Levittowners*, found that 44 per cent of residents intended to stay.

In Green Views we asked of intention to stay at least three years, and the figure overall was 62 per cent. Bryson and Thompson found low education and unskilled occupation predicted intention to stay—as had P. Berger in *Working Class Suburb,* University of California Press, Berkeley, Calif., 1960.

2

Planners and Purchasers

In a society increasingly critical of suburbia, the common image of new home buyers is of gullible victims of profit-mongering developers. Like the image of homogeneity, this is a caricature. A focus on people's choices and actions shows that most had made practical and purposive purchases within their perception of alternatives and options. Most got what they expected, even if it was not what they wanted, and very many got both what they wanted and expected. But their perceptions of alternatives, of course, were within the frameworks of ideas about family life. And their options, and the price to be paid for them, both financially and in terms of facilities and distances, were set by a development process over which they had no control. If these were gullible victims, it was to the dream they were buying.

Almost all were also victims to an image of property development in which the power of developers was unquestioned. Green Views was sold as a planned development, the provision of at least some facilities was heavily publicized, and the developer was very visible. The estate was historically placed in a period when urban planners stressed 'community' and sought to achieve it by 'seeking to impose an idealized vision of village life on the town dweller'.[1] This was also a period during which land development became both expensive and highly profitable. Green Views epitomized the process by which huge profits on rural land flow to those who can stand the massive costs of land development. It is clearly in the interests of such developers to accelerate the process of planning and reduce the provision of services funded by themselves while promising 'community' services (transport, schools, pre-schools, park equipment) that would come from public budgets. While bringing the pretty paddocks of Green Views to the people we talked to, the developer was featured as heavily promoting a prestige 'community' development, constantly protesting delays and fighting requirements.

This developer (I shall call the company DVP) was a high profile representative of a new category of urban managers, described in a study of that time as 'asset-rich institutions with huge investment capability, such as life insurance offices and finance companies ... swollen with assets and in dire need of outlets for them'.[2] But this is also a category of institutions with an image to maintain. The developer attempted from the start to create a 'special' image for Green Views, and to maintain a presence there. A representative, who came to be on first-name terms with leaders of residents' groups, was a regular participant in meetings and accessible for complaints. DVP was landlord of the only public spaces available (its own sales office and unlet space in the shopping centre). It thus controlled opportunities for formal and semi-formal meetings of great significance in the survival and conflict management of groups. So DVP was visible both as the profit-making agent of land development and as caretaker of the results of that development. Since it retained large landholdings for future stages of the estate it also had a very real interest in the continuing image of the estate. As visible developer DVP was open to constant criticism in the early years for broken promises and missing facilities; as caretaker of the public space it encouraged residents' groups, though the spaces it made available were always inappropriate for the intended uses (upstairs empty areas are hardly suitable for mothers with pushers!). As custodian of an image it was the target of disappointments.

Perhaps because of these overlapping roles, DVP acquired a mafia Godfather image of unlimited and rather suspect power, which was however highly useful if it was on your side, given that public authorities were widely seen as against you. Most people we interviewed had very little understanding of the development process. They had no access to it and saw no need to know about it, since they purchased through salespeople who were employed by builders erecting groups of houses on packages of land. They had no option but to pay the by now very inflated price, and most believed the promises. There was a widespread conviction that the developer was responsible for a vast array of features which it could not possibly provide (railway connections and schools, for instance, even the location of stations and the quality of the building materials in classrooms). But then this conviction had some justification. The publicity had promised such things (and individual salespeople apparently elaborated improperly on the vague promises) and the DVP representative was very visible in meetings about them (though always very carefully specifying his role as observer or provider of information). DVP was also given credit for facilities achieved entirely without its efforts. Like the man quoted at the end of chapter 1, many assumed that the advent of 'football teams, junior football, junior cricket, yoga' meant that 'everything's been planned'.[3]

People were also not at all clear about the relation between the company and the various public bodies—local government, state education and transport authorities—on which their facilities depended. Comments, critical or favourable, featured an anonymous 'they' which might be supposed to represent an unholy amalgam of profit-making capitalist institution and state public service providers.[4] Such comments reflected the visible evidence of the influence very powerful companies may have on public authorities. There was little curiosity about this relationship; the action groups worked on the assumption that the company was acting in their interests (firmly backed by the realistic explanation that this was only because it was in the company's interests). Thus in 1980, when there was still no primary school, DVP was approaching the Residents' Action Group (and our project) for figures on children's ages to support a submission to education authorities for a secondary school. Both schools had been promised in the brochures available since 1977. Severely embarrassed by the outcry in the estate at the absence of a school, DVP worked hard to appear as the residents' representative rather than the perpetrator of the unfulfilled promises.

This was not easy, since people commonly believed in the power of planning, and the ability of developers to dictate not only the provision of facilities but also the standard of housing and environment, as well as the price. For half our sample it had mattered in the purchase decision that the estate was advertised as a 'planned community'. What difference would planning make?[5] Almost all of the answers were practical and realistic ones about layout (31 per cent of all answers) and services (44 per cent). Only seven people mentioned housing standards and only three social composition. But when they talked of the standards of housing and type of people in the estate, most people implied that developers controlled these characteristics.

The only demand was that developers should keep their promises. Interestingly, they were not blamed for the *lack* of information—54 people said the information they acted on had been inadequate, but only 16 blamed the developer, and 17 their builder. (Another 15 blamed themselves for not finding out more.) A third felt they should have taken longer in the decision. But however long they had taken, many would not have had access to the information they wanted about the rate of provision of facilities, especially transport and schooling. DVP controlled neither, but promised both. And people firmly blamed DVP for broken promises. DVP was named in most such claims, even by the generally satisfied. A woman with school-age children, and 'more than happy' in Green Views, complained: 'We were promised the school a lot earlier and when we bought the house we were promised a lot more than we got at DVP. They let us down badly there. They still are letting us down, they're still letting the residents of Green Views down as a whole'.

Nor, it proved, could the developer control the price of housing. There was widespread bitterness at what was seen as a lowering of the standard of housing going into the estate, and hence the value of existing houses. A couple selling up had had their home valued at $65 000.

M: He said you won't get it, because the market has deteriorated, although it's worth it, you won't get it.

W: He told us a lot of people don't like it out here because it's flat and uninteresting.

M: it's got a bad name . . . Services, the services are bad, this is one of the reasons why we're selling, lots of things promised that have never happened . . . We were shown by, what are the land people, DVP, a [railway] station that was supposed to be built within two years, that two years has gone and there's no hope of a station. It was supposed to be on the estate. The bus service is very infrequent, it's no good, we're forced to run two cars.

There is evidence here of powerlessness and its social results, and of misunderstanding of political processes. Some of these facilities could not have been predicted. If a railway station was promised this was an outright lie. Some complaints, such as frequency of bus services, required action by public services. Only a third thought the developer had done a good job, 24 per cent thought it poor, the rest that it was adequate. And the ambivalence of DVP's image, combined with a conviction in the power of developers, meant it heard few thanks for the contentment so widespread in the estate. Those who were happy normally saw this as their own achievement of their own dream, not to be credited to an outside authority, no matter how active a participant it might be in the process of marketing the dream. Their happiness had little to do with that 'idealized village life': the friendly family community in a country atmosphere. Those who felt aggrieved normally blamed DVP but it was not community they had sought.

A better way of life?

The contented expected least from social planning. In 1981, 81 per cent said they were happier now than before the move. But was this because of the move? When we asked, 'Has it meant a better way of life for you?', two thirds said yes. Men were as likely to agree as women (though less likely to agree strongly) on both questions. Self-assessed class was not significantly associated with responses to either (though to both the 'middle class' were slightly more likely to say yes). But even more said it was a new *stage* of their lives, and those for whom it was a new stage were far more likely to see it as a better way of life. Not surprisingly, they were also far more likely to be first home owners and either childless or with pre-school children.

In what way was it better? The advertisements clearly alluded to status (better) and community (way of life); people did not. This is one of many areas where ability to listen to the words is essential. Of those who saw this as a better way of life only a handful were talking of anything that might mean community. Two mentioned planning, and another two country atmosphere; five talked of facilities. But most, and almost all of those in early family stages, were referring to their own transitions into a new home, a new family. Some made the distinction for us:

'It's hard to say 'cos I was just living at home, then was married and moved straight into my own home up here'. When the question was interpreted as meaning 'better than somewhere else to live', some were stumped by a feeling that they had only now started (adult married) life. 'I don't know another life since we've been married', said one woman; another, 'I don't really know, I've got nothing to compare it with—we were in a flat before' (as though that had not been a way of life at all). This was not only a woman's response. One young husband who had been living with parents before said Green Views was 'the only thing I know'.

Those who felt it was a better way of life almost always meant either home ownership or family stage, or both. The link of home and family was heavily promoted in the advertising; display homes pictured young couples or young families stepping through the doors, and playgrounds with toddlers in sunshine. But people were saying they had come here for the transitions, and found them and nothing else. The location of the transition could be almost irrelevant, and there was a cheerful cynicism about the suggestion that the developer had anything to do with it. Some sounded as though it was merely a necessary place, not attractive in itself (like the scraggly pine trees to which butterflies migrate by mass instinct). A better way of life? 'I suppose it's our own home, that's about all'. 'Only in the fact that I have a home of my own to bring my children up in. If I was living somewhere else in an area of my choice, I suppose I would be more happy than where I am now'. It was not just the young marrieds who interpreted the 'way of life' as meaning the house. An older man said: 'No I don't think Green Views has been a better way of life. It's only what we've made'.

Selling country atmosphere

If the better way of life was not credited to DVP, what of 'country atmosphere'? 'I think it's given us what we wanted for the time being, as far as being quiet and lots of natural trees and the house that we've wanted ... I mean for the money that we've got and the situation that we're in at the moment.' Even in such realistic accounts the slogan seemed happily accepted. Most agreed they had achieved the promised 'country atmosphere'. But what does this mean? In the survey data there are indications that the 'country' is no simple symbol. In the factor analysis of people's ratings of Green Views 'country' seemed to go with privacy and retreat *or* space and cleanliness. Noticeably missing was the rural idyll of community. It appeared in only one of the images of the estate derived from people's ratings: the package we called 'country village', of friendliness, well-planned community, cleanliness and greenery. That was offered by only 20 people, mostly young women. The other 'country' image was just green and growing, and linked to prestige.

In people's accounts, country almost always means greenery and space. That makes it easy to attain—you just go far out. Many of these comments contain unnoticed contradictions: 'I think it is so far out from the city it is like living in the country even though you've got houses around you. But it is just so peaceful when all the noise isn't there'. The major criticism in this regard was that DVP had failed to protect the splendid great eucalypts dominating the farm land, and an avenue of elms that had led to the homestead. A couple who had tried to buy a block with a eucalypt had found it priced beyond them; they were bitter now that the trees had been removed. 'They said there was a covenant (I don't know if that's the word) against cutting down the trees ... It was a con. It was probably the same as "the school's going to be there soon".' Her husband added, 'Where they had all that free space, or apparently free space, they've now turned it into 51 building blocks; they've done much the same there, they've cut down all the trees ... It was a cunning, cunning step on their behalf. They're very clever developers'.

But while trees raised tempers, nobody sneered at the equation of isolation and inconvenience with country atmosphere. Nobody seems to have criticized the image in terms of the inevitability that these green hills would become more suburban housing. If there was one area in which these residents did appear amazingly gullible, it was their extraordinary lack of curiosity about the plausible future of the estate. We were startled by the distress as the estate filled and the appearance of 'country' gave way to more obviously tight-packed housing. 'I just thought it was more like a really rural area, but now it's like just any of those places.' Several people were moving for that reason, and others now felt that they should have realized the future face of Green Views. No direct misinformation was asserted. But the promises of peace, quiet and country, well illustrated with photos of rolling farm land dotted with those huge eucalypts, had combined powerfully with the dream of a new house to veil the reality of suburban expansion. 'I didn't think it would be as populated as what it was', said a young woman, although she had seen the figures. 'I knew they were going to house so many people. But when I first sort of came looking here, it was a lot more open. There was a lot more open space and paddocks and it was cows running round the streets.'

The developer could take little glory from the better way of life; for country atmosphere DVP was seen as irrelevant; and neither slogan meant community. Very few criticized the (minimum legal) amount of open space, one aspect that was the developer's responsibility. But for providing 'a better area' (strongly in DVP's interest and largely beyond its control) it was seen as solely responsible and usually failing in that responsibility. And if 'community' meant anything in these purchase decisions, it usually meant 'better area'. Only 18 people circled each of 'unique' and 'small' in the offered descriptors. There was nothing 'special' about Green Views to 41 per cent, and the rest saw it as 'special' not because it contained community, but because it had 'better facilities' or because it was 'more attractive'.

'Facilities' for whom?

For some residents the estate *was* a better area. In the factor analysis of ratings of the estate 'better area' linked with two different features—quietness and provision of facilities. It is a matter of who is there and what is there for them. Most of those who thought it a better area praised not the planning but the people who had bought there. One couple, from Westburg, felt they were 'moving into the Toorak of the eastern suburbs'. Predictably, those coming from lower-status areas were more likely to see it as a better area. A man moving from a Housing Commission area said, 'It's a different atmosphere, people are different. It's quieter, people aren't sort of noisy. It's a different class of people.'

Facilities mattered for two reasons: provision for children and appearance. Broken promises about schools and transport festered. But Green Views did acquire some more visible and attractive facilities before smaller nearby estates: parks, sporting areas and a squash court, at last an infant welfare centre and a medical centre. At least locally it maintained a 'special' character. 'We get things easier, whereas I think people down there have always missed out', said a young woman. 'It's sort of like stepping out of one area into another.' Another said, 'Green Views has a lot more than other estates. There's more parks, there's more—there's something about Green Views; you have to live here to really realize Green Views *is* beautiful'. Local government agents regarded the estate, in the words of one male, as 'in danger of being spoon-fed'. After the early years the main complaint was lack of a school and transport.

There was widespread acceptance that new areas did not provide for women at home. The complete absence of formal child-care, the inconvenience of shopping facilities for women at home, the lack of any community centre, and the inadequate access to transport meant that to an outsider the estate's facilities denied women's needs even more obviously than did early suburban development.[6] Only one milk bar served the entire estate, and the shopping centre, when it finally opened, was not within walking distance from Stage 1 if you had a pusher. Older suburbs with corner shops offered more. But the women rarely said so, and complaints were not patterned by gender. The only women who regretted a move from an older area because they had lost local facilities were migrants. The milk bar was mentioned, in all our data, only in terms of the friendliness of the owner (often the only person people felt they knew here) or the problem of teenagers gathering there— much more often the latter. Nobody had expected or said they wanted more such corner stores.

There seemed to be two reasons for this acceptance. First, planning was premised on women leaving during the day, and this was seen as reasonable. Secondly, the lack of facilities was seen as the price you paid for a better area. (Too many milk bars meant too many visible places for kids to hang around.) Thus it was too simple to conclude that the planning of Green Views kept women 'confined to their traditional roles in the family as wives and mothers'.[7] In one sense it pushed them out by assuming they were mobile or in the workforce, and by making a traditional housewife's life maximally inconvenient and lonely. Thus planning for profit accelerates demographic change. But it constrained women's options if they sought outside work, because distance and transport to employment centres made employment often an option only for the childless, or parents who could be home late. And it contained them, if they stayed home, in an area planned for people who were not there. Residents seemed to see that as not only inevitable but reasonable.

At the extreme, some people objected to the promotion of a self-contained community not because it was a lie but because the idea displeased them. The Fence was seen by the developer as a claim to a 'special' status. 'It's "Green Views and bugger the rest", it gives people the impression of Green Views being the Toorak part of the shire.' (But there is no fence around Toorak.) These are the only quotations in which 'community' did mean something like 'village life', and in these it was unwanted. A woman saw both the estate's name and the Fence as objectionable, 'because, to me, that puts us apart. You know, it looks like that we're this little Community'. 'They' intended it 'for people to move in and stay. That is your home, and we have built this wonderful Fence around you, you know; you can stay in here and you can live here and never know what is going on in the outside. It is so shallow, the whole set up. We are going to build you a school, we are going to build you a shopping centre, we are going to have the bus, you know, we are going to do all of these wonderful things and you are just going to love the place.' Thus planning is linked to paternalism. 'Only a few people have had the guts to get up and put up a fence around their property.' She would have done so but they are now leaving and her answer is a manifesto for privacy: 'People need to say this is mine, this is my house, but here it is up and go, what is mine is yours and what is ours is everybody's'.

A special area?

She was unusual not in her rejection of community but in her disdain for the 'special' image. By far the most common criticism of Green Views as a whole was not that 'they' had sold it as 'special' but that they had reneged on this promise. Many complained of financial loss as a result: 'They've wrecked the area, quite frankly, with putting up a lot of cheaper homes, and there have been people who just don't look after their homes ... it doesn't give the image that it's supposed to, you know, like the beautiful place it's supposed to be'. This man had a valuation $10 000 below his purchase price a year later.

Those who rejected the 'special' label almost always saw Green Views as 'just another suburb'. A handful felt very resentful about this, and they were recognized by others as 'snobbish' people who 'shouldn't have come'. 'There were some people who came here very early on, who thought Green Views was going to be *not* an average suburb, but maybe an upper class area, and they've moved here with that thought in mind and it hasn't developed that way and they're bitter.' These comments contained strong hints of class divisions. A woman recalled: 'We were shown certain homes, and what sort of homes to build and what sort of gardens they'd [DVP] like, and we thought it was going to be pretty elaborate homes within the estate, and things didn't turn out that way. A lot of the homes are very Commission-like and you get certain areas of people that don't really care about their gardens or their homes'. A man was more explicit, 'I expected better things, you know. It started off nice ... but now I consider it a dump'. It was common for these complaints to emphasize the *type* of people that had come, and dismay that 'the same type of people were moving in as where we'd been before'.

There is no doubt that DVP attempted to create a 'better class' of area, and that it failed to reach the target it promoted. Glossy portraits of houses by well-known up-market companies had strongly implied they pictured Green Views before there were any houses there. Advertising jingles promoted superior status. A man who claimed that it had been presented as 'a little Toorak'[8] said this could be held as false advertising. Certainly it was wishful thinking, and clearly established that status is not so easily socially constructed. In the development process the image of Green Views was the subject of many large reports, but these provided little evidence of a 'quality' market for estate housing in the area. Whether it could have been created in the financial climate of the time is dubious. In the years after the estate began, as housing became more expensive and finance harder to get, the developer abandoned the attempt to restrict Green Views to higher-price builders.

Little boxes all the same

What makes an area look 'better'? Comments underline a paradox of housing values: uniformity is both safety and a sign of low status. The developer's attempts to impose uniform standards were universally approved: here the only criticism was that 'they' should have gone further. 'They tried to make it look different', explained a man, adding as though it followed, that: 'There's all sorts of covenants on the land. You know, houses have to be above a certain size and your fences have to be painted'. His wife added, 'I thought it was good that it was planned, in that you knew there were no sheds'. (The same year we talked to three people who nominated the 'tin sheds' going up as one reason for moving.) The gradual appearance of front fences at Green Views was a matter of debate in coffee groups and Residents' Association meetings, and when one appeared made of garden lattice it was much discussed.

Imposed uniformity extended to gardens. Fashionable (and fairly maintenance-free) landscaping with native plants was promoted by the developer and was almost ubiquitous, the sameness very noticeable to visitors, especially those aware of the ethnic diversity in the area. It certainly undid some of the carefully planned mix of house designs, but only one resident criticized it. 'I think the people that move in seem to all have a real urge to make their houses the same. They get a great load of rocks and a great load of tanbark and immediately try to make their house exactly the same as the one next door.'

Uniformity of standards was strongly desired.[9] But uniformity of appearance was a much feared sign of lower status. Diversity of housing styles was seen as essential for a better area, and often nominated as justification for the label 'beautiful'. 'It's just a beautiful area, the whole thing about it,' said a woman. 'It's just a place on its own ... If you like this type of area, it's for you. It's not posh or anything, it's your average suburb, I think, with a difference.' What's different? 'You're not looking at suburbia.' In her parents' suburb 'everything looks the same. Just about every other house is built the same way. This is completely different. You don't get two houses alike. You very rarely see two alike next door to each other'. What mattered was avoiding what many termed 'rows of houses the same'. Whether the developer had achieved sufficient variety was much debated, but everyone agreed that it could have been achieved, and the majority that in Stage 1 it had been. One woman commented approvingly that she couldn't believe how many ways 'they' could build the same house.

When we asked gingerly about the image of suburban uniformity, about a third expressed disappointment at uniform appearance.[10] But only one man saw the question as a criticism of suburbia. He cheerfully agreed: 'Let's face it, we're in suburban Melbourne, so it has to be. All the houses are the same, people live the same, we're in a rut!'. He had not wanted to be, but 'join the rat race and that's it'. Nobody gave the answer we expected, about 'suburban neurosis' and the isolation of women at home.

Two-thirds felt that the estate was a 'better area'. Two-thirds (mostly the same people) expected it to change for the better in ten years. Most saw enough variety in fittings, the angles of buildings or mix of designs, life-styles, layout or the growing gardens to avoid the appearance of what one woman called 'a nothing estate' or the 'Commission' housing in suburbs further west.[11] In Green Views 'There's not a lot of houses really the same. There is, if you like to go and point them out, but they're not all sitting in long rows ... like over in Westville, there's long rows of those dreadful places ... That seems to have been looked after, I think'. Some effort went into checking frequency of duplicates of styles, especially your own. 'There's not many of our particular design; like next door's the same sort of design but slightly different. There's more of that house around than what there is of our home'. One man could prove it: 'I know the roof tiling was all different because I tried to get some extra tiles for my place'. He drove round for two days and failed to find the same tiles to 'pick up'!

Uniformity of housing style was the feared symbol of status decline in the later rounds of housing, and DVP was widely held responsible for this. A woman protested, 'Stage 1 you don't notice it quite the same as Stage 3, which is down over the hill. Some of those houses look very, very similar, and you get two or three all in a row. The only difference is the fact that one's got the windows on the left and the other's got the windows on the right'. Like many of these early purchasers, she felt they had bought and contributed to an image that was now being betrayed: 'Stage 1, I think, comes out different. It comes from the original concept of what DVP were trying to promote, and they've altered their themes'.

If planners are powerful they should, it was felt, be able to achieve promised status. The comments reflect some of the dilemmas of arguments about the existence of a deity: if planners are all-powerful then they cannot be all-good. Few questioned their power.

The family community

Confidence is not mainly in developers and planners, it is in a type of development, parcelled in that phrase 'family community'. Community, I have argued, was not part of the goals of country atmosphere or a better way of life. There is little evidence that people sought community in any sociological sense of local belonging and interaction. 'Family community' occurred most often linked not with rural village idylls or caring networks but with a 'new area'.

Several assumptions are built in here. First, the very fact that it was new was frequently associated with being nice and better. Yet the same people correctly assumed that 'established' suburbs had higher status (Toorak is not new). And the isolation of new estates for women was a frequent theme in the media. So why is new better? The apparent contradiction is resolved by the context; most people meant that in the range of housing available to them, newer areas were a safer purchase. First, they were clean; less likely to be damaged (yet). Secondly, there was considerable confidence that if an estate was new it would attract and be planned for young families. On both counts they were realistic and right. 'The schools and welfare centres, they're not sort of run-down, dilapidated buildings. They're all new and well-maintained.' The planned facilities attended mainly to the needs of young children (and belatedly of young mothers).

Young people meant 'family community'. The choice of Green Views was based on predictions of its population more often than on confidence in its planning: 'I suppose I took into consideration the fact that a new estate would probably mean younger people, younger families—people our own age group, people that are obviously going to have families and their kids are going to grow up together with ours'. A man who described the older, working-class suburb he came from as 'apathetic', gave as a major factor in picking Green Views: 'the total concept of Green Views, you know, the self-contained community. We knew that everything would come, sooner or later'. But the confidence in the 'total concept' was less a faith in developers than a practical assessment of the population: 'We were no sooner here than there were groups forming and well-placed pressure, and everything seemed to come'.

In all this material, remarkably few people showed any fear

of a 'new' area. The comments ignored the needs of mothers and older people, but these people did not protest at their isolation. The obvious fact that newness was temporary was also ignored, as was the inevitability that children grow up. Only one resident equated newness with problems as toddlers grew: 'It has to get bigger. Sometimes I wonder how many you can keep behind a fence. The problem with the youth is that there is nothing here. Nothing apart from newness'. The likelihood that the needs of older children would not be met does not occur once in all the confident statements about the 'family community' from the developer or residents. There is frequent mention of things teenagers need—transport, entertainment, proximity to the city. But absence of these is mainly seen as a problem for the people in older age groups, and never as contradicting the assurance that the estate is for families.

But the children did grow. One woman expressed the disappointment: 'You always feel that when you're moving into a new area and it's not so built up and that sort of thing it is never going to be quite as bad, but what you don't think about of course is that they come from all over the place into these subdivisions and you just get a mixture...they come from everywhere, and the children are not going to change just because they've come to a nice place, are they?'. Deterioration was seen as inevitable unless 'they' provided better facilities. 'I think they're going to have a bit of trouble as the children start growing up. They need more community things for the children.' But most, like this man, acknowledged that 'That's one of the biggest problems of all the outer estates, I think, that there's nothing much for children to do'. Kids were, as one woman put it, 'bound to the boundaries'. Her daughter contributed, 'No McDonalds'. Teenagers agreed completely. Entertainment and transport were their two main complaints. In sharp contrast to the adults' questionnaire responses, they unanimously labelled Green Views as 'boring'. Yet the needs of teenagers were never featured in publicity, and provision of any activities for them took much longer than attention to the needs of small children.

Undoubtedly, Green Views had vandalism; any visitor was met by minor signs of it. But most people had only hearsay evidence of problems with teenagers: 'I don't actually know them but I've heard that there are a few families who have uncontrollable children, let's put it that way. It's uncontrollable teenagers'. The urgency of the problem intrudes. One man interrupted, 'I don't know if you've got a point in your questionnaire there on louts? Cos I think that could be quite a problem. Green Views has become a prime target for two kinds of louts. One's a car-borne lout and the other—who may or may not be a Green Viewser—'. His wife interrupted him: 'The other day two of the shops had their windows smashed and I mean they're big windows, and that's not the first time either'. They continued for some time, stacking up building-blocks of evidence.

Getting things done

The first group to emerge, at the instigation of young residents, was the Residents' Action Group. Later, in processes I explore in the final chapter, it was renamed Residents' Association; I have abbreviated both to RA. In the first three years it spawned a series of sub-committees, all focused on the needs of young families. Sporting groups (tennis, football and Little Athletics) were early successes. A playgroup for pre-school children commenced and, related to it, a voluntary baby-sitting group. Almost all the efforts for young children and their mothers had some success.

The developer had actively promoted residents' groups for those facilities. An uneasy relationship developed, the RA being used as a promotional ploy by DVP to symbolize the 'family community'. Several people told us they had been directed to it by sales representatives: '"You would like to join it, they're such a great group. They are keen to push the area ahead and to develop parks", etc. . . . There would be something special, I felt, that was what they were pushing. Because they always talked about the facilities that were going to be offered, such as schools and shops and parklands and the way of life and that there would be facilities for the children and therefore it would keep families closely within theirself'.

One of the women active in the early years recalled the pattern of progress and the ways the developer was entwined in it. 'Someone would say, "We'll have to raise money". And then someone else would come up and say, "How are we going to get the money? Everyone's asking for money around the estate. There's plenty of small groups who are having raffles and selling lamingtons. How do we get the money?"'.

And someone else would come up with the ideas, "Well, it's not really our job to get the money. Council should provide these facilities". And someone else would say, "Not only Council, how about DVP, they're the ones that are making a profit by selling the land, they should also do something"'. The two symbols of those years of fund-raising were DVP and lamingtons—a massive finance company and a small chocolate-and coconut-covered cake, packaged for marketing by fund-raising groups. (I return to the lamingtons in chapter 12.)

Lamingtons probably raised more money. One of the leaders explained that 'DVP are like all the big companies, only interested in making money'. When DVP offered to type and publish the newsletter (funded with difficulty by advertising, and collated and distributed by volunteers all at the cost of hours of RA leaders' time) there was a charge, $94 an issue, so cheaper means were obtained. But while it contributed little financially, DVP maintained an awkward partnership with residents' groups. It was dealt into most major issues, and passed them back, acting as a sorting office, with the RA in particular making constant small demands on DVP. Records of RA meetings contain 'DVP' in a majority of paragraphs. In 1981 the representative of DVP proposed abandoning the occasional newsletter put out by the developer and using the RA newsletter as a 'community newspaper'. The editor commented that 'there was no way she was handing any editorial rights over to DVP just because they donate a bit of money'. In the same meeting, later business produced several items nicely summarizing the ambivalent relationship with DVP:

There was a letter from DVP which stated that the Education Dept has not purchased land for a combined primary and secondary school...The Education Dept was about to start a reappraisal of the situation and DVP are collecting statistics about the area. Another letter was received from DVP about the open parkland, with the allocation of open space in the new subdivision. It said that open space had already been taken into account at the time of the development. Everyone said, 'And that means *no* extra land'. A letter was received from DVP and signed by [the shopping centre manager, a young woman], which said that while space is available on the first floor in the shopping centre, the community can use it. The letter used the royal 'we', and there was some comment about that ... It was accepted by the group that DVP were being as fair as possible.

For some time groups continued to express concern that the meeting space was available only until let, but there seemed no way that pressure could be put on the developer to provide permanent space, and there is no record of the groups asking for it. There was no protest when the large old homestead (a splendid building for a community centre) was sold and pulled down so that its expensive elevated site could be subdivided. When DVP put the rental of its previous sales office too high for Council to obtain it for community use, this was unchallenged. There were several episodes where the RA seemed keen to protect DVP, common interests overcoming antipathy. At the end of one meeting an invitation to Councillors was proposed for the next meeting to discuss a needed pavilion. One member suggested inviting DVP. The president expressed concern that Council might use it to get money out of the developer.

The partnership was uneasy and leaders of the RA grew increasingly aware of it. At one informal meeting the president summarized: 'We've got a bitter taste in our mouth from being friendly, inviting them along to all our meetings, and we are tired of being used'. The developer's representative was irritated by the constant demands and the lack of reward in commercial terms. When Jan raised the residents' need for a community hall, the representative answered, 'Yes, like they complained about the shopping centre, and they're not using that'. Because so many women were not at home in the daytime? 'But they're not even using it on Friday nights. They seem to be still patronizing their old shopping centres.' Was he annoyed? 'Yes, I am annoyed. Why should we make facilities available when only a small number will use it?'

There was no such immediate response to the evident needs of older children. It was two years after the first residents moved in before a youth group was started, regularly attracting up to fifty teenagers and few or no parents. The stimulus was vandalism. The initiative and labour came from adults with younger or grown children, and from one single childless woman, a primary schoolteacher. DVP, by then very concerned at the vandalism and complaints, agreed to use of the empty shopping centre space. Complaints about vandalism and noise on club nights were immediate, and blamed on inadequate supervision. The young parents who had initiated the group agreed wholeheartedly, but they could find no assistance. All had assumed parent help would be forthcoming but, as the young woman teacher explained, the model of starting groups now well established in the estate did not work in this case. 'When different people decided they were interested in forming something, what they'd do is set up a team, find somebody who's interested in running it, and then step out. Then they'd go into something else.' That strategy worked for young families, but failed in this context. The organizers were left with the only initiative in which not one of them had an immediate interest. The group called six public meetings; 'one or two adults turned up' and the two original organizers, who continued to run the club with very little assistance for some years. The rising attendance of teenagers was matched by a rapid increase in complaints about the club, and no assistance. Parents 'were using it just as a baby-sitting club, and wouldn't even give one night a year'. One couple helped with transport, a few others with equipment. 'And what you found out was that *most* people who helped didn't have any kids going to the Youth Club.'

The group built up to 35 regulars, with an awkward age range from 12 to 21 years. One of the older boys graduated to adult supervisor. But younger children annoyed older children and the space available was inadequate: 'We just muddled our way through'. It lasted three years before the teacher returned to study and sheer absence of adult supervisors forced closure, at least for the time being. Yet, as she argued, 'Most of the kids around this area don't have a lot of problems. They're not rushing to leave home. It's not like a lot of areas where you have your homeless kids, kids on drugs'.

The contrast could hardly be stronger. Parents of teenagers were 'just not there'. Parents or intending parents of preschoolers obtained kindergartens, playgrounds, equipment, and space for a playgroup and firmly reproduced the image of Green Views as a place for young children.

M: I still say it's a good place to live. It's got nearly everything it needs. It's got its shops and it's got its schools; it's got its pre-school and all the rest of it; it's got all its amenities...

W: I like it. I think it's a good place to bring up your kiddies. I don't think I'd like a teenager living here at the moment. There's really not much for them at all. I wouldn't want to live closer to the milk bar. There's quite a few vandals get down there and it's bad for the area. I know it's their parents' responsibility, but I think if there was more facilities for them, or a bus service that came in at a reasonable time, so they could go somewhere—the last bus runs what, 6 o'clock, 6.30, so they can't go out.

People found it easy to explain the absence of parents of teenagers. The most sympathetic said that parents of teenagers have too many demands on them, too little time. Sometimes recognition of the variety of activities going on in a new estate was added to this. The Youth Club organizer, hardly free of pressures herself, cheerfully explained: 'Parents have an awful lot of pressures these days and, no matter what the kids belong to, that group's saying, come and help us raise funds, come and help us do this, come and organize a stall. And I don't really think it's fair for parents'. But other explanations were less kindly, and also mentioned class. Some blamed upward mobility; parents selfishly pursuing their own standard of living who 'couldn't give a bugger' about the needs of the estate or about their children. Some implied that the parents of teenagers were more likely to be working class and more likely to be under financial pressures and to have two or more jobs between the adults. As the previous chapter showed, they were right. In the first years of the estate that association contributed to fairly competent group activity on behalf of the young families by young educated residents able to deal with agendas and meeting procedures, negotiation with bureaucracies and unsympathetic authorities. Parents of school-age children were much less likely to have these skills.

Those two streams converging in the estate carried with them sets of ideas about family life and social class. The young purchasers' vision of home ownership and family community excluded a future with teenagers. When organizers set out to find answers to teenage problems, they faced not just lack of effort by other parents but also puzzlement about what effort was appropriate. It was much less easy to entertain teenagers than toddlers. A young mother observed at a meeting on the problem, 'It's holiday time, when you get both parents working and the kids are left at home and there is no holiday activities for them to become involved in. The Institute of Technology ran something last term, but—'. Her husband observed drily, 'Not all children of vandalizing age are prepared to go to dancing classes at the Tech'.

On the other hand, the people who most clearly came to Green Views for a 'better area' and an image of green country quiet were those who had teenagers. And the teenagers, or at least those who talked to observers at the Youth Club,[12] were very aware of these parent goals: 'Oh, me Dad's not busy because Mum wouldn't let him have all the cars over to fix, like he used to. The house used to be stacked up with cars, and there's hardly any now 'cos we're trying to keep the place clean'. A second boy painted the same picture: the home, here, was 'a lot more trouble 'cos you don't want the rest of the houses in a court to be really nice and yours to be junkyards or that'. But the nice area resulting got a unanimous vote from teenagers—boring. 'It's boring, like we only sit down, muck around. That's about all. If we just sit down, muck around, 'cos we haven't got anything to do, most of the time we get into trouble.'

Notes

1. R. Frankenberg, *Communities in Britain*, Penguin, Harmondsworth, 1966, p. 197.

2. L. Kilmartin & D. Thorns, *Cities Unlimited*, Allen & Unwin, Sydney, 1978 p. 80.

3. The *Newtown* study showed much the same ignorance and puzzlement of planning as did the present study. See L. Bryson & F. Thompson, *An Australian Newtown: Life and Leadership in a New Housing Suburb*, Penguin, Ringwood, 1972. There is amazingly little literature on how people see the development process. For recent readings on the Australian process, J. B. McLoughlin, & M. Huxley (eds), *Urban Planning in Australia: Critical Readings*, Longman Cheshire, Melbourne, 1986. For a rare study of people's perceptions of planning see C. Werthman, J. S. Mandel & T. Dienstfrey, *Planning and the Purchase Decision: Why People Buy in Planned Communities*, University of California Institute of Urban and Regional Development, Berkeley, Calif., 1965.

4. I think it significant that in planning circles and literature the developer is always referred to as 'he', representing male power as well as a fictional actor that can communicate to others. I have avoided the convention deliberately—the development company was most certainly not an identifiable actor but a complex financial institution containing many contradictory attitudes and approaches to the development process and presenting in the estate as inaccessible and incomprehensible. People always said 'they'.

5. Wording of these questions (in the normally untaped section) was: 'Green Views was advertised as a "planned community". Was it important to you to buy in a "planned" area? How do you expect a planned community to differ from an unplanned one? How do you feel about the developers—have they done a good job? Do you feel there is anything *special* about Green Views that makes it unusual or unique? What sort of an image does Green Views have now?'.

6. C. Allport, 'Women and suburban housing: Postwar planning in Sydney, 1943–61', in J. B. McLoughlin and M. Huxley (eds), *Urban Planning in Australia: Critical Readings*, Longman Cheshire, Melbourne, 1986.

7. E. J. Harman, 'Capitalism, patriarchy and the city', in C. V. Baldock & B. Cass (eds), *Women, Social Welfare and the State*, Allen & Unwin, Sydney, 1983, p. 104.

8. Widely regarded as the highest status area in Melbourne, Toorak symbolizes wealth and gracious living. Sandercock in her analysis of the attempts of planners to cater for an executive workforce for Melbourne's industrial west records that since 'remedies advanced do not contemplate this elite actually coming to live among the

low-paid migrant industrial workers' relief was to come from better access to the east or 'some little separated "Tooraks" in the outer corridor'. L. Sandercock, *Cities for Sale*: *Property, Politics and Urban Planning in Australia*, Melbourne University Press, Melbourne, 1975, p. 152.

9. American studies have investigated the concern with standards; see especially C. Perin, *Everything in Its Place: Social Order and Land Use in America*, Princeton University Press, Princeton, NJ, 1977.

10. We had worried much about including such a question, apparently unnecessarily making the wording turgid! Late in the taped section of the 1981 schedule we asked: 'There's an image of new estates as houses that look much the same, with people living the same sorts of lives. Did you see it that way when you decided to come here? (Did you want that? Is it like that?)'.

11. The stereotype of Housing Commission areas as flat, uniform and with spare houses without facilities fits a decreasing proportion of the public housing in Melbourne. The study by Bryson and Thompson (*An Australian Newtown*) describes one outer Commission area in the mid-1960s not unlike parts of Green Views in appearance.

12. Interviews at the Youth Club were conducted in 1981 by Rosemary Grant and Brenda Meincke.

3

All in the Same Boat? Class and Classlessness

'It seems that a lot of people here seem to be the same', said a professional woman. 'They are very caught up in their own little worlds and families. I suppose you should expect that, but if you are looking at it from outside and you are not caught in that sort of thing it looks all the same to you.'[1] From the outside looking in, this is suburban uniformity. Yet Green Views contained far more diversity than its marketing, its appearance or the pictures painted by residents indicated. From the inside looking out, diversity was recognized, even celebrated, but not as 'class'. It took some time for the project team to adjust to how seldom the word appeared in people's accounts,[2] and how often assertions of homogeneity and 'blending in' were juxtaposed with stories that were clearly about class distinctions.

W: We felt pretty comfortable straight away, 'cos everyone's in the same boat. We had some very bad neighbours that we didn't think belonged, and they've shifted. No, as a whole, everybody seems to be roughly round the same age group and all in a similar situation, so it seems to blend in well.

I: Why did the neighbours shift?

W: Oh police squabbles. No, they were *lovely* people! I think they were sort of running from payments on hire purchase and the kids were in trouble with the police and it was a case of disappear before anything happens.

'We're all in the same boat' is one of the recurring phrases, always used approvingly, sometimes laughingly, to indicate comfortable similarity. But it was manifestly false. If the people of Green Views were in the same boat, it was most certainly not a one-class vessel, they did not share the same destination, and some were clinging to the sides or already going overboard.

Everyone belongs

By 1981 three years of participation in the estate had established that many people were isolated there. Seeking those, we asked, 'Do you belong in Green Views?'. To our surprise, 80 per cent said yes. And it was yet another gender-free question! There was no difference between women's and men's answers. Only three people were sure they did not belong; the remainder were uncertain. Either they were denying isolation, or they 'belonged' in other ways. Both of course might be true, but for now I want to focus on the meaning of 'belong'. There were many ways of belonging, but few were about 'community'.

The most common sense of belonging was a vague democratic sense in which 'anyone belongs': 'Anyone who wants to live here, I suppose.' On the surface this softens the divisiveness of a 'better area'. But the words seem to mean not that anyone is accepted, rather that those who can get here are. The entry ticket is home ownership. 'I think all sorts, in Green Views especially. There's such a wide lot of people live here, I mean there's all different nationalities and different occupations . . . Might be a businessman or I think it's a case of you can work in a factory and you can still own your own home'.

If home ownership got you in, family life meant you fitted in. Several women belonged 'because my home's here', or 'so long as the family's happy'. A very isolated migrant woman belonged because, 'My family, the love of the family, it's being together, that's being here'. She never saw the neighbours, 'They're very busy, working. I don't even know my next door neighbour. It's a shame but that's how it is. People work. They just don't see one another'. But without seeing them she could know she belonged, 'very much'.

The question received aggressive responses from a few: 'It's not up to me to say if there was any sort of person that didn't belong anywhere.' Some of these are statements about sameness, some more about a muddle of divisions, a sort of happy pluralism: 'All sorts. There's no distinction, really'.[3] Some sound more like defiant assertions of principle: 'I suppose anybody and everybody should belong here. I don't see whether this should be an exclusive area'. But most offer a sort of luke-warm democracy: 'anybody who wants to live here'. One man said cheerfully that he certainly hoped he belonged: 'If not I'm paying someone else's mortgage!' Who belongs? 'Oh, humans', he laughed, then finally resorted to categories of class, 'I dunno, I suppose lower- to middle-class people'.

Those answers that did nominate some who 'belonged' fell into five groups: class, life stage, social 'involvement', 'fitting in' to suburbia and values about property. In only two, those about life stage and property, was anyone excluded.

The workers and their friends

Few people talked of class, and when they did class distinctions sounded benign, even downright confused. Several felt the middle-class belonged ('average, middle-class people'). A handful thought, as one man put it, that 'workers belong here. It seems like a workingman's type of place'. Perhaps they meant the same people? One woman said, 'I'd say middle-class, while some others would say upper-class'. She laughed, 'You wouldn't be living in Green Views if you were upper-class. I wouldn't have thought that this was Rolls Royce terri-tory'. Another said middle-class though, 'I think when it first started, they were hoping it was going to be like a small version of Toorak'.

These are uncomplicated pictures of class, offering no gradations between Green Views and the 'natural habitat of Melbourne's wealthy elite'.[4] Toorak is here a symbol of un-reachable wealth, visited by tourist buses, not somewhere you would live. Yet it is the only high-status area named in all this material on 'belonging'. There is no picture of a continuum of rankings; rather, of an urban world divided into areas below Green Views—areas like it or a little better—and Toorak. References to the western suburbs abound; some people name new eastern suburbs considered a little more desirable, places for future moves. But only one man hints at the fine status distinctions in the rest of Melbourne, and the differences between 'new' and 'old' areas. He and his wife, both pro-fessionals, stayed less than five years. 'If you thought yourself above people, you probably wouldn't belong here—you'd feel you were too good for the people who lived in an area like this', he said, adding rapidly, 'No one, I don't think, in that sort of state, would come to a new estate like this. They'd aim more for the older places, the name places'. He mentioned a similar new estate: 'You think to yourself, oh what a terrible place that must be. They must be all poor and living in Housing Commission type houses, and they think they own the world. But this is the same sort of place'.

No one said that those who belonged were better than they. A man who called himself middle-class said that the majority of other residents were 'definitely working-class'. His wife added, 'There are no Toorak classes here'. Another woman said enthusiastically, 'There's quite a vast mixture of people here and I can't see why no one shouldn't belong'. Her husband put in, 'It's a cross-section of the community, and if you take my title as truck driver or labourer, in certain areas you possibly wouldn't belong, but that doesn't worry me 'cos I'm part of everyday living'.

Not one person mentioned class when asked who did *not* belong, though a few produced extreme, almost mythical categories. If 'average middle-class, working people' belonged, did anyone not belong? 'No, not really—unless you're sort of talking about ultra smoothies'; 'Jet setters'. A kindly process of social selection apparently excluded only those who would not want to be there, or would not make it: 'People that live here now are fairly well established financially, so that would limit say a one-income family with a large number of children getting into the place'. In Green Views class, it seems, did not divide; 'working-class' had nothing to do with revolution, and only sometimes referred to occupational skill. To several people, mostly women, the development was for those who had to *work*: 'We all work'. And it had a special message about women. 'You get the workers and you get the non-workers, as far as the women are concerned, but basically I think we're pretty much of a muchness'. That work is for the same goals, so arriving at Green Views produces, at least for some, a sort of contented proletarian consciousness.

M: I feel happier here than I would in Toorak, kicking ten dollar notes out of the gutter and that sort of thing. I'm a working person. I'm sort of getting to a position where I will be in a respected job in the community (like being a postmaster, they're looked up to). I hope it doesn't change my life-style. I'll still consider myself a worker, and

that's what sort of an area I'm in. I know there are chartered accountants, there's managing directors and there's whatever. But they don't
bother me. You know, I can talk to them or have a beer with them if
they want to talk to me, or whatever. But I moved here. It was an
area of young people. They all worked. They all had mortgages. I've
got a mortgage. They've got children. We're having children.

The domination of work and what it wins—the family home—
seems to unify in two ways. First, having achieved these,
people seem to have no further sense of reachable class to
which 'working men' could aspire, and certainly no sense of
grievance against capitalism: 'It's just people very like myself.
Once you get to know them. Just people buying their own
homes, and just the average wage-earner and the average
home owner. We sort of live within our means, with what we
can afford'. And secondly, that common experience of work,
home and family softens, even celebrates difference: 'Basically,
I suppose we're all in the same boat—to a degree. A lot of the
houses here are bought on the low deposit, so they're probably
mostly all strugglers, but then again, as I've said, there are a
lot of the more expensive houses'. This is not passive acceptance of common middle-class membership. What the data
show are a variety of processes in which highly active actors
create what might be designated 'do-it-yourself class'. These
differences, unlike real differences in material conditions or
real position in societal class structures, were understood, salient
and frequently discussed.

As we watched, an almost instant set of local divisions
happened in Green Views. Working from a kit of pre-packed
social assumptions, people constructed with amazing unanimity
divisions that had real results for the formation of friendships
and formal groups. Everyone knew these divisions existed.
Most described them with relish. When we asked, 'Do you see
Green Views as having very different areas?' they drew maps
that were strikingly alike. The vast majority followed the lines
drawn by developers on their price lists, and the maps celebrate
the power of urban managers to affect social divisions.

'If I bought a second house, I would probably buy in Green
Views', a young father asserted. Where? His wife laughed as
he said 'I wouldn't go down in Stage 3, which is over that way,
because I don't like it. It's getting down to the creek area
there. If I bought another house it'd be in this general area,

and it'd just be a bigger house'. I asked if that would be to stay near friendships, and she said that would not matter: 'Green Views is not so big'. He agreed and his hands drew in the air a social map, the same as the map drawn by almost everyone else. 'I wouldn't mind, say, moving up to the other side. I wouldn't go down that side.' Ignoring for now the implication that *he* would buy it and decide its location, I asked if he saw different areas in the estate. Silly question!

M: You can split it easily into three sections, I reckon. You can classify up on top, near the shopping centre, 'Snob Hill', 'cos you go up there and they're all big houses and one of them's got a servant or whatever it is up there! We did a paper drive once, I knocked on the door and the woman came to the door and we said, 'Have you got any papers for the pre-school?'. And she said, 'I don't know. The lady of the house isn't in'.

W: She had an apron on.

M: She had an apron on, so I said, 'Ooh well, that must be the maid, right, fair enough!'

W: Nice, isn't it!

M: No, well, up on the Hill up there the houses are bigger. They're double-storey houses and they drive bigger cars and they drive Mercedes and all the rest of it. Then I think you'd classify this place as the middle—this area now around here is middle order—

W: Going on the price of the house—

M: And then you go over to the other side, I'd say, which would be lower order ... They're nice houses, but the land's not as expensive, and it's getting down towards the creek and there's the electricity pylons, which take away the value of the places, I reckon anyway, and it's getting more over into Westburg. And a lot of people classify Westburg as a low area.

I: Do you feel you belong more in this part?

W: I do. If I go to the Health Centre or anything like that, and somebody'll say, "Whereabouts in Green Views do you live?" and you say Stage 1, they automatically know you're in this little area. You never say your street, you just say the stage and they automatically know, "Oh you're one of those are you?".

M: Or if they say Stage 2, "Oh, you're in Snob Hill". If they say Stage 3, "You're down in the lower class area at the back. Towards the tip!" [laughter].

This is a game people seemed to enjoy, as though within the security of knowing that everyone belongs you could play at guessing differences. The guesses were grounded in assumptions imported from the wider society: the status of Westburg, being on the wrong side of the creek,[5] the size and style of houses, the symbolic meaning of servants. But Green Views also produced its own clues; the Hill and Stage 3 were defined by DVP lines and builders' price sheets in turn drawing on attitudes to elevated land and status patterns in Melbourne. You would not become puffed running up the Hill; much of Stage 3 was more rolling than much of Stage 1, with better views. But the Hill looked east; Stage 3 irrevocably west. DVP adjusted lines, block sizes and price lists accordingly; purchasers were fitted to these assumptions, and the social maps followed.

Based on limited information, these maps were restricted by the anonymity of people and the visibility only of their most significant item of personal consumption—the house. Before any houses were occupied in Stage 2 we recorded people talking of the Hill. As the first streets took shape in Stage 3, residents disapproved of the 'Commission-like' rows. Three quarters of our Stage 1 sample went 'never' or 'virtually never' to Stage 3, and nearly half as seldom to Stage 2, though the shopping centre was there. The only data for such confident labelling were appearances of houses, accrued information about prices and social knowledge.[6]

These data mislead, of course, hardly hinting at traditional indicators of life chances, occupation and education.[7] The divisions are called 'class', though with reluctance, the word appearing late in the descriptions. But they are not based on position in the labour market. Normally that is unknown. Nor is there much knowledge of indicators of status—life-style, decoration, taste. These are accessible inside the house. In Green Views, size of house and car indicated not what you did or your qualifications for doing it, or what you did with what you got paid, but how many people did it and for how long they had been doing it. Number of incomes and life stage were the obvious dividers, and people talked much more often about whether 'they both work' than what the jobs were. Two-income families 'belonged' in the sense that they were typical of the area, though they were least likely to belong in a social sense, and they knew so little about each other that there was no other basis on which to assess belonging. A mother of school-age children said 'ordinary people, anyone' belonged. 'Basically they all work hard to live here and most parents work.' It took no time to belong: 'I always wanted to live in Green Views'.

Thus in a society in which the new poor are single-income families, the newly anonymous in class terms are dual-income home-owners. And workforce participation muddied the two streams flowing into Green Views so that hard rock shelves of unequal life chances could hardly be seen. For now, the older second-home owner clearly had more resources than the young professional couple with babies and one income. But the apparent equality was a temporary phenomenon, and everyone knew that. In this context it makes sense that descriptions of life stage were more divisive than those of life chances.

All in the same life stage: Old is over 40

Nobody said people at all life stages could belong. Rather, many assumed falsely that there was only one life stage: 'They're all young couples, first homes, and we're all battlers . . . So we really all belong here'. In about half of these replies class was mixed with life stage, and the two were combined with workforce patterns, as in, 'I think middle-income, average-income earners. Young families mainly—two-income earners.'

If belonging was about being in the same life stage, many were too old or too young. One woman did not belong 'in this court, which consists of a lot of young married people with children; I feel perhaps that I am a little bit old, I'm a little bit out of my era'. A man declared that in a 'community-type estate, a place to live where children, etc. and families are the main criteria' those who 'race around in cars etc.' did not fit in. His wife explained, 'Well someone that basically is not aware of kids'. The only unmarried man in the 1978 sample summed up local life: 'The mothers stay home all day and talk about each other, and the men come home at night. I've not made friends with anyone here, only because I'm a single person . . . It's too far out from entertainment, from the city. The pubs are a bore. There's nothing single-wise'.

All these comments share three assumptions. First, homogeneity of age group is good. The language hints at an effort to avoid prejudice: 'You've just got people the same age, or roughly the same age and young children ... Not that I'm against—you know, I think it's nice to have older people around as well, but it's nice to see lots of mothers walking around with babies and to be a part of it'. Family community means young families, disconcertingly narrowly defined! 'It would be, probably, a 40 and under community. There's exceptions, of course. And they're very friendly.' A young woman, describing the ones that 'don't fit in', explained (to a researcher uncomfortably near the cut-off age)[8] that 'there's not one old couple in this street, whereas in other streets, there's probably the occasional old couple—when I say old I mean over 40'. She thought 'they may not want to fit in'.

Secondly, age group is 'read' as stage of family life and of home ownership. 'It's mainly people of my own age, in that same stage of life, just bringing up a family. Not ones moving into their second homes. I think the ones that are bringing up their families, that can sort of see ... a light at the end of the tunnel, in respect of being able to pay off their house and perhaps moving out eventually, when their kids grow up.'

And thirdly, there is a strikingly limited picture of life stages, young and old, with no range in between: 'It's more beneficial to the younger families. I can't see too many benefits for older people here. The major problem of transport would probably hinder most of the older people' (the problems of driving for the over-40s?). The 'old' are seen as unchanging, while the image of the young commonly includes an accurate map of the life-stage track they are on: 'There seem to be a lot of young ones. When I stay home and go for the bus, it's mostly young mums with a pusher—maybe a pusher and one toddler or just a pusher, or a pusher and pregnant ... You perhaps see somebody, and they're just a couple, and they're all going trudging off to work, like you are, and then the next thing, the wife's home and there's a baby'.

That apparently pervasive phrase 'all in the same boat' turns out, on examination, to belong mainly to the young, and entirely to the first-home owners.[9] The pressing priorities of the present are all-demanding and levelling: 'It's people just very much like myself. Once you get to know them. Just people buying their own homes, and just the average wage-earner and the average home owner. We sort of live within our means, with what we can afford'. This common burden means 'everyone belongs' *and* (because) 'nobody's home'. 'The sort who belong are family people, young people with families. It seems like a lot go to work.'

Nobody's isolated

The third sense of 'belong', through social interaction, was the one we intended. Few interpreted the question our way. When they did, there was always an assertion that there were no *barriers* to belonging, unless you made them yourself. It sounds easy. 'I think you belong the first day you walk into your house', said a mother of school-age children, adding, 'everyone belongs'. 'It's up to the individual person' was a recurring comment. Not one statement in this context implied that other factors might contribute; if you do not belong, it is your preference, option or fault.

And the picture remained gender-free. Both women and men said as much, though both implied that the work of belonging was done by women. A husband said he belonged 'more to the house', then asked if we meant 'to the community of Green Views'? His wife replied, 'Oh yes, I know people; I know faces that you can recognize and smile and say hello'. The only barrier recognized is not being there—for women. All men worked full-time, but only two saw work as stopping them from belonging because they worked unusual hours. One couple debated the question:

W: I do! I'm very well-known around here [laugh]!

M: My wife does, yes, she supports the local Green Views shopping centre! But I really don't spend enough time at home—

W: Everyone knows me.

M: To really feel part of anywhere, wherever I've been, irrespective of whether it be Green Views or anywhere else.

'Both working' was a reason many gave for not belonging. Apparently regarding his Asian background as irrelevant, a professional man explained, 'We're stuck with our jobs, 9 to 5, and by the time we come back we may not belong because we didn't get ourselves involved'. That is your own fault: 'some people live in their own home and they don't know anybody and they don't want to try to know anybody'.

Where luke-warm democracy smudges the differences in life chances, these statements deny the existence of suburban isolation; the theme recurs throughout this book. A woman who had recently stopped work said: 'It wouldn't take long if you didn't want it to take long, because I think everybody's so nice you could make friends just walking up the street if you wanted to. But as I said, I never had the time for anything like that because I worked'. Such statements were most often made by people with no experience of being isolated. They came too from those involved in 'community' action groups, with the clear implication that civic effort is rewarded by belonging. 'Being involved' usually meant belonging to organized groups, and was seen as entirely a matter of choice. Anybody can belong, a woman said, 'as long as they're friendly, willing to participate in the area and sort of help develop the area properly. Instead of sitting around, waiting for it to be done'. Getting involved is easy. 'There's lots of things to join in and do and meet people. So it's up to the individual person. My husband's very outgoing so he just took himself off there and introduced himself and I did the same thing at the tennis club...But I do know other people that won't join in anything, and they're finding it very hard to meet people and sort of fit in'.

And if they do not? A sharp edge to this pretty picture is the conviction by several that you 'have to belong' in Green Views. 'Because of isolation, and the fact that it's a community type of environment, you've got to belong here', said a young father. He explained, 'Well the atmosphere lends itself to belonging—for survival in the area'.

So who does not belong? If those in the sample felt excluded, they were not saying so. Those few who said they did not belong all said they did not want to, with only one exception (a sad story told below). To stop here would give a picture of bulk belonging. Almost everyone who wants to, can say they belong in Green Views. Most of those who did not belong fitted the accusation that they were anomalous or not trying; they were people not in the 'right' life stage or in the full-time workforce, or both. The young would belong in future; 'We moved in, and once I stopped working and started going to other things in the area, you belonged more because all your contacts were in the area'. The old, presumably, would leave.

Belonging in suburbia

In a society stocked with stereotypes about suburban conformity, suburban mediocrity, suburban neuroses and malaise,
surely those moving on from this first step into home ownership,
or unable to move because resources were limited, would be
anxious to dissociate themselves from suburbia. Yet only two
took this position strongly, both women whose images of society
were explicitly in terms of class differences, and who saw the
estate as lower class. Far from denying that this was a one
class boat, they agreed, and wanted to leave.

Both saw the life of suburbia as about 'being involved': 'Not
belong—committed would be better, as in a gaol'. This woman
had been in several groups, but saw them as 'very insulated.
Everything done is within Green Views ... Most people I talk
to had a choice about where they were going to live, and this is
where they chose to live. And most *really* belong here; their
mentality is towards the little suburban house, and mine isn't.
Most people seem interested in getting things going and
kindergartens and pre-schools and all the works, 'cos they
know they're going to be here and their kids are going to grow
up here. And I feel sort of—we'll be moving soon'.

The other woman also used an analogy of a total institution
for the estate. When they moved in: 'I thought that it was a
dust hole; now I think that it is a concentration camp'. Her
husband put in, 'With a fence around it', and she echoed this,
adding, 'I am sounding like a snob now, aren't I? I guess it's
that the type of people who live out here aren't what I have
been used to'. He agreed. 'A lot of them are just people who
have moved to Green Views hoping that this is the house that
they are going to stay in all of their lives. They have not got
any ambition'. She had overheard a friend saying of someone
else, "I didn't think they could afford to live there", you
know, as if Green Views is some sort of big deal'.

Her problem was about privacy; not isolation but inability to
avoid interaction. She compared this with the better-off spacious
older suburb where she grew up and the (also better-off) semi-
rural area to which they hoped to move. 'The people here are
just so different, they are so different! I just couldn't believe
it, they are so matey, so terribly matey, to your face!'. She is
'sort of stuck here with the baby' and the five other babies in
the court are seen not as an opportunity for social contact but

as basis for competition: 'all you get is "mine can do this and that"'. Her husband put in, 'You are a snob', and she reacted with predictions about the class future of the estate, as though it followed from the interaction pattern. And the linking theme is the teenagers. 'I look upon this place as a future Farwest — the kids here are really rough; there will be a battle between the Farwest kids and the kids of Green Views. I think that the wall outside just breeds a false feeling of security about what is going to happen. I might be going off the handle here, but as I see it, it is Northern Ireland against Southern Ireland'.

Belonging and standards

Here luke-warm democracy disappears. Neighbours with a messy yard 'don't deserve to live in a nice area like this', said a woman who had earlier said, 'I've never sort of looked at anybody and thought, well I wish you didn't live at Green Views. I don't know enough about the people and that to know'. A recurring phrase is 'they don't care'. 'Everyone did the right thing by getting the houses looking reasonably neat. But there's a few people who don't care. Like across the road, there are two old ripped cars and all the rubbish in the driveway. They started off when we first shifted in; they worked on their garden, but it's just gone back to mud and dirt and there's no driveway. I'd hate to see what the back garden's like.'

Thus life stage links with appearance; teenagers are very visible. Like the song, Green Views was as much about the families in the little boxes as it was about architectural homogeneity: 'And they all have pretty children and the children go to school'. Young families have pretty children. It is young families who belong, but not only in the sense that they have the numbers. Young families and the retired are no threat to property values; here the strikingly limited picture of range of life stages makes sense.

I: What sort of people belong here?

W: Oh I think young families. You know. And retired people.

I: Are there any people who don't belong?

W: Yes, idiots. Irresponsible people. I feel they should be somewhere where they do fit in, but it's not the type of area...I just don't believe that people who can't look after other people's things, you know, like the playground equipment—that's here for the kiddies, not for teenagers to wreck. And I think they should be tried to be kept out of the area.

In the 'family community' there seem to be very few children old enough to wreck play equipment. But the future in which those 'little kiddies' grow into teenagers is much feared. The fear of teenagers, the inability to control or understand them, is certainly in part a fear of their transitional status.[10] The single teacher who organized the Youth Club confessed, 'I was petrified of teenagers. I had nothing to do with teenagers at all. I hadn't even had anything to do with older primary kids. I thought "Ooh teenagers! Oh my God! What are we going to do?"'.

Many, however, assumed that crime was a necessary result of teenagers either coming in or growing up. 'The child population is going to explode', a woman predicted. Her husband added, 'We're already starting to see the effects of that. Large numbers of kids hanging around the shops up there...a house or two every week is broken into in Green Views'. The link between child age and crime is obvious to him: 'When all these children reach school-leaving age and don't get a job and they hang around the place all day, the problem will get worse and worse for sure ... the place could end up turning into another Westburg'. Even children agreed. A woman recounted hearing a 13-year-old warn a friend against leaving his bag outside a shop; the friend answered, 'Well, we live in Green Views now, not Farwest'.

The cross-threading of themes confuses this material. However independent the variables may seem to sociologists, in Green Views life stage is also about social class. The benign picture in which everyone belongs is blotted by the conviction that areas 'go downhill' as kids grow up. There are three different arguments here.

First, some people objected to what they saw as recent, lower-class arrivals in older age groups. That there was an association between lifestage and the socio-economic and educational background of the pioneer residents probably fed this impression. It was likely to be strengthened as the gloss of the highly promoted elegant new estate wore off, cheaper land was released, and the 'country' image more obviously contrasted with suburban reality. One mother of teenagers admitted she was 'not very keen' on the area: 'The whole atmosphere seems to have changed somehow. It's hard to put a finger on it, but there's a lot of new people coming in and there's a lot of the older people moving out as well. There's a lot of night-time, you know, young kids (hoodlums, actually) screaming'.

Secondly, some people objected not to specific people but to the changing age composition, seeming to equate life stage directly with class. A father of teenagers offered the link of new with young: 'I mean, this is a new area, and you wouldn't expect to find kids that would vandalize'. His wife added, 'I mean, the houses don't cost two bob around here and you expect kids to congregate round Commission areas and that'. Everyone agreed that, as another woman said, 'It's not going to get any better once all these children get older. There's nothing for older children here'. Although she added, 'They may not be so disadvantaged as the Farwest ones, because there's so many disadvantaged families there with broken homes and lots of other problems'.

The third theme in some of these packages of ideas about life stage and class was the threat to family life in the estate's 'going downhill'. A high rate of marriage breakdown was assumed,[11] as was its relation to women's employment and mortgage repayments. A minister of religion said authorities 'call it mortgage row' and linked this immediately with teenage problems: 'We could quite easily hear this screeching of tyres nightly, even over the noise of the television'. Although in choosing the estate 'that wasn't a consideration', he had hoped it would be 'a little bit better than, say, if I can use another suburb, say Westville. I would have expected *more* of the people who lived in Green Views'. Why? 'I thought that Green Views would have had a little bit more—I'm trying to avoid using the word 'class', that's not what I mean.' But it is what he means. The squirming at mentioning class serves to under-line how important it is to those trying not to mention it. A woman told of having her car stolen, 'It's just those little things, they make you think of it as a *lowly* type of suburb'.

Only a few of the young (with more faith in developers) were optimistic. The mother of a young baby felt they had time: 'If it keeps on improving, then they'll have enough local entertainment to keep him amused.' Several who had sought this new area of young people would later flee it when it began to look more used and less young; they would move on to another new area (taking with them their own growing children). One man had chosen another new residential area: 'I have yet to see what I would call working class out there. Not, again, that I'm saying we're a better class than anybody else, I'm not'. He explained: 'Probably because I'm a businessman and I'm dealing with business executives and directors'. This environment will not do, 'because of the basic style of neighbour and their children. I wouldn't like my children to mix with them because they would be the sort of kids that if it was inner suburbs would be at the state school, and I would never send my kids to a state school'.

The association of 'family' with class is often apparently unrecognized, and if recognized it embarrasses. Women seemed to be embarrassed more often than men. A young mother said anybody belonged here 'apart from perhaps (this might sound dreadful) the Housing Commission type homes'. She tried to explain: 'They cause so many problems with the type of people. That sounds awfully class conscious!'. Such areas, she felt, created problems: 'All the people that aren't sort of a strong family often seem to go to them. The mum works and dad works and the kids are often left on their own. They're the ones that let themselves in and let themselves out of the houses, so they cause lots of behavioural problems because the parents don't know where they are and often don't care. It's a gross generalization, but there's lots of kids—like at Farwest, where it seems to be happening, all the behavioural problems'.

The same awkward equation of parental pressure, women's workforce involvement, poor discipline, family stress and teenage problems produced far more hostile responses from men, including the familiar theme that 'they' should control these problems:

M: If they got rid of half the backsides out [of] the joint, no more idiots on trail bikes, the juvenile kids got some parental supervision and a good kick in the backside occasionally—and I could give a few of them a good lick round the ear when I get some bloody backchat— it would probably improve a hell of a lot ... I don't blame the kids, I blame the parents. The parents need a kick in the backside, not the kids. You've got a work situation when you've got both parents working and they don't give a bugger.

Several people welcomed the selective processes that removed 'undesirable people', who were 'noisy and things like that'. A couple who 'fight and argue a lot and the whole neighbourhood can hear it' and whose kids were 'just roaming around the area' had left; 'they couldn't, from what I've heard, keep up with the payments'.

Creating a one-class boat

The democratic acceptance of 'all sorts' therefore applies only to the sorts that are not visibly different. In this context the frequent assertion that 'we're all in the same boat' looks like a bizarre lie; yet it is also a strongly-held belief. It means 'we all have the same goals', we are all home owners, and we are all in the same life stages. It masks the facts that many are not securely in this dream boat, that a third of these families are past the stage of cute controllable toddlers, and that those are the ones who are staying, and their children are the most in need of facilities. That class is conflated with life stage indicates the power of these beliefs. Nobody seriously means that the young in society are the middle-class. But what is seen is the maintenance of the home and the age of the children; so long as there are no visible signs of lower-class behaviour the word need not be used.

Of course those who offered categories of people who always belonged, at least by implication, had categories for those who did not. The majority of these statements were not aggressive about those they excluded. But they were always about either life stage or property maintenance. The two were firmly linked, and the link was class. So the democratic picture oversimplifies processes by which belonging was filtered.[12]

'Who doesn't belong?' Only one occupational category was nominated, the only occupation which brought visual evidence of class membership into the estate: 'the truckies'. Of several complaints about trucks, none explicitly asserted they looked lower class, but all implied it. 'Wherever you look there are trucks,' said one woman (obviously falsely). Complaints about several large trucks parked by owner-drivers were filed with the RA, which duly protested, and attracted resentment. One driver and his wife now planned to leave Green Views. She saw their trouble in class terms. 'We have been told by the parking officer that the Residents' Action Group complains all the time about it; it detracts from the area, we are a low class of people that they don't want living in Green Views.' She repeated this (though there was nothing in all our observation of the RA meetings or correspondence to confirm it) and her words include class: 'This Residents' Action Group, they think they're sort of millionaires. They're all mortgaged to the hilt, and they look down their nose at all the people here...If you get rid of the Residents' Action Group, I'd say Green Views would be a nice place to live, and just ordinary, every-day people, it's just a mixture here—everyone'. The story included serious harassments that she blamed on the intervention of the RA group.[13]

Anonymous phone calls came first, whenever her husband was away, and while she was ill; they continued for three hours one night, and she had to answer the phone in case her husband 'had broken down with the truck or something'. Shortly afterwards she had a miscarriage, and on her return from hospital her husband was sent a wreath with the message: 'On the death of his wife'. The police were called, but on this and a second florist's order the next day, the name and address were false. A silent phone number was installed; weeks later she met the recipient of her old number who said, 'We are being driven insane by anonymous phone callers. They ring up and when I say I'm not you they say "Don't tell lies", and all this string of obscenities follows'. A sympathy card arrived saying 'Flowers first, accident and funeral to follow'. After a period of obvious police visits and surveillance 'it just stopped, so the police reckon whoever it was had seen the police coming here on and off'. But she remained puzzled: 'All my immediate neighbours are lovely. We've never had an ounce of trouble from them'.

All home owners

There is nothing new in the suggestion that property owner-ship masks class differences; both those committed to class conflict and those promoting stability have asserted this for at least a century. Marx and Engels said so. Politicians have always said so. The housing industry boasts it. Urban sociology has for some time been fascinated by the suggestion that class struggle is defused by either or both home ownership and debt. The ideological function of home ownership has been portrayed as incorporating the working class into the dominant order, fragmenting it into mere status groups and substituting for class consciousness a privatized preoccupation with the 'personal life'.[14]

Green Views is the home of home ownership firmly in the context of capitalism. And it certainly *sounds* classless. But the apparent homogeneity of life there is no simple phenomenon. The widespread unwillingness to use the term 'class' combines with eager and curious discussion of apparently petty differences in resources and life-style. The insistence that residents are 'all in the same boat' is seen as compatible with sharp differences in real class situation. And the pretty, democratic picture of an estate in which everyone belongs sits oddly with evidence of hostility towards and resentment of some who are there or might come.

The easiest interpretation of the evidence is that Green Views was enjoying the smooth processes by which affluence bestows on parts of the working class both middle-class status and privatization.[15] But a high proportion of the residents thought of themselves as workers, and most who identified with a middle class accepted most of the others they labelled as workers with apparent equanimity. Moreover, hardly anybody saw life chances on the estate as being equal. This is a picture of people *seeing* class, but not *saying* it. Differences in life chances, never far from people's portraits of the estate, were rarely specifically stated. Rather, they appeared in odd places, like a dye staining the colours of those portraits and making them run into other shapes.

The divisions that mattered most were divisions between home owners. Most people saw divisions within the estate, and behaved in terms of them. They also readily and often urgently drew social maps dividing Melbourne home-owners; they had come to Green Views following those maps. The area was not Toorak, and nobody thought it could be. But while nearer, geographically and socially, to Westville and even Far West, it was to be very different from these. Both were largely areas of private home ownership but lower status. Those who were satisfied felt confident that they were moving away from such areas: those most dissatisfied felt either that Green Views was not sufficiently distinguished from them or that the 'type of people' in those suburbs were now following them here. For both, the myth of homogeneity was constructive.

From the inside looking out, little of the society's class

system can be seen. This has been one of the consistent, and valid, criticisms of 'community studies'; most studies either assert that the local patterns of inequality are microcosms of the wider society or simply ignore those wider societal patterns (of both class and gender).[16] It is my intention to do neither, but the nature of my data makes it possible to see the class structure of which these people were a part only indirectly— through their local lives. These pictures offer no experience of relations beyond the Fence. The patterns of acceptance of class differences and active creation and celebration of status divisions in Green Views are not separate from the structures of class, but part of the way they work.[17] Ethnographic data in a locality give a sharp picture of local divisions and a distorted, distant reflection of wider ones. So they work rather as the skindiver's mask does, to clarify the underwater world (giving an entirely false feeling of belonging in it) but to offer no access to the shapes above, lending unreality to that other world (and an entirely misleading sense of its irrelevance).[18]

But the data do offer a chance to explore processes by which people define and impose 'equality' and aspects of inequality long ignored by the sociology of 'public' life. This is partly to argue that the male-sociology concepts of stratification of 'public sphere' mislead, since they ignore the 'people work' of the 'private' sphere;[19] much of this book is about that dichotomy. But I want to argue further that those concepts mislead *also* because they ignore the sphere of local interaction in which people can and do work to obscure, erase or reinterpret the reality of class placement in capitalist society, including the reality of women's labour and its crucial contribution to maintaining the consumer demand from the 'private world'.

'All in the same boat' did not ever mean all in the same class situation, or even the same current financial situation. It meant something between 'all under the same pressures' and 'all in the same dream'. Those who used the phrase were the young parents, and they were referring not to occupation or income, which they recognized as varied, but to home ownership and family life, whose goals they held in common. So real differences in the chances that they would be moving on or going up did not matter for now. 'All sorts' can belong, so long as they share those goals. But they share also, of course, the dangers. 'All in the same boat' is about a common struggle, if not a common destiny—we are in this together. The experience does not make us alike; that 'the same boat' did not refer to attainment of middle-class membership is quite explicit in many statements. Nearly half of these people cheerfully call themselves working class, and there is no evidence of attempts at closure against those whom a survey researcher would classify as such. But there is much evidence of a sense of danger from visible signs of working-class residents. All sorts belong, but not the sorts associated with wrecked cars (if they bring their wrecked cars with them). It is a family community, but not a place for older kids who damage things. You are welcome to be a truckie, but not to park your truck in the court. And, to turn to the subject of the next chapter, there is widespread acceptance of acceptable migrants.

Notes

1. Her words echo the terminology of Perin, linking socially constructed status to the categories of land use management. 'There are two ways of thinking about social status: from the outside looking in, and from the inside looking out. There are the social pigeon-holes people are defined to belong in, and there are the social principles with which they negotiate their relationships with one another'. C. Perin, *Everything in Its Place: Social Order and Land Use in America*, Princeton University Press, Princeton, NJ, p. 168.

2. The literature in qualitative analysis contains little on the dangers of theme-finding without control, and nothing on the problem of the missing theme. Team discussions record our frustration with this one, laughing accounts of how we could 'get them to say it' ('sounds like...'). We assumed in the early stages that people were constrained by egalitarian ideas; as the discussion below shows, this was certainly true of some. But for a while our assumption prevented our seeing the power of other dominant ideas to mask such divisions *and* the significance of dividers deriving from those ideas. The 1981 schedule did not use the word 'class', people had been asked to say what class they were in in 1978, when the survey interviews were not taped.

3. One way of noticing when a theme is emerging from experience in the field is the joke labels it acquires in the research team. We began calling this the 'licorice answer' (all sorts) before we recognized its significance in the puzzle of 'classlessness'.

4. *Age*, 23 February 1988. Toorak occurs as a referent in the same way in Newtown: 'We wouldn't change for any house in Toorak'. See L. Bryson & F. Thompson, *An Australian Newtown: Life and Leadership in a New Housing Suburb*, Penguin, Ringwood, 1972.

5. The creek in question, a minimal and intermittent watercourse, has significance here beyond its unattractive appearance. Melbourne's suburbs are notoriously divided in socio-economic status by minor waterways, especially when they take the geological line between the flatter west and the more rolling land of the higher-status east.

6. A splendid contrast is provided by the portrait of naked local class divisions in an industrial company town where occupations and income are known and divisions are imposed by male work roles. See F. Campbell & R. Kriegler, 'Illusion and disillusion: The ideology of community in an industrial town', in M. Bowman, *Beyond the City*, Longman Cheshire, Melbourne, 1981, pp. 71–96, and R. Kriegler, *Working for the Company*, Oxford University Press, Melbourne, 1980.

7. Within the functionalist tradition of sociology the husband's oc-

cupational role as the 'boundary role' linking family to outside world is the primary 'status carrying role'. See T. Parsons, 'Age and sex in the social structure of the United States', *American Sociological Review*, vol. 7, 1942, pp. 604–16. Following this logic, stratification studies for decades have used rankings of male occupational status to place households, a practice denounced in feminist critiques, but, as chapter 2 showed, followed by people. See R. Crompton & M. Mann, *Gender and Stratification*, Polity Press, Cambridge, 1986, for recent discussion.

8. Both Jan Salmon and I were under the dreaded age of 40, a factor that became important as the project progressed. It offers a nice example of unanticipated problems of research design—factors you can hardly alter when you find they matter. Factors we had expected to be problematic—our places of residence, family structures, education and professional work status—mattered little, but age and life stage were crucial in establishing rapport.

9. This phrase is a splendid example of the danger of thematic analysis where there is no rigorous method of checking the occurrence of themes that 'take hold' of the data, and of the way this can be avoided by computer handling of unstructured data. A string search of all text on file showed the phrase was not as ubiquitous as I had expected, at least in recorded sections (though its use in the conversations and meetings not taped cannot be measured of course). There are sixteen occurrences of 'the same boat' in the text files, one referring to specific women, the rest to 'all' residents. All recorded uses of it were by parents of young children. Jan Salmon and I are both recorded using the phrase during meetings at Green Views, apparently adopting it as local dialect, though unaware that we were doing so. At the start of the project it had been a phrase familiar to neither of us, and much discussed. Intriguingly, it is a phrase noted in memories of the battle for home ownership by Australians who built houses in the immediate post-war years, and interviewed by Pamela Rehak for Stoking up dreams: Some aspects of post-war housing in the suburbs of Melbourne, PhD thesis, Monash University, Clayton, Vic., 1988.

10. For an analysis of transition in the context of urban developments, see Perin, *Everything in its Place*.

11. I return in later chapters to the idea of the Family. Rates of marital dissolution are impossible to document; there was one case in our reinterview sample, two couples were separated by 1981 and several other cases occurred in the group networks and other people we knew. For obvious reasons the stories of marriage strain, breakdown and sexual rumour have been omitted from this account.

12. The questions asked exaggerated this effect in two ways. First, the

democratic message was summonsed by the flag verb 'belong'. Virtually everyone had a way in which they and everyone else belonged. And secondly, having assumed (wrongly) that everyone would offer divisions, we asked 'Who doesn't belong?' only if the speaker implied that someone did not. This fine example of how reasonable, but regrettable, logical assumptions distort fixed schedules undoubtedly deprived us of the chance to question the blanket 'everyone belongs'. Belated insertion of the prompt after several such replies produced some of the data used here.

13. After this interview, we intervened, arranging a meeting for her with the president of the RA, who was both appalled at the story and anxious to help. The theme of the class membership of the RA is picked up in Section 4.

14. The Marxist argument was developed by Castells to incorporate the ways ownership divided the working class, tying the individual to the capitalist financial system and to private commodity consumption. The debate in Britain focused on the ways in which the attainment of ownership by some might be said to create 'housing classes'. M. Castells, *The Urban Question*, Edward Arnold, London, 1977. For the British debate, see R. Pahl, *Whose City?*, Longman, London, 1969; J. Rex, 'The Sociology of a zone of transition', in R. Pahl (ed.), *Readings in Urban Sociology*, Pergamon, Oxford, 1969; and on the subsequent debate C. Bell, 'On housing classes', *Australian and New Zealand Journal of Sociology*, vol. 13, no. 1, 1977, and Rex's response in the same volume. For summaries of other material see N. Duncan, 'Home ownership and social theory', in J. Duncan (ed.), *Housing and Identity: Cross-cultural perspectives*, Croom Helm, London, 1981, pp. 106–7; R. W.Connell, *Ruling Class, Ruling Culture*, Cambridge University Press, Cambridge, 1977; L. Kilmartin and D. Thorns, *Cities Unlimited*, Allen & Unwin, Sydney, 1978. J. Kemeny, *The Great Australian Nightmare*, Georgian House, Melbourne, 1983. Rehak documents the post-war political debates in Australia in Stoking up dreams.

15. The classic studies in Britain exploring and challenging this thesis were by J. Goldthorpe *et al.*, *The Affluent Worker in the Class Structure*, Cambridge University Press, Cambridge, 1969.

16. C. Bell & H. Newby, *Community Studies*, Allen & Unwin, London, 1971; L. Bryson & B. Wearing, 'Australian community studies—a feminist critique', *Australian and New Zealand Journal of Sociology*, vol. 21, pp. 349–66.

17. 'The finest-meshed sociological net cannot give us a pure specimen of class, any more than it can give us one of deference or of love. The relationship must always be embodied in real people and in a real context...Class is defined by men as they live their own history, and, in the end, this is its only definition.' E. P. Thompson,

The Making of the English Working Class, Penguin, Harmondsworth, 1968, pp. 10−11. This is not to argue, as A. F. Davies did (in *Images of Class*, Sydney University Press, Sydney, 1967) and neo-Weberian writers (though not Weber) have tended to imply, that the study of individuals' relations and interpretation of them is enough for understanding class relations. But it is most certainly to argue the need to see active actors in class systems, and to heed people's accounts of both class and status—indeed to do so dissolves the conceptual distinction between the two, an argument presented by C. Eipper, 'Class processes: Key issues for analysis', *Australian and New Zealand Journal of Sociology*, vol. 18, no. 2, 1982, pp. 214−27, esp. p. 226.

18. The metaphor applies also to the researcher's partial involvement with the people studied; on several occasions when I met residents in other contexts I experienced a sharp dissonance—rather as the diver does if the mask is held at the water's surface so both worlds can be seen.

19. M. Stacey, 'The division of labour revisited or overcoming the two Adams', in P. Abrams *et al.* (eds), *Practice and Progress: British Sociology 1950−1980*, Allen & Unwin, London, 1981. See also her and others' papers in Crompton & M. Mann, *Gender and Stratification*.

4

On Not Being Different:
Migrants and Acceptance

The pretty democratic picture of 'belonging' included lack of prejudice. Ethnic diversity sometimes was offered as *part* of the belief that 'everyone belongs': 'all people, really, because there's all nationalities for a start'. Acceptance of migrants had a lot in common with acceptance of 'all sorts' in class terms; if they were not obtrusively different they could belong. 'They're getting into every area, aren't they. But you don't have any problems. Most of them are probably nicer than Australians, I suppose. I must admit we don't know any migrants—they're all basically Australians.'

When directly asked whether they mixed with different people, almost all residents interpreted the question in terms of ethnic differences. Only 44 per cent said yes. But another 44 per cent said they did not mix with anyone in Green Views! Nine per cent said people here were all the same, leaving only four people who said they avoided mixing with those who were 'different'. Only four of those who did mix were negative about it. Half of the sample said they found those people 'just like anyone else'. The rest stressed either broadening experience or culinary variety: 'You learn from it most of the time'; 'It's good for the children to have different friends'; 'We've eaten with Italians, eaten with Greeks, eaten with Lebanese. And we all laugh and cry'. Most enthusiastic were overseas-born or young couples who were more likely to be moving on. 'I like migrants, I think they make the world be different. I'm a migrant myself and I like meeting my own people, which there's not enough of them ... We got Chinese food, we got fish and chips'. A young woman said proudly, 'The proof is, I'm Australian, my husband's Italian ... The whole of Australia's a combination, it's either live with it or get out! I prefer to live with it. Well, I've learnt a lot'. She could cook 'a great Italian meal'.

Similarly, if people disapproved of the 'proportion of migrants here' few were prepared to say so. Interpretation is difficult, and any bias would be towards tolerance.[1] 'That's a baited question, isn't it', laughed one man. 'I suppose it depends on your racial prejudice a bit. To me, there's too many.' But only 18 per cent were negative; 29 per cent said they were very positive; most showed no antagonism. 'I think they've got us outnumbered actually', said one man, but added, 'It doesn't worry me'. A good thing? 'Probably in the long run, yeah ... I think the general Australian adopts the Australian adage, I'm alright if you are, sort of thing.' The general Australian as represented here was sharply aware of the migrant presence. The 'joke' about being outnumbered occurred several times: 'I think they're entitled to live here—as long as we don't get overrun', laughed one man. His wife added, seriously, 'Which we could be, in ten years' time'.

Like the statements about 'belonging' these responses cover a range from enthusiasm to luke-warm democracy, with more at that end: 'It doesn't matter, whoever can come can come, it's a free country I believe'. When we asked who does not belong, nobody nominated migrants. A common phrase was 'migrants don't bother me' or 'don't worry me' (like bush flies, so long as they are not too numerous or aggressive?); 'I haven't seen too many, there's a few different types, but they don't worry us'; 'I've worked with migrants and I can't knock them because I've never run afoul of them. So migrants don't worry me'. But the tangle of ideas about 'nice' areas and their symbols included the very strong conviction that 'too many migrants' made it a 'lower' area, and that Green Views was in danger of this. The woman teacher who ran the Youth Club remembered being warned by a 'girlfriend'. 'I was looking around the northern suburbs and I hadn't looked at Green Views and she said, "Don't look at Green Views, there are too many migrants". I said, "Well, what difference does that make?". And that made me look'.

Some arguments tied ethnicity into the class and life-stage knot. 'I'm not too sure of the type of people coming in, but just by reading things there's probably quite a high percentage of migrants or tradesmen . . . It's grown a lot from that original thing where there were just mainly younger couples'. More migrants 'coming in' threatened: 'The place has a very bad image and it's going to become a migrant area, a bit like Westville, mostly second generation migrants'. 'They seem to be moving into the older areas—most of them move into the older areas—and then eventually they're taking over everywhere else.'

Yet for most people the migrants 'belong'. The inconsistency is easily explained. When we asked explicitly about attitudes to the ethnic origins of residents,[2] that luke-warm democracy remained, a pastel picture of tolerance and often enjoyment of difference. But the tolerance was always conditional.

'The migrants'

Nobody had trouble picking 'migrants'. There were few who balked at the blanket term. And an extraordinary number of people easily estimated the proportion of migrants in this and their former area. To refer to 'the migrants' as a group bothered nobody, not even migrants! Most used the term before we did, and when we asked how they felt about 'the proportion of migrants' not one person remarked on the diversity of background and experience which meant that to talk of 'the migrants' of Green Views made little demographic sense. As chapter 1 showed, there were overseas-born residents across all occupational and life-stage groups, and across educational and self-assessed class categories. The overseas-born shared less with each other than most shared with the Australian-born (also, of course, not homogeneous). Physically and socially they offered a variety ranging from a few who were easily identifiable as 'different' to many who could not be so labelled unless their country of origin was known. Yet nobody responded, as we expected, by saying 'What do you mean by "migrant"?' or 'How the hell would I know?'. One woman, herself Italian-born, thought the proportion was 'half and half'; 'I notice it, you know. Walking around, you can pick them'.

The assumption that you can pick a migrant—or the house of one—is intriguing. The British-born, distinguishable by physical features or language were identified by several people: 'They're all poms'. 'There are an awful lot of poms here actually', said a woman who went on to map her court, 'One's Italian and the other's Maltese, all the rest are Australians'. Her husband cut in, 'Well the people across the road there were Indian, weren't they?'. 'They kept to themself', she said. Nor, surely, can you 'pick them' by the house. At the time of the reinterviews there were only two houses in Green Views that stood out from the 'natural' brick (both were white and often labelled as 'probably Italian'); otherwise the rigorous uniformity of the houses defied distinctions. Yet people who said they 'didn't mix' with migrants knew where, and sometimes how, they lived. 'Migrants don't bother me because they always seem to be the same as us. I mean everybody who goes past the migrants' homes, they're as nicely kept as ours.' A wife said her neighbours were 'totally different to us'. How? 'They like night life, they go out and spend, they like to drink and stuff like that, and we don't.' Her husband contributed, 'They haven't got a colour TV, that's why they're out all the time'. But she thought that 'They're just different because they're both European and they live a different sort of life'.

And asking whether there were 'more' or 'less' migrants here than in the former area we got easy answers. People clearly *did* such estimates, and acted on them. Those who had moved to Green Views to escape 'migrant areas' were sharply aware of the number of migrants who had also moved there. Only 35 per cent of the sample said there were fewer migrants here than in their former area; 21 per cent said it was the same proportion; 39 per cent that there were more. But only 4 per cent did not know the answer to the question, though it would have proved very hard to answer statistically.

These features combined in an amalgam of certainty rather like the certainty with which people mapped the 'areas' of the estate, and hardening equally quickly. Estimates caricatured, attitudes to one national group hid variety, luke-warm democracy was easily overtaken by the conviction that 'the migrants' had the numbers: 'I don't think I'm racially prejudiced but I'd say one in four is only Australian, and the rest is something else. It is! We've got Chinese, Indians, Greeks, Italians, an awful lot of Indians and an awful lot of Asians. An *awful* lot. In this street alone, I think there's only three of us who are Australian'.

The wife of a builder illustrated all these processes. 'Because of the unemployment rate, I'd say it's only about one third of

Australians in Green Views, just say from walking around the supermarket. If you want to look at it from that point of view, I'd say a third Japanese, Malaysian, a third Italians and a lot of Indians. Nothing against them. They all make a community. But I think we've got enough because otherwise we're going to be outrated. I mean you drive around [inner suburb] now and it's nearly an all-Italian suburb. And then you've got your Greek areas. I wouldn't like Green Views to become like that at all'. Her builder husband had a lot to say about the Italians who 'do all their work for cash' (that is, tax dodging), and she admitted, 'I'm a little bit against Italians coming to Australia... Like I think you'll find a lot of Italians own their homes a lot sooner than what Australians do. Maybe they're prepared to work seven days a week too, maybe three days a week's cash straight in their hand and they can afford to do that'. She had a Malaysian neighbour who sent her pay packet home. 'You've got all these people working in Australia. You've got a lot of Australians unemployed, there seems to be a lot of New Australians employed, but the trouble is, the money's still going out of the country. Maybe it's the building trade and builders' point of view, you see a lot of Italians coming out here and working, then they send their cheques back to Ma and Pa back home ... That really bugs you.'

The migrants who don't matter

Most of these comments are backed by overt assumptions that to be acceptable migrants must be assimilated. Governments may have moved beyond the language of assimilation, but it reigns in Green Views among the Australian-born and migrants:[3] 'If the person anglicizes themself to a certain extent, I'm prepared to overlook where they come from'. Which migrants are acceptable? Five requirements predominate: that they are not 'new' migrants, offer no 'language barrier', do not live in 'ghettos', stand for the common values, and are not lower class. On passing these tests, anyone belongs!

A clear implication of many statements was that second generation migrants do not matter: 'You know, you're not getting fresh migrants, or anything like that, that don't speak English. You're sort of getting people that have spent their childhood here anyway and are sort of married, it's just moving somewhere to live'. The problems with migrants being 'fresh' are clearly that they are hard to turn into the soil of community, and also that they are more noticeable, even offensive. With the second generation there are 'not hordes of them or anything, but they're integrating well into the area'. Several people explained that the Green Views 'migrants' often had only one parent born overseas, so were more willing to 'blend'. A woman said the proportion of migrants 'doesn't seem to be that high. It doesn't really worry me at all. Most of them don't seem to be first-generation migrants ... they blend in with the Australian culture as well as their culture, which I'm all for. The thing that sort of does irritate me slightly is when people bring in their own culture and they come to get a better life, but they don't want people with an Australian way of life as well'. Many comments indicated acceptance of a natural flow of the second generation to this area and way of life: 'They're all coming over. I've noticed that the mums and dads live in Westville and it's like the children that are coming over here to buy ... We do come from a migrant family, both of us, and to me—go to Westville, it's like Little Europe over there. They should be out mixing in all suburbs, instead of just being a little cluster together'.

Language problems were mainly forecast in the school: 'The only thing that I would worry about would be if we had a lot of children that have the language difficulty at say state level, when you're sending your children to state school and in some areas the children have to play outside while they teach the others English'. Several parents cited troubles at the school as their only objection to migrants here: 'There are migrant children at the school, they're having a very hard time at the moment. The children are becoming a very nasty school ... I think it's the language problems'. The possibility that it was a parent problem was not raised.

For many, 'no ghettos' was the absolutely inflexible condition for acceptance: 'I think, without being biased against ethnic groups, I think if 10 000 Swahilis or something shifted in, it wouldn't go down too well'. Some saw a historical trend away from ghettos, perhaps reflecting their own movements outwards from ethnic concentrations: 'It's great to see Chinese people and Italians and Greeks moving out of their little cliques in the city or wherever they live, to come out and spread a bit'. And the overseas-born were among the strongest objectors to ghettos: 'My God there's a lot of migrants around here; Asians, lots of Asians around here, Greeks round here, Italians, there's only a few Maltese, like me'. Is that a good thing? 'Yes, once the nationality doesn't come in the middle, it's OK.' Equal proportions of 'migrants with Australians, so that migrants can integrate' was the goal of several people: 'I think what is wrong is that migrants come in and more migrants buy houses and the Australians will not. You can say goodbye to the houses and you go ahead and start building a little Italy (laughs), or a little Chinatown!' (he is Chinese).

They should mix beyond their own group, preferably 'contributing': 'The ones I've seen so far are a younger set. I haven't seen all that many of the older type of migrant, if you know what I mean'. His wife did: 'I'd say the ones that are coming here are good for the area anyway because they're willing to—there's not many that come here that aren't trying to do something for the area. Whereas in the older suburbs, they slot themselves in their houses and don't want to talk'. He inserted the word she had avoided: 'in their little *ghettos*'.

M: So long as they just become part of the community and get involved in community groups and activities and don't isolate themselves and say, 'We're Italians', or 'We're Greek, we only mix with Greeks'. Or even the English; with the English; there are a few of those. As long as they mix with everyone and don't isolate themselves from the rest of the community, I think it's good.

So the migrants that do not matter are not only living like Australians but are also (unlike most residents!) prepared to work for the community. And the crucial fourth and fifth requirements follow easily from the lightly hidden demand for assimilation. They should accept Australian values and must not lower the area. The values that matter concern property standards, and several people praised migrants for these: 'If anyone's letting it down I reckon it's the Australian people— the Australian-born people—themselves'. His wife agreed. 'You don't see any of the Italians' houses and that with their parked cars in front of their places and things like that.' He added, 'I think they're extremely—especially the Italians— houseproud'. Houseproud, but identifiable? Better still are the invisible: 'I'm not against them living in the area, depending on the way—I mentioned before that there are people who look after their homes and things like that; if they blend in with the community, I think, as far as I'm concerned, they're good, they're welcome'.

A few people implied that in severing themselves from 'ghettos' the Green Views migrants had become more privatized than the Australian-born. An Asian migrant saw how this could lead to hostility: 'They see these guys, they own everything in their houses, they don't believe in the never-never, they're always not going out or spending money or anything like that, whereas the Australians are more outgoing'. A woman who said the area was 'mainly migrants' added: 'The ethnic group we seem to have here, it is their own block of land and their own house, that is very important, their own little piece of Australia'. The suburb has selected the desirable migrants: 'It's a fairly quiet environment, I know we've got lots of different nationalities, but I think that's good. I don't think anybody has the right to say that nobody belongs in a certain place. We haven't got any criminals or anything like that'. And (foreshadowing the ideas of 'good neighbours' in part II), another woman described hers: 'They're lovely people, but they're Turkish. And there's a language barrier. Lovely people, couldn't wish for nicer neighbours'.

The private home was the common basis for belonging. 'All this mix—all these people—have one thing in common: they're strivers, and they're achievers. So you're getting, from the ethnic group, those members of the ethnic group who wish to advance themselves and own their own home'. He is talking about class, the *sameness* of class position.

M: This is middle-class living. First of all, the fact that we do represent the middle class of Australia, which I consider is about 70 per cent of the people of Australia ... excluding the very wealthy and excluding the very poor. The parameters are that we all own our own homes, or are buying them; these are economic paramenters. We either own one or two cars, we either have a caravan or a boat as a rule ... and we all have to go to work five days a week. There's a proportion —a high proportion—of the womenfolk go to work too. So we have economic things which keep us in line: we're paying our homes off, so we can't race off to Europe for six months of the year ... And the other thing is that, even though we're all different ethnic groups or peoples in Green Views, for some reason or other there seems to be some sameness in our position in society. In other words, the Italians next door, they seem to be in the same middle class of Italians. Now I came from an Italian area ... we had very

low working-class Italians as neighbours ... I'm not criticizing them
for their education or whatever, but just—it's a difficult thing to say
what is class, what differentiates one class from the other...The
people next door are definitely in the higher bracket of the Italian
community.

Migrants would matter if they became too numerous (it was
strongly in the interest of Green Views migrants that this
should not happen) or too visible (those who were 'different'
were likely to become as privatized as possible, and those 'like
us' were highly likely to sever themselves from the stereotypes
and company of the unacceptable migrants). Like the 'workers',
the migrants were accepted so long as they were disguised in
the common values of family and home. But they were carefully
monitored; some of the detailed accounts of ethnic origins of
residents sounded uncomfortably like dossiers.

Ethnic origin became an issue every time people felt that the
status of the estate, or the quality of family life, was at stake.
Comparison with Westville was clear: 'Over there you have
the communities within the communities, here we are trying to
build one community'. Zoning of children to secondary schools
highlighted the difference between the acceptable migrants of
Green Views and the migrant areas beyond. The Education
Department decision was to send Green Views children to
schools across the creek. A leader of the RA explained: 'Some
have moved to get away from the concentration and they get
to Green Views and the department is going to zone their kids
into a school where they would be outnumbered again, basically
they would be going to migrant schools and the reaction was
quite spontaneous'. Another office-bearer seriously compared
the situation with the bussing of American children to deseg-
regated schools: 'Here is somebody who buys a nice house in
Green Views so that they will be away from the ghetto areas
and their kids get bussed into a ghetto area school and this is
causing a lot of trouble'.

Yet most people had moved here expecting migrants. One
man, when we asked 'What sort of people did you expect to
find here?' answered simply, 'Wogs'. His wife laughed.

Go Home Wogs!

Along the great green expanse of the Fence somebody had
written, in huge letters, 'Go Home Wogs!'. In the set of

questions about migrants we asked for reactions to this. We hardly expected a range of responses to such overt evidence of prejudice. But to our surprise we found it. Six people said they approved. One man hesitated and said, 'This is going to be a very biased interview'. His wife put in, 'He agreed with it'.[4] Another man said it was 'only vandalism' but after the tape was turned off his wife laughed and said, 'He probably wrote it'.

A few gave a sort of 'liberal' dismissal that spread thinly over hostility or helplessness: 'I suppose it's freedom of speech. I've said it meself sometimes'; 'It doesn't really worry me, everyone's entitled to their own opinion, so if they want to write something like that—well I suppose really it's a bit disgraceful, but I can understand how people get upset because they seem to be taking over the country, all the migrants'. Several tried not to be prejudiced but were concerned at the proportion of migrants in the area, and hoped Green Views would retain a lower proportion than the western suburbs: 'Over in Westville where I work we have them coming in to work all the time. Sometimes I am glad to get home, and I'm not prejudiced'. Again, the migrants who mattered were those who were visible.

W: A bit unfair, I suppose they've got as much right to be here as we have.

M: As long as they speak Australian.

W: As long as they live the Australian way of life.

M: No, they can live their life; as long as they speak English, I couldn't give a damn.

W: I call my father a wog. It doesn't really mean anything. Well, they called anyone from Europe ... a wog. They don't normally stipulate Italians.

M: It suits them sometimes ... When you get these grease balls that are walking around with their black dresses on and couldn't speak a word of English ... In my job you run across that many different nationalities ... You try to speak to them and they say, 'Oh I can't spikka much English' and you think, 'Well what are you sitting there for?'. They come to Australia. At least they should try to learn English before they get here. Otherwise they shouldn't be allowed.

Most startling were answers that saw the painted message not as prejudice but property damage: 'I probably have really little reaction to it—only that it made a mess on the fence'. 'The only thing that I was annoyed about was that they'd defaced the fence'. One of the women most active in community groups rang the Council and asked them to paint it over; 'It wasn't so much the sign itself, I object to people painting graffiti of any type on the fence'. Another couple, both involved in the groups, had exactly the same reaction: 'The message on it really didn't mean anything to me; I just thought of it the other way that, you know, there's some nut that's gone and had nothing to do and defaced the fence'. 'Someone being stupid', his wife added. Here the interviewer put in, 'Did you have any feelings about it at the time? I mean you looked at it and you saw it there, what did it do to your guts?'. The wife's answer was: 'I just thought it was horrible to think that people write those sort of things on fences and things'. In each answer the wording explicitly pre-empts consideration of the hurt to migrant residents or the effect on community relations.

Fourteen people gave such answers, and three of them were themselves first-generation migrants. 'I would have liked to catch the fella in the act! I think it was very stupid, actually, very destructive. I'm very very annoyed with some of the kids, some of the things that they've done, like that, like ripping down some of the signs and bending all the street signs.' But what about the content?[5] 'Oh I don't think that really bothered me, no. Just the fact that it was defacing other people's property.' A wife butted in after the question, 'Wished they hadn't messed the fence up, it was a dumb thing to do'. The husband agreed, 'That's our regret, because these sort of things—', 'cost money', she finished. One man was explicit about the class message: 'It didn't offend anybody. It just annoyed people that they wrote on the fence. It starts giving the area an approach of a slum, writing on walls and fences'.

Another set of answers shrugged it off as 'just kids' or grumbled about the delinquency indicated. 'I reckon the kid whoever done that should have got a foot right up the backside', said one woman. 'Just kids' always implied that the slogan was meaningless. 'Kids or students', several concluded, one man adding, 'It wasn't a political thing'. 'You see so much of it' was a reason for dismissing the message; 'It's everywhere you go, you'll see signs, not just Green Views, it's everywhere, I think it's just society'.

But about half those asked were clearly angry. 'Disgusting' occurred in fourteen answers, 'disgraceful', 'awful' and 'shattered' in another six. 'Bloody disgusting' came from several, and most of these contained no argument. When they did, common values of family and home were appealed to. A woman who had not noticed the slogan said 'I don't think it's very nice'. Why? 'There's good and bad everywhere you go. I mean you take people as they are. So what if they're Chinese or whatever. You see a decent home and people.' Only two of the large number of overseas-born protested and both denied that it hurt them personally: 'I don't care if somebody write this on the board because I no feel a wog'.

Almost everybody assumed the sign referred to Green Views and its ethnically heterogeneous population; only three people questioned this. Several thought they knew exactly which residents were being addressed: either a 'ghetto' of houses rented by Turks in one court or, at the other extreme, 'up on the hill, where the big houses are, there are groups of migrants there, lots of them'. Everybody knew what 'wogs' meant; the abusive term was accepted as part of the vocabulary by those who used it and those who condemned it. Almost everybody 'read' it as 'southern Europeans', though this term of abuse has a chequered history.[6] It meant Asians to only two very hostile men.

M: What people see is, you see an Asian here, whether he's Vietnese [*sic*.] or not, well you class him as Vietnese. It's supposed to be the boat people coming to this country and you see him go past in a nice new Commodore station wagon and they've built that new house in the court and you think, now how can they get here...There's no way I can go to England and squat in there and get a job and a new car and a new house.

Three people used 'wog' without hesitating. 'It wouldn't bother me, there'd have been no reaction if I'd have seen it, I don't think I would say anything', said a man. His wife agreed: 'No, I've worked with wogs. They're only here, the same as us, to get a better living and to bank a bit of money and enjoy their own property'. And only a handful of answers addressed the *label*. Some people commented that children used the term. 'Kids of what, 10, you can hear them in the park, saying "wogs this and wogs that" and he's generally of ethnic background anyway, I mean—last of the heap'. A Greek-born woman said, 'We get some of that at work. There's some people born here, they think we're Australians. And they talk at lunchtime at work, they say "wogs at school do this" and "wogs do that" and I sit there sometimes and I feel like talking about it, but I don't'.

A few people tackled the message: 'It's terrible really, we've brought a lot of culture and a lot of good things to this country'. Several of the Australian-born and two overseas-born respondents argued that 'If you want to call anyone a wog, we're all wogs really'. One woman saw the labelling process as the problem: 'The whole racial thing starts when you just sort of put tags on people. If you didn't put on tags and call them wogs or Greeks or whatever, well I don't think there'd be any racial tension at all really'.

There was only one answer recording a response in terms of relations within the estate. Bill, an early president of the RA, said, 'Oh I thought it was disgusting myself, because this sort of thing isn't good for the relationship between the new members of the community and the community itself'. And only one woman saw the slogan in terms of her own migrant neighbours. 'I laughed! It was just the right time! Isn't that *terrible*!'. Her story is, so far as I know, highly unusual in Green Views.

When does it matter? The story of one court

In our records this is the only dispute in which misunderstanding and antagonism clearly derived from ethnic difference, and in which violence resulted. It is recounted here *because* it is anomalous, an extreme case of the way suburban living can create and exacerbate social tensions, and because the participants offered such full and open accounts of their troubles that they throw a sharp light on those processes.[7]

Mandy is at home with young children, and active in the child-based local groups. She is one of the few who answer a question about good neighbours with a negative example, a 'terrible neighbour'. The first description is 'They're New Australian people', and the first evidence given is unusual behaviour: 'I used to say hello, but instead of even looking at me, she would turn her back and walk inside. Now that hurts'. So the normal processes of court life were violated from the start, and it matters more because the children are the same age. 'They own the court and if our children do go out there,

there's a fight started.' Later she cites another unwritten rule —
reciprocity: 'She's never had my children in her house except
for her daughter's birthday twice.' Why not? The answer is a
third rule, about family priorities: 'Well, I think they're just so
busy spotlessing the place all the time. They work crazily on
their windows every day just about'. So the values about
children and house are challenged. So too are values about
discipline, violated by unacceptable intervention with another's
children. When they moved in, her daughter, then a toddler,
'rode over the road as fast as she could, 'cos she saw these
little kids . . . and the grandmother came along, and she picked
her up, picked the bike up, smacked her on the bottom and
brought her back across the road and plonked her on the front
lawn'.

Later she says, 'I've seen her wield a piece of wood on my
son's backside . . . when she thinks nobody's looking'. Four
years on, disputes continue around the children. 'I don't know
why they don't want them around.' The phrase 'I don't know
why' recurs, but Mandy wonders 'if it's because we have so
many friends — people coming and going all the time; we're
involved in things'. Could they misunderstand? 'I don't know.
I think they think Australians don't like them, but they do.
They wanted to.'

So what went wrong? Two very ordinary incidents are brought
up several times in hours of interviews: the loss of a child's
shoe and the noise of a party. The shoe story, in turn, makes
sense only in the context of an earlier episode with Mandy's
large dog, which got out and jumped on the Greek woman's
daughter. 'The mother came out with an umbrella, trying to
belt the dog and I said, you know, "I'm sorry", and she started
on me . . . I said, "ooooh, you keep *your* stupid little dog
away" — 'cos they had this little dog who used to sneak in
under the fence, 'cos it's only a tiny little thing, and it used to
eat all the dog's food, rip my trees out.' The little dog was
outside, as was her son, who was 'at the stage where he was
taking his shoes and socks off'. She 'went mad at him'; he ran
down the road barefoot and when she returned with him one
shoe was gone.

W: I thought, 'Oh here we go, the little dog's taken it'. So I went
looking, and I couldn't find it. So I knocked on the door, and I said,
'Can I go in your backyard?' — 'cos the gate was shut — 'and see if your

dog's taken his shoe in there?' 'cos I had a feeling, 'cos he'd already pinched the next-door neighbour's shoes off the front door-step. And she said, 'No, you go away'. And I said, 'But it might be in the backyard; the little dog might have taken it'. It was all really nice, you know, as good as you could be, 'cos I wasn't going to have a fight about a shoe! I just wanted the shoe back so I could put it on him. And she said, 'Oh you bloody bitch, go away!'.

After an hour of searching, near tears, she found the shoe in the Greek woman's yard and demanded that the little dog be constrained. 'So, of course, she threw back at me that day my dog had been outside, and then she said, "Oh we'll get the better of your dog". And then, a week later, it disappeared. I mean, it's too coincidental.' A second dog, equally big, 'disappeared too—mysteriously again'. She is convinced their present dog will 'probably go too'.

The second incident was a party. Mandy's pregnant friend next door was at home with only her small son. The noise was 'terribly loud. I mean, *we* didn't worry about it because there's no use hassling about it; it'll be gone in the morning; it'd be nice if it wasn't so loud, so late, but it was. The houses are too close, anyway'. But the friend's house 'is right on theirs, and the noise was *so* loud, she bashed on the window, 'cos I suppose, you know, you don't go outside when you're on your own ... So they started chucking things at her window and she got really upset and she rang her husband, and he rang us, being friends'. Mandy went over 'to calm her down, 'cos when you're pregnant things are about ten times as bad'.

So far, a tolerant response, and help offered. But Mandy's action was already interpreted as aggression; 'They weren't pleased about me going over there'. In a later conversation she mentions a factor that doubtless contributed. They had already formalized the dispute. 'I never said before, but we sent a solicitor's letter asking them to stop it or else. We got desperate. I was getting upset. I was always ringing my husband about it because I was so frustrated because I didn't want to run out and retaliate, but I didn't know what to do ... there's always sort of been two against one, kind of thing: two adults against me'. Her neighbour's husband now called the police. 'I mean, fair enough, his wife's on her own. He can't come home. What else can you do?' To justify getting 'involved' she invokes friendship *and* already growing enmity. They had been 'asked to be involved' by friends and, of course offered help 'because they're such good friends ... and because we hated these people anyway!'. There is also a sense of justice: 'I mean, why shouldn't they be harassed? We've been harassed so much by them, I knew how she felt, and I was sort of thinking, "Oh you rotten people" ... and then, of course, because we'd got involved, one of the guys laid into my husband'.

Who 'laid into' whom is now impossible to determine. Nobody was hurt, 'It was more of the push and shove thing', but the situation was changed. For the first time in three hours' conversation, Mandy throws in the term of abuse: 'So I called the police again. Because I wasn't going to have my husband punched up by three big fat wogs!'. She laughs sheepishly and explains to me, 'I mean, that's what we call them now. We're at that stage that, you know, how you can't do anything about it, it's so frustrating; you start saying things. Well that's what we've got like. I mean, the kids have too. It's terrible'. She knows the term is offensive. At another time she says that a neighbour had told her the Greek husband, when an inner-city child, used to 'run around looking for fights because people called him a wog ... he's probably had a lousy time anyway, probably with his parents trying to make it here, I guess. But to bring his kids up with the same attitude, it's a bit crazy I think'. She feels that the bad language on the Greeks' part justifies her use of 'wog'. Just last week 'the older woman came out, and she said to my kids—and my kids hadn't done anything this time, I *know*—I mean, of course, all kids fight— she came out and said, "you effing b's, you get out of here". "She can't speak English, and she wouldn't understand swear words", that's what her son-in-law told me. But she's always said things like that to the kids'.

Language is a theme throughout the stories. 'Another big fight happened one day and their cousins were still living here, and they were playing footy, and our kids were *trying* to play out in the court, but of course it's *their* court!' She laughs and mimics, 'You know, "you go away, and you p-off", and all the rest of it. They used the words. They do, quite casually. For people who don't understand any English ... perhaps it's another language, all those words!' The sarcasm is mixed with guilt. 'The kids only started—I probably even started them, you know, saying that, because I was so frustrated. You know how you sort of think, "I'm not going to call them one of those ... Wog! You rotten wog!'" She can't remember the first time she said it, thinks it was when the children were told not to play on the footpath, '"Oh shut up you silly old wogs", or something, you know, "I can't stand you". I even told them to go back once, because I didn't like them ... 'cos I just didn't want them to be here anymore. But that's about all.' Her husband uses the term frequently in his version of the incident during another conversation. She would never use it of Greeks who keep to themselves. 'We have Greeks next door, and they're fine. They work a lot.' But the others don't fit. 'I can't understand why they don't want to know anyone. It just doesn't make sense to me, and if they don't want to, why don't they just stay away, instead of hassling people.'

Were there any solutions? 'We considered moving and thought, why should we be moved out of our home?' There is no room for friendship. 'I feel sorry for them because I'm sure there must be something they need. Once I would have thought, if anything could happen to make them be friendly it would have been nice, but now I don't care. They can rot! ... And then you wonder if it's because you've done things in the area, and you're happy and you've got friends and people come and go and you go out and I don't stay home all the time, I've got things to do ... I start to think, well maybe it's all my fault. You know how you start off, knowing you haven't done anything and you start to really get down and think, perhaps I have done it all. Perhaps I'm really horrible, like she says I am. But I don't think I'm that bad!'

Here, clearly, are migrants who 'matter'. They failed on each of the criteria of invisibility. They offered a language barrier and mixed only with their own extended family and ethnic group. While there was no insurmountable language barrier with the wife, the grandmother spoke little, and often inappropriate, English, and was the more visible of the women. The household undertook piecework, so although both women were home during the day the wife shared little of Mandy's experience and challenged her values about family life—a theme I return to in chapter 7.

W: She said to me one day too, oh, something about I'm a rotten mother, and I don't look after my kids. And I thought, well maybe I am a rotten mother, but I do try. And I think my being involved in what my kids do, surely that's good enough. And my staying home with them ... And she sits on her sewing machine—her industrial machine over there. She said, 'I work 18 hours a day.' And I said, 'Do you now'. I said, 'When do you sleep?'. 'Oh I don't need to sleep. Three or four hours a night.' And I said ... 'Your kids don't need that money' ('cos she said she was earning the money for them). I said, 'They don't really need that. They only need love' ... She said, 'Oh I buy them houses and a land' ... Perhaps she's just one of those people who want to make money. She said she's not going to live here: she hates Australia and she's going back to Greece.

The story vividly illustrates the processes by which prejudice is constructed, especially when the other side is also seen. This Greek family was not in our random sample, but the wife had been interviewed during a separate project sector.[8] She was bitterly unhappy with the estate and deeply regretted the move there. The location was as desired; she had been afraid in the inner suburb where they previously lived, as 'there was always a lot of trouble: robberies, the hotel was down the road and there were drunks lying in streets, men chasing women drunk, and this thing that exists in Australia where one doesn't get out to help'. Green Views was better: 'It's good here, you don't hear of people stealing, fighting, of trouble'. But it did have disadvantages: 'I was near the shops, transport, near the city, all of which are missing at Green Views'. But her unhappiness was not due to geographical isolation. Here, as never in her experience before, she said, 'the Australians separate the New Australians'. She was sure this was not usual, knew 'there exist some Australians that don't consider what the other person is, whether he's Greek or Italian or Yugoslavian, they consider them people. But here there are Australians who have New Australians as wogs, to say it better than they do. I've changed many houses, here in Australia, but I've never come across this as I have here. They don't want me ... They feel we are much lower'.

Deeply distressed by her daughter's experience in the first years, she was taking the child from the local school to send her to a private school.

W: There exist prejudices among the children, I've made complaints to the teachers. My daughter argues with the other children because they call her wog and an idiot, that she's Greek and because of that she's dirty, and such things are said by children that I think are learnt off their parents. Because a child ... doesn't know what a wog is, he must learn it off his parents and have it explained to him by them so he can understand it. Yesterday I went to school at lunch time to give her her lunch and I found her crying because they had called her wog and hit her in the stomach. She complains to the teacher and the teacher tells her you don't hit them, and the same to the Australian kids.

Mandy is right, the Greek woman wants to return. So does the girl, she says, even though Greece is not her homeland.

W: I'm old, I understand their talk, but she's only eight years old and never known Greece, she's been born here, and she tells me to return to Greece because they don't want us and call us wogs. She's eight years old and can't understand and from now she's started to grow hatred inside her for Australians. This has only happened in Green Views. It's as if all the prejudiced Australians have come to live in my neighbourhood.

It is hard to find a good friend, she says, one that respects you. She tells the story of those incidents building up: the same dog, the same party. An observer has no way of discovering what in fact happened, but there are clues as to how misunderstandings accumulate like arsenic: 'It all started with one neighbour's dog and it's ended with us grown-ups in the trouble. First dog, children, then parents'. It is easy to match the two accounts and to see how each makes sense of events. Mandy's is in terms of women's anxiety and resentment and men's growing anger. Her neighbour's is about an exuberant family celebration. 'Prior to a week ago I had a party and at 10.30 they brought the police because we bothered them. I had 25 people at home only, all families. My children were asleep, and you can see they're small, so I could make a *lot* of noise! I had the stereo but not loud. And they brought the police.' She appeals to rules of neighbourhood reciprocity: 'Prior to that my other neighbour had a party until 4 in the morning and we couldn't sleep but we didn't say a thing. Well, he's entitled to have a party, why should I complain? But I was thoroughly shamed when bringing the police'.

Again, I want to emphasize that this story is not typical of the experiences recorded. But then, neither were the wreaths and threats to the truckie's wife. Both are about the importance of not being visibly different. Almost all of the Greek-born women interviewed regretted losing the proximity of shops, transport and the company of other Greeks. The exceptions were two women who very firmly did not want to call themselves Greek. All had come not for contacts with those they knew, but for clean, open air and new houses for family living, just like our whole sample! Some had felt no prejudice. Compare the woman quoted above with one of the same age group, fairly young and of similarly modern dress and appearance. She had no criticism of Green Views. But her Greek neighbours criticized her for trying to escape her background. 'We don't really go with the traditional Greek type things', she explained. What had attracted her to Green Views was the absence of European influence. 'Everyone's very friendly here', she said, 'the schools, anything that you sort of get involved with'. She had met no Greeks who did not like it. The children spoke no Greek, liked the school and had lots of friends.

Her neighbour was older and, in contrast, very sure of her ethnic identity: 'I'm Greek and I have it as a proud thing'. She felt no antagonism: 'everyone around here are friends, even the Chinese'. But she did not think she was accepted. 'I have no contact with Australians. I have no Australian neighbours. But I think no one likes foreigners or other races. Doesn't matter how well you know each other, they can't love you.' Men had different experiences. Perhaps prejudice applied differently to women and men; the experience of loneliness certainly did. Several Greek men felt no problems, were content with life, the achievement of the house and all Green Views had to offer.

One Greek woman was selling up. 'Some like us—most don't', she said simply. 'They don't want us. They envy us that we can afford to live here, that we have our own homes and jobs, they don't like us moving up.' The interviewer recorded 'the anguish she felt at the thought of living in Green Views for ever. Repeatedly she spoke of feeling like a prisoner there. "Life is very hard for me here. You see I go closed inside, how can you live, every day inside without seeing anyone?"'.

Notes

1. As in all such research it is extremely hard to assess this effect. The impression that migrants are widely accepted was supported by the absence of comments about them in the group processes where we were participant observers; our records never show the migrants as a topic of conversation except when there is concern for the isolation of migrant women. On the other hand, almost certainly our presence submerged prejudice: the term 'wog', for instance, is apparently common currency in the estate but occurs very seldom in these interview transcripts except where we raised it in the context of the slogan on the Fence.

2. These questions followed the questions about a 'better way of life' and home ownership in the taped section of the 1981 interview: 'Do you mix with people in Green Views who you see as different from yourself? How do you find that and what do you get out of it? How do you feel about the proportion of migrants here? Are there more or less migrants than where you used to live? A couple of years ago a sign appeared on the Green Views fence saying 'Go Home Wogs'. How did you feel about that?'.

3. Australian policy and vocabulary have changed with governments — see J. Jupp, *Racism in Australia*, Allen & Unwin, Sydney, 1985.

4. That we had anticipated no openly prejudiced responses to this question is shown by our including it in a schedule when two women students with Greek-born parents were among our interviewing team. Neither had stereotyped Greek features, and one, Emmy Herouvim, had the misfortune to strike this interview. She dealt with it directly, 'I'd better get out!', and achieved the required shift to another topic. It is impossible of course to know how much our presence determined the responses, but if its effect was to obscure prejudice, a lot leaked through. One man suggested laughingly that the sign had perhaps been written by 'La Trobe Uni. people, wanting a reaction for their survey!'.

5. In both these cases the interviewers, Lyn Kennedy and Pam Fanning, had the wit to ask the prompt which we had not included, having had no warning of this response. The results nicely show the value of both flexibility and partiality in interviewing. The wording of their probes indicates how startled we all were by these responses. Tapes also record another interviewer, Barbara Steele, as saying 'It's all right, I'm English', when an Italian resident protested at the sign. Nor had precodings allowed for it; had we not been taping, the property-standards answers would have been impossible to separate from those disapproving of the evidence of prejudice.

6. The term appears to have originated in Britain. *The Macquarie Dictionary* gives it two meanings as a term of abuse, first 'a native

of North Africa or the Middle East, especially an Arab', and secondly 'a person of Mediterranean extraction or of similar complexion and appearance [? short for golliwog]'. My folk memory was that it referred to 'wily oriental gentlemen', a colleague produced 'worthy', and a British migrant suggested 'western'. In Green Views one Chinese-born man laughed and said the sign: 'didn't worry me because "wog" to me means "Recognized Oriental Gentleman". Did you know that?'. It seems to have been a 1950s import to Australia; 'Wogs begin at Calais' came with it. It was not a term of racial abuse in my childhood. The term was then (and still is) Australian slang for a germ or mild infection: my mother recalls that she could not understand the hilarity from British visitors in the mid-1950s on being told my sister and I were 'in bed with a wog'. The shift to its use as a term of abuse for southern European migrants, and especially Greeks, belongs to recent decades and may now be becoming more lighthearted. It has certainly been co-opted by some migrants; one respondent objected to having migrant friends 'referring to themselves as "wogs" when my children are around; then I have to try and explain to my children that you don't call people wogs'. Five years later a highly successful Greek theatre group had a long-running comedy in Melbourne called 'Wogs out of Work', but in 1981 the term was certainly shatteringly offensive to most migrants.

7. I would like to thank especially the two women whose stories made this section, and who talked so openly about the disputes that troubled both so seriously. The context needs explaining; there was no intention to set out to collect and contrast opposing versions of a conflict, and I would have found such a research design ethically problematic. That different interviewers had gathered both sides of the same drama was pure chance, only realized as the details were fitted together by me during my interview with 'Mandy' (at which stage I told her I thought I had heard her neighbour's experience from an interview conducted by my student). Both women knew we were interviewing for research reports, both very carefully gave their side to the story, and both very seriously wished for an end to the troubles they reported.

8. These interviews with Greek-born residents of Green Views were done by Marie Daviditis, and she contributed thoughtful discussion of them. Some, but not the one quoted here, were conducted in Greek.

5

Little Boxes Made of Ideology?

Across diversity stretches a conviction of homogeneity, across unequal chances, acceptance and tolerance of those in the same dream. The story so far is of the power of the common goals of home and family to unify or to veil disunity. The next three chapters turn to those goals. Are they really the same for everyone, and are they staying the same?

Home ownership, like motherhood, had until recently an almost unspotted record in Australia as 'a good thing', and (like motherhood) was therefore little researched. Both have been taken for granted, though both impose formidable requirements at some stage on most of the population. It seems likely that one reason for the dominance of both requirements on young adults—that they have families and that they live their family lives in private homes—is that the two are strongly interconnected. And the connection seems obvious in Australia.

That Australia possesses one of the highest rates of home ownership in the industrialized world has long been a source of pride to politicians and the press. Australia has also proved one of the slowest, among western countries, to shift from traditional family structures. It shows the same patterns of change, but change seems stalled. Marriage rates are declining, divorce rates increasing. On present trends, up to a quarter of Australians may not marry; a third of marriages will end in divorce. Childlessness is acceptable option for an increasing number of young couples, though it is hard to estimate for how many. But Australia remains overwhelmingly a marrying society, and one in which family means nuclear family, child-lessness is deviant and gender determines people's social places.[1]

Both motherhood and home ownership have been attacked and explained in terms of the dominance of ideology, but the links between them and changes in them are little explored. Partly this is because work on ideologies of both family and home is rarely related to evidence of what people think, let alone what they do. Partly it is because the two have not been assessed together, so ways in which they support each other are little understood, and ways in which people live within and remake them are rarely considered. But partly it is also because the idea of ideology has descended from being one of the most powerful critical levers of social thinking to become one of the concepts in sociology most often lacking definition and most intransigently incompatible with research data.[2]

Proper paths to private places: An ideology of the family?

Family sociology, committed to monitoring the ways ideas change, sees a quite different society from that pictured by critical literature on family ideology committed to exposing non-change.[3] In one, dramatic change undermines social stab-ility, in the other, dominant ideas constrain. They see by dif-ferent methods: family values studies rely on survey evidence, while writing on family ideology, if it has drawn at all on evidence, has sketched broad historical sweeps or pictured women's lives from unstructured data. They communicate little. Thinking about families was lit up by the fascination of the women's movement with the ideological constraints on women's lives. A wave of works declaring the effects of dominant ideas set out to expose their social results. The tasks of showing that the ideologies are in fact there, and how they dominate family life—and of establishing their content and the extent of their power—were not often part of the agenda. Women's studies used the concept of ideology as Marx designed it to be wielded, as a weapon for social struggle and an explanation of stuck societies.[4] Thus this literature had and still has little to do with data. Its assertions about dominant ideas of patriarchy were backed by varied theories about the origins of these ideas and their relationship to capitalism. It splendidly forced a rethinking of the family from being seen as a rather boring functional necessity to being seen as the 'focal point of a set of ideologies that resonate throughout society'.[5] But the literature was vague about which ideas formed the set. And it overlooked or denied the processes of construction of ideologies and the relationships to them of active individuals. Thus it tended to portray women, as a category, as victims of unchanging ideology.[6]

These questions were tackled unevenly in a newer stream of feminist research which used ideology as a research tool. Australian studies of accounts from women and men, documentary sources, policy statements and historical records, have investigated ideologies of motherhood, of home and work, of family lives in different settings, and the effects of such ideologies on those apparently outside them—on politics and policy, and on family tasks and workforce patterns.[7] Historical research has established the complexity of the processes by which dominant ideas emerged and were changed by those who interpreted them and those whose lives they sought to remake.[8] Reviews detect similar patterns in family studies which have not sought 'dominant ideology', but have found massive constraints on the behaviour of people living socially approved family lives, as well as on the options of those who choose not to live such lives.[9] Contributions to the growing body of literature on women and the built environment have drawn together evidence of women's places and how women are situated.[10]

The evidence is uneven, several very different theoretical approaches are represented and quite normally the concept of ideology is used without any attempt to define it. Some writers are content to say an ideology exists and then illustrate it with data. Few have asked what evidence is required, how ideas are linked, why linked ideas determine behaviour, how they reach individuals, how they are evaded or challenged, or what is to be done with survey evidence that shows change and widespread rejection of just those ideas claimed to be dominant.[11] Almost all offer far more understanding of women's than men's experience. But collectively writers indicate background sets of ideas about family behaviour. Two themes strongly recur and both help make sense of demographic evidence. One is that family life is dominated by thinking in terms of two 'spheres'—the private world of home and the public world of work. The second is that there is a proper order to the steps in family life.

Private/public, family/work, hers/his

Dichotomies dominate the thinking about 'family', and when the family is seen as one side of a dichotomy it is always the sweet side, the 'haven in a heartless world'.[12] The sociology of the family started that way, celebrating the stabilizing function of women's place as the soft, 'expressive' centre of the private family home, its necessary separation from the men's 'instrumental' world of work and men's 'boundary role' in linking the two.[13] Understanding of the origins of modern families was illuminated by writing on the fusing of rural and domestic idylls in which women, home and community stood against the uncaring worlds of industrial work.[14] Feminist scholarship has used the theme of private and public worlds as a theoretical lever for the analysis of women's and men's different access to power, status and authority.[15] The critique of suburbia grabbed this theme to attack the ways the city 'has been shaped to keep women confined to their traditional roles in the family as wives and mothers'[16] in suburbs 'based on an accentuation of woman's role as mother and homemaker'.[17] Thus the private haven was pictured as women's business, and strongly linked to an idyll of peace and repose.

That dichotomy has become a fascination in the literature, and the number of references questioning it must surely now exceed those applying it unquestioningly. Indeed the sources most commonly cited and criticized for the promotion of that dichotomy never presented it as an accurate description of anyone's worlds, let alone women's.[18] Thinking in terms of 'two worlds' has been attacked as a myth obscuring the reality of the state's invasion of the home, the real and *changing* interpenetration of family and work in women's lives,[19] women's vulnerability in private 'havens', and the reality of male power.[20] Critics have questioned the application of the dichotomy to the understanding of urban space: 'The idealized opposition of female, domestic, private, often suburban worlds and male, productive, public, usually urban worlds does not really describe the lives of many people'.[21] Nor does it assist in understanding the no-man's land between family and paid work, the 'non-residential domestic sphere' that occupies much of women's lives and is also always changing,[22] or the ways 'her' privacy was always experienced in interaction with the public world.[23] Rather, some have argued, women are 'positioned at the intersection of two social worlds';[24] the 'boundary role' is hers, not his. Empirical studies of women's 'incorporation' in men's work and of rural settings have clearly shown the dichotomy just does not make sense of the data.[25]

So why do discussions of the dichotomy persist? Three reasons seem likely, all themes that will recur throughout this book. First, while the distinction of public and private spearheaded a critique on the traditional family, there have been few critical studies of that traditional family form. The studies that query the assumption that the family is a private world are all of anomalous families—mothers on welfare, black families, ministers' wives and rural town life! A suspicion remains that the hard core of the nuclear family is still home to the private haven, and that suspicion is maintained in the critique of suburbia.[26]

Secondly, the dichotomy is seen as not only misleading but dangerous. Like the 1960s debate over conflict and consensus approaches in sociology, it risks becoming an attack on straw theories. Nobody ever seriously suggested that society was characterized only by consensus. But there was growing concern that this ruling theoretical approach made it much easier to see consensus than conflict, and that at least some of its proponents, in the social sciences and in places of power, might want society to be like that. Somewhat similarly, critics of dualist images of women's and men's spheres point to the tendency of dichotomies, even when critically used, to obscure the crucial areas of confusion and change that fit neither sphere. Those who use dualisms to describe women's place may confirm that placement, especially by policies allocating care for the dependent young or old to 'the community', which means women at home.[27]

Thirdly, whether the world is in fact so divided and whether the researcher is helped or blinkered by looking at it that way, some people do. While dichotomies oversimplify women's experience, they appear in women's accounts of their lives, and they do make a lot of sense of men's. However distorting and inappropriate to the patterns of social change, the division of private and public worlds remains the background to family life, the way we interpret its demands. Ideas about women's and men's places, duties, opportunities and options seem to confirm the assumption that the private world of the family is and should be segregated from that other real, hard world of work, and that it is and should be maintained by women.

Studies show a set of ideas hanging together, making sense of each other—ideas about gender, family roles, children's needs—in which are clearly distinguished women's place and the man's world it is in, home from the outside world, unpaid from paid work, the rewards of love from those of money. They involve a 'cluster of replication'[28] beyond the arrangements of domestic life, shaping ways of thinking about work, leisure, provision of care and the built environment. Both women and men see women's paid work as anomalous, not real work, and women's employment patterns, earnings and experiences of work reflect that belief.[29] Both women and men see child-care as women's work and home-care as strongly preferable.[30] Household work is still mainly done by women whether or not they are in paid work; 'ideology has sustained this split—women are supposed to be working for love'.[31]

But should we conclude from this that the traditional division of worlds, with women in the home, is 'seen as inevitable, as naturally given and biologically determined'?[32] The same studies show a very great variety of values and behaviour. Where such ideas are heard, the evidence is of idea-debates rather than a simple domination of one set. The same packages of ideas, or ones that sound much the same, fit together in factor analysis of statistical data and in people's accounts.[33] People see them as separate sets, one identified with 'old' ideas, and one with 'new'. The 'old' are the popular props of the dichotomy, confining women to the private world, giving mothers passive qualities (patience, being there) and absolute duties (the care of her children). The 'new' ideas open options, sometimes for men to take a greater part in the processes of making and maintaining the private world; more often for women to take on, as well, tasks 'outside' it.

The dichotomy of public and private therefore cannot be jettisoned, but it is crucial that the image of 'spheres' be seen as 'an object of analysis not a conceptual tool'.[34] It disguises, rather than directing enquiry to, processes of change. Merely to label ideas as 'old' is to debate with them.[35] Shifting values, and considerable confusion and conflict about them, mean that traditional ideas are 'both strong and weak',[36] dominating behaviour yet apparently easily reworked, at least by some. Surveys show increasing proportions of samples questioning. The old ideas are more likely to be supported by the young, by women not in the paid workforce, by the Australian-born, by those with a religious affiliation and those with less education.[37]

But we know more about where these ideas have been stretched or broken than how. Certainly not all the young or educated are questioning traditional ideas. Nor is questioning confined to those rejecting traditional family forms; how could it be? The changes of the last decades occurred across the society, spurred by policies removing restrictions on divorce, abortion and employment of women;[38] the effect was to increase autonomy and reduce dependence on family units of all kinds, making them in some ways more private, and in other ways less so.

Under the term 'privacy' the dichotomy packs a cluster of ideas and masks the contradictions between them.[39] In the present context three need to be clearly distinguished. The first idea is that historically associated with the bourgeois ideal: of family privacy as the sweet setting for the growth of peace and caring; privacy *for* haven, community, emotional security. It is in this sense that the dichotomy is seen as historically located in the bourgeois family,[40] and as offering the ideological justification for patriarchal domination. The second sense is about autonomy and independence: privacy for a purpose, privacy *to* build stable family units. That people confuse these ideas is clearest when autonomy is seen as selfishness.[41] Men and women call many of the 'new' ideas selfish: childlessness, small families, mothers' employment. The third sense is the one that made a verb, 'to privatize'; privacy *from* others, the antithesis of community. The apparent contradiction is built into the sets of ideas; privacy in this sense belongs in the bourgeois ideal.[42] Family life is about all three.

Proper paths to private worlds

That traditional ideas are both strong and weak is most clearly shown in the conviction that there is a right order for going through family life. In Australia, as most people still see it, everyone marries, and married people have children: marriage indeed means children. Those proper paths are natural, and marriage is still widely seen as 'an almost inevitable step in the transition to adult life'.[43] Though far fewer are taking them, and many more delaying them, there is a lot of evidence that people accept the order of these steps on the ladder of family life, and very little evidence that they reject them. Those who stray are very aware of the prescribed path they have left and tend to rejoin it. Many indicators of change show a pulling back to that path. Most changes in marrying, having children and employment are changes in the timing of the steps into family life, rather than a rejection of those steps or the order in which they are trodden. A marked feature of stability is the sense of the 'proper time' for family stages.[44]

The strength and weakness of traditional ideas shows most clearly in patterns of mothers' workforce participation. In the late 1970s workforce participation of mothers looked like an unstoppable trend. But as the pioneers moved into Green Views the increase in married women's workforce participation rates in Australia had slowed to nearly a halt for the preceding half-decade, and the strong association of employment with life stage remained. The proper path was for young women to work until child-bearing, 'drop out' with young children and then re-enter the workforce, preferably part-time, when children started school.[45] It was as though, at least in this setting, the 'new' ideas had intruded as far as they presently could into the 'private world' of the family, allowing women 'out' so long as children did not need them 'in'. The resilience of the 'old' remained the most striking feature of family change. But change continued: by 1986, 40 per cent of mothers of children aged under five in couple families would be in the paid workforce.[46] The weakness of those ideas is clearly shown in the ways women seek exemption: working 'for the children' is a common explanation, working part-time is not 'real work', and working is required, before children, by the major financial commitment of most couples—buying the home. 'The rise of the woman worker has eroded the ideological supports for male dominance and female domesticity.'[47]

The great Australian ideology? Home ownership

If those two themes, private worlds and proper paths, summarize 'family ideology', 'the home' is very clearly part of both. It epitomizes, makes possible, the private world; home, like family, is natural. 'Home is where the good woman should be and there is nowhere else to go.'[48] The reformers of Australian family life saw home as 'a place of rest and refreshment from the cares of the world',[49] and language today says so. That world is 'outside'; a home is a 'family home'. And the home is a necessary step, firmly in place at the start of the necessary path. In the United States Perin showed that home ownership was viewed by urban managers as a mechanism for placing people on the proper 'ladder of life'.[50] There is little research in Australia or elsewhere examining ideas of home, but people whose words appear in family studies link home to private family life, and the proper steps on the family ladder: 'I don't think a home is a home without children'; 'We were both ready to have a child by then ... Getting the house was the main thing'.[51] Observers have long asserted that the two are linked: 'Australia is the small house. Ownership of one in a fenced allotment is as inevitable and unquestionable a goal of the average Australian as marriage'.[52]

'The Great Australian Dream' is to own your own home; the observation is commonplace, but few studies have asked why, and fewer have examined just how widespread or uniform that dream is. In most studies the only evidence is the indisputable fact that until recently an ever-increasing majority of Australian adults was attempting home ownership. Owner occupancy (owner or purchaser) rose to over 70 per cent in the mid−1960s, and still accounted for 68 per cent of households at the census of 1981 (the year of our reinterview). In the state of Victoria, the context of Green Views, the census figure was 71 per cent, and a household survey in 1983 (a more accurate source) gave the Victorian figure at 76 per cent (42 per cent owned outright, 34 per cent were purchasing).

The conclusion easily follows that 'the Great Australian Dream is almost universally held'.[53] But the fact that everyone tries to own their home may merely indicate the absence of alternatives. Does an ideology presenting home ownership as 'an innate desire' hide the failure of the capitalist system, and government policy, to create viable rental alternatives? This argument on home ownership in Australia has done much to put it on research agendas, but it throws little light on the ideas and actions of people buying houses.[54] There are few overseas studies of people's personal accounts, and these have tended to show that 'although there may be a "dominant ideology" the value systems of many people are ambiguous, fragmented and inconsistent'.[55]

Why do people seek ownership, how much does it matter, and why? And how is the dream related to family? Answers have appealed to the dichotomy of private and public. 'The family and the good citizenship that home ownership is believed to instil are equally idealized and, thereby, equated. A sacred quality endows both the family and its "home", sacred in the sense of being set apart from the mundane and having a distinctive aura'.[56] As the container of this private world, the home is necessary to the ideal of private family life. But few studies have explored the links, or the ambiguity here of 'private'. In 'individualistic' societies the haven may be invaded by its significance as a status symbol?.[57] Autonomy may mean privatization for men, escape from the home for women. Such questions have not been asked, because the nexus of family and home is seen in the centre of the traditional family.

The family was experienced as a little community, a self-contained unit which fulfilled the needs of its members for security, warmth, intimacy. People had higher expectations of domestic happiness based on marital compatibility and close relationships with their children. Home was a 'nest', the cherished possession, the place where you could express your 'real' self, the place where you chose to spend your time.[58]

Here is the basis for feminist attacks on suburbia: 'The Australian suburban dream created at one fell swoop the Australian housewife's nightmare'.[59] But such attacks bypass questions of how widespread is suburban isolation, and how inevitable, and why suburban homes are so passionately desired. When these questions have been asked, the simple equation of private home with the 'private world' is obviously inadequate.[60] Game and Pringle acknowledge that 'the suburban dream *does* have a material base. But precisely because it is ideology it offers only a partial account'.[61] And precisely because it is ideology it will be related to social structure. Is this a dream for all people, equally powerful for all and equally accepted?[62] For women as well as for men? If new family ideas are questioning women's places, especially for the economically favoured, ironically those least able to afford home ownership may be those most committed to it ideologically. Thus the optimistic picture of the increasingly 'symmetrical' family led by the middle class obscures real barriers to attaining the goals of the 'ideal family'. The increasing contrast between the family lives of people in different social classes will be magnified as home ownership becomes less easily attainable.[63]

But these trends do not mean that we have two *sorts* of family lives. Critical writing has tended to produce an interpretation of family not unlike the 'dead heart' image of Australia, dominated by a massive, intractable, unchanging core. Neither deserts nor families are homogeneous or unchanging. From the fact that the educated and middle class more easily question traditional family ideals it does not follow that the workers 'are stuck with the "ideal middle class family"' in suburbia 'while the middle class moves on to bigger and better things'.[64] It would be rash to assume that those remaining within traditional family forms are only (let alone all) the economically disadvantaged. It is obviously wrong to assume that family values became frozen there in the 1950s. Yet each of these assumptions has crept into critical writing on the family. To assume that the favoured are moving *en bloc* from traditional family ideals flies in the face of the demographic trends and evidence of values. To assume that the ideology of the family haven is all-powerful in unchanged suburbia denies the most obvious feature of suburban living; people do not need studies of changing family values to tell you that 'everybody works'. If the optimistic picture of progress to symmetry and equality is unreal, so too is the image of little boxes housing traditional nuclear families, filled all day with women.

In summary, then, diverse sources discuss the power of the idea of 'home' and its association with the goals of family life. But 'ideology'? There is no evidence that the same values stretch across society, no examination of the processes by which they might change or of the possible patterns of ideas of home, and no enquiry into how that dream of ownership may be received, translated into social behaviour, or made and remade by people making family homes.

The idea of ideology

If powerful ideas about family and home do indeed dominate Australian social life, those ideas will be displayed in the private housing estate. If they dominate Australians uniformly, they can certainly be expected to be uniform there. This will not establish the power of the ideas across Australia, any more than an excursion to the known nesting grounds of penguins will tell us how widely they are spread across the continent. But it is the best way of finding penguins, if there are any to be found. So long as you know what to look for. In the case of ideology this is far from obvious. Ideology is always seen as made up of a set of ideas that dominate behaviour, but few writers specify the set or how ideas are linked. And fewer say in what sense ideology is claimed to dominate: does 'dominant' mean affecting all behaviour, or determining it, or doing so across society, or representing the interests of the dominant group? In the Marxist original, though not in subsequent developments of it, ideology was dominant in all these senses. Few current research studies claim this—but nor do they say what they do claim as the power of ideology, or how they might explore the connections of ideas and the complicated ways they are received. If the concept of ideology is to be used as a research tool, just what ideas are said to dominate? In what sense do they dominate? And what is the evidence that they do? Having specified what to look for, it is possible to approach the methodological question most studies avoid—how do you catch an ideology?[65]

I am here using the concept in its 'weak' sense because that seems demanded by what we know about family life. The packages of ideas about family and home appearing in the different studies suggest that such ideas have resilience, staying-power, and the ability to influence behaviour even when manifestly inappropriate to people's needs or obviously more suited to the options of other sorts of people. But people very clearly do receive, respond to and work within these ideas in very different ways.

My working definition is simple: ideologies are sets of ideas that hang together and hang around, influencing behaviour. They are, as far as we can see, untidy sets, or sets of sets of ideas, offering 'different, often overlapping, intersecting frameworks of understanding'.[66] Rarely will those ideas clearly fit reality; they mask, obscure, distort, though no ideology will be totally false. The strength of the myth promoted will depend in part on its closeness to the reality obscured, and our inability to see it as myth. (So that word 'natural', recurring in the discussion above, may be an indicator of ideology in action.)

To use 'ideology' in this weak sense as a research tool is difficult. The 'stronger' assertions that ideology necessarily exists, serving the interests of rulers and determining behaviour, tidied the task of the researcher. Locating ideologies became largely a job of locating the powerful. There was no problem in finding how dominant they were, since, like fall-out, they necessarily affect everyone. A 'weak' concept still contains the recommendation to ask whose interests are served by pervasive values, but it will direct attention to messier processes by which sets of values are passed on through the social structure and confirmed, changed and challenged by active individuals. Ideology, I would argue, operates less like fall-out than like garlic, hanging around, sometimes dominating, often attractive but hard to dismiss.

Some areas of social life (more than others) are influenced (not determined) by such sets of ideas, loosely linked and hard to disentangle, and at least in part unquestioned or unjustified by large sectors of society. The origins of ideologies will be misty, their results a veiling of segments of our lives in un-questioned assumptions. Ideologies will always be related to but rarely perfectly be in the interests of those with power— even in the highly unlikely event that their interests are cohe-sive. Ideologies, by their nature, change slowly and unevenly; their resilience to sudden revision or challenge is both the reason for their influence over behaviour and the guarantee that they will never clearly reflect the interests of a particular power group.[67]

Nor will ideologies ever be simply accepted by anyone, let alone everyone. Nobody is only a recipient of ideology; ideo-logies are not made in heaven or by power élites, and beamed out at a vulnerable population. They are mediated through, changed by, and recreated by people in active relationships to these idea packages, not merely by victims of them. 'Ideology does not function in a simple manner by being imposed upon the individual; rather it is continually created and recreated by its subjects through their participation in its partial repre-sentation of reality.'[68] Moreover, people never receive ideas uninterpreted; they get different versions from different sources. They knowingly or unknowingly affect the reception, reinter-pret or translate the message, and they rarely do that alone.

If ideologies are as described they are characterized by three features challenging enquiry. First, they are by their nature opaque; they offer a version of the social world as real. The only ideologies easily accessible to researchers will probably be dead or dying; live ideology is hard to see through.[69] Secondly, ideologies are not things, but relationships of ideas, people and their socially structured lives, and so are always in flux;

impossible to locate by simple statistical descriptions of sets of ideas at a given point in time. Thirdly, they will be hardest to see from within. In Hall's words, 'We are all of us, most of the time, *in* ideology'.[70] So the webs of 'reality' presented to us are invisible, until perhaps we run into them by defying them, or get outside them by social transitions whose experience may work for ideology the way dew does for spider-webs, by highlighting the threads against the social scenery.

The following chapters ask whether, in Green Views, there are commonly held sets of ideas about family and home, what the links are between them and what their consequences for action are. But they also look for patterns of ideas and ask what evidence there is of weakness as well as strength of traditional ideas. How are they being remade? The assumption is that people always, in very complex ways, negotiate with ideology.[71] The process will be uneven and the effects will be socially structured. Thus the study of ideology requires study of the social networks that mediate, defend and distort messages. Part II of this book is about local relationships, exploring network management both as a way of negotiating with ideology *and* as a result of such negotiations.

Finally, a methodological point. Catching ideology requires different *sorts* of data—statistical data and people's words—played off against each other.[72] It will also require careful evaluation of what is netted by these means if it is to be called ideology. At the very least, four questions must be asked. First, do those ideas cohere as a *set*, a package of ideas, rather than merely a selection of the researcher's variables? Secondly, could the apparent dominance of a set of ideas be merely the artefact of the method used, the question asked, who asked it or the setting it is asked in? If so (and almost always that is possible) can other data from other methods be used to check the themes identified? Thirdly, do those themes *really* dominate across the data, or do they just look dominant because of the researcher's predisposition to see them there? And finally, is there any evidence that those ideas have anything to do with behaviour, let alone influence or determine it?

Notes

1. For recent commentaries on patterns of change, see P. McDonald, 'Families in the future: The pursuit of personal autonomy', *Family Matters*, no. 22, December 1988, pp. 40−7; papers in A. Burns, G. Bottomley & P. Jools (eds), *The Family in the Modern World*, Allen & Unwin, Sydney, 1983; L. Richards, *Having Families*, rev. edn, Penguin, Ringwood, 1985.

2. The background of the concept is explored by N. Abercrombie *et al.*, *The Dominant Ideology Thesis*, Allen & Unwin, London, 1984. Its many uses in feminist research are explored by Helen Marshall in Not having families: A study of some voluntarily childless couples, PhD thesis, La Trobe University, Bundoora, Vic., 1986. I have discussed its use in family sociology and the failure of this work to communicate with critical feminist writing on ideology in 'Family and home ownership in Australia: The nexus of ideologies', in M. Sussman, K. Boh & G. Sgritta (eds), *Strategies in Marriage, Family and Work: International Perspectives*. (Special issue of *Marriage and Family Review*, forthcoming 1989.)

3. J. Bernades, '"Family Ideology": Identification and exploration', *Sociological Review*, vol. 33, 1985, pp. 275−94.

4. For the history of the use of the concept in the women's movement see C. Burton, *Subordination*, Allen & Unwin, Sydney, 1985; and M. Barrett, *Women's Oppression Today*, Verso, London, 1980.

5. M. Barrett & M. McIntosh, *The Anti-Social Family*, Verso, London, 1982, p. 29.

6. For these developments in theorizing about gender see for example R. W. Connell, *Gender and Power*, Allen & Unwin, Sydney, 1987; and L. Alcoff, 'Cultural feminism versus post-structuralism: The identity crisis in feminist theory', *Signs*, vol. 13, pp. 404−36.

7. On the ideology of motherhood, B. Wearing, *The Ideology of Motherhood*, Allen & Unwin, Sydney, 1983; on work, A. Game & R. Pringle, *Gender at Work*, Allen & Unwin, Sydney, 1983; on working-class families, C. Williams, *Open Cut*, Allen & Unwin, Sydney, 1983; on childlessness, H. Marshall, 'not having families; on singlehood, Y. Stolk & R. Penman, *Not the Marrying Kind*, Penguin, Ringwood, 1984; on policy, C. Baldock & B. Cass (eds), *Women, Social Welfare and the State*, Allen & Unwin, Sydney, 1983; on education, C. O'Donnell, *The Basis of the Bargain*, Allen & Unwin, Sydney, 1984.

8. K. Reiger, *The Disenchantment of the Home*, Oxford University Press, Melbourne, 1985; J. Matthews, *Good and Mad Women*, Allen & Unwin, Sydney, 1984.

9. For reviews of the literature see Connell, *Gender and Power*; L. Bryson, 'The Australian patriarchal family', in L. Bryson & S. Encel (eds), *Australian Society*, 4th edn, Cheshire, Melbourne,

1984. For work in this category see J. Harper, *Fathers at Home*, Penguin, Ringwood, 1980; and G. Russell, *The Changing Role of Fathers?*, University of Queensland Press, St. Lucia, Qld, 1983. It is important to note that most of the research studies of changing family values cited in reviews, including Richards, *Having Families* and J. Harper & L. Richards, *Mothers and Working Mothers*, rev. edn, Penguin, Ringwood, 1986, draw on data from the mid-1970s.

10. C. Allport, 'The princess in the castle: Women in the new social order housing', in Women and Labour Publications Collective, *All Her Labours: Embroidering the Framework*, Hale & Iremonger, Sydney, 1984; and C. Allport, 'Women and suburban housing: Postwar planning in Sydney, 1943–61', in J. B. McLoughlin & M. Huxley (eds), *Urban Planning in Australia: Critical Readings*, Longman Cheshire, Melbourne, 1986. Matrix Book Group, *Making Space: Women and the Man Made Environment*, Pluto Press, London, 1984.

11. In a review of Betsy Wearing's pioneering work I considered these problems in detail; see L. Richards, 'Mothers', *Australian Society*, vol. 3, 1984, pp. 40–1. In a recent contribution to the theoretical debate Wearing reports her current research on the ways that women negotiate with ideology and discusses the constraints of her previous theoretical framework; see B. Wearing, Beyond the ideology of motherhood: Leisure as resistance, Paper to the annual conference of the Sociological Association of Australia and New Zealand, Canberra, 1988. Another major rethink-piece is offered by A. Game & R. Pringle in 'Beyond *Gender at Work*: Secretaries', in N. Grieve, & A. Burns (eds), *Australian Women: New Feminist Perspectives*, Oxford University Press, Melbourne, 1986, pp. 272–91.

12. C. Lasch, *Haven in a Heartless World*, Basic Books, New York, 1979.

13. The classic statement of this functionalist version is T. Parsons, 'Age and sex in the social structure of the United States', *American Sociological Review*, vol. 7, 1942, pp. 604–16; for discussions see D. Morgan, *Social Theory and the Family*, Routledge & Kegan Paul, London, 1975; G. Bottomley, 'Feminist and sociological critiques of the family' in A. Burns, G. Bottomley & P. Jools (eds), *The Family in the Modern World*, Allen & Unwin, Sydney, 1983.

14. L. Davidoff, J. Esperence & H. Newby, 'Landscape with figures: Home and community in English society', in J. Mitchell & A. Oakley (eds), *The Rights and Wrongs of Women*, Penguin, Harmondsworth, 1976, pp. 139–75.

15. It has been used as a conceptual lever, most importantly by M. Rosaldo, 'Woman, culture and society', in M. Rosaldo & L. Lamphere (eds), *Women, Culture and Society*, Stanford University

Press, Stanford, 1974, ch. 1. See also M. Stacey, 'The division of labour or overcoming the two Adams', in P. Abrams *et al.* (eds), *Practice and Progress: British Sociology 1950–1980*, Allen & Unwin, London, 1981; E. Gamarnikov *et al.* (eds), *The Public and The Private*, Heinemann, London, 1983.

16. E. J. Harman, 'Capitalism, patriarchy and the city', in C. Baldock & B. Cass (eds), *Women, Social Welfare and the State*, Allen & Unwin, Sydney, 1983, pp. 104–29.

17. A. Game & R. Pringle, 'The making of the Australian family', in A. Burns, G. Bottomley & P. Jools (eds), *The Family in the Modern World*, Allen & Unwin, Sydney, 1983, p. 96. See also Allport, 'The princess in the castle'. For a research essay stressing the participation of people in construction of this ideology see P. H. Rehak, Stoking up dreams: Some aspects of post-war housing in the suburbs of Melbourne, PhD thesis, Monash University, Clayton, Vic., 1988.

18. Rosaldo explicitly described it as an exercise in ideal types, and Saegert's most cited article is a criticism of the duality; Rosaldo, 'Woman, culture and society', in Rosaldo & Lamphere, *Women, Culture and Society*, ch. 1; S. Saegert, 'Masculine cities and feminine suburbs: Polarized ideas, contradictory realities', *Signs*, vol. 5, Spring 1980, pp. s.96–s.111. For a recent critical assessment see L. McDowell, 'Towards an understanding of the gender division of urban space', *Environment and Planning D: Society and Space*, vol. 1, 1983, pp. 59–72.

19. I have written in more detail about the ways the dichotomy misleads understanding women's workforce participation in 'No man's land', introduction to Harper & Richards, *Mothers and Working Mothers*. See also papers in A. S. Sassoon (ed.), *Women and the State: The Shifting Boundaries of Public and Private*, Hutchinson, London, 1987.

20. On the relation to the state see C. Baldock & B. Cass, *Women, Social Welfare and the State*; on interpenetration of worlds, R. Rapp, 'Family and class in contemporary America: Notes towards an understanding of ideology', *Science and Society*, vol. 42, 1980; on work, Game & Pringle, 'Beyond *Gender at Work*: Secretaries'.

21. Saegert, *Signs*, p. s.111.

22. Harman, 'Capitalism, patriarchy and the city'.

23. G. Turnaturi, 'Between public and private: The birth of the professional housewife and the female consumer', in A.S. Sassoon (ed.), *Women and the State: The Shifting Boundaries of Public and Private*, Hutchinson, London, 1987, pp. 255–78; Reiger, *The Disenchantment of the Home*.

24. H. Graham, 'Do her answers fit his questions? Women and the survey method', in E. Gamarnikow *et al.* (eds), *The Public and the Private*, Heinemann, London, 1983, p. 145.

[25.] On 'incorporation' see J. Finch, *Married to the Job: Wives' Incorporation into Men's Work*, Allen & Unwin, London, 1983; on rural settings, B. James, ' "Public" and "private" divisions in a single-industry town', paper to the Sociological Association of Australia and New Zealand, Brisbane, 1985; K. James, 'Public or private: Participation by women in a country town', in M. Bowman (ed.), *Beyond the City*, Longman Cheshire, Melbourne, 1981, pp. 71–96.

[26.] M. Simms, 'The politics of women and cities: A critical survey ', in J. Halligan & C. Paris, *Australian Urban Politics: Critical Perspectives*, Longman Cheshire, Melbourne, 1984, pp. 129–40.

[27.] J. Finch & D. Groves, 'Community care and the family: A case for equal opportunities', in C. Ungerson, *Women and Social Policy*, Macmillan, London, 1985, pp. 218–41; J. Finch & D. Groves (eds), *A Labour of Love: Women, Work and Caring*, Routledge & Kegan Paul, London, 1983; L. Bryson & M. Mowbray, 'Who cares? Social security, family policy and women', *International Social Security Review*, no. 2, 1986, pp. 183–200.

[28.] G. Dalley, *Idelogies of Caring*, Macmillan, London, 1988, p. 22.

[29.] Game & Pringle, *Gender at Work*; Harper & Richards, *Mothers and Working Mothers*.

[30.] L. Bryson, 'The Australian patriarchal family' in L. Bryson & S. Encel (eds), *Australian Society*, 4th edn, Cheshire, Melbourne, 1984 and 'Gender divisions and power relationships in the Australian family', in P. Collins (ed.), *Family and Economy in Modern Society*, Macmillan, Houndmills, Hants 1985; Harper & Richards, *Mothers and Working Mothers*; Wearing, *The Ideology of Motherhood*.

[31.] Bottomley, 'Feminist and sociological critiques', in Burns, Bottomley & Jools, *The Family in the Modern World*, p. 26.

[32.] Barrett & McIntosh, *The Anti-Social Family*, p. 27.

[33.] For Australian statistical data, see Helen Glezer, 'Antecedents and correlates of marriage and family attitudes in young Australian men and women, *XXth Internaltional CFR Seminar on Social Change and Family Policies*, Australian Institute of Family Studies, Melbourne, 1984. For accounts see Richards, *Having Families* and Wearing, *The Ideology of Motherhood*. For British studies of similar sets M. Boulton, *On Being a Mother*, Tavistock, London, 1983; A. Oakley, *The Sociology of Housework*, Martin Robertson, London, 1974, *Housewife*, Allen Lane, London, 1984 and *Becoming a Mother*, Martin Robertson, London, 1979; J. Busfield & M. Paddon, *Thinking About Children*, Cambridge University Press, Cambridge, 1977.

[34.] Barrett & McIntosh, *The Anti-Social Family*, Verson, London, p. 90.

[35.] L. Richards, Ideology at home: Family and home ownership in the Australian context, Paper presented to the National Council on Family Relations, Atlanta, Georgia, November 1987.

36. A. Burns, 'Why do women continue to marry?', in N. Grieve & A. Burns, *Australian Women: New Feminist Perspectives*, Oxford University Press, Melbourne, 1986, p. 222.

37. For surveys of the evidence see Burns, 'Why do women continue to marry?'; McDonald, *Family Matters*, pp. 40–7; introduction to Richards, *Having Families*.

38. McDonald, *Family Matters*, p. 45.

39. H. M. Hernes, 'Women and the welfare state: The transition from private to public dependence', in A. S. Sassoon (ed.), *Women and the State: The Shifting Boundaries of Public and Private*, Hutchinson, London, 1987.

40. Several works question the assumption that 'private' and 'public' retained the same meanings; see J. B. Elshtain, *Public Man, Private Woman: Women in Social and Political Thought*, Princeton University Press, Princeton, NJ, 1981.

41. McDonald uses Kant's definition of autonomy—'the individual's capacity for self-direction' and rightly points out that it is: 'not the same as individualism, narcissism or selfishness. The latter are all values. The individual may choose to use autonomy in a selfish or selfless way'. *Family Matters*, p. 45.

42. G. Dalley has made the case for the linking of familist ideology with 'possessive individualism' and explored the philosophical links involved in *Ideologies of Caring*, Macmillan, London, 1988.

43. Busfield & Paddon, *Thinking About Children*, p. 118.

44. P. McDonald, 'The baby boom generation as reproducers', *Australian Family Research Conference*, Australian Institute of Family Studies, Melbourne, 1983.

45. That path was so clearly specified in the accounts in the *Having Families* study that working with a child under five was used as the criterion for 'working mother'.

46. For the workforce patterns of this period see 'No-man's land', introduction to Harper & Richards, *Mothers and Working Mothers*; P. McDonald, Can the family survive?. AIFS Discussion paper no. 11, Institute of Family Studies, Melbourne, 1984, and for trends since, McDonald, *Family Matters*, pp. 40–7. Seeking challengers to the old ideas Wearing, using Mannheim's framework, sought but found no 'utopian' values, despite specifically sampling for 'feminist' and 'working' mothers, though in her more recent paper she recognizes that her theoretical framework led her to overlook ways women negotiated exemptions. Both the studies on which *Mothers and Working Mothers* is based had a cross-section of socio-economic status, and both produced the same picture of confusion, with many defiant and debating the 'old' ideas but none clearly living out the new; there, the theoretical

framework encouraged pictures of variety and neglected the ideological context.

47. K. Gerson, 'What do women want from men?', *American Behavioural Scientist*, vol. 29, no. 5, 1985.

48. Matthews, *Good and Mad Women*, p. 142.

49. Reiger, *The Disenchantment of the Home*, p. 37.

50. C. Perin, *Everything in Its Place: Social Order and Land Use in America*, Princeton University Press, Princeton, NJ, 1977.

51. Both these quotes are from my own work (*Having Families*, p. 98; and Harper & Richards, *Mothers and Working Mothers*, p. 71); the contribution of home ownership to family ideology was not part of the theoretical focus of those studies, so went unnoticed.

52. R. Boyd, *The Australian Ugliness*, Penguin, Ringwood, 1968.

53. J. Kemeny, *The Great Australian Nightmare*, Georgian House, Melbourne, 1983, p. 1. A debate has run for some years over with Kemeny's position; see for example T. Ward, 'Comment on Jim Kemeny's "Home ownership and finance capital"', *Journal of Australian Political Economy*, no. 3, 1978; D. Haywood, 'The great Australian dream reconsidered', *Housing Studies*, vol. 1, 1986, p. 213; Rehak, Stoking up dreams.

54. While there have been few research studies of home ownership motives in Australia there are several sources of commentary on them. The strongest research 'case' for home ownership has been put by H. Stretton, *Ideas for Australian Cities*, Georgian House, Melbourne, 1975. The interpretation of the industry was presented by W. J. Kirkby-Jones, in 'Housing Australians—an industry overview', Paper for Housing Industry Association, Sydney, 1981.

55. J. Agnew, 'Home ownership and identity in capitalist societies', in J. Duncan, *Housing and Identity*, Croom Helm, London, 1981, p. 63.

56. Perin, *Everything in its Place*, p. 47.

57. J. Duncan, 'From container of women to status symbol: The impact of social structure on the meaning of the house', in J. Duncan (ed.), *Housing and Identity: Cross-Cultural Perspectives*, Croom Helm, London, 1981, pp. 36–59.

58. Game & Pringle, 'The making of the Australian family', p. 96; on housing values in those years see Allport, 'Women and suburban housing'.

59. B. Kingston, *My Wife, My Daughter and Poor Mary Ann*, Nelson, Melbourne, 1975, p. 2. Reiger's account (in *The Disenchantment of the Home*) of the changing idea of the home provides a far more complex picture of the processes by which women remade the link of good family and private home, and Rehak's thesis (Stoking up dreams) on the post-war years includes accounts from architects and home-building couples.

60. Reiger, *The Disenchantment of the Home*, pt 1, traces the contra-

dictory processes by which 'the home' was modernized and made hygienic and efficient in the pre-war years, and the invasion of the 'private world' by professional advisers and inspectors.

61. Game & Pringle, 'The making of the Australian family', p. 96.

62. It is startling how few ask this question. See P. Williams, 'The politics of property: Home ownership in Australia', in J. Halligan & C. Paris, *Australian Urban Politics: Critical Perspectives*, Longman Cheshire, Melbourne, 1984, pp. 129–40.

63. B. Cass, 'Housing and the family', Social Welfare Research Centre, Kensington, 1980; T. Burke, L. Hancock & P. Newton, *A Roof Over Their Heads: Housing Issues and Families in Australia*, Australian Institute of Family Studies, Melbourne, 1984.

64. Game & Pringle, 'The making of the Australian family', p. 97. See also B. Cass & H. Radi, 'Family, fertility and the labour market', in N. Grieve, & P. Grimshaw (eds), *Australian Women: Feminist Perspectives*, Oxford University Press, Melbourne. A strikingly similar argument is put by B. Berger & P. Berger in *The War Over the Family: Capturing the Middle Ground*, Penguin, Harmondsworth, 1983 with a different conclusion—celebration of the survival of the best in bourgeois values. The confident prediction of working class following middle class to family symmetry was the thesis of M. Young & P. Willmott, *The Symmetrical Family*, Penguin, Harmondsworth, 1973.

65. One methodological innovation to catch background ideas is reported by J. Finch from a study of family obligations in 'The vignette technique in survey research', *Sociology*, vol. 21, no. 1, pp. 105–14.

66. S. Hall, 'Ideology in the modern world', *La Trobe Working Papers in Sociology*, no. 65, 1983, La Trobe University, Bundoora, Vic.

67. Reiger provides insight into the ways that those promoting ideologies are themselves recipients in her story of the contribution of Vera Scantlebury Brown, *The Disenchantment of the Home*, ch. 6.

67. Reiger, *The Disenchantment of the Home*, p. 23.

69. D. Morgan, *Social Theory and the Family*, Routledge & Kegan Paul, London, 1975.

70. Hall, 'Ideology in the modern world', p. 26.

71. S. Hall uses the same verb for a somewhat different process in *Culture, Media, Language*, Hutchinson, London, 1980. Marshall's analysis of the childless, Not having families, has explored the range of ways in which people outside normal family life may negotiate with ideology. I discuss evidence that those inside do so too in the introduction to *Having Families*, and in 'Australian family studies', *Contemporary Sociology*, vol. 14, 1985.

72. Richards, 'Ideology in the modern world', p. 26.

6

Whose Home? The Meanings of Ownership

M: I don't know whether it's a journalist's theory that all Australians strive for their own home. I think, when we were buying our house, Australians, per head of population, were the greatest home owners in the world. I think they still could be. So, it's sort of a thing that's born into you ... Well I've never come across anybody yet, whether they own a house or don't, that don't want one.

Home ownership in Green Views is a natural step in family life and a necessary one, both obvious and inescapable. There is a widespread assumption that, like marriage, it is a goal for everyone. The purchase of the house was the overwhelming preoccupation and justification for decisions and the common link felt with other residents. Only a fifth of those interviewed had ever even considered not owning, in most cases only as a temporary expedient. Very commonly, they 'explained' wanting to own by the fact that they had always wanted to own. 'It's our life. It's something that we've always wanted'; 'It means everything really. Security. You've got a home to come to'.

'The Great Australian Dream—to own your own home! I think we're the country with the highest home ownership per capita.' This woman was right, if she meant 'of societies like ours', and right in adding, that 'Foreign-born people own more of their own homes than Australians do'.[1] A British couple had migrated mainly to own a home: 'In England, it's so hard to buy a house'. An older Greek man had never thought of renting: 'When you are your age, it's different, but when you come to my age, I think you need more relaxing, more privacy. Everyone in my country swears, you know, it's very good to have my own house'. A Chinese migrant said, 'I think that is one of the main things in life—that a person has to have his own home'.

Like the material on classes and migrants, these answers offer no harsh picture of inequality. Only five people gave reasons for owning that were about status or prestige; for only one was it the first answer, and then status was for the family: 'Prestige. For my children, I suppose'. Perhaps status is not earned by doing what everybody naturally does? One aspect of status was finally raised by a direct question: 'Do people respect home owners more than those who don't own their home?'; usually, until this question was asked the issue had not appeared in the interview. Even then only half the survey respondents agreed, most saying *some* people thought that.

Attitudes to renters, as a category, were not hostile. The same phrases used to indicate acceptance of lower classes and migrants turned up for renters: 'they don't worry' or 'don't bother' us. Here too those that do not worry anyone are those on the proper path. Normally people expected that non-owners were all potential owners; nobody would want to rent. 'It doesn't worry us. We've got friends who haven't got homes', said a young man, adding, 'And we know they're eventually going to strive for one. It's just a matter of time and getting money together'. One woman respected her 'friends that are in flats and things like that' more, 'because they're going to end up in a better house in the long run'. Most people had been renters: 'Anybody who thinks any less of somebody who rents is pretty sick, in my book. 'Cos we've rented for so long ourselves'. Eight of those who did agree that people respect owners more than renters hastily dissociated themselves from this view. Two used the words that traditionally deny prejudice: 'some of our best friends'!

Another ten specified that respect came not from 'people' but from bankers.[2] 'It's only when you go to the bank manager and ask for a loan, then he will give you a more favourable consideration if you tell him you own your own house. But otherwise, your friend would not think much more of you if you told him that.' Nobody questioned assertions that 'the bigger the debts that you've got, the more money you can borrow', and 'with a house, you're stable'. One man operated on that assumption himself: 'When I interview people, I look at people who've got something round their neck, and they're going to have to work hard to keep their job'.

But while renters as a category were understood, renters in Green Views were highly suspect. They were uncommon, always transient and usually obviously different. There were three in the 1978 sample, but in the reinterview sample, only one renter remained (in a company house). They were apparently also not easily included in social interaction. No one nominated a renter among the four people they knew best in Green Views.

W: Oh yeah, there's a big stigma about renting. Especially around here, where people do *own* them ... You never come across anybody who actually admits to just renting as a permanent structure. It's always, 'Just for the moment, until we can get enough money', or whatever. But people tend to look down on the ones who haven't been able to save up enough for their deposit. And 'Fancy getting married and having kids if you don't have your own house!' sort of thing. Maybe nobody ever *says* anything to the ones who do rent. It's just there's an opinion around.

That opinion was about the proper paths; family life is entered via home ownership. A woman explained, 'If I meet someone and they're buying their own home, you think, oh well, they've got a few brains'. In clear contrast, 'Couples that get married and just never sort of knuckle down or bother to think, well, we'll buy our own home, well I haven't got much time for them'.

Why do you want to own?

Given the taken-for-grantedness of owning, 'Why do you want to own?' is an odd question. 'I don't know that I could give you a reason for wanting to. I suppose it's just like, as they say, the Great Australian Dream. It's just something you do. I couldn't rent for a long, long period. I mean, not on a permanent basis.' The question was sometimes answered (like 'Why did you get married?'[3]) with, 'Everyone does'. But everyone doing the same thing for different reasons is not evidence for ideology, and when reasons are given, they sound very muddled. 'I suppose it's the Great Australian Dream; we always expected to own a house, or own property, so we just bought'. Explaining, this man added two different reasons: 'It's the done thing. I don't know, it would irk me, I think, to pay rent to someone else', and then added a third: 'It just sort of came naturally. The obvious thing is to buy a house and own it'.

Studies from other western countries similarly offer a jumble of answers,[4] indicating that it is unwise to assume anyone has *one* reason for owning a home, and reasons are usually much less practical than they sound.[5] The few studies reaching behind simple coded categories share two themes: that it is natural to own, and that it is necessary for family life.[6] Holmes found two thirds of her young, British, working-class respondents gave 'financial reasons', and one third 'freedom to choose' and to 'do what you like with the place'. Asked what they liked about owning, they stressed independence and control. But the words they used suggested a 'widely-held view about the "naturalness" of home ownership'.[7] In the United States Rakoff reported that while the obvious meaning in unstructured interviews was investment, behind this came a tangle of inconsistent answers concerning family life, social status and security, refuge and control. He argued that the house 'is a dominant symbol of a variety of problematic and conflicting life experiences—personal success and family happiness, mobility and permanence, privacy and social involvement, personal control and escape'. This bundle hardly fits cleanly into the 'private' world in a two-world picture. The 'multivocality of the house as a symbol reflects the ambiguous meanings Americans attach to the private sphere'.[8]

All these themes, even the words, recur in Green Views. Here too people gave 'hard', practical reasons, with more complex ones behind them. Coding up to three responses for each, we collected 305, of which a third were coded 'financial investment/security'. Another 18 per cent were in terms of 'security of tenure'; other down-to-earth replies ('can do what you want with it' and 'owning something/possession') accounted for 24 per cent. Replies explicitly and only about social life and identity rated very poorly: 'achievement' and 'status' together were merely 7 per cent, and the 'soft' answers of 'privacy' and 'stability' only 17 per cent. Moreover, in first responses the practical reasons dominate:[9] over half were coded as 'financial investment/security', with another 15 per cent as security of tenure. So when the soft answers came in they were more often second or third thoughts. Since there was so little variety, patterns are hard to find. There was no significant association of reasons for owning with life stage, class or education. Only one variable—gender—patterned the answers; those patterns are discussed later in this chapter.

But what people *said* sounds less practical. Each of our coding categories hid multiple meanings, most complex in the most popular categories. Examination of the text of replies raises three issues, none of which has been discussed in the literature. First, it questions the validity of handling these questions by quantitative methods alone. Secondly, it throws open the assumptions about which reasons are 'hard', which 'soft' or 'emotional'. Finally, the distinction made in several studies between 'practical' or 'financial' reasons and 'family' reasons becomes absurd. Security is about family, independence is about family, investment, privacy and being established are about family life. Listen to people, and there are few meanings put on owning a home that are not tangled with ideas of family life.

A conversation between husband and wife makes each of these points.[10] These are Asian immigrants, both full-time employed, with a young child. Why do they want to own their own home?

M: Without going into finance ... I think you manage togetherness. I think it holds you more together, the home, than what you were if you were renting. Even though your costs are far greater in a house ... your responsibilities are also greater. But I think it closes your family closer together. You are closer together and working together.

W: It's good, I like it. (Baby) can run around. You can do what you want.

M: It means everything really. Security. You've got a home to come to.

W: You go out, you come back. You see you have the house.

M: It's an achievement. I think it's the biggest step to marriage. That's the biggest step, and your second biggest is usually buying a home. It means everything ... Just starting from the bottom, I suppose, and working your way up ... We always wanted a home.

W: We were always thinking about a home ... Independence, anyway—very important. Better for all of us.

There are many keywords in operation here. But one, 'security', is obtrusive in all the accounts. Security is the off-the-hook answer to 'Why own your own home?'. It was the only one-word answer commonly given, and the term was used but rarely explained, in a majority of responses. As a one-word answer it is cryptic; we had to probe for follow-up comments to establish even whether this was financial security or security of tenure. A lot of answers are about both, some about neither; 'security' has many meanings, frequently combined.

Security: Your money or your life?

Financial security has at least three faces in these accounts. Each has its keywords: rent as 'wasted money', 'security for the future', and 'building up'. The apparently simple argument about wasted rent is most common, but it is usually combined with the other two, and all are less about money than family life.

The wasted-rent argument is so completely unquestioned that the catch-phrases come tumbling out. People repeatedly described renting as 'wasted money', 'dead money', 'money in another person's pocket' or 'down the drain'. (Each of the phrases occurs in one or another of the overseas studies—these are *international* keywords!) One man produced 'dead money down the drain'. A woman offered 'We were sick of our money going down the drain, lining someone else's pockets'. The absurdity is fine evidence of the acceptance of recurring phrases. The assumption that renting is financially disastrous seems indeed to preclude any reasoning about its advantages.

'Dead money' arguments expand easily to 'investment', but usually this too was offered more as a keyword than an argument. Several sounded puzzled about the investment they firmly claimed, but confident that it was responsible planning:

M: I just couldn't see the sense in paying rent for 35 years and that's unrecuperable money. And this is an investment. We've got that money—even though you pay three times as much back for it, it's still—one day—going to be ours, and you're sitting on $50 000. And by the time we've paid it, $50 000 will not be a lot of money. But at least it's an investment.

'Security for the future' was the obvious meaning of financial security, but these were always family futures. They came from all life stages. The childless couples emphasized excitement with what one young woman in a very bare house called 'starting from the beginning with nothing, and moving up to what we've got now'. Those with children stressed the need to be stable: 'It's something to own and can't be taken away from us. It's a home for the children and we don't have to move around any more'. So life stretches into old age. If you get the timing wrong you pay for it: 'If they've got teenagers, obviously they'll go without more'. If you make a false step you retrace it. One woman, forced to sell because of financial difficulties, firmly intended to purchase a house again: 'It is sad to sort of lose all this, but then this is not the only house in the world. I mean, if you own your own home, that's what's important ... You've got to buy yourself a house because when you're too old to work you couldn't afford to pay rent on a pension, so this is why, I think, everybody strives to at least own their own home'. And the long view takes you to the next generation, life cycle in action. 'Security in the future—not only for us, but for the kids later on in life. You know, we won't be here for ever'. A retired man recalled his setting out on the proper path. Owning your own home was 'a fundamental thing when I was 16 years of age. And my parents taught that to me. My first thing in life was to buy a home, and then everything came after that'.

Recurring words were 'new start to life', 'being settled down', 'base' or 'foundation' and 'permanence'.[11] Not one statement contained regret for the settling, though most people had enjoyed the first step of married life in a flat without children: 'I suppose those two years we were both working, and having a pretty gay social life ... But it just seemed to be a natural progression'. Ownership was the basis for unity and stability: 'We want to be a family, and a good foundation is owning your own home'. One of the men who had missed the proper path in early life stages said the house meant, 'Stability, it just basically comes down to stability. It's something that everybody shares in the whole family, sharing'.

Many saw those messages in early socialization. One couple, both of whom were the eldest of large families (9 and 11 children), talked of the effort to save: 'There were a lot of little ones looking up to you and our parents had given us the best they had and they didn't have a lot of money, so we had to do on our own...each of my sisters and brothers that have got married, *and* his family, have all done the same'. Two men cited their parents' failure to achieve home ownership as reason for their own determination: 'Like, my parents always rented, for as long as I can remember', one said. 'I wasn't going to bring up my child in a rented house.'

There was as much agreement about these maps of paths into family life as about the maps of the social areas in the estate. Getting a house was like throwing a six to start the game.[12] A young couple had been living in a caravan at his parents' place. Buying the house changed their lives: 'It's helped us *plan*. We tend to plan things now'. That means planning family. 'It was a prerequisite of getting married', said a woman, explaining that 'Both our parents have always owned their own homes. It was a goal that we both saved for from the time we were engaged. It was just something that naturally followed'. And children naturally followed the stage of saving. In Green Views the timing of 'family' was clearly in terms of mortgages, women's working and dual income.[13]

But as this game was pictured there were no snakes to slide down. In all this material there is no case of anyone questioning the necessity of the home ownership step for family stability or the certainty that once on the housing ladder you will 'eventually' own the home. 'Security. If I own my own home, if there's payments hanging over my head, I know if anything happened, no one could take the house off me. And therefore my family will always have somewhere to live.' No one could take it? His confidence is amazing, in a setting where mortgagee auctions were quite commonplace. But no one mentioned in this context the *in*security in having 'payments hanging over' their heads, though almost all had them.

In the interviews with people selling up, we found three whose finances necessitated it. In each case they blamed their own over-commitment or bad decisions. None regretted having tried for home ownership or felt they should have been advised against it. They had their foot on the housing ladder, however painful the process. A man leaving the estate because his marriage had broken up gave the tension over the house purchase as the main reason for their troubles. But he was still going to buy another house, and of course marry again. His reasoning echoes many of the themes in earlier chapters: 40 is old, work is required, life stretches ahead dominated by the house: 'I sit down and think to myself, what am I going to do when I'm 40, I'll have nothing'. He saw the burden as inevitable: 'You've got to work hard the rest of your life, like 30 years is a long time to pay for a house, isn't it really? And not many people get it in under 30 years'.

Nor is there any comment on the vulnerability of home purchasers who in the majority of cases depended on two incomes to meet mortgages, or vulnerability of family ideals possibly incompatible with the requirement for two incomes. The home owner's progress is clear, from 'nothing', through sheets on the window, to becoming 'established'—usually on two incomes. The order of steps is essential: home before family. In one of the few allusions to a world in which the home was out of reach, a woman said, 'If you get married and start to have a family immediately it is virtually impossible to save the deposit for a house. So these families that actually have got the deposit on their house, even if the repayments are pretty steep and they're having a terrible struggle, they've still got their foot in the door of their own block of land and their own house'.

Financial reasons collapsed easily into social. Like Australians generally, these people believed that the best thing to do with your money was save towards a home.[14] They hardly had to justify this since they saw no other way. No one included the financial advantages deriving from the political subsidy of home ownership. When people said their reasons were 'purely financial', other factors always slipped in at the end. A childless teacher I shall call Cathy responded quickly: 'We'd been through the thing of paying out money for rent . . . We wanted something that would be our own eventually . . . to actually get in and get started on owning something . . . that was the reason. We wanted financial security'. But as she thought about it, her answer became more complex: 'We had never earned a wage before, we hadn't had much money, yes, so it was definitely a financial security thing. Plus we felt that if we were going to have children ever . . . you definitely could *never* have children in a flat.' Later, those reasons linked into 'permanence' and social pressures: 'In my friendship group and my family group the pressures that I'm getting from other people are, yes, it is good to own your own home and there is something unstable, perhaps, about renting'.

Security means control

Control also had two meanings, each with its keywords: a negative version ('no one can put you out'), and a positive (you can 'make it yours'). Both, in turn, were obviously about independence from a landlord. The first, but not the second, was normally followed by phrases such as 'especially with a family'.

'Throw, kick, put you out'—the keywords abound for what landlords do to renters. Being 'put out' of a rented house (like a dog!) was widely dreaded, though nobody had experienced it. A vivid, violent (and inaccurate) picture is drawn of vulnerability to the unreasonable whim of anonymous landlords. 'You can be put out at any time' was asserted by three people. If you own, 'You don't have to worry about the landlord throwing you out all the time'. Even the hazy early messages of childhood were cited by only one woman, whose mother 'was always throwing up things in front of us, like people who were thrown out of their houses because they couldn't pay the rent'. Her husband, she said, 'feels the same because his father had the same idea, coming out from Italy with nothing'. The husband confirmed that 'It's security and, like she said, nobody can kick you out'. The certainty of 'they can't take it away' if you own it is matched by the conviction that 'they' can throw you out if you do not: 'A rental agent can put you out of the house when the owners say you've got to get out. If you're in your own home, it depends on you keeping up the payments on whether you stay. I think when you own your own home it's just a basic security. You got your garden—it's just your own piece of Australia, your own piece of the land ... I feel as if this is my base to go from'.

The second meaning of 'control' was about independence, about 'being able to do what you want with it'. Keywords again; several phrases stand for freedom from interference. One women remarked, 'Put a nail in the wall, people always say'. Not always; we had only four other comments about nails in walls, but forty about other ways of 'doing what you want with it'. They include having wild parties (two comments) and being able to repulse neighbours (one comment only in this context, but a recurring theme in others). One man rejoiced that if he was in a rotten mood he could 'put a brick through the wall' of a house he owned. He had never tried to put bricks through rented walls and, like most, had no evidence of serious restrictions in rented accommodation. But most had rented, and had felt a niggling constraint: 'It's not permanent when you're renting . . . You can get kicked out the next week if they feel like it. And you can't do anything. You put a bit of paint on the wall and they'll have a fit'.

The home as haven? Here the answers sometimes allude to privacy. But they are rarely about the first of the three meanings of privacy, the sweet idyll of privacy *for* peace, haven, caring. Rather, they evoke privacy *to* be yourself and privacy *from* others. They offer themes about adulthood; independence, control, individuality.

Fourteen people volunteered 'independence' as a reason for owning their home. Some of these explicitly compared their own home with their start to married life in their parents' homes (in two cases in a caravan). All linked ownership with the transition to adult status; a young man said that 'Buying me first home, basically it was sort of a new start to life'. He explained that 'It's mine—no one can take it away . . . security for the future. It's just yours, and you can do whatever you want, without anyone always bugging you'.

Nails in walls can be hooks for pictures or symbols that indicate 'ownership is the authentic metaphor for identity'.[15] A lot of these answers report pleasure in 'putting yourself into it', that is not trivial. A woman said: 'It's something that everyone deserves to have. It's something that is actually yours and doesn't belong to anyone else. It's something that you can choose and change around to suit yourself'. Twenty-three people talked of 'getting it the way you want it' and 'making it yours', another 10 of more specifically 'putting your ideas in practice', and designing the house and garden: 'It's ours—something that really works for us. It means a lot and what we do to the house, what renovations we do, we *enjoy* doing it because it's ours'. Several said this was the only thing you *really* own, or the only place you can express yourself; here 'self' must be taken seriously.[16] Half of the reinterview sample said they had definitely wanted a 'new' house, that is, not previously occupied; a few of those added that they would have preferred to design their new house rather than buy one ready-built, to 'make it individual'. But the newness was what mattered; and again the idea is of building up: 'You can build your own identity, and not have the feeling that you actually belong to somebody else'.

'You' or 'we' in these declarations of independence always refer to the couple. That children are not mentioned is partly of course because they are seen as neither participating in nor having preferences about 'doing it up'. But they do not even feature as potential occupants in these statements. The house is never portrayed as part of their identity. Just as the family community is for little kiddies, the dream of the home that is 'ours' sometimes has no place for older children.[17]

There is little sense here of 'a privileged emotional climate they must protect from outside intrusion, through privacy and isolation'.[18] When protection sounds most urgent it is autonomy that is at stake. One of the two women who called the house 'the start of my own life', had an easy answer to 'What does this house mean to you?': 'Everything. If I didn't have it, I think I'd just give up really'. Her only explanation is, 'It's my house. I don't have to answer to anybody'. Owning is necessary for autonomy, and autonomy is about control; privacy here means freedom from interference. It is rarely given alone as a reason for owning, often appears almost by accident late in an explanation. Talk of investment leads to talk about paths into family life, which links with privacy and independence (often all in the same breath) as though they were the same reasons. A man wound up a speech on inflation with the summary: 'From a financial point of view we felt it was an advantage, and just from the point of view of having your own identity really, and having more freedom to do what you like and when you like and what renovations or whatever you want, well you're free to do those without going through a landlord. Just having your own privacy, too'.

A particular sort of private world, this: designed for adults to make families in self-sufficiency, 'building it up' together. Autonomy is often linked to 'togetherness'. 'It's ours. It's our home'. Five people said the purchase of the home was the start of doing things together (though presumably they had done many other things together before they bought). A man called it 'Our first sort of building up of something together in our marriage. We came in here with four bare walls and not much money and all the rest, like most people, and slowly built it up'. Being 'ours' meant 'Freedom, I think, more than anything. If you had to rent a house, it wasn't ours. And here we can come and go as we please and I don't have to worry about committing myself to anyone. It's ours. It's our home. You don't have to worry about anything'.

There is also pleasure in seclusion. You do not have to go out of it, and do not want to. Several eulogies of suburban life carry clear messages about a privatized world. A recent immigrant compared it with life (with children) before owning.

M: Because you've got a bit of land, a house built on top and you want to do something, you want to do the garden, the back garden, add this one, put this, put that, so you're more interested in what you've got. Before, you rent, you're only interested in get home, having dinner, watch TV. Saturday and Sunday, get the car out. You don't have that interest in getting home, "I have to do this and I have to plant that tree." ... Not that we have to, we like, we like to do things in the house.

His children were school-age, and such contentment was more usual at that life stage but not restricted to it. Cathy again:

W: You live a kind of transient life, I think, when you're a renter. It's definitely an in out job. You're never home ... Whereas this is a more, I suppose, settled way of life and more solid way of life ... a different way of looking at things altogether ... We tend to stay in the home more than we would have in our flat. We're quite happy to stay home in the afternoon, and just enjoy being here ... It was something we really looked forward to, to having our home and sort of building a future ... something that we can really work on, something that we can put a lot of ourselves into and get some return out of ... You know, this is going to be yours, this is going to be ours.

What's the difference between a renter and a home owner? She said 'Stay-at-homeness, I think'.

This is no monolithic set of values. There are some people firmly responding only in terms of practical finance.[19] A few talk only of personal achievement, and a handful only of status. But some themes persist in a high proportion of cases and link with each other: on exploring one, we find another; the background of one contains another. There is a variety of emphases on meanings of the home but no indication of competing or clashing interpretations. Almost all the accounts are also about family, the dominating theme about proper paths to worlds within which people have control. Those threads inter-weave so tightly that it is grammatically impossible to pull them out: family is in the same sentence, the same phrase, as investment, control, security. The fabric is tight and strong and, as in all fine-woven fabrics, the individual colours merge, giving the impression of uniformity to a complex set of ideas.

But there are signs here of how people work at the fraying edges of the ideological fabric. Particular private worlds are portrayed in most of these accounts; not the sweet dreams of family haven in the 'old' ideas, but proper paths and necessary conditions for adult, independent lives. Where have all the havens gone? The answer appears to be 'Gone to husbands'.

His dream and hers

> If only through his work in some nook of the economic machinery, the individual must find a way of living in this alien world ... The private sphere ... is mainly where he will turn. It is here that the individual will seek power, intelligibility and quite literally a name—the apparent power to fashion a world, however Lilliputian, that will reflect his own being: a world that, seemingly having been shaped by himself and thus unlike those other worlds that insist on shaping him, is translucently intelligible to him (or so he thinks); a world in which, consequently, he is *somebody*, perhaps even, within its charmed circle, a lord and master.[20]

It is not only by outmoded grammatical convention that the individual in this much-quoted eulogy of family homes is male. Both the historical literature and that of conservative sociology contend that in modern society the home has become not just *a* haven, but the *only* emotional haven for individuals, the only refuge from a heartless world.[21] But it is men who are portrayed in refuge there. And feminist sociology firmly explains this in its exposure of the 'private world': the home is not her haven, rather her place of hard domestic labour.

Yet so far the picture of Green Views is almost gender-free. The reasons for coming, the patterns of satisfaction, the images of the estate show no gender differences. This is *their* dream, *their* choice, *their* path to family life. Women and men speak for the couple: 'we wanted', 'we decided'. In the coded re-sponses to 'Why do you want to own your own home?' there are no male or female reasons; all were given by both women and men. Women were more likely than men to give reasons to do with the haven of home—privacy, stability—but these soft answers were only a minority of responses.[22] So too were reasons about status.[23] The gender differences fade beside the fact that both men and women were far more likely to give answers coded in the apparently hard categories: investment, security of tenure, or 'you can do what you want with it'.[24] Only one respondent (a woman) gave privacy as a first reason. But while a little nifty recoding can produce statistical significance for a gender difference in these figures, the statistical data looks as though only some women, and even fewer men, see soft meanings of the home.

So where does the difference lie? The critical literature shows that the home must mean different things to women (placed in the private world) and men (providers of shelter by their labour in the public world). Other studies have indicated such differences. They suggest a woman puts more emphasis on the home as a private place, a base for identity, a place to improve and express herself.[25] But if she is not at home? Most studies of meanings of the home assume that women are there. If they are normally in or likely to return to the workforce, what happens to their ideas of the 'private' world? Studies of workforce participation clearly show that in dual-income families the double load of paid and unpaid work is largely carried by women. And mothers' patterns of paid work, and attitudes to it, unlike fathers', are always shaped by the perceived needs of the children.[26] We might except then that while women would stress the needs of family life, in their thinking about housing, they would not experience the home as haven. So a first guess can be made at the puzzle of privacy: if the 'private world' of the home was rarely pictured as an intimate haven, is this perhaps because women, at least, rarely see it this way? And while we might expect few differences in women's and men's reasons for *wanting* home ownership, we would expect the home to mean different things to them.

This was in fact the case. An earlier, vaguer question—'What does this house mean to you?'—seemed to access themes that do clearly distinguish men's from women's answers.[27] It produced two instant responses: 'Everything' and 'It's mine'. Three further key words appeared: the familiar 'security'; and two new themes, 'work' and 'home'. Of these, only one, 'everything', came from women and men. Seven men and five women said 'everything', and another four men used phrases such as 'an awful lot'. They apparently meant it quite literally, just as they literally meant it was the start of life. But each of the other key words covered sharp patterns of gender difference.

Her security and his

'Security' was offered, unquestioned, by both women and men (though more often by men, perhaps because men more often give one-word answers). In the answers to 'What does your house mean to you?', twelve women and sixteen men said 'security'. But to men it meant financial security (all but two), to women stability (again, all but two). One husband answered, 'Big mortgage', and his wife, as though agreeing, said, 'Well, we feel secure'.

When they said their houses meant security, men, much more often than women, gave explanations that included financial investment and/or control over their shelter. Both were also commonly offered by women, but the combination of the two, in the absence of other, softer themes, was a male answer. 'Security ... no one can kick you out. You're paying money to yourself rather than someone else'. Men emphasized much more often the financial disadvantages and vulnerability of renting and lack of control, of not being able to 'do what you like with it'. Again these contrasts are not absolute: but women more often disliked the lack of stable tenure and wanted control over decoration and taste.

Pronouns matter. Dead rent arguments came from a dozen women, with the same words and lack of logic, and often even more fervour, but most said 'we' as though they spoke an agreed-on view, and all but two talked first of the uncertainty of renting. What started as a wasted-rent argument for women easily turned into one about being on the proper path; for men it referred to autonomy. A woman who said her husband had refused to rent, explained: 'We had to have a house of our own. He wouldn't live in another person's house'.

For women and men security referred to necessary steps on the ladder of family life, but they tended to see those steps differently. For men it was more likely to mean 'getting established', 'starting out', 'setting up' as an independent marital unit. For women it was usually a necessary condition for having children. As with all these differences, the contrast is not absolute. Statements about the problems of flat life and the delights of being an independent household came as often from women, but they usually included children. When men mentioned family life stage they indicated a burden of responsibility. One woman whose own response to walking in the door was absolutely simple—'Oh lovely! Home at last!'—said she wanted to own 'Mainly for my husband. He wanted to start everything as fresh as what he could. You know, from the bottom up. So basically from bare dirt and keep going'.

Women seemed to see longer paths through life stages; they used images of families with needs, not of autonomous couples. Most women's statements about home ownership as a step in family life involved children as the next step. A woman currently in a company house said she would rather own it: 'Just to know that whatever you do to it is going to be permanent'. The interviewer laughed, 'Put a nail in the wall, people always say!', but that was not what she had meant. She was talking about family and freedom: 'I'd like to have a few, a couple of acres or something so that the kids can get out and do things— just a sense of permanence'. For another woman the house meant 'security' and, in the same sentence, 'It's sort of our aim from marriage to get a house and then have our family'.

The security of not renting, for women, was about stability and space for bringing up children. No men say this, though many women grammatically deal their husbands into this view: 'Well, to provide a stable environment for our children—our forthcoming family. We both wanted children and we didn't want to be in the position of paying out a large amount of money on rent when we could be paying it off on something of our own'. Several women, like Cathy, really meant 'you couldn't have a baby in a flat', and others clearly pictured the planned stages of family life in terms of home. 'I wanted a house for the baby to grow up in', said a young mother. 'I didn't want him to be born while we were in the flat.' When they were first married and she 'wasn't expecting' she had been 'quite happy in a flat, just the two of us'. And if they hadn't had children? 'Oh we would have bought a house eventually, but not as quickly as what we did.' Four men talked of space for children to play or of future inheritance, and one of giving children 'a home, a base'. A few said *they* would find family life unacceptable in a flat: 'If we hadn't have bought here, we would have bought somewhere else, even if we had to hock ourselves sort of into oblivion. I don't think I could handle living in a flat—not for too long'.

These themes should not be interpreted as showing men distanced from the family. On the contrary, the family had central significance. How do you feel when you walk in the door? 'Well I've come back home', said a man, explaining: 'It's home. Because the family's there'. Many statements from men about the importance of their homes involve children. But the *ways* in which security meant family were usually different for men. Men were more likely to link family to home when they had older children; it was the younger women who made that link. Fathers more often stressed the importance of inheritance ('something for him'). It is hard to resist the summary that women see themselves *living*, with families, in homes; men stress *leaving* the home to the children. While this is too simple it does introduce a further contrast; for men, but rarely for women, the home is their *own* possession.

Whose home?

To the question 'What does the house mean to you?' both women and men replied: 'It's mine'. But they meant different things. Unqualified, it was mainly a men's response. Men came home to *their* house. Nine men said just 'It's mine', another eight used the word or identified the house as only theirs—'I'll own it, me and the Insurance Company'—but not his wife. In the 10 cases where women said 'mine', only three included no other family members (two of those were in very unstable marriages.) Pronouns matter here too; another 18 women said 'ours' or 'we own it'. Family intrudes on women's sense of owning but not on men's. Women mentioned children in nine of the answers to 'What does your house mean to you?'; men in none.[28]

If a woman talked of her house as 'mine' it usually meant that it was her creation, represented her taste and her effort (not his) in 'doing it up', and her relationship with it. In this context men never said they loved their house or it made them happy. (Ten women did.) But men very frequently said they felt 'proud' of it. The complicated meanings of 'together' emerge in those pronouns. 'It was something we were doing for ourselves', said a young wife. 'You know, all his new ideas . . . We're doing things together now.' Women often said 'It's my home', a very different statement, more about making a home out of a house-object. Some couples explicitly agreed that the house was, in this sense, hers.

W: I've poured a lot of love into the house and it has given me a lot back . . . this house represents me . . . It is just how I wanted it and I like it for that. You know, my husband sort of said, 'If you want that, fine, do it, have it . . . Yep, you're in the house all day, most of the day, so it is up to you'.

When women did refer to 'my' home it was to recall the dream of married life. 'I've always wanted to buy my own home. I think it's every girl's ambition when they get married, to have their own home'. For men 'mine' (in a few cases 'my bit of Australia') was about control: 'I look at it and say it's mine. Like, we lived in my in-laws' for a year or so after we got married. Now, when I walk in, I know it's mine'. The most obvious male meanings of 'mine' were those associated with security—my money, mine to remain in, mine to control. When women said 'mine' they almost always also said 'we' and 'work'. 'Mine, I own it', said a professional in part-time employment. 'We started from scratch, and we've got a lot of things done, bought everything, worked hard for it.'

The two sides of the dichotomy, work and home, are linked in these accounts as means and end. But they are different means to an apparently different goal for women and men. 'Traditional family ideology' associates work with men and men with public worlds. But in this context they are reversed. Work was a woman's response. Two men said the house was, as one put it, 'a symbol of what I've worked for, probably for the last seven or eight years'. And three talked about 'putting work into it'. By contrast, 16 women said 'work', meaning one or all of 'doing it up', paid work for mortgages, and housework. Doing it up was a serious business and meant enormous effort and expense by couples often very short of both time and money. When men talked about their labour on the house it was always on the exterior. Feminist writing on architecture has argued that women are identified with interiors of houses, whereas 'in the market, as any estate agent's window shows, the exterior is mainly what counts'.[29] In Green Views both women and men agreed.

But women, especially women at home, were more likely

than men to stress the 'work to be done' (to make the house acceptable): 'We've still got a lot of work to do outside in the garden and what have you, but when we moved in, there was absolutely nothing, and we nearly bought an established home. It would have been a lot easier. But we thought, we may as well start from scratch. A little bit of a struggle and what have you. A bit of an excitement, I suppose, we don't really regret it'. Only men talked of these duties with resentment. One, now selling up, answered 'How do you feel when you walk in the door?' with 'Broke!'. He laughed and added 'Too much bloody work. A lot of responsibility and a lot of work to get it the way I wanted it...We'd just been working a lot, that's all. Busy getting things for the place. At the time, I was working six days a week and I didn't get home until 8, 9, 10 o'clock at night. I only had one day, Sunday, to do things'.

Not surprisingly, only women said 'I'm working for it', implying they would otherwise be at home or that their earnings were absorbed by mortgages. Some indicated that only the home could justify the load they carried in domestic and paid work, but it was always seen as justified. A young woman explained: 'I think it's just everybody's dream to own your own home eventually. I just don't believe in working all your life and then looking back and having nothing for it. Because, as far as I'm concerned, for every day that you work, you've got to sort of have something in return. Just to come home to your own home, knowing that it's yours...was determined to work till I got one'. A moment later she added, 'Yeah. Both of us together anyway'.

Men rarely talked of working for the home in this way, and when they did it was coupled with the idea of gaining a haven *from* work: 'Well it means home to me, something to work for, come home to enjoy'. The contrast is easily explicable. Women's paid work very frequently was required by mortgage repayments, which in turn were seen as the only reason for her being in the workforce.[30] 'This is something I did with my job or with my sacrifice', declared a migrant woman. 'This makes me feel more happy.' Interestingly, only for women did having to work cast a shadow of doubt on 'security': 'Security, you know, we've worked pretty hard to get it, and we've got to work hard to keep it. It's a big thing'. That the home justified the price was clearly expressed in the happiness of a woman for whom the double load continued unremittingly:

W: We lived in a flat for many years, trying to save up the deposit for a house. I worked nightshift and minded the boys in the day. My husband had two jobs. We were under such pressure, all living together in a tiny space ... [Moving here] changed our whole lives. We had a home for the boys, a backyard for them to play in and the parks and everything else. It was our first home, the first thing we'd owned and we worked so hard to get it ... It's home and security.

Hardly surprisingly, domestic work was frequently mentioned by women, never by men. Only one woman (the teacher whose mother had stressed the insecurity of renting) denied caring about her house. But in doing so she accentuated the importance of its being 'mine' in terms much more typical of men's answers. Emphasizing her freedom from housework, she responded to 'How do you feel when you walk in the door?' with 'Depends which day of the week it is! If it's Friday night I feel terrific because the house cleaner's been in'. Defiantly, she added: 'I'm not a house-conscious person. It's just somewhere to live. I'd be happy in a tent, I couldn't care less'. But a little later the tone changed, 'I guess it's nice. I enjoy having something of my own'. No man referred to the labour involved in the maintenance of the home. The contrast was nicely illustrated by exchanges when a husband was present during an interview with his wife. What did this house mean to her? 'I can't look!' she laughed, 'There are six messing it up and only one cleaning it up! There's just not the time'. He said, almost as though she had not spoken, 'Well, I always look forward to coming home'.

Her home and his haven

'Home', was the other response apparently not affected by gender but meaning very different things to men and women. They used the word almost equally—33 to 35—in these answers. But only two women who said 'home' meant haven from outside work—and they referred also to the further work 'inside'. One woman said simply 'It's my home'. How did she feel when she walked in the door? 'Tired.' Otherwise, when women said 'home' and 'work' in the same statement it was because the home required their labour, and justified it. Men just did not say that. On the other hand, some men did clearly say that the home was an escape from work. Asked what their houses meant to them, a few men produced answers straight out of the feminist literature on the dichotomy of private and public worlds! One man said simply: 'It means my own home, own retreat—a place that I own myself. A retreat, a place where I'm a king'.

Men used words such as 'rest', 'retreat', 'warmth', 'comfort' and talked of having 'somewhere to come home to'. 'It's me home. I'm quite proud of it. It means a lot ... Good to be home, you know, I've got somewhere to rest'. Another man, who said his house meant 'home'; explained that this meant 'peace, isolation from the outside world'. One answered, 'Extra bills! A lot of work!' but then, more seriously, 'I suppose it's privacy to relax in. Not the old adage that a man's home is his castle, I wouldn't quite go that far. Certainly a place to relax'. Men 'come' and 'go' to the home. 'It means that I have a house. I have somewhere to go, to come home really. I like it, it keeps me warm, I suppose'. Women used these terms less, as though, even when they were 'out' in paid work, they were more often in or of the home. An older man answered instantly, 'This house means to me comfort, peace and serenity in every way'. He went on, 'I feel, when I walk in the door, that I have separated myself from the rest of the world as I knew it beforehand, and I have my own peace of mind and my own pleasantness and comfort. Meditation, if you like, or whatever. It is very peaceful and it's very mind-settling'. His wife agreed only in part; privacy for her had a different meaning: 'Well, I think that it's nice and peaceful. I like that part: to just come in my door at certain times, because you feel like getting away from all the traffic when you're our age'. But the agreement was only superficial; his haven was her cage: 'Personally, to me, it's far too quiet and I've never been happy here. But that's just for me, my point of view, who's home all the time'.

Often linking with the 'everything' response, some men expressed a passionate need for a refuge from work. One man's house meant to him, 'My everything, that's all I've got!'. When he walked in he felt, 'Very relaxing'. Another said, 'It's everything we've got, like all our money's in it'. When he walked in the door he felt, 'It's good to be home from the rat race'. Several said 'I've come back home', or 'Happy to be home', and three of these had answered simply 'everything' to 'What does this house mean to you?'. But as one man recognized, this was one-sided. 'All depends what sort of a day

I've had at work—and I've had some rippers! I'm usually happy to be home. I think you've got to be, or you wouldn't live here ... I'm happy. But poor old [wife] is not getting it, are you love?'. His wife was at home.

Only two women's answers suggested personal refuge; both were from 'dual-life women' carrying both full-time employment and the domestic load.[31] Both were about peace from the hassle of everyday life, to 'put your feet up'. But 14 men talked about a private world away from their public work life. The contrast is not absolute. Only a minority of men talked of havens. They did not seem a particular group of men; the wives of many were employed; they came from all life stages and education groups. The haven image hangs around for men, available perhaps for those whose work pressures justify it, or whose wives 'at home' are devoted to maintaining it. But with those two exceptions, havens never happened in women's notions of home unless they were havens for the rest of the family. Compare these comments:

W: Well, I love it. To me, it's a real home, where my husband and my children can retreat from the world, if we have to, or we can invite our friends.

M: I like to be home. I like to come home. I like a sort of smallish, darkish place—like a cockroach, I suppose! ... But I think home's very important. It's a place that I can come back to, and hopefully, if I'm left alone, just sit and get over everything else.

In some accounts, always by women, these ideas were tied to very traditional family values, and then the requirement of private home was simply unquestioned fact. Women are more likely to talk of the home in terms of 'doing things together', as though part of the pleasure is the convergence of couples' hitherto disparate interests and leisure activities.[32] Privacy here is for togetherness, and it is privacy provided by the woman, *from* the hard world of work. Her work, in turn, is *for* the home and *for* the family. Literally, for at least some women, the home in this sense means a family life; without it, there is no place of peace to hold the family together.

Grace is a Greek-born mother of school-age children, who has always stayed home with them. 'I think it's important for everybody to be able to buy their home'. I ask why, and her explanation emphasizes again the complexity of these ideas:

W: It means so much, I think. It means a family life. You get so much. I mean, whatever we do, it's for our children as well ... I mean, we're a family. So everything we do, our home is important. Everything about our home means a lot. You show the children so much in your home.

I: And you'd feel you couldn't do that if you were renting?

W: Oh yes, it's not the same. Although you'd be clean in a rented home and try, it's not the same ... You take pleasure in knowing your garden's nice, and in the summer you can sit out and enjoy your home. And you don't really have to go away from home because you have that many things here now. You can enjoy your barbecue and have your friends in and people don't have to go out.

The recurring themes are of proper paths to worlds whose security is essential both for family and for autonomy. The dichotomy of private and public life has new shapes here, different for women and men. Privacy means autonomy and togetherness and it involves work for women, not only as administrators of homes and managers of family status, but also in jobs fitted into the corners of proper paths through family stages. In all the fascination with the social effects of home ownership, there has been no interest in the possibility that it might affect women differently from men. From their accounts, women seem to carry the contradictions of the dream. Practically, the possibility of ownership drives (or beckons) women out of the home into mortgage-paying employment, and justifies this. It commits them too to the labour of maintaining status. For dual-life women the different meanings of privacy are exposed: no haven here, but autonomy, control, bases for building families. Yet ownership still seems to commit many women to the proper paths enshrined in traditional ideas of family life.

Those themes stretch across a variety of finer meanings, as does the pervasive sense of an urgent need to own,[33] obscuring differences in goals and priorities, just as the assumption that everyone owns their home obscures inequalities of life chances. And couples create their joint, but gender-patterned, versions of the dream. The man who compared himself to a cockroach (as though ashamed of his need for refuge?) is asked how his wife, a teacher, would reply:

M: I suppose it's security, and it could well be the same for me ... But I think she needs a home too ... the house is more important to her than to me. I sort of slipped into it as a natural progression, but to own your home is something—she wants to *own* things, and *have* that sort of thing. So the home, the physical home, is a fair bit to her and the home—not a house, a home, sort of thing—is a lot to her too. She, I think, likes family life.

Ideology at home?

Ask about home, and women and men talk, albeit in different ways, about family life. While the reasons for owning varied, the necessity of a home for a family was taken for granted. Several people said they did not care about investment; nobody said the home was not essential to family life. 'For them to grow up in' was sufficient reason for owning, as was simply 'it's good for the kids'.

Ask about 'a good family life', and women and men talk not about new homes but about old ideals. In that context only five even mentioned the home, and they made it just part of the furniture of family. 'As long as you're happy and content within your home', one man said. For another, a good family life was 'The one I've got. Job, house, home, financial security', as though the package deal was obvious. Only one man, on being explicitly asked, specified ownership:[34] 'I think you've got to have your own house. It's something that's yours and something for your kids and that. You know you don't have to worry about where you're going to live next year'.

Definitions of good family life also rarely included, but always assumed, that a good family has children.[35] To specify that for a family life you need to have children would be like the proverbial recipe that begins 'first catch your chicken'. To specify the prior purchase of a home would be like inserting 'first buy a casserole'. The steps—marriage, then the home, then the children—are assumed: 'Sort of filling the goal that we had when we first got married—waiting five years, saving for a home and achieving that goal, and starting a family'.

Notes

1. She was right, but only about some ethnic groups; see T. Burke, L. Hancock & P. Newton, *A Roof Over Their Heads: Housing Issues and Families in Australia*, Institute of Family Studies, Melbourne, 1984.

2. In terms very like those of Perin's urban managers they asserted the importance of being a debtor—but their conviction that bankers and people differ casts some doubt on her assumption that her urban manager respondents represent the popular 'lending library' of background ideas. C. Perin, *Everything in Its Place: Social Order and Land Use in America*, Princeton University Press, Princeton, NJ, 1977.

3. L. Richards, *Having Families*, rev. edn, Penguin, Ringwood, 1985.

4. J. R. Seeley *et al.*, *Crestwood Heights*, University of Toronto Press, Toronto, 1956; G. Pratt, 'The house as an expression of social worlds', in J. Duncan (ed.), *Housing and Identity*, Croom Helm, London, 1981; B. Ineichen, 'Home ownership and manual workers' lifestyles', *Sociological Review*, vol. 20, pp. 391–412.

5. In one of the earliest studies Rosow tidied answers into precoded categories; he found his sample of upper-income Americans averaged 4.5 reasons for ownership each. Almost half of their reasons were 'emotional (psychic, family and ego)' followed by 'status-prestige'; 'financial considerations' were 'less significant than commonly supposed'. I. Rosow, 'Home ownership motives', *American Sociological Review*, vol. 13, 1948.

6. See especially C. Perin's *Everything in Its Place*. For a detailed summary of literature on home ownership meanings see J. Agnew, 'Home ownership and identity in capitalist societies', in J. Duncan (ed.), *Housing and Identity*, Croom Helm, London, 1981.

7. A. Holmes, *Housing and Young Families in East London*, Routledge & Kegan Paul, London, 1985, pp. 69, 70, 145.

8. R. M. Rakoff, 'Ideology in everyday life: The meaning of the house', *Politics and Society*, vol. 7, 1977, p. 86.

9. Holmes' study, *Housing and Young Families*, also remarked a difference by order of responses.

10. It also alerts the listener to the difference between his and her reasons, and the apparent invisibility of those differences to the speakers; they appear to reinforce each others' statements while saying very different things.

11. The data here recall strong themes in Richards, *Having Families* about the necessity and inevitability of 'getting set up' and 'established' and 'settling down'.

12. See L. Richards, 'The impossible dream', in D. Davis (ed.), *Living Together*, Centre for Continuing Education, Canberra, 1980.

13. Ineichen *Sociological Review*, pp. 391—412, found 40 per cent of his sample were deferring a first child for housing reasons. Over a third of Holmes' mothers said this; see Holmes, *Housing and Young Families*.

14. It is not my aim here to examine whether they are 'right'—that task has been tackled by Burke, Hancock & Newton in *A Roof Over Their Heads*, and by J. Kemeny, *The Great Australian Nightmare*, Georgian House, Melbourne, 1983, as well as very frequently in financial papers and the popular press.

15. J. R. Wikse, quoted in Duncan, *Housing and Identity*, p. 63.

16. In another context I have argued that sociologists should listen when people talk of 'identity'. See J. Harper & L. Richards, *Mothers and Working Mothers*, rev. edn, Penguin, Ringwood, 1986, ch. 10. David Hickman located 'personal investment' as a category of reasons for home purchase in his current study of choice of location in another area of Melbourne.

17. The house designs confirm this image; the trend to 'family rooms' overlooked by the kitchen was dominant in these years, and all designs in the 'display strips' emphasized space in lounge rooms but provided tiny rooms for children.

18. P. L. Berger & H. Kellner, 'Marriage and the construction of reality', in H. P. Drietzel (ed.), *Recent Sociology No. 2.: Patterns of Communicative Behaviour*, Macmillan, New York, 1970, pp. 49—72.

19. The schedule was at fault here; there should of course have been a prompt for those, asking whether they would *not* purchase should financial conditions clearly make renting a better bet! I suspect that 'financial security' here works rather as 'for the children's education' does—as a reason for women's employment; it is an easy and acceptable explanation, but never a complete one.

20. Berger & Kellner, 'Marriage and the construction of reality'.

21. This is one of many areas where a related study of lives beyond the estate and lives within the marriages would have expanded analysis. Without these, we cannot judge the possible other sources of 'private' lives for these people or the relation between these and family, but there is no assumption here that the home is their only such source, and very little that they say indicates this.

22. Of the total 305 reasons, only fifty-three were in these two categories—thirty-five of them from women, eighteen from men. (Interestingly, those giving such reasons, women and men, were significantly more likely to say they had never considered not owning their home.)

23. Women indeed more commonly (thirty-six) than men (twenty-seven) produced reasons coded as 'achievement/attainment', 'status/prestige' or 'owning/possession'. The low proportion of

status reasons for owning does not of course mean the house is not seen as a status symbol; indeed, when a later list of items included 'For most people, the home is a status symbol', 62 per cent (women and men) agreed.

24. These accounted for over 60 per cent of all reasons (105 from men, eighty-four from women). 'Financial investment' was the reason given first by 51 per cent of women, 64 per cent of men.

25. B. Lloyd, 'Women, home and status', in J. Duncan (ed.), *Housing and Identity*, Croom Helm, London, 1981. The different arenas for 'privacy' and 'freedom' of women and men are explored in a critique of Rosaldo's work by A. Yeatman, 'Gender and the differentiation of social life into public and domestic domains', *Social Analysis*, no. 15, 1984. See also S. Saegert, 'Masculine cities and feminine suburbs: Polarized ideas, contradictory realities', *Signs*, vol. 5, Spring 1980, pp. s.96—s.111; D. Hayden, *Redesigning the American Dream: the Future of Housing, Work and Family Life*, W. W. Norton & Co., New York, 1984.

26. The studies also show the extreme difficulty of designing research that adequately pictures household labour and the distribution of burdens and negotiation of tasks and responsibilities in the intimate setting of marital power relations. To do so well requires very detailed and invasive research—another study in itself. An early decision was made in the present study not to attempt to include necessarily inadequate sketches of domestic situations alongside the data on home and local relationships.

27. They are very different questions, one about reasons for doing what is socially very strongly prescribed, the other seeking personal responses to the achieved house. We invited those personal responses deliberately by the prompt: 'How do you feel when you walk in the door?'.

28. All the quotations below in which men mention children are from responses to 'Why do you want to own?'. On women and home ownership, see S. Watson, *Accommodating Inequality: Gender and Housing*, Allen & Unwin, Sydney, 1988.

29. A. Ravetz, 'The home of woman: A view from the interior', *Built Environment*, vol. 10, pp. 8—17, esp. p. 8. See also the special issue on 'Women and the American city', *Signs*, vol. 5, 1980; and S. Ardener (ed.), *Women and Space*, Croom Helm, London, 1981.

30. This 'visible' reason for work is highly likely to cover many others—if the mortgage had not required it she would probably have done paid work for other reasons; see Harper & Richards, *Mothers and Working Mothers*.

31. The phrase is Laura Balbo's; see her 'Crazy quilts: Rethinking the welfare state debate from a woman's point of view', in A. S. Sassoon (ed.), *Women and the State: The Shifting Boundaries of*

Public and Private, Hutchinson, London, 1987, p. 51.

[32.] This was a strong theme drawn by M. Young & P. Willmott in *The Symmetrical Family*, Penguin, Harmondsworth, 1973.

[33.] R. Forrest has questioned the assumption that purchase of the home is a qualitatively different experience from any other commodity, not merely a bigger one, in 'The meaning of home ownership', *Environment and Planning D: Society and Space*, vol. 1, 1983, pp. 205−16. The point is important, as is his suggestion that there will be major differences in people's perceptions of this purchase. The present data certainly suggest such differences, even in a relatively homogeneous setting, but here the home purchase is imbued with a special significance.

[34.] This is almost certainly because an unscheduled prompt was used−in retrospect it seems obvious that to probe the taken-for-grantedness of ownership was necessary.

[35.] Richards, *Having Families*.

7

A Good Family Life: Hers and His

If the home is a necessary condition for family life, and two incomes are necessary for the home, the home will normally be empty of the family for whom it is necessary. So you would hardly be surprised to find, in the 'family community', that 'nobody's home'. The dream of the private haven, if it is as described in the critical literature, is indeed an impossible dream, in which family homes commonly contained no family for most of the daylight hours until the mortgages were under control. A modern tragedy?

If so, it is a tragedy whose results, including evident contentment, are varied. Many regretted the empty homes. But most saw them not as a tragic contradiction but as an inevitable result of the proper pursuit of goals. The story so far is not one of simple contradictions. Most people got what they wanted and what they expected. The images of the estate were mixed and satisfaction uneven, but what was sought and seen was an environment that provided a setting for ideas of family life stressing the proper paths (including paid work for women) to a particular private world.

In the reasons for ownership the private home appears a more complicated container than the literature suggests and no tranquil haven of repose for women. Most images of home life are not violated by the woman's employment. Indeed, for the young childless there is no contradiction. The home comes first, chronologically and in priorities. To have the house, among other reasons, most of the women were in the workforce prior to having children, and children were delayed while the dual incomes were essential—a workforce participation pattern now established in Australia.[1] 'The sorts of things that matter most to people out here are getting their ultimate goal, their own home. You can carry on from there, finishing it, getting it ready for the time you have a family.'

But then, if children are a necessary condition for family, contradictions loom, and ways out have to be negotiated. A woman, angry at the continued burden of house payments, told the interviewer that they were seriously considering not having children. But 'it's selfish, you're only being materialistic if you don't have kids'.[2] If family requires children and home ownership requires two incomes, the crucial link is what *children* require. To escape the contradictions they had to have negotiated exemption from the requirement that mothers be home.

Certainly for some women this was impossible, and the price was massive stress. When women were at home it was usually because there were pre-school children. Parents of pre-schoolers were most likely to report worries about finances. Mothers of school-age children were much more likely to be in the workforce, and some had serious worries about children. A woman selling up because the mortgages had proved too much said they would buy again as soon as they could afford it. For now her main concern was child-care: 'Don't let Nana know this— before she had her first heart attack she used to take them over the holidays ... I used to pay for them, but then it got up to $20 each, I worked for them to be looked after'. Mothers' duties and employment now directly conflicted: 'They just have to stay home and boy it's awful; I'm just a nervous wreck while it is happening, I hate them being at home. I don't like them having no one to look after them, it really worries me the whole time. But ... we couldn't live if I gave up the job, you know. And I've always been one that's never permitted the kids to go home from school on their own or anything'. The house was the clear centre of the contradiction: 'It's really bad for the children I think, really bad, but I just can't do anything about it now; this house is too heavy, this load is too much'.

Her dilemma was set in a firm package of ideas about the needs of children and her own duties. Her employment was necessary for the struggle to keep the house, but it had to be fitted into her management of the home, which in turn was fitted into a division of labour and authority. There is no room here for negotiation: 'I couldn't take another job—I mean I've said many times I'd do it, but you know life would be unbearable. I mean I'd be so cranky, they'd never see me at all; I'd never get the housework done, no washing or—it would be really awful. But he wouldn't permit it anyway'. This sounds like traditional ideology as portrayed in the critical literature. But is it dominant? Hers is the only such statement of unresolvable dilemma in all the data collected.

Togetherness

When people were asked to define 'a good family life' it sounded very modern. Answers were easily produced (like reasons for owning homes) and (unlike those) were extraordinarily uniform. All were in terms of relationships; there is nothing here on the traditional places of women and men. Rather, they uniformly stressed 'togetherness'.[3] What appeared was a different sort of private world, a dream of a self-contained family capsule fuelled by love and communication; a very modern machine. Two of the coding categories collected 78 per cent of first answers and 88 per cent of second. These were 'doing things as a family' and 'companionship/communication in marriage'. 'Sharing tasks in the marriage' was the only other frequent coding.[4]

With such unanimity it is hardly surprising that these answers show no patterned variations in the coded data. 'Togetherness' and its variants appeared as the image of good family across life stages, ethnic groups, class and educational levels, and in responses from both women and men. The data are so uniform that they do not allow tests for factors that surveys show are associated with traditional ideas, in particular religious affiliation and education.[5] 'Togetherness' and related ideas[6] recurred in almost all transcripts. (Two people said the family that plays together stays together!) 'Communication' was the only other common keyword. A handful of mentions of 'happiness', a few of 'financial security' and some of 'loving and caring' made up the collection of themes.

These answers, then, were remarkably consistent, apparently omitting (or obscuring?) traditional gender places. They *could* show that a 'sharing' idea of family is becoming dominant even in this most suburban of settings. Or they could indicate the masking power of common goals; 'togetherness' could work, like 'all in the same boat', to cover different meanings.[7] That suspicion could be tested in two ways. One is by comparison with accurate, detailed knowledge about what people actually *do* (and think and feel) in their houses, and that requires a different study.[8] The other is by listening to words: what do people *mean* by 'togetherness'?

Whatever else it means, 'good family' in these answers does not involve the maintenance by women of private havens for men. Only four answers made women's place in the home part of 'good families'. By contrast, 11 emphasized that the husband should be at home 'enough'. No one aware of the critical literature on the family would dare assume that 'enough' meant 'as much as the wife'. But if this is traditional ideology it includes at least gestures to the sharing of family time. Certainly 'good family' does not mean equality. Only six answers even alluded to equality: four of these combined 'respect for each other' and 'sharing work'; the other two said togetherness should combine with independence. But togetherness was also compatible with extreme role segregation. One woman summarized: 'Wife not working; at home, a homemaker. He's a good provider. A close-knit family; depends on togetherness as a family. Time with your husband'. And togetherness here is no unreachable star. Two-thirds said they had now achieved their idea of good family, and the contentment and sense of achievement glows in many transcripts.

The only obstacle was time; if 'together' is the keyword of family life, its enemy is lack of time together. When those who had not achieved their idea of good family were asked what they would need to do so, time dominated the picture. It was much more important than financial security or the wife not having to work.[9] Sometimes this is the mother's time with the children: 'The quality of the attention you give the children. I think the most important thing is perhaps doing things together, no matter what they be, whether they're just simple things like playing little games and talking to each other at home'. But time worries are not usually about mothering time. Asked if they had 'enough time' with spouse and children, only 4 per cent of the sample thought the wife had completely inadequate time with the children, but only 2 per cent that the father's time with them was inadequate. In a later section of the interview only 11 per cent said they worried about 'never having time to relax with my family'. Adult time was a matter of concern to 70 per cent, and half of these said it was completely inadequate. Only 10 per cent thought it enough. There is a clear message here that children get what time is available, draining the available time away from partners, and that good family life contains a dream not only of children but of dyadic intimacy much harder to attain.[10] A woman summed up her needs for a good family life: 'Not having to work so hard, and spend more time together as a family unit, do things together'. Another enshrined an Australian catchphrase in the dream of family: 'The ideal is No Worries. I would love to be a hermit and relieve the pressure and have a real family unit'. She highlighted a nice irony: hermits do not have families.

On these answers, good family is about a particular sort of private world—private from others and self-sufficient. The 'old' ideas here sound weak. But to see their continuing strength, ask about motherhood.

Good mothers

During a phone call, Joanne, a teacher currently at home, commiserated with the project co-ordinator, whose after-school care arrangements were going wrong. She commented that since starting school her own son 'has really needed a mum. I'm not a real mother type but I'm rather glad I wasn't working'. Jan threw in, laughing, the question we were then piloting for the current interview. 'I said facetiously, "What's your definition of a good mother?", much as to say aren't we good mums, worrying about our children? She said quite seriously, "One with a happy kid. It doesn't matter what she does"'.

There are three reasons for quoting the incident. First, the fact that both Jan and I had young children not only sensitized us to the problems of mothers but meant that nobody could assume we were seeking the 'old' ideas condemning employed mothers. So if we skewed the data in any direction it should have been towards 'new' ideas of independence for women. Secondly, the discussion indicates the complexity of ideas of 'good' mothers. Most, like Joanne, *had* a definition of a good mother, and most combined aspects of an old 'real mother type' and a newer reality featuring employment.[11]

But thirdly, Joanne's comment was one of only a tiny handful of definitions that incorporated 'new' ideas about independence for women and interest in children, rather than only listing passive qualities of patience, listening, and being there.[12] Almost everyone (93 per cent) said they were (or, in the case of the husband's answers, that their wife was) a good mother, and everyone could describe one.[13] Only one woman protested at the question—but because it was too hard, not because there was no *one* 'good mother' to be described. The question produced a portrait of dominant 'old' ideas quite startling in its uniformity.[14]

As with the reasons for owning your own home, these answers show very different patterns of first and later responses (up to three were coded; see figure 3). On first response, 'loves them' is far more likely than any other answer, and 'there when needed' is followed by 'patient'; these three account for more than three-quarters of the first answers. The 'new' ideas together rate only a tenth, most concerning active mothering—playing and reading with children. Nobody suggested that a good mother has her own life. On second and third codings, love and patience feature less; discipline and active mothering more. Several specify that a good mother does not work, fewer that she 'teaches her children', and three that she 'has her own life'. So the 'new' ideas progressed from 11 per cent of first to 24 per cent of those giving third answers. But only half of the sample gave third answers. Most could summarize a good mother very quickly. One man said she was 'Caring, understanding, always there'. A woman said that, 'A good mother is very patient and understanding with her child; to be loving is important.'

Not only are these ideas strikingly 'old', they are also amazingly uniform. The uniformity increases when text is examined, because the answers we had treated as 'new' turn out to be very compatible with the 'old'. Playing, reading and teaching were almost always associated with devotion of time: 'Has to be there for the children, teach them right from wrong'. Time turns out to be the essence of mothering.

Love is uncomplicated: not one of these statements tries to explain or justify that most common specification that a mother loves her children. Many put in 'of course'. (We can assume that more did not include it for this reason.) Love is also uncommitted to either 'old' or 'new' ideas, but is comfortable in the company of both. In such blanket statements it is impossible to judge if these are two different ways of loving. 'There's got to be plenty of love', said one mother, but she mentioned first 'always being there for her children'. Discipline, too, comes with both old and new ideas. The word is used more often by men, referring to the grubby stuff of mothering 'understanding, discipline, hygiene'. Women are more likely to tuck it in among the softer things 'Loving, caring, spends time, disciplines them'. Women said 'maintains discipline' a few times, men never. Perhaps for women it means control and order, for men punishment?

But having time and giving it is the dominant theme. As previous studies have shown, so too in this data—ideas about giving time are strongly linked with peaceful and passive mothers in private homes. These comments are not restricted to the groups where studies have shown strongest allegiance to 'old' ideas: 'Patience; loving, attentive, listening and spending time', offered a professionally-employed young woman; 'Loving, warm, able, spends time with them', said a white-collar male whose wife was at home. There were no comments from women as to what the good mother's time should be spent on. But the few comments from men were all about housework and tended to include services to themselves in the mother specifications: 'Someone who looks after the children and does all the housework', said a man whose wife was employed full-time. Three specified that she should be a good cook; three more added phrases such as 'Looks after kids, always there, listens to my problems'. Here is a first indicator of the effects of education on family ideas; those six were all men who had not completed secondary education. Only one matriculant, a man, includes housework, and his ideal is a much more active woman: 'Attentive and effective, organized runner of the home, makes an effort to identify opportunities for children, trains them properly'. The only woman to mention housework (also a matriculant) *separates* it from the good mother: 'Patient with all their little ways, doesn't worry too much about the mess, cleans up afterwards, plays with them, loves them'.

Though the uses of time varied, the amount was generally agreed; the good mother gives *all* or *enough* of her time. There is room here to negotiate; how much is 'enough'? But if giving enough is a challenge to women in the workforce, being there 'all the time' is impossible. Yet many definitions included it, some, interestingly, combining it with the idea of teaching, not merely passively being there:[15] 'Must be there all the time and must take time to teach the children'. A part-time employed mother said 'Loving and I suppose patient. It's harder than being a good father because we're there all the time'.

All of us? But 'nobody's home'! The very common phrases— 'there when she's needed' and 'all the time'—carry messages about priorities and options. The few comments specifically banning mothers' employment turn out to be the top of an iceberg of assumptions that, ideally, they should only mother. So an answer that seems not to preclude workforce partici- pation can be the justification for staying at home, as for the mother of school-age children who said being a good mother was about 'Caring for the needs of your family—of your children. Being there for their problems, whatever they are'. Later she added that 'some mothers are very bad'. She couldn't take a job because 'I'd have to make the proper provisions'. A first hint of the ideology-production in women's groups: 'I can name mothers on the estate that don't do that. Not that I *would*; none of my business'.

'Devoted' and 'committed' have three mentions each, and 'always' accompanies giving time and being there. A young father said a good mother was 'always there, doesn't go out to work ... Some mothers don't have time for the kids and just put them in a creche'. Several called these mothers 'selfish', and the good mother, by contrast, 'patient with children and devoted to them every minute of the day—very unselfish'. She is also 'ungrudging', 'not grumpy', 'doesn't lose her temper' has a 'pleasant personality', 'doesn't abuse them' doesn't 'scream' and 'never gets upset, always quiet'. All these were from low-education respondents, but matriculants contributed 'won't lose temper' and 'calm in a crisis, gentle, fair, doesn't yell or storm'. There are fewer prohibitions on good fathers (all from the low-education group), three about drinking and two about violence; one woman summarized: 'doesn't drink, doesn't smack'.

Over three-quarters of all respondents said it was hard to be a good mother, several adding that it is harder nowadays. The ghost of the good mother specifically haunted the employed women. A mother of school-age children, employed full-time, (of low education), said good mothers must be 'extremely understanding'. But she turned then to practical problems: they must also 'have their children's lunches cut, which I don't often have time to do. Do homework with them. Spend time with them. Do all those little extras which working mothers seem too busy for.'[16] Very few people showed, as Joanne did, even a wry awareness that some mothers fail to match the model. And fewer questioned it. None of the fathers indicated that they did not expect their wives to fit their model perfectly.

Only a handful of women distanced themselves from their 'good mother' ideal. So the statements in any way *questioning* the passive, omnipresent 'good mother' hardly represent a feminist's 'utopia'.[17] They come from six women, of whom four are matriculants. Both low-education challengers were full-time-employed. 'Plenty of tlc, chastise as it's necessary, don't give in to all their needs', said a mother of school-age children, adding, 'Being home with the children does not always prove a good mum'. The other had pre-schoolers, and sounded more worried than challenging: 'Must look after them and care for them as best you can. It's difficult when both are working, so you must make the most of "out of work" times'. The four matriculants, all at home, seemed more able to distance themselves (but four is a puny negotiating taskforce!): 'Probably all the things I haven't got!' laughed one, 'Patience, tolerance, loving, interested in children, I suppose that covers it'. A childless teacher did challenge the question: 'That implies there are bad mothers, there aren't—just mothers who cope at different levels'. But her definition of a good mother was: 'Coping in the house in the traditional role, feels fulfilled, gets total satisfaction out of that role'.

Perhaps the 'new' definitions are those that do not include 'being there'. If so, there are six, a motley lot, split between education groups. The most radical is 'Active and independent, has her own life-style'. But this man added 'caring, looks after the kids'. And that is it! In this setting there is effectively no challenge to prescriptions for the mother role very clearly challenged by a substantial number of people in all previous studies.

His time and hers

If ideas of mothering remain dominated by the traditional model, is *fathering* changing to relieve the new pressures on families? 'Togetherness' suggests a shift to equality. And statistically the data about good fathers make such fathers look extraordinarily like good mothers. The balance of 'old' and 'new' ideas (in the table below) is much the same: first, second and third answers are distributed between categories very similarly for mothers and fathers. The pattern across answers also looks the same. For fathers, as for mothers, love was a leading first answer, but less common later, while 'taking time' was a leader in all three answers for fathers; it beat 'love' as a first response. Moreover, people *said* the roles were alike. Sixteen replied 'same as a good mother' (intriguingly, most had low education). Several others used the same terms for at least part of both descriptions. The same keywords also appear in mother and father descriptions—time, understanding and patience—with understanding a little more common in fathers' descriptions, patience a little more in mothers'. Time is mentioned in more definitions of good fathers than of good mothers (again, mostly by those with less education).[18]

Good Mothers and Good Fathers

First, second and third answers to the question, 'What's your idea of a good mother/father?'
(per cent of those giving an answer)

	First		Second		Third	
	Mum	Dad	Mum	Dad	Mum	Dad
Loves them	35	27	16	12	15	9
Disciplines them	4	5	13	12	16	4
Patient	17	10	14	7	3	9
There/makes time	25	29	26	23	24	16
Not working/not always out	3	–	6	3	7	2
Teaches skills	1	1	5	4	1	4
Plays, reads	10	13	13	21	20	31
Own life/leaves work	–	5	1	3	3	14
Other	5	11	6	15	11	11
	100	100	100	100	100	100

The similarities are important. But the differences are fundamental. The table produces the unisex picture by juxtaposing very different answers for women and men in three categories: those about time ('being there' for mothers and 'making time' for fathers); those about being absent ('not working' for mothers, 'not always out' for fathers); and those about lives away from home ('has her own life' for mothers, 'leaves work behind' for fathers). Each of these pairings of ideas proclaims the difference between her place and his.

Study the words and those differences are clear. Time is not only the linking theme but also the centre of differences. Mothers take time, spend or give it, fathers make it or find it. By implication, mothers *have* the time to give; father time has to be specially created. Fathers are not required to 'think of their children all the time', let alone 'be there to care and help all the time' or be 'patient with the children and devoted to them every minute of the day'. These are all descriptions of a good mother (and all from people with little education). The six matriculants who talked of time did picture mother time less enclosed by duties. All said she 'spends time', the phrase most commonly used across the sample in relation to men's time (though he 'spends as much as possible').

'All the time' is used about fathers only in pleas that they don't spend it *all* outside the family, and only by the less-educated. He 'loves his children and doesn't neglect them by going out all the time'. Being 'there when needed' is only once used in reference to fathers (by a young childless woman working full-time). A father is required by low-education respondents to 'spend as much time as he can with [the] kids'; there is open season on a mother's time. He should find 'time to give help'; her time is the default. Several people said he should help when she was unable to manage or at least that he should be able to if he had to! 'A good father takes his children out and knows how to look after them if the mother is sick', said a mother at home with grown children. This was not only an older-generation response; a young, educated woman offered, 'He can relate to them, and helps out while the mother is doing something else—he takes time'. He has to be prepared to 'give up his own time'. There is no mention in these statements that she has any of her own, or that there are other calls on it.

Moreover, where good mother definitions rarely specify *what* she spends time on, fathers' time is more purposive: 'He sets standards and is around enough to show care and affection'. Fathering, several said, requires quality time: 'Time to give help, bath, feed, shower them, do things in the mother role'. 'Help' of course also specifies the default—she has responsibility for the children; he has to be 'prepared to help his wife', 'tries to help' or 'takes time to give help'. (These are all low-education responses.) And time also seems more under the control of fathers; 'if possible' is a frequent phrase. Mother definitions never say *when* she spends time, whereas a father 'makes time for them [the children] after work'.

The assumption, even by mothers who are not, is that mothers are always there. It is not an assumption restricted to the less educated or to those with old ideas. The part-time professional woman who said that it was harder to be a good mother because 'we're there all the time', said a good father was the same: 'loving, patient, time for the children'. Good fathers, she said, were mainly her age group: 'They help with the family'.

Indeed it was common for very strong differences in meanings to be hidden by the assumption that mothers' and fathers' roles are the same. One young woman described a father as 'having much the same qualities as a mother has'. But she continued, 'I know they can't, at work, but I think when they come home, making time to listen and know their kids, know their personalities, especially being ready to listen'. Her definition of a good mother repeated several of those phrases, but with very different import:

W: The ones I'd call good mothers to me always have time for their children. They've put them first. Like me, they've sat back and thought, 'You don't have them for very long as dependent on you'. And they listen, and take the time ... And in after-school activities they are involved where their kids are involved. I don't think it's hard to be a good mother.

Being a father is never a full-time job in these accounts, and there are very few father descriptions that imply children have top priority. Only one woman (a full-time employed mother of pre-school children) suggested a good father 'puts the child's needs first'. But her idea of a good mother was 'someone who devotes her time, gives lots of love, is there when needed, fulfils her child's needs'. Being a father is more contained. Mothers are described as having 'endless patience', and for them, but not for fathers, 'patience and understanding' are linked as though by hyphens. For several respondents 'understanding' is a one-word description of a good father, but never of a good mother.

On the other hand, fathers and only fathers are assumed to have *real* full-time jobs. 'A good provider' (or just 'provides') occur in nearly 60 per cent of responses from both low- and high-education groups. 'The father should be the breadwinner', is a migrant man's definition. Only one person (a young tertiary-educated woman currently at home with school-age children) questioned the assumption that a father is first a provider: 'He's the same sort of person as a good mother. Doesn't necessarily mean a good provider in the material sense'. Her husband was in a blue-collar occupation. To no other respondent did the provider role seem distinct from fathering, and to none of the rest did its priority need explanation. The commitment of fathers to providing is absolute and is taken to explain their inability to give time; it is affected by neither education nor age group. A young, educated mother, currently at home, sadly said she could not cite her husband as an example of a good father: 'He enjoys her when he's got time to spend with her. Three nights a week he's not at home, and all day Saturday he can't spend at home with her'. But he does help: 'He'll chip in and pull his weight, as far as chores go with her. He knows how to change her and bath her and feed her and dress her and those sort of things ... He finds it hard relating to her'. But she says elsewhere: 'I think we, as a generation, are a lot better off, because the fathers, or the majority of them anyway, are taking up more responsibility as a parenting role'.

From this material it is very hard to tell if this woman is right. Even if they are starting to say such things, these fathers seem to be taking up very little responsibility. Young people are as likely to use the keywords of 'old' answers, and while the few very different replies mainly come from the young and educated, they are few. A quarter said it was hard to be a good father; over three-quarters that it was hard to be a good mother.[19] As a father of young children put it, 'at this phase in the child's life' his part was 'complementing the mother's role'. They were both very aware of the implications of what he was saying but not challenging them.

M: I think the child is looking for a father at the end of the day because it's been a one-sided affair during most of the day, so he's looking for relief. (Wife laughs.) In walks Dad, and immediately he wants to play and show what he's learnt during the day—show off I think—Dad provides an opportunity. But there's a father's role, changing the nappies, just the same as the mother's role. (Wife exclaims!) ... It's just as hard as to be a good mother, I suppose, except the hours are shorter.

What's new?

These responses come two decades after Betty Friedan wrote: 'It is easy to see the concrete details that trap the suburban housewife, the continual demands on her time. But the chains that bind her in the trap are chains in her own mind and spirit'.[20] Here in the suburban centre of the 'typical' family it is reasonable to expect a strong commitment to traditional family roles. But not such *uniform* commitment. If 'new' ideas had a hold on the Australian family they should be heard from this young sample, with a range of education and occupation. Yet there is much less evidence here of 'new' ideas of parenting, much more of the power of traditional models of good mothers, and much less of changing ideas in young and educated groups than in comparable data from the mid-1970s or in recent survey research.[21]

If the young and the educated are espousing new family values they are not doing so at Green Views. Here, at least, the powerful ideas of family are the traditional ones; ideas of independence for women and egalitarianism for marriages are rare and almost always mixed with old values. And these goals are by no means limited to older or less-educated people. A tertiary-educated father of one pre-schooler, his wife at home, offers as a 'good mother' 'someone who is patient, loving and understanding, there when she's needed, doesn't go out to work'. His idea of a good father? 'Shares child-care duties, loves the children and teaches them things'. A good family life is 'sharing life together, being financially secure so you can enjoy time with the kids'. The three fit together, make a set: a picture of the little community. Combined with the need to work for the home, it still contains those contradictory requirements.

Yet the data give an overwhelming sense that the dream is, if not achieved, at least within reach. People seem able to work with the demands of the apparently eternal triangle of home ownership, family and necessity to work.

Who's home?

The material on family life is unlike the material on home ownership. The home had many meanings, but answers on family picture only one good family life. Stretched across differences of life stage and life chances are very common convictions about what mothers and fathers *should* do, what family life should be.

But to ask about family life is to invite agreed-on definitions.[22] To check the impression of uniformity and to find how people work within those apparent contradictions, I made a search in our records for all the ideas to do with women's paid work.[23] The retrieval was massive. The material was gathered in all possible settings and contexts over five years: informal meetings, taped sections of the sample interviews, other more unstructured interviews, participant observation in friendship groups and phone conversations. 'Working mothers' are a major topic of interest and concern in Green Views. But though the material was so very different from the answers to direct questions about family, it showed the same intransigent uniformity of replies.[24]

The strongest theme of this rag-bag of material is that women's employment is undertaken from necessity, not by choice. The necessity is largely about owning and furnishing the home. Much of this material contains and explains the tension between the sharing-sounding goal of 'togetherness' and the two worlds of women and men. Family 'together' means that women are there. A woman who defined a good mother as 'someone who devotes her time' and a good father as 'putting the child's needs first', reflected on Green Views:

W: I think we're all basically living the same sort of life because we're compelled to. I mean we're all getting up, going to work, coming home. All the women are going back to work, basically through financial—the lady in the Health Centre said 'They're all back; six months and they're back' . . . We have no other choice . . . You don't want it that way but that's the way it is. You know, if you want your own home and you want all the comforts that go with it, we're all compelled to live the same life-style. We go to work, we work hard, we have the weekend off, we go back to work Monday morning.

The tone is one of regret or resentment, rarely anger, but equally rarely approval, enjoyment or enthusiasm. Many statements are wryly resigned to the effects of mothers' employment, and *very* few condemn it outright. It may be that some people approve but feel unable to say so. But only one man approved without qualification (and then he says a lot about her place!): 'You have to find something to keep her occupied, and if she's home you reduce the topic of your conversation'. They were childless.

It would be easy to oversimplify this material. Nobody came out fighting for women's right to work. But almost all women were either employed or hoped to bring in at least some extra income in the future. Nobody pretended to live in a world in which mothers stayed at home. Three-quarters of the men said all or most of the women they knew 'go out to work'. Nor did most people say they should stay home; only 9 per cent were prepared to say a woman should never work after marriage. On the other hand only 21 per cent said she could work any time, or that it is up to her. The rest qualified their approval in terms of age of children, with the most common response being 'only after children are at school'.[25] Over half the sample agreed that 'Too many women with young children are working these days'. Neither employed women nor men whose wives were employed were less likely to agree. But education mattered; the matriculants and those calling themselves middle-class were significantly less likely to agree. Where the respondent was less-educated or working-class, wives were also less likely to be in the workforce than women of the same life stage, despite the likelihood that they needed the money more.

There is, in all this material, hardly a sentence that questions the assumption that women's work is bad for the family. The nearest to approval are ambivalent statements. A young mother justified her return to work saying: 'They've got wardrobes full of toys but that's not enough; they wanted something new all the time and you can never keep up, you know, they got bored so quickly ... plus they wanted other children to mix with'. Her children had been difficult since she took a job, and she felt guilty taking them to child-care. 'I say, "Well you don't have to go if you don't want to go; I'll stay home" ... All the way there in the morning I tell them that I love them and things like that, you know, I think it makes them feel more secure.'

The comments about effects are almost all about children, and almost all of them are negative. Only four are about marriages. Three women had given up working because of the tensions in their marriage. One man, separated from his wife, blamed the house:

M: Mainly because we were too concerned to get this house, being brand new and on dirt like, to get our garden established and all that sort of stuff . . . you lose your personal contact with each other, to go out and enjoy each other's company, and that sort of stuff, you know. She worked and I worked, and on weekends it was working in the house. And then you go to work again on Monday.

If there were children, nobody claimed any advantages from the mother's working except material purchases, though for a decade research and commentaries had stressed other benefits to mother and child. Nobody talked with enthusiasm about their job. This was partly because, like most married women, they had taken jobs for convenience of hours and child-care distances and time of travel. The price of mothers' working is a theme-tune of the women's groups and hangs as a threat over the well-being of the family and the lives of those women who do stay home.

'It's always the kids that suffer'

Again, time is the dominant theme in the argument that her work destroys their family community. *All* such statements assume that the wife continues to carry the domestic load, and that the suffering of children arises because she fails to do it adequately. But there is never evidence of this suffering and it sits oddly with the sense of achievement of 'good family'. Hints of class differences leak in; it is *other* people, the ones who are 'sort of not strong family' who have the problems. Several women commented acidly about neglected latch-key kids ('How many women forget their duty to children and go running off to work?'). But nobody cited a real case.

M: There seems to be a lot of pressure, and I relate that back to the mortgage or whatever. Both husband and wife working, kids coming home, you know, and they've got to let themselves into the house at 3.30 in the afternoon. Mum's not home until 5.30 or 6 o'clock, Mum's too tired to prepare tea, and there's a lot of problems . . . it's always the kids that suffer.

There are strong and undocumented claims, too, about the impact on social life if the 'little family worlds' are too privatized. One man, who had just sold his house, said he and his wife had found it 'very hard to break through' to people 'because most of them were working couples, and we didn't see them; they weren't there through the day and of course we were busy in the evenings'. They had made no friends, just 'pass them in the street and wave to them'. People were 'very much tied up in their own little worlds, concerned with their problems, perhaps how they're going to pay next month's mortgage ... When they came home at night they were too tired. Just sit down, put the feet up and watch television and that was it'. A teacher took the argument further: 'Because they're so tired and they're overwrought with their financial problems, and then perhaps a little bit of emotional stability missing, the children are suffering'. She will be home with her children, indeed suspects that 'back in my deep dim past I may have chosen teaching with that in mind'.

Many of these themes are gloomy echoes of previous studies. So too is the conviction that 'today' it is harder to be a mother. A woman whose 'good mother' definition was 'someone who spends time with her kids, is prepared to put a little bit of sacrifice in', emphasized 'communication': 'Just be there ... when they come home from school if you can be and have a hot drink of Milo with them and just talk when they want to talk'. That, she said, was hard. 'I think it's the rush, you're rushing everywhere and get all ragged. Our mothers' time was the time to be a mother, it was quieter.' Some, but by no means all, go a further step to imply that struggle causes delinquency. But there are few straightforward arguments that delinquency is caused by women's workforce participation and those that are put refer to lower-class parents with poor discipline. The embattled organizers seeking parental help in the Youth Club recognized the story: 'I'm sorry, my dad can't come 'cos he's on night shift and me mother's on day shift and they pass each other in the night, but the mortgage has to be paid'.

One young woman was renting a house for sale. Her idea of a good family life was more 'modern' than any others in the survey sample: 'family involvement with each other ... each one is sort of equal and an individual at the same time. That responsibility isn't rigged to one person, it's shared, where things are discussed openly and not hidden'. She and her fiancé were 'working to buy a house here . . . and have children', but she saw in Green Views a family life she rejected: 'Up in the centre, at night time . . . there's kids of all ages, no parents of them around, some of them are doing things that, you know, children of that age shouldn't know anything about . . . and you say, you know, "Where's Mum?". "Oh, she's at work but she sent us up here to play". I think in a few years there'll be a terrible delinquency problem'. The obvious conclusion is the proper path: 'If I was to have children, I wouldn't consider working till they were at least at school, then I—probably one parent should be with the children if they're here. They need someone to be there when they want to talk, when they want assistance with things'. There is no sign that the 'togetherness' ideal makes this any less *her* duty. She is clear on the familiar timing of steps: 'It would probably be difficult because, with interest rates going up on housing loans and things like that all the time, I feel both parents would have to work, to begin with anyway. Especially if it was their first home. And I probably would consider not having children at first'.

The then president of the Residents' Association (RA), Susan, was mother of one school-age girl. She was the subject of continuous criticism for her working and her style of leadership in groups. A friend recognized how these criticisms were combined:

W: They just see her as a very bad mother, they don't see her *there*, just being with her kid, and that's noticed even by people that are not necessarily malicious . . . Because she was so different, and didn't conform to what they thought mothers ought to be (even if they're working 'cos lots of mothers work in Green Views) to their kids . . . It's more a sense of responsibility towards her child, much heavier than just the mothering business.

During the years of the project Susan dealt in a range of ways with these ideas. In the early years she avoided women's groups, pruning her network to those met through her full-time employment, evening work for the RA and 'outside' friendship. She tried to include her daughter in her group work, but finally had to resign: 'I didn't want to expose her to it, mainly because of the ridicule. There was a lot of comments about how I shouldn't be doing it and she was suffering'. Later she left the estate.

Not really working

To these incompatible demands, women had really only one answer: part-time work. A young mother who had had no year since marriage in which she had not earned some money told the interviewer: 'No, I didn't work. I did a Party Plan for a little while, which was irrelevant, you can't really call that work.[26] It was just an interest. I didn't work until the youngest was 19 months old'. That was part-time and she moved into full-time but found it 'too heavy' (an adjective that often turns up in this context). 'I won't go back to full-time ... between going to work and the housework, I didn't have the time to spend with my husband and the children and it just about caused a major divorce I think, a rift. I just didn't have the time to spend with him and though he never expressed it he wanted time with me, it showed in many ways, so I gave the job up.' Part-time she had done waitressing from 5 p.m. to 8 p.m. A neighbour 'kept an eye on the kids until my husband got home and took care of the kids, that is why I worked those hours'.

But part-time is not only about *time*; it is also about the degree of commitment required by the woman. A mother who had been an executive secretary (and loved it) planned to return to work after her children were older. Not now, since her husband did shift work. And not as a secretary, 'Because you have to be involoved; you have to walk out the door and from then until you come home you don't think of home'. As Australian figures and previous studies clearly show, the sought compromise is part-time work.[27] Discussing the effects of part-time work on the community, I asked one woman 'What sort of women get part-time jobs, meaning 'as opposed to full-time'. Interpreting the question differently, she laughted: 'Well, whoever can get them! I think a lot of them, once the kids go to school, if they can get some part-time work, they're interested in getting it. I think things are tough around here, with people in these new homes'. She had read my question as asking 'Which women work?'.

Full-time work is just not a considered option in her statement or in the lives of many mothers of young children; they will work only if they can get 'a bit of part-time'. And in the Green Views study, as in Australian studies generally, women's workforce participation patterns mirror this compromise and its costs. Women move in and out of the workforce reflecting family demands, availability of acceptable child-care and accessible work with the right hours. The price is not merely part-time pay, but lower job security, inability to find networks that will be supportive of their workforce life and vulnerability to the ideologies of the family maintained within the estate.[28]

Sometimes there are hints of doubt about the priorities. 'I don't think they really want to be with Mum all the time', said the woman who was 'a nervous wreck' from leaving children after school. Later she said her family life would be different if she didn't work, but was puzzled to explain why. 'If you're a housewife you could do everything in a day; you wouldn't have to do anything except cook dinner'. Much later she added personal things: 'It *would* be different, I'm sure, because to start off with, I'd make a point of sewing and I love crochet and I'd do all those things I'd really like to do, but now by the time I get home I'm too tired to concentrate on them'. A glimpse here of a possible private world? Certainly her home now is private in one sense—visitors are discouraged: 'I could possibly find it a bother if I did have someone who kept popping in and out all the time because I really don't have the time with working and looking after this house and running the kids to their sports and playing sport myself and shopping; no there's just not enough time.'

Community: Who wants it?

In the material on women's employment the second most common assumption (after the assumption that children suffer) is that women's employment means loss of community. 'Most of them are working people' has the logical conclusion that 'everyone just seems to keep their heads down'. People say it of themselves: 'Everyone is working hard; weekends we go out'. An Italian-born woman summarized the compromise: 'I love this house, I love the area. I never see the neighbours. They're very busy, working...nobody knows anybody'. Her needs were minimal: 'It's nice to be able to know who your next-door neighbour is and what their name is. I don't, because we've never even met'.

These comments have none of the fervour of those concerned with the effect on family; sometimes they even sound ambivalent. And the ambivalence is not only from overloaded two-income households. The woman whose neighbours kept their heads down was herself at home, but knew nobody 'past two doors' and was very sure people did not want to know each other. She had worked until recently: 'Since I've had my child I've got to know a few more people. It feels quite good. At one stage I was the only person home in the street out of seventeen houses'. But she had enjoyed the privacy; later in the interview she commented: 'Before, you could sort of come and go, knowing you were by yourself and you could come in and go out as you felt like it'. Not now: 'You feel as though you get watched quite often. Just talking to another few neighbours, they sort of feel that too. It's always someone looking out of curtains or something'.

Clearly implied is that people ought to want the community they do not get if nobody's home. But do they want it? Privacy also means autonomy. 'I don't know anybody', said another woman at home, laughing. 'I suppose I'm too busy! That doesn't sound too good does it! I don't know, really everybody *works* here, this is one of the problems I think. You know, everybody here works.' But she said she was not really lonely: 'I've got my mum, and I have a fairly busy life otherwise, I've got aunts to visit and a sister to visit, and friends outside of Green Views. Green Views's not, I mean, I don't feel that I'm trapped here, or anything like that. I don't think you need to be'.

There is a strong theme in this material that 'nobody's home' is a self-fulfilling prophecy: women who stay at home are so lonely that they are more likely to go out to work. It is a claim very hard to examine. In each of the cases where this was given as a reason for return to the workforce it was either one of many reasons or sounded defiant. A husband explained: 'I think you feel a little bit of the economic thing here, where lots of houses are empty during the day. Therefore if I'm not here, for a non-working wife, she might wander into the street and meet people, but because of the economics, people are working'. His wife, whom I shall call Jane, agreed quickly: 'That's one of the main reasons why I thought I might as well go to work, because it's so isolated and boring being at home, and I didn't have a second car, and it was a hassle going on buses to go shopping, and I didn't have the money to shop once I got to the shopping areas'. He laughed, 'Now you've got the money, but you haven't got the time!'. Nor does she have time for any of the intense local group activity that make her life in the last three years sound far from isolated. Her story suggests a strategy by which she actively worked her way out of traditional ideas:[29]

W: I used to go on Monday afternoons to the YWCA thing, I'd work Tuesday morning in a creche, I'd play squash on Wednesday morning, I'd play squash on Tuesday nights, I'd have Thursday off. On Friday I'd play competition squash, and I was doing so many things that I thought I might as well go to work...I dropped out of the kindergarten committee at the end of last year because I didn't have anybody at kindergarten this year, and I joined the mothers' group at the school and I was going down listening to the reading too on Thursday; oh, Thursday I *didn't* have off! I joined the mothers' group there too and then the job came up, so I dropped out of that 'cos that was a daytime thing.

Perhaps her involvement in community activities also exempted her from criticism? When she was applying for the job, a friend said: 'No one knows; the women around here will scream when they find out, because she has three little ones. She is always running around and having her children minded'.

Negotiating with ideology

Not going to the mothers' group is an obvious way of dodging dominant ideas of women's place, as are squash and women's leisure groups. But in the material so far appear a range of less obvious ways to deflect the sanctions of disapproving husbands, neighbours or infant welfare sisters. You can redefine those ideas as 'old', or claim exemption on grounds of the age of your children, or the arrangements you can make for them, or the nature of your work—not really work, or just for now. Or you can appeal to that other part of the ideological tangle: the necessity (for family) for financial security in a home of your own. All these techniques can be strengthened if you also manage your networks, moving with people who approve, avoiding those who do not (probably including the mothers' club). New networks may offer other ideas that allow you to move further in that direction. Looked at this way, it is clear why education and class are relevant to values: they will affect the settings and the audiences, and the networks that mediate ideology. Not all women feel trapped and few of those seek to

escape traditional family life. But few are comfortably encapsulated in the 'old' ideas. The processes of negotiation, and
their relation to earlier themes, are shown most clearly by
looking through a single case.

It is not of course a typical case: no woman's experience was
'typical'. Each of the women portrayed in this book was tracing
her own path through the particular pattern of pressures and
opportunities that her family life and its ideological setting
presented. Those patterns varied, and so too did the women's
desires and skills for negotiating a preferred path. One of the
most active negotiators was a young woman I shall call Robyn.
In the early years of the estate she had been one of those most
constrained by traditional ideology.

Three years on, chatting about the women's groups, Robyn
distinguishes the playgroup from an activity group run by the
YMCA for women 'ready to accept that they want to get out
for themselves'. It is a group in which women can indulge in
laughing conversations distancing them from mother duties.
(After one meeting, Jan noted 'a lot of ribbing about their
mothering abilities. Robyn described herself as "the one who
screams at her children in the middle of the street"'.) Women
in the playgroup are different, she says. They don't 'really
want to admit' the need for activities for *them*: 'Because you're
not supposed to do things for yourself when you've got kids.
Everybody tells you that your kids are the most important and
you should stay home with them and that you should be a
good wife and mother and do the housework and be happy
with your children: you don't need anything else'. Everybody?
'I think probably our last generation are the worst.' There was
pressure from her parents, 'not in words, but in feelings. And
I *still* get it. And from Ken's parents. And from some women
around me too, yes. Some, not many, because a lot of them
are workers around here'. One of her friends 'does *not* believe
women should go to work when they've got kids. I don't
agree. It just depends on a lot of situations really: who minds
them, when they're minded, when you work, how often you
work ... If you can get child-minding worked out well and all
the rest of it, what does it matter; if the kids are happy,
they're not going to suffer from it are they?'.

The appeal to a higher value—children's happiness—neatly
sidesteps the disapproval: 'My mother-in-law used to say to
me, "What are you working for?". I'd say "to get some things

for the kids", 'cos that was basically why I went, to buy some new furniture for them and things like that'. Different explanations fit different audiences. 'It depended on who I was talking to. You have to pick your person, otherwise you get hassled!' The 'last generation' is distanced. She talks to her parents 'probably once a week—that sounds dreadful!' and sees her mother regularly ('It's only half an hour's drive, I think it's worth it to go over there'). Asked if she has a lot to do with her in-laws, she says sharply, 'Only when I've done something wrong. My mother-in-law lets me know. My mother agrees to disagree. They both stayed home all the time with their children and never went to work and "You don't need anything, you survive with what you've got"—but oh boy, isn't it a drag!'.

Such arguments could never have been produced when Robyn and her husband were first married. Family came first, then home, and both were and still are unquestioned. She recalls the decision to buy a home in a vivid account of the ways people are 'called out' by ideology:[30] 'We didn't have any ultimate thing to get a home. It was later, when we'd been asked, "What are you going to do, are you going to buy a home?" and we suddenly realized, "Oh yes, we'd better do something about it!"... We thought, "Oh dear, well I'm working part-time, I might as well put the money away towards a house"'. Later she says: 'The reason we decided we wanted to own, we felt that why pay out dead money to someone? Why not pay out those thousands we were paying in rent, to own— even if we're only paying interest, at least the ultimate gain is there. And also, I suppose, everybody likes to have something they can call their own. I suppose we all buy our houses because of that, don't we?'. Do people respect home owners more? 'Well I never thought about it before. But now I think I do because I feel that they're doing something with what they're working for.'

She had two babies before they moved to Green Views. 'Of course it's better, being in your own home, I think, with your own children. It doesn't matter so much if you haven't got kids. All I wanted was a backyard for the kids to play in.' They looked for about six months in established areas, to be close to family and friends, but found the prices too high. Looking back, she reflects, 'We went in with our eyes closed, I think'. But now she is one of those most clearly able to see how the dream of the home had worked to obscure both the real future of the estate and their own financial future:

W: No matter what house we looked at was lovely to us. It was great. 'We'll do this and that and that to that', sort of thing. It just looked good 'cos there weren't a lot of houses here. It was so open and we just looked at the gorgeous-looking houses, and thought, 'Oh this'll do'. I think I liked the idea of there not being so many homes around, but I never thought it would grow so quickly. That's why we want to go to the country. It never even registered with me that housing was done, more often than not, in estates. Because Mum and Dad said, 'Oh we bought our block of land here', and other people bought around.

But the major error was in 'not thinking of finances later, when I stopped working'. And finances indeed proved seriously strained. Robyn worked part-time after marriage but stopped with her first pregnancy. Her language reflects containment in the private world and the resultant vulnerability to the ideas it represents:

W: All I did was stay home. We rarely went out, except perhaps to visit my mum or his mum. Once you don't go out, you lose it, you just don't know what to say to people ... The longer you stayed home the harder it was to get out to talk to anybody. And the odd times you did go out, you didn't know what to say to them, and you had a rotten time anyway. It was your own fault, but you just didn't know how to.

The move to Green Views brought Robyn's first attempt to get 'out'. She had no driver's licence. 'I went out and got that, 'cos I couldn't take it any longer, not getting out.' But there was nowhere to go and few daytime friends: only thirty families had moved in, and during the day 'there was nobody there'. Her language makes men irrelevant in the estate's life: 'Everybody worked in the court except for me, and I was the only one with children at home'.

W: I thought that you were *supposed* to stay home with the kids, and that was the right thing to do, and that I should be happy doing the housework. And I found I couldn't *handle* being happy doing the housework and not talking to anybody. I think that's a lot of trouble with women; they don't realize that, or they've been told so much that's what they should be doing, they're too frightened to go and do something for themselves 'cos people will think they're thinking of themselves and they shouldn't be.

Part of the power of the ideologies of home and family is that they work through local relationships. Robyn became part of the local groups from the beginning, winning confidence and competence but only partial support for any challenge to traditional ideas. Most of her friends are at home since 'It's hard to mix with people who work full-time, because they're busy and you're busy'. As more move into the workforce an increasingly embattled residue of women at home maintains old values and surveillance. 'If you were to tell somebody you went out and played .cards on Friday night or something, they'd think, "Oh yes, did you? And what did you do with the kids?" ... That sort of third-degree thing. Like when I'm going to school—"But who minds the children?"'

Robyn has by no means rewritten her own ideas. She is unsure what to do with the night-class training: 'I couldn't imagine myself getting anything much done at all at home at the moment. But I would like to do something. I want to stay home for *them*, that's the reason, 'cos I get too much pressure if I go out! And then you have to be prepared to devote time. And I wouldn't like to get out and get a job where I had to give so much time that I wouldn't be able to give time to the family'. A good family life? 'Interests everybody can share; we all take an interest in each other.' A good father? 'Puts into the home as much as the mother does not in time but in value.' And a good mother? 'Tries to put family first.'

Notes

1. See C. Young, 'Work sequences of women during the family life cycle', *Journal of Marriage and the Family*, vol. 40, 1978, pp. 401–11 and L. Richards, 'No-man's land', introduction in J. Harper and L. Richards, *Mothers and Working Mothers*, rev. edn, Penguin, Ringwood, 1986.

2. That childlessness is considered 'selfish' is very clearly established in several studies, both of parents (L. Richards, *Having Families*, rev. edn, Penguin, Ringwood, 1985; J. Busfield & M. Paddon, *Thinking About Children*, Cambridge University Press, Cambridge, 1977) and of the childless (H. Marshall, Not having families: A study of some voluntarily childless couples, PhD thesis, La Trobe University, Bundoora, Vic., 1986).

3. The section of questions in the 1981 schedule asked first about good mothers and good fathers, then about family time and finally the following questions: 'What's your idea of a *really* good family life? Would your present life have to change much to be like that? What chance do you think you have of getting that sort of life?'. Except for group-member interviews this schedule section was not taped; quotations are from the interviewer's transcription of the answer. Taped transcripts are strongly preferable for the sort of analysis conducted here, write-ins losing the fuzzy edges of answers that are often important in interpreting ambivalence and contradictions.

4. The precodings (on the basis of postcoding pilots) were: companionship/communication in the marriage, sharing tasks in the marriage, doing things as a family, wife doesn't have to work, children well brought up, children self-sufficient, good health, financial security, less time pressures. 'Doing things as a family' rated 42 per cent of first answers (and was the most common coded category for each of the three answers); 'companionship/communication' 36 per cent; 'sharing tasks' 15 per cent of first answers, 5 per cent of second, and 24 per cent of third answers. No other coding had more than 7 per cent on any answer.

5. Effects of religion are inaccessible here, given the limitations of the statistical data and the fact that people never talked of the effects of religion on family ideas (interesting in itself). I am grateful to David Morgan for querying the invisibility of religion in this material. It is most certainly not irrelevant; the 1978 survey showed that 17 per cent of children, 23 per cent of husbands and 27 per cent of wives attended church at least once a month.

6. 'Togetherness' featured in 49 transcripts; 'close' in 11; 'sharing' 15; 'time together' in 10; 'enjoying each other' in 11; 'communication' in 20; 'happiness' in 7; 'financial security' in 7; and 'loving and caring' in 14.

7. They could also indicate what I suspect to be a feature of family values surveys: when dominant ideas are in flux, expressions of values, especially to a nice middle-class interviewer (usually female) are likely to echo 'acceptable' ideas while behaviour lags behind. This is of course more likely to affect studies offering people statements for comment: 'A woman is only fulfilled when she is a mother' is very hard to agree with in public! See H. Glezer, 'Antecedents and correlates of marriage and family attitudes in young Australian men and women', *XXth International CFR Seminar on Social Change and Family Policies*, Institute of Family Studies, Melbourne, 1984.

8. We included questions on household tasks, child tasks and decisions in the Stage 3 survey, but omitted them from the major reinterview on the grounds that, unless set in a major section probing the family dynamics and preferably including joint interviews and actual observation or daily diaries, the data were so simplistic as to be merely suggestive. In the absence of these, codings must be interpreted—just like the ideas of 'good family life'—as indicators of ideas about what people feel they ought to say, as well as what they like to do and what they actually do. My own conclusion is that such data can fairly reliably be taken as indicating a point beyond which 'new' ideas could not be stretched; there is no chance that more people share tasks equally than say they do! In the Stage 3 interviews 30 per cent were coded as saying that the wife did all or most of the housework, 32 per cent that the husband 'helped' a bit, and 36 per cent that they shared it equally. For child tasks the figures were 62 per cent, 18 per cent and 18 per cent; for decision-making 2 per cent, 2 per cent and 82 per cent, with another 10 per cent saying the husband does most or all of the decision-making. These patterns differ from other studies—see L. Bryson, 'The Australian patriarchal family', in L. Bryson & S. Encel (eds), *Australian Society*, 4th edn, Cheshire, Melbourne, 1984—almost certainly because Stage 3 couples were even more concentrated in the early life stages than those in the main sample.

9. Up to three were coded from each person: less time pressures scored 46 answers and 'more time together' 20; 'financial security' and 'wife wouldn't have to work', 11 each.

10. This has been a major theme in literature on marriage since the 1950s; see E. W. Burgess *et al.*, *The Family from Institution to Companionship*, 3rd edn, Van Nostrand Reinhold, New York, 1963.

11. I am using here the terms used in Richards, *Having Families*, and in Harper & Richards, *Mothers and Working Mothers*; they were the terms people themselves used. Those interviews were conducted five years before the Green Views project began, but the ideas are startlingly similar.

12. These were developed from Richards, *Having Families*, but asked in a different order: 'Do you think of yourself (your wife) as a good mother?', 'How would you describe a good mother?', 'Do you know anyone you'd call a really good mother?' and 'Is it hard to be a good mother?'. Sadly, for reasons lost in history, when we repeated the questions with regard to fathers we omitted the first and third. The scheduled interviews contained a set of four questions on 'good mother' ideas.

13. This is different from the pattern in Richards, *Having Families*, where ideas of good mothers were sought before examples, and I did not specifically ask if people thought of themselves or their wives as good mothers—just if they knew any. Only a handful said they or their wives qualified, and it was common for people to say they could think of no example or to produce models who were very old or dead. I suspected this was partly because the ideal was stated first, and was then hard to fit to real women. It may of course be that in this respect new ideas are penetrating women's images; without controlled data this remains guesswork.

14. On the basis of piloting and previous studies, we precoded two general categories—'loves them' and 'disciplines them'—then three categories associated in previous studies with 'old' ideas ('patient', 'there when needed' and 'doesn't work') and three 'new' ideas ('teaches skills', 'plays/reads with them', 'has her own life'.).

15. This combination is explored in detail in Richards, *Having Families*, where I called it the 'career mother' approach; some women, usually educated, were devoted to mothering as a skilled profession. It has echoes in Helen Marshall's data from voluntarily childless couples, whose apparent acceptance of ideas associated with traditional family ideology—the necessity for sacrifice and commitment, especially by mothers—was given as a reason for *their* decision not to embark on parenthood. See Marshall, Not having families.

16. The cut lunch seems to have symbolic value—it occurred also in Richards, *Having Families* data. The school canteen and its volunteers proved a major source of conflict and resentment between women in the estate.

17. Wearing sought such 'utopias' in her sample from more varied backgrounds and found none, though she did find more questioning or distancing from the model (as did Richards, *Having Families*) than the present sample shows. See B. Wearing, *The Ideology of Motherhood*, Allen & Unwin, Sydney, 1983.

18. In 'good father' definitions from the lower education group 58 per cent mentioned time, compared with only 28 per cent of the more educated. 'Good mother' descriptions show the same pattern, but fewer include time, even counting in 'being there'. From the low education group 18 per cent mention 'time', 22 per cent 'being

there'; from the higher education group 14 per cent mention 'time' and 9 per cent 'being there'.

19. Seven per cent saw fathering, 43 per cent mothering as *very* hard, 56 per cent saw fathering as *not* hard, but only 28 per cent said that of mothering.

20. B. Friedan, *The Feminine Mystique*, Dell, New York, 1963, p. 26.

21. Both Wearing's *The Ideology of Motherhood* and my own data are from that period, and both contain considerable evidence of 'new' ideas and confusion about them. See introduction to Richards, *Having Families* for a summary of studies.

22. The methodological implications are important—to schedule an interview on motherhood is effectively to append the invitation with 'BYO ideology'; my own and other past studies should be interpreted in that context.

23. The NUDIST system allows not only retrieval of material indexed under a particular category, but exploration of themes by progressive abstraction of finer categories, creating new index 'nodes' and allowing retrieval of the text they refer to. See L. Richards & T. Richards, 'Qualitative data: Computer means to analysis goals', Paper to the Sociological Association of Australia and New Zealand, Sydney, 1987.

24. It is also of course skewed. This is inside-looking-out material, the view of women's work from within the estate. Women who are not employed are more likely to be in women's groups and also to attend evening meetings. But the data covered here come also from the taped sections of sample interviews, in which employed women were strongly represented.

25. See Harper & Richards, *Mothers and Working Mothers* and Wearing, *The Ideology of Motherhood* for Australian data.

26. The comment epitomizes this form of women's work: see chapter 12 for a further discussion of 'party plans'.

27. See Harper & Richards, *Mothers and Working Mothers* for evidence and also for discussion of the inadequacies of this solution and problems with the part-time compromise.

28. Harper & Richards, *Mothers and Working Mothers*.

29. On the uses of women's leisure groups in this process, see B. Wearing, 'Beyond the ideology of motherhood: Leisure as resistance', Paper to the annual conference of the Sociological Association of Australia and New Zealand, Canberra, 1988.

30. The phrase—and the highly influential idea—are Althusser's. See his 'ideology and ideological state apparatuses', in L. Althusser, *Lenin and Philosophy and Other Essays*, New Left Books, London, 1971. For discussion of recent theoretical developments and their application to family ideology see R. W. Connell, *Gender and Power*, Allen & Unwin, Sydney, 1987, and K. Reiger, *The Disenchantment of the Home*, Oxford University Press, Melbourne, 1985.

Part II

A Family Community?

8

Whose Family? Whose Community?

The people who bought the house-and-land packages brought with them, it seems, packages of ideas and ways of negotiating with them. In those packages traditional ideas were reshaped, not rejected. The packages differ from the family ideology identified in the literature. They picture a different private world, saying little about domestic retreat (and then not for women), a lot about autonomy, for women and men—but not for mothers. The accounts are dominated by themes of privacy and time. But the packages retain the assumption of one pathway to family life. Marriage, home purchase, dual-income beginnings lead to the start of family, then the 'return' of women to the home (like library books to their proper places). They will re-enter the workforce in partial commitment as babies inevitably grow up: the mother's time is committed to mothering.

So both her autonomy and her ideas of family 'togetherness' must mean different things from his. She is bound to the wheel of life cycle as he is not. Women's negotiations with the ideology were all in that context. The requirement for the home, and the requirement that her financial contribution cease with motherhood, mean that a wife is committed to a particular form of double dependence on her husband.[1] He becomes controller of her labour and provider both of the material conditions for it and of the home, the necessary condition for a good family life. These sets of ideas show remarkable uniformity.

But such complex and changing dreams would not produce

uniform effects even if social behaviour were a perfect reflection of dominant values—which it is not. The image of homogeneity in Green Views, of bulk belonging and acceptance, masked real dividers of life stage, life chances, gender. Those dividers will affect how people work within the packages of ideas of family and home and the ways they rework those ideas. So it is unlikely that local relationships will be uniform.

What then of the critique of suburbia, the picture of a uniform nightmare of private isolation born of the dream of the privately-owned home? That critique splendidly exposed the aspects of suburban life ignored by male-dominated sociology and the ways in which planning attended to the needs of male commuters. It identified the ways women are placed not only in home worlds but in urban space, and how they are associated with suburbs. Private/public, hers/his, suburban/urban? In popular symbolism 'women and suburbs share domesticity, repose, closeness to nature, lack of seriousness, mindlessness and safety',[2] all about having time and giving it. That symbolism shed light on the years of suburban explosion[3] and showed the links of suburban life to the resilience of the 'old' ideas of mothering. But it was always 'too clean, too fictional'.[4] As suburbs radically altered with changing family patterns that dichotomy has become less helpful for understanding the variety of lives that can be contained by the ideology of family, and the variety of ways people negotiate with it.[5]

Uniform nightmares for look-alike families?

There are three hidden assumptions about uniformity in that critique, all, ironically, features of the functionalist sociology feminism most strongly attacked. The first is that isolation is always bad, and community is always good and always wanted. Second is that the Family, uniformly private, isolated and nuclear, dominates behaviour. And the third is that people uniformly receive the ideological pressures to privacy, so are uniformly unable to find or build supportive social networks. None of these assumptions stands up well to experience or research.

The first assumption, that community is always good, is embedded in both popular culture and sociology. Community is presented as something we all want and once had. The dichotomy plot thickens: then/now, community/isolation links with private/public, home/work, his/hers, urban/suburban. 'Community' is undoubtedly part of the ideological tangle of family and home, but it is much less clearly desired than families and homes. While many people in Green Views were concerned about isolation and many were isolated, few clearly craved community. As earlier chapters show, 'community' in Green Views referred to an amalgam of clean, green, facilities and friendliness, not to intimate knowledge or friendship.

In sociology community refers to bigger things: 'all forms of relationship which are characterized by a high degree of personal intimacy, emotional depth, moral commitment, social cohesion and continuity in time'.[6] Only in recent years has the assumption that community is good been challenged by studies indicating the advantages of anonymity and linking them to autonomy.[7] But anonymity and autonomy are opposed to traditional family ideas. Suburbia was portrayed, in the 1920s and again in the 1950s and 1960s, as a place for community *and* domestic retreat. The commitment of planners to these ideas continued though family forms changed.[8] The first critiques of suburbia were not of loneliness but of compulsory community and frenetic status-seeking activity.[9] As concern at the isolation of women in suburbs grew, the critique acquired a central paradox which has never been tackled. The nightmare of isolation is pictured in a context of stifling community and vulnerability of women to competitiveness, gossip and surveillance. Ironically, in both portraits the assumption of homogeneity remains: sweet, warm homogeneity has become hard, conformist homogeneity, *the* suburban dream, *the* suburban woman's nightmare in the dead heart of the Family.

The second assumption, of uniformity of family, is even more obviously false. Of course there is no such thing as the Family, and of course researchers now acknowledge the proportions of single people, informal marriages, childless couples and other family forms. The idea of the Family, its location in the private/public dichotomy and its placing of women, is identified as the core of patriarchal ideology. Yet mainstream and critical studies alike reaffirm homogeneity. In American family sociology the isolation of the nuclear family has been shown to be a fiction, but the debate did little to dent the model of a single nuclear family form, united by common norms defining segregated roles. Typical isolation was replaced by typical modified extended family relationships.[10] When implications of suburbia for women were at last exposed by feminists they often restated the assumption of homogeneity in the new language of hegemony. One ideology defined one set of roles in an oppressive institution.

Thus both streams supported the third assumption, that people in suburbia, all Family people, are uniformly isolated. Portraits of suburbia did not seek variety. Most research into social supports focused on kinship links, clearly showing that modern families are not uniformly de-kinned by mobility,[11] but not exploring other relationships or how those might be shaped.[12] Most set out to describe the structures of networks, not to explore the processes by which they are managed by active individuals—especially women.

Network management is never done

The sociology of community has a remarkable record of ignoring women. Partly this is because it has not seen their experience as different. Community has almost always been pictured as his, with the assumption that it is also hers.[13] Few studies have even remarked that his community may not include the daily interactions of local life. As one working-class woman told Jean Martin, 'a man's not a neighbour' to another man, 'just somebody working in his garden'.[14] But sociology's ignoring of women is also partly due to the fact that often it has not seen women *or men* in those social areas where women are active.[15] To see women's local lives requires looking in different places, places not often defined as worthy of research.

Feminist writing has recognized women's local relationships as work, but to date has produced few studies of this local work. Researchers focusing on class in studies of women's lives and marital power easily bypass the petty patterns of neighbouring for the strong strokes of societal conflict.[16] We know women in general do much more of the work of making and maintaining ties than men do and that this pattern persists into old age.[17] But we know little about women's job of managing the interface of private and public worlds, or the ways in which that job changed as paid work for married women became normal.[18]

In discussions of women's 'service' work of caring, feeding, transporting and building support structures the most cited studies are classic accounts of strategies for survival by women in situations of poverty where men are effectively powerless.[19] It is important not to assume that these glowing portraits of women's networks depict the lives of all women. It is equally important not to assume that 'community' is a lower-class habit. What are the strategies of women in other settings, notably in the new suburbia where 'everybody works'? Studies portraying vestiges of stable support structures in the traditional working class[20] are counterbalanced only by portraits of that other suburbia, the busy, buzzing routine of the middle-class female family administrator running community groups or running her children to after-school activities.[21]

When needs, goals and available resources are so different people will construct different strategies for making and using social links.[22] Understanding of these will in turn be governed by the 'rules of relevance' of relationships, the 'principles or rules that are used implicitly by the interactants in ordering a relationship, and which serve them as a basis for knowing how to act in, and what to expect of, a relationship'.[23] In what follows, I am drawing on approaches to social networks emphasizing the effects of social contexts, the constraints on choice and the processes of defining and altering the rules of relevance of relationships. But there are two important gaps in those approaches. First, even those studies theoretically committed to seeing networks as the results of individual choices and constructions have pictured them only at one point in time. So we still have a very limited understanding of the processes I have termed 'network management', by which we make, maintain, alter, remake and unmake our social links.[24] Like gardening, these processes require time and skill. The tasks are not only to provide the conditions for growth but also to weed out or prune back excess growth, selecting rewarding plants, thinning branches and clearing needed space.

Secondly, the focus on individuals' choices and constraints has diverted attention from the ideological settings of the rules of relevance. Almost all of the network links that matter to people will have important ideological loadings. People may adapt to, or even defiantly reject, social knowledge about relationships, but will never totally ignore it. And some types of relationships carry a heavier load of social knowledge than others; individual strategies will be much more constrained in those. Network management is always complicated. But the ideological setting of types of relationships further complicates any strategy worked out in terms of the needs/goals and resources equation.[25]

Networks will always be to some extent the products of processes by which people negotiate with ideology. But network management will also be one crucial way of negotiating as they select or sever the links through which societal prescriptions are filtered, understood and enforced. Interpretation of these processes will always be difficult since ideology is always partly opaque. And understanding those processes will be harder in areas where little is known about the ideological backdrop. That is certainly true of neighbouring.

Everybody needs a neighbour?

Perhaps the clearest result of the failure to examine a range of social and ideological contexts is the assumption that neighbouring offers default relationships for those—and only those—unable to do better. Thus viewed, neighbour relations are 'residual, relations people have in addition to, or instead of, more rewarding ties outside the neighbourhood'.[26] That assumption is part of the idelogoical baggage carried by male and female researchers[27] into community studies, and by residents into new estates. It denigrates daytime relations between women as silly, time-filling trivia. Thus, with little data on the meaning or processes of local links, Fischer could conclude that because local contacts were fewer they were less supportive than contacts in wider contexts. When Allan set out to contrast working-class kin and friendship relations with middle-class ways of allowing acquaintances to 'flower out' into friendship, he did not hear strong gender differences in accounts of neighbour links. Women talked of controlled, ceilinged friendships with neighbours, far more complex and vulnerable than the more easily defined and developed—or avoided and severed—relations of male neighbours or the couple interactions of middle-class sociability. But to their husbands (and Allan) they were not real friendship.[28] The assumption that neighbouring is a residual relationship has also helped confirm the myth that neighbouring is irrelevant to men. In societies dominated by men's breadwinning roles everyone assumed that breadwinners had bigger things to do. So men's part in producing and policing the ideology of private worlds was ignored, as was women's in making and maintaining the social positions of their families, managing the ambiguities of the private sphere that is both protected haven and public statement of status.[29]

On the surface 'neighbours are merely people who inhabit the same locality, and by comparison with co-workers and co-religionists, their interactions are distinctly not norm-governed'. But 'the term has become saturated with emotional and normative connotations which obscure this simple truth'.

Neighbouring—interaction with neighbours—need not involve neighbourliness, 'a positive and committed relationship constructed between neighbours'.[30] In fact, some studies have asserted, neighbouring normally will not involve friendship: 'Neighbourhood friendships are usually casual, not very intimate, and based largely on the low cost of interacting with those nearby'.[31] People are likely to be very conscious of the ways they work at neighbour relations, and the limits to them. This should mean that neighbouring is *par excellence* the artefact of network management. It embodies some choice and control, but also elements of constraint ('you're stuck with your neighbours') and costs that are hard to evade if relations are unsuccessful.

But neighbouring is, or supposedly was, also equated with community, caring, citizenship and responsibility, and strongly linked to ideas of good family life and the comfort of women's worlds. Relationships between neighbours literally link families and homes with the public world. The rediscovery of neighbourhood by planners aiming to create family community or to soften suburban mass housing is a celebration of that link. What might be termed the Sesame Street image of neighbourhood has been strongly revived by those working for urban renewal and local action, imbuing neighbouring with the ideological trappings of family. 'To be neighbourly is a natural human trait. It combines our concern for others and our concern for self ... Likewise, the neighbourhood is a natural phenomenon. It is organic, growing naturally wherever people live close to one another.'[32]

By comparison, modern city life makes neighbours 'just vaguely familiar strangers. They scarcely know, hardly see and rarely depend on one another'.[33] So the neighbour relationship is set between privacy and community, and suburbia is set in that context. The peculiarities and built-in contradictions of neighbour relations are clearly part of the tangle of ideas about family and home. What people do with neighbours will reflect the ways they negotiate with those ideas.

Notes

1. The phrase is Gamarnikow's, cited and discussed by C. Allport, 'Women and suburban housing: Postwar planning in Sydney, 1943−61', in J. B. McLoughlin & M. Huxley (eds), *Urban Planning in Australia: Critical Readings*, Longman Cheshire, Melbourne, 1986, p. 236.

2. S. Saegert, 'Masculine cities and feminine suburbs: Polarized ideas, contradictory realities', *Signs*, vol. 5, Spring 1980, pp. s.96−s.111, esp. p. s.97.

3. C. Allport, 'The princess in the castle: Women in the new social order housing', in Women and Labour Publications Collective, *All Her Labours: Embroidering the Framework*, Hale & Iremonger, Sydney, 1984.

4. Saegert, *Signs*, p. s.97.

5. For recent discussions of the dichotomy in urban sociology see E. J. Harman, 'Capitalism, patriarchy and the city', in C. V. Baldock & B. Cass (eds), *Women, Social Welfare and the State*, Allen & Unwin, Sydney, 1983, pp. 104−29; L. McDowell, 'Towards an understanding of the gender division of urban space', *Environment and Planning D: Society and Space*, vol. 1, 1983, pp. 59−72; M. Simms, 'The politics of women and cities: A critical survey', in J. Halligan, & C. Paris, *Australian Urban Politics: Critical Perspectives*, Longman Cheshire, Melbourne, 1984, pp. 129−40.

6. R. A. Nisbet, *The Sociological Tradition*, Basic Books, London, 1966.

7. Allport, 'The princess in the castle'.

8. C. S. Fischer, *To Dwell Among Friends: Personal networks in Town and City*, University of Chicago Press, Chicago, 1982. See also C. S. Fischer *et al.*, *Networks and Places, Social Relations in the Urban Setting*, Free Press, New York, 1977, pp. 79−98.

9. There was a major debate over the existence of 'suburban man' (*sic*) and suburban life-styles in the post-war years. For discussions and data see P. Berger, *Working Class Suburb,* University of California Press, Berkeley, Calif., 1960; H. Gans, *The Levittowners*, Vintage Books, New York, 1967; and, more recently, D. Rothblatt, D. Garr & J. Sprague, *The Suburban Environment and Women*, Holt, Reinhart & Winston, New York, 1979.

10. In that debate a very important contribution was the study by E. Litwak and J. Szelenyi, 'Primary group structures and their functions: Kin, neighbours and friends', *American Sociological Review*, vol. 34, no. 4, 1969, pp. 468−81. That study is discussed in chapter 9. For summaries of the debate from a feminist viewpoint see G. Bottomley & P. Jools (eds), *The Family in the Modern World*, Allen & Unwin, Sydney, 1983; B. Thorne, 'Feminist re-thinking of the family', in B. Thorne & M. Yalom (eds), *Rethinking*

the Family.

11. For Australian evidence and survey of studies see H. Kendig & S. Mugford, *Ageing and Families: A Social Networks Perspective*, Allen & Unwin, Sydney, 1986; A. L. Howe, 'Family support of the aged: Some evidence and interpretation', *Australian Journal of Social Issues*, vol. 14, no. 4, 1979, pp. 259–73.

12. See A. Steuve & K. Gerson, 'Personal relations across the life-cycle', in C. S. Fischer *et al.*, *Networks and Places: Social Relations in the Urban Setting*, Free Press, New York, 1977; for a discussion of literature see L. Richards & J. Salmon, 'There when you need them? Family Stage and social network', *La Trobe Working Papers in Sociology*, no. 68, 1984, La Trobe University, Bundoora, Vic.

13. This argument has now been exhausted: see R. Frankenberg, 'In the production of their lives, men (?). . .sex and gender in British community studies', in D. Barker & S. Allen (eds), *Sexual Divisions and Society*, Tavistock, London, 1976; S. Delamont, *The Sociology of Women*, Allen & Unwin, 1980; L. Bryson & B. Wearing, 'Australian community studies—a feminist critique', *Australian and New Zealand Journal of Sociology*, vol. 21, 1985, pp. 349–66. Some studies, discovering gender, have returned to append it, for example H. G. Oxley, *Mateship in Local Organization*, 2nd edn, University of Queensland Press, St Lucia, Qld, 1978. Some have been sufficiently receptive to their own data to see gender—see K. Dempsey, 'Gender relations: Examination of social closure by men against women', *La Trobe Working Papers in Sociology*, no. 75, 1986, La Trobe University, Bundoora, Vic. A very few started out with it gender as a primary concern, notably R. R. Pahl, *Divisions of Labour*, Blackwell, Oxford, 1984, in Britain, and C. Williams, *Open Cut*, Allen & Unwin, Sydney, 1983, in Australia.

14. J. Martin, 'Suburbia, community and network', in A. F. Davies & S. Encel (eds), *Australian Society: A Sociological Introduction*, 2nd edn, Cheshire, Melbourne, 1970, p. 315.

15. The phrase is Lyn Lofland's; see her 'The "thereness" of women: A selective review of urban sociology', in M. Millman & R. M. Kanter (eds), *Another Voice*, Anchor Books, New York, 1975.

16. See Williams, *Open Cut*.

17. For example J. McCaughey, *A Bit of a Struggle*, Longman, Melbourne, 1987; Kendig & Mugford, *Ageing and Families*; P. D'Abbs, 'Family support networks and public responsibility', in *XXth International CFR Seminar on Social Change and Family Policies*, Institute of Family Studies, Melbourne, 1984, pp. 509–36.

18. For summaries of writings from geographical traditions see Women and Geography Study Group, *Geography and Gender: An Introduction to Feminist Geography*, Hutchinson, London, 1984.

19. Most commonly cited are three very different studies: M. Young

& P. Wilmott, *Family and Kinship in East London*, Penguin, Harmondsworth, 1962; L. Rubin, *Worlds of Pain: Life in the Working Class Family*, Basic Books, New York, 1976; and C. Stack, *All Our Kin: Strategies for Survival in a Black Community*, Harper & Row, New York, 1974. See for example L. Balbo, 'Crazy quilts: Rethinking the welfare state debate from a woman's point of view', in A. S. Sassoon (ed.), *Women and the State: The Shifting Boundaries of Public and Private*, Hutchinson, London, 1987, pp. 45–71.

20. On the community theme in sociology see R. Nisbet, *The Sociological Tradition*. The theme of class differences in local relationships is thoroughly explored by G. A. Allan, *A Sociology of Friendship and Kinship*, Allen & Unwin, London, 1979. On Australian differences see Martin, 'Suburbia, community and network'.

21. See for example Gans, *The Levittowners*; J. R. Seeley *et al.*, *Crestwood Heights*, University of Toronto Press, Toronto, 1956. Margaret Stacey's work has contributed substantially to the 'seeing' of women in communities; see her *Tradition and Change: A Study of Banbury*, Oxford University Press, London, 1960; M. Stacey *et al.*, *Power, Persistence and Change*, Routledge & Kegan Paul, London, 1975; M. Stacey *et al.*, *Women, Power and Politics*, Tavistock, London, 1981. See also the papers in R. Crompton & M. Mann (eds), *Gender and Stratification*, Polity Press, London, 1986.

22. For the original study in this tradition and a review of literature since, see E. Bott, *Family and Social Network*, 2nd edn, Tavistock, London, 1971. For a summary of network studies see P. D'Abbs, *Social Support Networks: A Critical Review of Models and Findings*, AIFS monograph, Australian Institute of Family Studies, Melbourne, 1982; and for an exploration of the interplay of factors see P. D'Abbs, Give and take: A study of support networks and social strategies, PhD. thesis, University of Melbourne, 1983.

23. Allan has adopted this concept from Paine; see Allan, *A Sociology of Friendship and Kinship*, p. 15. For a fuller exploration of issues in network research see L. Richards, 'Families in a suburb: Network management and its varied results', *La Trobe Working Papers in Sociology*, no. 64, 1983, La Trobe University, Bundoora, Vic.; and Richards & Salmon, 'There when you need them?'.

24. L. Richards, *Having Families*, rev. edn, Penguin, Ringwood, 1985, intro.; and 'Families in a suburb'.

25. See J. Finch, *Family Obligations and Social Change*, Polity Press, Cambridge, 1989.

26. Fischer, *To Dwell Among Friends*, pp. 98–9.

27. I suspect, and my own experience confirms, that professional

women are *more* likely to face problems in seriously listening to their data on neighbouring relations than are professional men because they are more likely to have rejected those relationships and their encapsulating social results, and to be seen as rejecting them.

28. See Richards, 'Families in a suburb' for a detailed critique.
29. For an exception see K. James, 'The home: a private or public place? Class, status and the actions of women', *Australian and New Zealand Journal of Sociology*, vol. 15, no. 1, 1979, pp. 36–42; and K. James, 'Public or private: participation by women in a country town', in M. Bowman (ed.), *Beyond the City*, Longman Cheshire, Melbourne, 1981. On the ambiguity of the private sphere, see J. S. Duncan, 'From container of women to status symbol', in J. S. Duncan (ed.), *Housing and Identity: Cross-Cultural Perspectives*, Croom Helm, London, 1981, p. 51.
30. M. Bulmer (ed.), *Neighbours, the Work of Philip Abrams*, Cambridge University Press, Cambridge, 1986, pp. 18, 19; here I am adopting his careful definitions of terms.
31. R. M. Jackson, 'Social structure and process in friendship choice', in C. S. Fischer *et al.*, *Networks and Places: Social Relations in the Urban Setting*, Free Press, New York, p. 70.
32. H. W. Hallman, *Neighbourhoods: Their Place in Urban Life*, Sage, Beverley Hills, Calif., 1984, p. 11.
33. Fischer, *To Dwell Among Friends*, p. 98.

There When You Need Them?
Neighbours and Social Support

The stereotype of the uniformly isolated nuclear family in the uniformly lonely suburban setting fits badly in Green Views. But loneliness certainly dominated some people's experience, and everyone had a feeling of isolation. Their words make it clear that many also felt that it was somehow their fault if they were isolated. Green Views was not *that* far out, transport was not *that* difficult. But distance is a matter of perception, and transport needs are about the routines of daily life; women especially felt distanced, and those unable to remake their lives to deal with the problem always implied that it was of their own making.

Two women puzzled over their feeling of isolation. 'My husband keeps reminding me it's only 13 miles out of Melbourne. It's not that far out. But I sort of do feel like at the end of nowhere sometimes'. Why? She reasoned that the problem was transport: 'When you have to go back and forth all the time—well, I visit my parents nearly every second day'. Her neighbour agreed: 'I wouldn't just say now, like, I've got nothing to do I might as well go for a ride to the shopping centre...just for a reason to get out of the house'. The first woman too was talking about the difficulty of planning and justifying women's daily activities: 'For a while there I was very isolated, and very lonely for a while because I felt a lot of my friends found it too far to come out here. And for me to see friends, whereas before it'd take me five minutes to go anywhere I wanted to go, it takes me now twenty-five. And you've got to consider petrol...You don't generally make a trip anywhere unless you can do quite a few things at the one time'.

An early brochure featured a railway line closed pre-war; now the nearest train station was several kilometres away as the crow flies and further by road. The bus service was twice daily when the estate opened, hourly by the time of the second interview, but still a cause of great dissatisfaction and, since it was also little used, under great dispute. In 1978 transport was the most frequently mentioned complaint (27 per cent), and it proved the most persistent. By 1981 it accounted for 44 per cent of complaints.[1] Asked to rate the estate on the availability of public transport, over three-quarters said poor or bad.

Men and women were equally likely to criticize transport, though women were far more disadvantaged. They needed it more; when there was one car, almost always he drove it. And women were served by public transport far less adequately. What there was catered to men's travel both in routes and in timetables. As the women quoted at the beginning of the chapter made clear, and geographers have recently documented, women's journeys are shorter and more scattered and their timetables unpredictable whether or not they are in the paid workforce.[2]

By 1981 the tramline had been extended to the next suburb 'in', requiring a bus connection. It was used 'never or almost never' by 84 per cent of men and 72 per cent of women in our sample, but nearly two-thirds said they wanted it extended to Green Views. (It had crept half-way there by mid-1989.) The bus did loop round the estate but was rarely used even by women; two-thirds of women and over 80 per cent of men and children used it never or almost never. Why would they? In 1978 only 39 per cent of households had a second car, but by 1981, 58 per cent had at least two, though for many families this had meant a crippling financial burden. So the estate had entered the dilemma of public transport provision widely recognized in literature on planning: what there was appeared inadequate, and the necessary response was to do without it.

The obvious result was that, still inadequate, it would remain underused and therefore underdeveloped, as the residents now relied on cars. A freeway route was at this stage planned down 'the creek', alongside the estate and straight into the city (as the male flies!). Nearly half our sample (and the local MP) were unaware of this, though it featured in street directories.

When we asked for attitudes to the freeway, expecting to find a strong protest about 'country atmosphere', we found that only 15 per cent disapproved, while two-thirds approved unconditionally. There was no gender difference but when women's answers were recorded they had often approved because 'he'd use it'.[3] That of course would help them. Ninety per cent of men drove their own car to work in 1978, and only two-fifths of them took under 20 minutes.

The less obvious result of the transport dilemma was to divide the experience of women. It is now widely acknowledged that women are much more the victims of inadequate public transport than men. But the literature has largely ignored dividers other than gender.[4] In Green Views, life stage and resources meant that poor public transport was of some benefit to some women, justifying the commitment of income to a second car and freeing them from the transport routes designed for men, as they carried around or catered for young children, shopped and visited. For those without jobs, that freedom was curtailed by the necessity to 'consider petrol'. But they were not as constrained as those women without cars who relied on public transport and increasingly became aware that as others obtained cars they left the estate during the day. In 1978, when fewer women had access to cars, only a third were not in the workforce. By 1981 half the women were out of the workforce but cars took them out of the estate. Thus transport combined with awareness of shifting family values to make 'nobody's home' a self-fulfilling prophecy.

Isolated from what? Blood and water

Most people could get out of Green Views, so most did. Most had bought close to where they had come from, so had real opportunities for continued contact with family and friends. While only 7 per cent nominated proximity to friends or family as a reason for choosing Green Views, most people achieved both. Forty-one per cent of wives' parents and 46 per cent of husbands' lived either in Green Views or in a nearby suburb. And two-thirds of both his and her parents lived somewhere in Melbourne. Yet most people felt distance. 'Why did you have to go so far out?' was a question several had been asked. Again, it was seen as their fault.

'Losing touch' with family and friends was a frequent theme, but people almost always lost friends first. Family, or at least parents, were rarely lost; these were nuclear families but not, in Parsons' sense, isolated. Two-thirds of the 1978 sample said there had been little effect on contact with parents, and only 12 per cent said a lot, a few of these actually seeing their parents more often. The main effect was to make daily contact a little less likely, weekly contact more likely. Nearly half of the parents, his and hers, were visited at least weekly before and after the move. Less frequent visits stayed at exactly the same level.[5] The range of parental contact was considerable: at the extremes, 35 of the 1981 sample of 150 visited *both* his and her parents at least weekly, and 12 never visited his or hers. It was also quite predictable. If the parents were available, they were, in almost all cases, visited. And the telephone made up the difference; there was weekly contact by phone with two-thirds of wives' parents (daily contact with over a quarter), and 53 per cent of husbands' parents (daily contact with 13 per cent).

In 1981, 48 per cent rated Green Views good or very good for proximity to parents, another 16 per cent OK, and only 9 per cent had no contact with parents on either side. Nearly all of these were households in which spouses were overseas-born. Being overseas-born made it more likely that you never saw your parents, but no less likely that you saw them frequently; if parents were available, the overseas-born were much more likely to visit them.[6] Proximity to family was not often picked as a factor in choosing the estate, but for at least half it had been achieved. Three-quarters of couples with pre-school children had parents in Green Views or a nearby suburb. Life stage was associated weakly with degree of contact with husband's parents, strongly with degree of contact with wife's. Couples with young children tended to live closer to their parents and to see more of them; the parents were more likely to be alive and still in their own homes, and the young marrieds to have made only a first move away from there. But 'family' here was specific: all the relevant kin were parents, usually mothers, and usually the wife's mother.

W: Well I did try to get closer to mother's...but not particularly to anyone else, you know. I mean my brother, for example, I was disappointed he didn't buy over this side of town but of course he couldn't afford it, it was just too expensive, and I don't see much of

him since he's been over there. But you know, they do have to make
their own lives so you just say to yourself well that's how it is. So it
hasn't really bothered me much; I don't like living in people's pockets.

She offers a nice insight into the relation of mothers and
daughters and assumptions of kin links. Her mother, now
living with them, will move with them to Queensland, but will
first go to help a sister in Sydney:

W.   She doesn't want to leave here now, but the sister rung three
times in the last three days checking on when mother's coming, and I
said to mother when she rang me in the office the other day, I said,
'Now I think that she needs you up there, she's been very sick and
there's nothing like having your Mum around when you've been very
sick', I said, 'You've just got to go, Mum'.

The links were not just about visiting, but also about help
flowing both ways. That these married children would care for
elderly parents was commonly assumed. Their words leave no
doubt about the strength of kin ties. They also indicate the
importance of proximity when caring is necessary.[7] Two families were leaving Green Views to care for parents. In one case
this was looking ahead; the wife's father lived in a southern
suburb (about half an hour's drive) which her husband described as a 'bloody long way away. You might as well be interstate'.
The comment illustrates the gendered perception of space: he
drove further to work every day. But she agreed, 'I need to be
closer in case he is ill, because I can't go over there every day
if he is sick'. In the other case there was an interstate move
required.

W: My mother is very, very ill and she lives in Queensland and I've
got to go up. I've got two sisters and we're all very, very, very close,
extremely close, and they can't, their circumstances don't allow them
at this stage to sell their houses and move. So I've been up there to
see my mother and so has my husband and we decided that, yes, our
circumstances will allow for another change in our lives at this stage,
so we're going up there. He's going to go into business.

Help more commonly flowed the other way—from parents to
the grown children. But such aid, little noticed in the literature,[8]
seemed firmly set in accepted rules. Help with money was

obvious: twenty-three couples had a loan or gift from parents towards the house deposit, and another four had saved by living with their parents before purchasing. But there was no evidence of reliance on parents for regular assistance in carrying the women's burdens of family and home. In the absence of any close, formal child-care, and given the proximity of parents, we assumed kin would provide day-care for many. But of the 70 wives in the workforce in 1981, only five used kin for child-care for pre-school children, another three for after-school care of school-age children. The most usual arrangement was to shuffle women's time if the child was too young to be left alone, with informal care filling the gaps: 'When I was working part-time from 5 to 8 of an evening, my friend was only two houses away, she kept an eye on the kids until my husband got home and he took care of the kids, that is why I worked those hours'.

If the hours, or the non-kin carers, were not available, usually the wife did not work. Despite the concern about 'latchkey kids', in our sample only 17 school-age children were unattended.[9] In each case the parent felt they were old enough to 'look after themselves'. Most families had fall-back arrangements if child or carer was ill, but kin were used in such an emergency by only five mothers of pre-schoolers and seven of school-age children. Most commonly (31 families with pre-school and 38 with school-age children) the nuclear family coped: one parent, usually though not always the woman, stayed home.

These patterns show more about the rules of relevance of kin relations and assumptions about women's work than about distance. Over a third of the sample would use kin for baby-sitting if they went out socially at night. At night, of course, their own mothers were more likely to be available to babysit. But the difference also indicates the ideological backdrop to working women: in order to go to work most needed assistance, but some women at least could not ask. Where wives did *no* paid work it was more common for them to expect kin aid in daytime child-care.[10] These women at home were also more likely than women in the workforce to expect child-care help from friends at Green Views, at least in the daytime. But this was still uncommon; only 12 did so. Friends outside the estate undertook child-care for only one woman in the workforce and one at home.

Friends outside

Not everybody had lost their 'outside' friends. Nearly three-quarters of respondents said in 1978 that the move had not affected contact with friends, and in 1981 Green Views was rated well for nearness to friends by 59 per cent. But only those with no children at home had increased their friendships outside; a fifth of the men and a quarter of the women had felt outside friendships dwindle. Just as with kin, the move had not changed the proportion seeing friends at least weekly (40 per cent did so in 1981).

Many people felt they had been shedding friendships at this stage on the family path. Several factors combined to isolate them; the time demands of family, the distance they had moved 'out', and the different rules of visiting friends, especially for women — 'My friends I don't visit as often, because naturally, you don't visit friends unless you get an invitation, and vice versa. But with family, you can just drop in'. To these factors was sometimes added social distance. The couple 'such a bloody long way out' saw the south-eastern suburb she came from as 'the other side', relegating Green Views to Melbourne's 'west'. She had lost touch with friends who had moved 'east', rather than north. 'We don't get together as often. It sort of has to be a special occasion ... Particularly now — the baby has made a difference too. Because I just can't get up and go'.[11]

Everybody knows somebody

Did local relationships make up for the lost contacts? In 1981 only 8 per cent rated the estate poor or bad for friendliness; only 11 per cent worried about 'not being accepted'; 15 per cent about not 'having anyone round here that I can talk to'. Few people, on these figures, sound isolated, although there are always a few, and the meaning of friendliness is unclear: 41 per cent did not circle 'friendly' as applying to Green Views. Through these data persists the impression that friendliness did not mean 'community'.[12] Certainly, best friends were rarely in the estate. Three years on, only 15 women and 10 men said their best friend was in Green Views (and for one man and two women a Green Views best friend had moved). But as the estate emerged from paddocks, so too did positive attitudes to neighbouring. In our first interview this sounded like 'family community'.

In 1978, when all the houses had been occupied less than two years, exactly half the sample claimed to have met more than 10 people, and two-fifths more than 20. While these could have been very fleeting contacts, other questions confirmed the impression of a lot of neighbouring. Asked how much contact they had with their present neighbours, over a third said they 'chatted regularly', and over a third that they 'visited regularly'. Only a quarter said they had 'little or no contact'.

Being 'neighbourly' was a new experience for a high proportion of the residents.[13] Many had come in out of the neighbourly cold when they moved to Green Views. When we asked about contact with previous neighbours, both the 'chatted' and 'visited' categories scored less than a quarter, while 43 per cent of residents had had little or no contact. Only 16 per cent said they were lonelier now than before the move, and only 9 per cent said they were lonelier than when they first came. But then 44 per cent said they were *never* lonely. This is one area where ethnic background mattered. A quarter of those who were overseas-born or whose spouse was, but only a tenth of those from households where both were Australian-born, said they were lonelier now than before the move.

Not only were most people apparently not isolated, they were also very active joiners. More than half of the sample had some member of their family in a local group.[14] Not surprisingly, since most of the local groups were geared to children's needs, the younger households were more likely to have group members, and women were more likely to belong.[15] Again, ethnic background appears as a main divider. If either husband or wife was overseas-born the household was much more likely (56 per cent) to have no family member in a group than if both were Australian born (33 per cent).

But this early 'community' also had firm limits. Three years later, neighbour contact had often not developed since our first interview. The levelling-off of local relationships seemed more by control than lack of opportunity. Nearly half said they knew 'a lot' more people in the estate than they had known in 1978, and another third said that they knew 'a few more'. Only one knew fewer. But more than three-quarters knew 'much the same circle' as in 1978. Those who were overseas-born, or married to an overseas-born spouse, were no more or less likely to say that it was easy to get to know others or that they knew more people, but they were more likely to know the same circle of people in 1981.[16]

So the picture of considerable social contact (at least for some) was about contact that had largely been made soon after moving in. The reinterviews confirmed that. In 1978 only 12 per cent disagreed with 'it is very easy to make friends in this community', though another 24 per cent did not know. By 1981 they knew and only 4 per cent were unsure, but 21 per cent of those remaining in the sample disagreed. More disagreed with 'I am very attached to this neighbourhood'—22 per cent in 1978, rising to 32 per cent three years on. Only 19 per cent had all or most of their friends in Green Views. Few seemed shut out; the estate was rated good or very good for 'friendliness' by 79 per cent, and for being 'community minded' by 65 per cent. But over half said that if they were very unhappy or worried nobody in Green Views would know. Most wanted it that way, and here ethnic origin made no difference. Just over a third said that it had not been important to them to get to know people in the estate, but only 15 per cent said it had not been easy to make contacts. There was a significant association between the two: those for whom it was important were more likely to find it easy. Of course this happy experience was not everyone's—at the extreme, eight people for whom it had been very important found it very hard. Nor were there any single factors clearly predicting who had felt it important or found it easy.

The most obvious effect was of life stage, but life at Green Views was certainly not determined by life stage. Life stage was not associated with whether most of your friends, or your best friend, were in Green Views, though the households without children were more likely to have most friends beyond and less likely to have best friends in Green Views.[17] Nor was life stage associated, at least statistically significantly, with whether it was important to get to know people. In each family stage over a fifth thought it very important. And in all but the 'empty nest' households over 30 per cent found it very easy. But this question suggests one pattern: parents of pre-schoolers were much more likely (85 per cent) to find it easy. They were also more likely to have established and maintained 'the same circle' of friends, and life stage *is* statistically associated with the answers to that question. But it is an association only for women, created by the mothers of pre-schoolers.

Gender divided experience in complex ways which warn against assuming it has constant effects or that local relationships matter only to women. Overall, women and men gave similar answers, indeed while women were as likely to say it was either important or very important to get to know people, men were *more* likely to say it was very important. But life-stage groups in which women were most likely to say it was not important were those where men said it was, a twist to suburban life that is highly relevant for family harmony and for women's home lives, and a theme I return to in the final chapters. Getting to know people locally was very important to the women with young children, and to the men who were childless or had school-age children. The fathers of young children saw it as less important. They were also less likely to be lonely. They were either preoccupied with the opportunities and constraints of work or (perhaps *therefore?*) content with the private home. For men, but not women, there was a significant association between life stage and loneliness.[18]

And what of the omni-explanation for loneliness—nobody's home? Here, as in several other areas, the data offer little support for the claim that women's employment destroys community. While many gave the absence of neighbours during the day as a reason for *feeling* isolated, there is little evidence here that the employed women were less socially inclined or active than women at home. Whether or not a woman was employed made no difference to whether her friendships were in Green Views. But as I have argued in chapter 7, it is unwise to assume that part-time work for women affects them in the same way as full-time work. Analysed separately, part-timers proved *least* likely to say that their friends were mostly or all out of Green Views (because they had young children?) and women not in the workforce were *most* likely to say (because they retained the opportunity to visit?).

Who will be there when you need them?

The general picture then is nearer the developer's blurb than the stereotype of uniformly isolated individuals in suburban nightmares. But neither stereotype fits most people. And it would be rash to assume uniform social contact, let alone uniform attitudes to it. To get at those we need to know what people *do* with and for their neighbours.

In the 1981 reinterview, questions about the aid people expected from kin, friends and neighbours were replicated from an early and very influential study by Litwak and Sze-lenyi.[19] Their contribution to the debate in the 1960s over the isolation of the nuclear family was to argue that primary re-lationships were adapted to 'modern' societies. Kin might be distant, but they would, if they could, assist with long-term crises: meanwhile, friends, if close, or neighbours, would help with short-term crises. Challenging the assumption of the iso-lation of the nuclear family, they nevertheless, like Parsons, maintained that there was a modern 'dominant family form', not isolated and nuclear, but modified and extended. And they found it when they asked people in the United States and Hungary how much aid was expected, in different-sized crises, from each source. Starting with those assumptions our data tell the same story. Analysed like the original study, the Green Views patterns of aid expectation were remarkably similar. As predicted in that study, a high proportion (75 per cent) expected 'very much' help from neighbours in short-term (one-hour) emergencies.[20] The proportion expecting 'very much' help dropped off when the crisis was longer.[21]

If patterns are looked for, however, they dominate the data. Starting with the assumption that 'the family' covers varied and changing patterns, a different picture emerges. At least in our data, and quite probably in the original study, the figures did not show simply that people tailored their expectations of aid to the particular relationship, relying on handy sources for small tasks, calling in possibly distant kin for major crises. When the data were recoded to show patterns of expectations from each source across three emergencies, it appeared that *more than half* these people had the same expectations of both kin and friends no matter what the length of time involved.

Expectations of neighbours most clearly followed the ex-pected pattern, but even there 35 per cent gave the same answer for all situations, and 16 per cent always expected 'very much' aid. For the short-term crisis that should be the neigh-bours' speciality, only half the sample expected neighbours to be more help than either friends or kin. Eighteen per cent expected most help from neighbours for a week; 14 per cent for three months. Some people, it seems, have neighbour relations in which support is expected even in long-term crises. Some, also against the predictions, expect little or nothing from neighbours no matter how minor the emergency.

Such strong associations between patterns of aid from different sources suggest that it is too simple to assume that other primary sources compensate for absent kin or are nicely lined up to deal with crises of different duration. Instead, these data suggest, as a few recent studies have indicated by other methods, that the social environment may be cumulative.[22] Altogether, only 12 per cent of our sample conformed to the predicted pattern, with expectation of help from kin increasing, but from neighbours and friends decreasing as emergencies lengthened. Overall, support seems much less evenly distributed than predicted. In the short emergency a quarter look thrice-blest, expecting 'very much' help from all three sources, and an eighth expected this for a three-month emergency! At the other extreme, a few expected nothing from anyone.

The search for patterns demands thought about the nature of these questions and the local lives they are about. Who will need what sort of aid in each situation? Since to help requires not only proximity but also knowledge that help is needed, what sort of local relationships will convey that information? What situations are such that, given the resources, people will prefer to buy help from strangers rather than accept it from neighbours? Very many of these questions have gender or life stage or both as components of the answers, and all are set in the context of knowledge about neighbouring and kin relations.

Gender determines who helps. Like the study we replicated, we asked about help available to the wife; it is interesting but not surprising that answers from women and men were the same. But their help expectations were all about gender.[23] In every case where a particular person was nominated, this was a woman. When it was a neighbour, she was often 'the neighbour' as though there were no male neighbours. Women kin were most often named, and almost all were the mothers or mothers-in-law of respondents. Though, like the original study, we did not ask for specific nominations, in 60 cases a mother was specified for at least one emergency, and in almost all it was the wife's mother, even where it was clearly less convenient for her. One man said: 'My mother or sister would come and help' for the week-long emergency; for three months, that 'Her mother is too far away, but she might come down in a case like that'. The wording of these answers says much about the rules of relevance that make women 'kin aid dispensers'.[24] Mothers would know and come: 'Mother would come and stay' occurs several times, 'get Mum' and 'send for

Mum' three times each. 'Send for Mum in South Australia' is said just as confidently, as is 'Mum would have to come' and 'Either my mother would come to stay or I would go and stay with her in the country'. Nobody would 'send for' a neighbour or asserted that a neighbour would 'have to' help.

Where the amorphous category 'relatives' in the codings did not mean mother, it almost always meant parents. 'The parents would be the only ones you can rely on', said one man. Another said that 'One of the parents would come from Malaysia' for a three-month emergency. Although many fathers would have been available and retired, apart from mothers the only kin named were half a dozen sisters, one aunt and two grandmothers. Perhaps the clearest statement of the way this works came from a woman who answered, 'I'd cope. Ring my mother', as though coping and summonsing mother were part of the same process. Although many people are confident of neighbour help, answers about neighbours never carry this certainty. A man whose replies fitted the original study perfectly had answered to the hour's emergency: 'The neighbour would help out for that short time'. About the week-long emergency he said, 'Perhaps neighbours would help, but we'd really rely on her mother', and for the three months, 'Her mother would be called on to help'.

Life stage was ignored in the study we had replicated, but proved in the Green Views data to be the best key to locating those blessed with support. Those with only pre-school children were far more likely than any other life-stage group to expect very much help from all three sources in any situation and were the only group that never said they did not expect help from any of the three. Life stage was significantly related to expectations of aid from kin in all crises. It was significantly associated with expectations of friends and neighbours in only the hour-long emergency. Then, expectations were very high when there were young children, low when children were not there, suggesting that young parents have greater opportunities to make helping relationships and reciprocate, as well as greater need for them. But these relationships do not seem to stand up to bigger crises. The same shaped pattern lingered for longer crises (the young parents expecting more) but it was no longer significant because for everyone there was less aid expected.[25] When there is a young child in the house an hour is, several said, 'as much as you can ask of a neighbour'.

So it surprises less that neither women's workforce participation nor ethnic background proved significantly related to help expectations. Both might be expected to have a lot to do with need and resources, but it seems that the constraints on what you can *ask* apply to everyone. Workforce participation of women failed to shape these answers in any clear way. Ethnic background had one effect: households where one spouse was overseas-born were slightly more likely to expect kin aid in short-term emergencies, and less likely to expect it for three months (those who had kin available expected more of them than did couples who were Australian-born).

But these patterns of gender and lifestage were also affected by life chances. Pursued statistically, the interaction of life stage and class proves complex.[26] Life stage seems much more to affect the aid expectations of the better-off. This is most obvious in neighbour relationships. Those who see themselves as 'middle-class', whatever their life stage, expect more of both friends and kin than the 'working class', but not of their neighbours. The association of short-term neighbour aid with life stage turns out to be produced by the more educated and those who call themselves middle-class. When husband's occupation is controlled for, the association of neighbour aid to life stage was significant *only* in families where the male is a professional. These families were least likely to expect very much aid from neighbours in a short-term crisis. But those of them with young children were most likely to expect it.

Those with more resources seem, when they have young children, to have shelved restraint temporarily, but when children are older they have restored it. The few professional families with school-age children are more likely than any others in that life stage to expect little or no aid; at that stage they have the resources to seek support further away from home. But when women are at home with young children neighbours may be a necessity. They will find the exchange of help easier if they are better off, they may be more competent at negotiating relations if they are educated, and perhaps the fear of becoming embroiled in intimate relationships is less if they are also moving out of the estate or returning to a professional job. Thus the young mothers with resources may be most likely to seek and find neighbour aid.

Neighbouring, then, is patterned by the interaction of gender, life stage and life chances. But only so far? Certainly there is no one neighbour relationship, uniformly different from kin and friendship. People's words suggest that in some situations the neighbour can be the most intimate, needed and used support. But they also indicate common constraints on neighbour relations, constraints that apply across the estate and would apply even if everybody were home. While behaviour with neighbours depends on needs and resources, it seems worked out within a very strong web of ideas about neighbouring defining firm limits to growth, a web some can stretch but no-one can escape.

What do the neighbours do?

One way of checking the dominance of ideology is to search for variety. Are there different responses to the requirements of privacy and community, different styles of suburban life? We asked people in 1981 to nominate the four people they knew best in Green Views. Then they checked a long list of statements, circling those that applied to each of the four relationships. The items covered the ways they had met, things they had in common, what they did, and in what contexts.[27] Cluster analysis produced six very different styles of local relationships.

Five features of this typology stood out. First, 'community' is uncommon. To start with friendship and 'community' types is to start with the types located last, and those into which fewest people were dealt. The three types in which most people fell seemed to have little to do with 'community'.[28] Secondly, community seems only to occur when there is a common life stage. Thirdly, gender, life stage and resources always interact. All three dividers were relevant to all types, and women's workforce participation cut across them. Fourthly, there seem strong constraints on friendship with near neighbours. If the locals known best were near neighbours they were not likely to be known well. And finally, belonging to formal residents' groups had little to do with the sort of relationships people had with others in the estate. In each of the types there were at least two people prominent in the groups, and one is used in the illustration here.

The family lifers

Only one type suggests family community: it was the last located, and only 14 people were in it. They mix socially as couples with those they know best in Green Views, are often in each other's houses, share equipment, tell jokes, local news and 'very personal things', and expect to stay friends should one family move. These are mainly friendships between women at home (all but three are women), almost all with same-age children, mostly in the same school. They have found people like them; most 'live the same way' as their friends and are the same nationality, and that means Australian-born, except for two from English-speaking countries. They are 'established', mostly second-home owners. Most of the men are professionals and none of the men has more than one job (in every other type at least three do). Almost half of the contacts were made through groups, and all but two of the families have a member in a local group.

They all say it was important to get to know local people and most knew many more three years on. Not one is lonelier than when they first came, nearly half have all or most of their friends here. Few say no one here would know their troubles. They belong here, it seems, both in the sense that they do not have ties elsewhere, and that they are committed to the estate. They are less likely than those in any other type to be in contact with parents, and most have lost contact with 'outside' friends. Most will not move in two years, and would buy again if they saw the estate today. Their images of the estate sound like the brochures—'clean', 'well planned', 'friendly', 'community'. But (*because* they are committed?) they are critical about space, lawfulness, environment issues and community apathy. Only nine say that Green Views meant a 'better way of life' for them.

It was not a better way of life for Jane and her husband, though this was the first house they had owned. Both are English-speaking migrants, with no kin in the country. It was a second marriage, so she was older than most mothers 'starting a family': Green Views was somewhere to live. Her strategy of local relationships was limited by her life stage and built on its opportunities: 'I had to make my friends within walking distance'. Space was shaped by children: 'In those early days, the ones I did get to meet were the ones that I could go to easily, pushing a pram'. But stage of children distanced: 'The children didn't really have neighbours of the same age to play with, and what do you talk about with people that are older than you? You haven't got very much in common'.

W: The first six months were terrible because we didn't have any family ... All the houses were here. This one wasn't occupied immediately, and that one ... they weren't married and the man was living there and he was sort of involved in all these single man's activities ... And over here we had a very house-bound woman. I'm sure she had that phobia about going out of the front gate because she had three children. The children weren't allowed out the gate either. And we never saw them ever ... Two girls over there were both working. The next couple were both working, the next couple were both working ... I was the *only* one.

They still have no close neighbour relationships, and he thinks 'it's probably something we've worked at ... Not to have too many people sitting in your house or on your doorstep, you know, being too involved in your life'. Jane feels her neighbours 'don't want to get involved'. He agrees: 'Each family unit wants that separation, to keep people at arm's length'. Presence of children guarantees neither contact nor friendship. 'Three or four' women in the court are at home with babies now, but 'there's nobody home usually. If somebody's at home in their house, they don't see anybody else around'. She doesn't know what the others do: 'We're on speaking terms with all of them. You know, I stop and have a chat, as I go by, 'cos I'm always going up and down, mainly chasing children and looking for children'.

Children formed the basis for almost all their local friendships, but through deliberate group activity. Jane attended an advertised meeting to form a playgroup and started on 'the whole roundabout' of playgroup, baby-sitting group, kindergarten. The first friendships were the ones that lasted, and, in his terms 'become more concrete'. *All* the original contacts were hers, and only a few friendships 'flowered out' to home invitations to couples. The crucial resource is time—her time. As he remarks, 'Any working wife would have a lot of trouble to make those friends because you just wouldn't have the time'.

It goes without saying that a man 'wouldn't'. But nor did most women. They were, she says, 'too shy to open their lives to something like this'. Certainly she is not, but she is also older than most women in this family stage, and has professional experience behind her. Another woman says of her: 'She's the sort of person that would be everywhere, that'll go up and sell an old age pensioner a raffle ticket for free swimming lessons, and would succeed. Jane's the sort of person who wouldn't worry if she didn't know anyone'. She is a notorious organizer (mothers run for cover when she comes into the kinder, according to one of them).

But she has no 'best friend' here. The closest, a 'very good friend' (who makes just the same distinction in describing Jane) is several years her junior. They have a lot in common, a life-cycle stage, suburban life, and attitudes to it, which include determined avoidance of isolation. Jane seems to have a deliberate strategy of local relationships, can analyse them and cheerfully terminate links. With the last child at school, she has returned to work, welcoming the end of her involvement in local groups: 'I was doing so many things that I thought I might as well go to work'. The original (women's) friendships are retained, with contact still through children: 'I still see the girls on and off. The children go around to play on Sundays and Saturday afternoons and I wander down to round them up and see everybody'.

The local jokers

The second 'community' type is about a different sort of friendship—adult, usually couple, relationships that are relaxed but not intimate, mixing socially (not only in the daytime), telling jokes with same-age local friends, but not intruding on 'very personal things'. This is another small group: 11 people, of whom 6 are women. They are not often in, but do watch each other's houses, lend equipment, and are the most likely of any type to have friends, and 'a lot', even a hobby, in common. Over half of their friends were known before the move to Green Views, many through work. Most of the rest are neighbours, a few are members of shared groups. None were met through children.

They are starting up the ladder. All the women are under 30 and all the men under 35. Only one is a second-home owner. When they came, all were childless, all the women employed; three years on all but five have 'dropped out' as they have children. They may of course also be changing their style of local relationships, but not to Jane's. In half these households husband or wife is overseas-born. Occupations are mixed. They demonstrate the complex interaction between needs, resources and network strategies and the crucial influence of life-cycle stage on each.

This type seems to rely less on kin than on neighbours, or to be self-sufficient. But their kin are there; this type tops the others on contact with parents. Almost all say the number of their outside friends has dwindled. Very keen to get to know local residents, they also found it easy; they all say they know more people, and no one says that they are lonelier than when they first came to Green Views. They got what they expected—suburbia. The best thing about it is the house: many would not buy there again and say husband or wife has regretted the decision. They are likely to agree that 'nobody is home' during the day—hardly surprising, since they are themselves mostly absent. Yet for two-thirds it is a 'better way of life'.

Cathy, a teacher, interprets that phrase in terms of the next step on the 'proper ladder', after what she calls 'a flat existence': 'You're never home. We were studying at the time, so *we* weren't'. They had looked forward to 'having our home and sort of building a future'. They have no intention of staying at Green Views permanently. She enjoys the house, loves decorating it and has tried to make it special. And she feels she belongs: 'We have a lot of friends that we mix with'. These are limited, 'same boat' friendships in which other similarities are not important: 'We're as diversified as teachers and accountants, electricians, truck drivers; the guy next door can't read and write. The girl on the other side goes to uni'. But all are 'home-seekers'.

These are very different friendships from Jane's, linked neither by children nor by groups. Cathy's early involvement in groups was just to make 'contact', and she dropped out when meetings began. Loneliness is brought on yourself: 'Most of the people that we have encountered have been very receptive to any form of friendship that you've offered to them ... even if they don't want to see you and they don't want you in their home, they would never ignore you, you know'. But then she will never be at home all day in Green Views; the following year they will have moved interstate. Should they return to Melbourne they want to buy 'further out', where most of their young professional friends are. The cheaper housing in Stage 3 has disappointed them, tending to confirm their parents' concern about the estate: 'At that time I was pretty young and I don't know whether I could honestly say that I'd thought terribly much about it. I don't think that I'd seen that many different kinds of life-styles'. She is sharply aware now of 'the Hill, as we refer to it ... where you've got your two-storey, 50 to 60 square places, which is the kind of home I lived in before, and I know that they're very different to the one I'm living in now'.

The good neighbours

The third, most 'friendly' of the type— the good neighbours— is different in two respects: it is not a life-cycle type, and it is about near neighbours. It is also a more common type: 22 people were assigned to it, half of them women. This is one of the most 'working-class' types, and one of the most 'Australian'. Seldom the same age as their local contacts, or with children of the same age, they have rarely met through children. Three-quarters of the people they name are near neighbours, and usually only one is a close relationship. They lend equipment and mix socially as couples with one or two and, being near, watch each other's houses. But they have not found people like them. Just over half of their nominees are the same nationality as they are and they 'live the same way' as only a handful of later-named friends. Lacking common life stage to build on, or children to forge links, they seem to do more serious neighbouring, telling jokes and local news only seldom. But they all say Green Views is 'friendly'; they found it easier than any other type to get to know people and are most likely to say they are 'never lonely'. Not one is lonelier in Green Views than where they lived before. None have all their friends in Green Views, but they are more likely than any other type to have lost touch with 'outside' friends and to say getting to know people in Green Views was 'very important'.

These people are fairly isolated from kin, especially from their own parents; few visit parents weekly or expect aid from kin in minor crises. But they are happy here and likely to stay. People in this type, more than any other, are satisfied with Green Views and are definitely not moving within two years. Their expectations were right: they came for price and space and 'peace and quiet'; they would buy here again. This is the only type in which nobody has regretted the move.

Grace has never regretted it and is very happy with Green Views. She feels 'involved', and uses that term, as well as 'close' and 'belonging', very frequently: 'I have made a lot of friends in Green Views, because I've got involved. The same people who are involved, you come across all the time'. Her friends are made through many groups, though 'a lot have dropped off', and she reports few close friends. Her activities are all child-related: 'They like the idea of you being there taking part . . . "oh, my mum's helping on the canteen"'. Where they previously lived there were 'older people, and we sort of didn't get involved'. Here she feels a 'closeness': 'Everybody's sort of close and you don't have far to travel and you get to know each other, and it's good'. But neighbour relationships dwindled as people became established: 'As far as actual *neighbours*, there is no neighbour here, close by, that I'd know what was happening, to help'.

Like Jane, Grace sketches the court in shades of workforce participation: 'On this side, they both work. The other side, they both work. This side, they both work. She's home now with the baby. The other side, they both work. See, there was nobody here; everybody worked. There's no neighbours because no one's home'. Like Jane, though, Grace shows ambivalence about 'good neighbours': 'Someone that comes to see how you are—not when you're just sick! Just asks, in general, how everyone is and not one that pops in every five seconds. Not a person that seems to ask a lot of you, because I think a lot of people tend to use people'.

Unlike Jane, and in a different way from Cathy, Grace has an enormous stake in her home: it is Grace who says 'It means a family life'. But the private world must spill into community involvement: 'There's so many people that don't know a lot of people. And it's a shame. If we can get in touch with them, if they come out, then they're involved. We drag them in, and they're real happy just to know somebody, but we can't sort of go along to everybody as they move in, because not everybody wants to get involved'.

Functional friends

The 'functional friends' people have made relationships that are sufficient for their needs. They name near neighbours as 'best-known', but in this case there are no obvious barriers to knowing them better. Most 'live the same way' and are the same nationality as their contacts, a few met friends through children, most are the same age and have young children. Yet they seldom say they have friends in common with those they name or would stay friends if they moved, and over half are seen less than once a week. They seem least anxious about local relationships. None say it was hard to get to know people in Green Views and half say it was not important. Their friends are mostly outside the estate, no one has a best friend here and no one gives as their 'most neighbourly' act inviting a neighbour in. They expect that no local person would know their problems, and define good neighbours in terms of not intruding. In times of need they expect no kin aid, but no aid from friends and neighbours either.

These brisk functional friendships are set in strong enthusiasm for the estate. All 16 see Green Views as friendly and say it is a 'better way of life'; they would definitely buy there again, few regret the move, none are definitely moving in two years, only three possibly. They came primarily for location; it was handy and the price was right, and they appreciate peace and quiet. This is a white-collar group; few call themselves 'working-class'. Most wives are at home or in the workforce part-time. Just over half are first home owners; few are migrants or married to migrants; they do not mix much with 'different' people.

Gary and his wife are content, at least at this stage. In their conversation the recurring words are 'kiddies' and 'bonds': 'It's a good place to bring up your kiddies', he says. 'Kiddies' means early life stage, and certainly they are staying for that. Later, perhaps, they will move. They have many complaints— about facilities, schools, apathy, the teenagers 'hanging around' and the 'vandals'. They came to Green Views before they had their first child. Both joined the pre-school group before the wife was pregnant, confident of the coming steps: 'Half of the people that went didn't have children. Now a few of them on the committee have got kiddies his age group, so at least we know them'. But they 'couldn't really belong' at the start, she explains, 'because we both worked. A lot of them were already home with their kiddies ... It makes a difference when some-body else has got a few children. You have your bonds, I think, then'. But children were not the only bonds. The im-portance of its being a new and 'young' area is repeatedly stressed: 'You're all striving for the same thing'.

Gary and his wife came expecting to make friends, but did

not find it easy. She says: 'I had to start doing gardens'. Committee friendships never developed: 'I think we probably get on better with the neighbours'. They still have more friends outside Green Views and regard those friendships as closer and more sociable *because* they are outside. Both are very sure that neighbours can be *too* close. Like Jane and Grace, Gary's wife is at home and enjoys occasional social contact, but limits it by strong beliefs about neighbouring danger. His goal is 'knowing the people and having a fair degree of friendship, and knowing you can get a bit of help here and a bit of help there, and vice-versa, is all that's required from your neighbours. I don't think you really have to get into the stage where you're over-friendly'.

The triers

The triers are people most likely to nominate neighbours as those they know best in the estate, but least likely to have social friendships there, and also least likely to expect very much help from neighbours. Into this type are dealt 20 people linked by factors that suggest they were unlucky. Of all types they are least likely to be the same nationality or to 'live the same way' as those they name. But they tried to establish local relationships. They rarely say they 'prefer to keep our distance'. Being near, it would seem, for them means seeing contacts frequently (but not to talk personally), swapping local news, sharing child-minding but (perhaps *because* they are near?) avoiding personal things. The neighbours they name have little in common with them: few have children the same age. But they came at the same time. These people are more likely than those in any of the other types to name as 'known best' in 1981 the same four people as in 1978. Class matters here. Over half the males are in blue-collar jobs and over half *call* themselves 'working-class'. Gender also matters—the majority are men, and nine of the 20 wives are in the workforce, six of them full-time. And the type has the highest proportion of migrants— mostly European—with more than half the households having one or both spouses born overseas.

They are joiners: eight of those dealt into this type are group members. Generally they have kin close by, but not friends. Most found it was not easy to get to know people, but said it was important. Lonelier now than when they first came, they expect little help from neighbours. They sound dis-illusioned. Many plan to move within two years and say they would not buy here again; it was not a 'better way of life'. A third say their expectations were not met, and a quarter have had regrets; they are likely to call it 'lonely' and 'boring'. Three actually say they were happier before they moved. More than any other type, this one suggests there are several paths to a style of local relationships. An upwardly mobile migrant couple 'moving up' to Green Views might fit the pattern, as might an Australian-born couple lacking the young children who apparently facilitate friendship and finding that their neighbours in this new smart estate are migrants with whom they might share equipment but would hardly talk about personal things.

One such resident is Bill, self-employed, his children in their teens. His commitment to Green Views is almost entirely for the house. He is very aware of class: 'People I've met in Green Views are employed, certainly, but some are more managerial or self-employed or a better job in industries or better pos-itions—not professional perhaps but commercially employed people rather than people who are just pick and shovel workers'. Like Cathy he is sharply aware of ethnic differences: 'We must accept migrants as our whole life-style really. Because it's our government that brings them in'. But acceptance does not mean friendship: 'You know, I've got one neighbour here who's a migrant and we always exchange a bright word when we see each other, but we don't sort of come running in to each other at all ... We don't seem to have neighbours who are always in and out of the place really'. But they are happy: 'We know the people about us. We know our neighbours—not well, but we know our neighbour to talk to'. For the 'most neighbourly' thing anyone has done for them, he offers: 'The neighbour next door has offered to look after the dog when we've been away, if I want it. Nothing much more than that'. And his most neighbourly act? There is a sense that he feels he gives more than he gets: 'I helped him put his lawn in. I got all the neighbours involved in that one-tonne truck for rubbish collection because of the strike. I've taken all their rubbish down to the tip'.

A good friend would be quite different, and he feels he has many where they last lived. Those are social friendships, de-fined in terms of leisure and sympathy: 'Oh, I think somebody, you can enjoy their company, really. Somebody who you can relax with ... and you can go and cry on their shoulder'. Their social life is entirely outside the estate, involved in older kin and past networks: 'We always say we've stuck to our circle'. Both are working: 'We don't have a lot of time to entertain; we don't get that exchange of entertainment'. Elderly parents take up weekends. Like Gary, at the other end of the life cycle, he recognizes that young children would facilitate closer relationships. The teenagers 'are sticking to the groups they knew before they came to Green Views'.

The picture is of a man who just lives there. Yet he was one of the most active in the early groups, and the disappointment perhaps is related to that experience: 'I think of some of the marvellous things we did. We pushed some things forward. And I did ask a question in Council, one night'. But he dropped out of the group because of 'personality conflict', feeling he had met a cross-section of local people but having close relationships with none: 'Most of us had a certain amount of community effort, which was the only thing in common with us. We were all from different walks of life'.

The distance keepers

The most consistent and apparently straightforward of the types, the distance keepers seem, on the surface, to epitomize the popularly pictured evils of suburbia. The 22 people allocated to the type effectively have no local friendships. They know neighbours best, have little to do with them and little in common. While it must be quite hard *not* to see your neighbours more than once a week, less than a third see any contacts that often. Some people know each other but few mix socially, and they do little else for each other but watch each other's houses. Even though they live near to those they know best, hardly any lend equipment and most only 'exchange greetings' rather than talking. With only five of the 88 contacts do they talk about personal things. This is the only type in which many agree with that most 'un-neighbourly' statement: 'we prefer to keep our distance'. There is no clear demographic identifier. This is the only type different from the sample on religion, with a high proportion of Catholics. Few call themselves 'working-class', though two-fifths of the husbands are in blue-collar jobs. They are mainly first home owners. There are more women than men and most women are at home.

This type epitomizes default relationships. In the absence of any other local interaction, they know best those who live nearby but with whom they have little in common. Both opportunity and choice look circumscribed. More than any type, this one raises questions about loneliness and autonomy, and the processes of avoiding or terminating local relationships. But these people are not stereotypical isolated suburbanites. They are the *most* likely to expect assistance from some source in all crises. Only one respondent expected no aid from any of the three sources in any crisis. They are not surrounded by kin; they have the lowest levels of contact with parents; less than a third see the husband's parents weekly, and many parents are overseas. They are also not friendless, but *all* of them say that all or most of their friends are outside the estate (two saying they have no friends) and few have found those friends dwindling since the move. No other type shows such strong independence of local relationships. Most say it was *not* important to get to know local people. For most, no one in Green Views would know their troubles, which is hardly surprising since only two have their best friend there.

They seem to have asked little of the estate and seem not to be committed to it. A third may move in two years and over half say they are not attached to the neighbourhood. They care about privacy and are most likely to agree strongly that owning their home is important. One of this group is Keith, the man who described his love for his home as 'like a cockroach'. He went on to explain what his work means: 'I live in motels—not a lot, but a fair bit—and I certainly don't like that sort of thing. I couldn't live by myself'. He prefers to be at home and private: 'I don't have friends and I don't go out at all virtually. I haven't been out for six or eight months. I've been for maybe two drinks on the way home from work, and then straight home'.

Yet he has been a highly active group participant. Like Bill he has *met* many people as a result but established friendships with none. People 'pass through' his community efforts—'some people go and some people come and so on'—but relationships are deliberately kept superficial: 'I can say hello to anyone in the street as I walk down to the shop or whatever, and they'll always say hello back and maybe exchange a word or two. That's as far as it goes really'. He is more 'involved' now than before, but not committed to staying at the estate (they do move, a year after this interview, to a higher status area further 'out'). He is sharply aware of the socio-economic status and image of Green Views (he and his wife are both professionally trained) and much of his group activity is to combat what he sees as local social problems. They do not have teenagers, but he spends one night a week in the (fairly thankless) task of organizing and running the controversial Youth Club. Like Bill and Cathy he shows a sharp consciousness of the class of residents: 'I don't really have plans of staying here for ever and a day. I don't really think, if I moved out tomorrow, I'd cry over it'. But this is a rejection of roots, not of Green Views: 'I mean, when I say that I don't know that I belong here, I don't know that I belong anywhere.'

They found it fairly easy to get to know people, and his wife organizes social occasions: 'We've had a couple of parties here, getting on towards Christmas time and so on, where we've gone round and invited all the people in the street, just to sort of have a bit of a get-together because we are living in the same place, and to try and create a bit of community friendliness and so on'. But it is not a friendly court he says: 'Over the last year or so, it's sort of gone off ... There's a lot of people aren't here a lot of the time; they're working or whatever, or they go away on the weekend'. How do such relationships 'go off'? Keith regards it as a woman's problem, and the contacts they do have are his wife's business: 'Apparently, at one stage, there were a few problems with a few of the ladies, between themselves. You know, sorry, but as ladies sometimes are, they seem to get their claws out for one reason or another'.

She would say she has many local friends, he insists he has none. And (like Jane and Cathy) he is sure isolation is a question of personality: 'I've got a lot of acquaintances, but I haven't got any real friends—no one I can go and tell my troubles to or go out on the grog with one night'. 'Real friends' are defined very clearly: 'Someone you can trust, someone you can talk to, someone you can go out with, without worrying too much about them making a fool of you or you making a fool of them'. He is very sure such friendships do not belong in neighbour relations. You have to be able to 'live your completely separate lives'. A good neighbour is:

'One that doesn't bother you. That'll come to you if they want help, but if you want help, they're available too. Maybe that you can borrow from or lend to and have in once in a while, maybe over the summer, for a barbecue or whatever, but isn't on your doorstep all the time'.

Nobody's close to a neighbour

There are no simple stories in this material. The variety of local lives reflects the interaction of life stage, gender and class, not the effect of any factor singly, and ethnic origin is clearly relevant. Much less obviously relevant is the factor widely blamed for suburban loneliness. There is little indication that people are deprived of sought friendships by their own workforce participation or that of the woman next door. Across the whole sample, where the woman was in full-time work, the respondents, men and women, were slightly *more* likely to have local relationships that involved talking about personal things than if the woman was at home. If she worked part-time it was much more likely. Women's workforce participation had no relationship to having friends in common or talking about local news; indeed its only clear relationship was with minding children!

But the variety of local lives is set in a common framework of understanding about local relations that seems unaffected by the dividers. The strongest message is that neighbour relations normally are not close. Those who have close relations find them elsewhere, those who know their near neighbours best know them very little. In each of the different types a good neighbour is at a distance, 'not one that pops in every five seconds', in Grace's words, not 'on your doorstep all the time', in Keith's. Jane's husband combined the two: their goal was 'not to have too many people sitting in your house or on your doorstep'. Like the ideas of family and home, and obviously related to them, common ideas of local relationships stretch across varied behaviour.

Notes

1. This was partly because the more obvious causes of complaint—no phones, no shops—had been dealt with at last. There were as many complaints in 1981, but the theme of isolation emerged as facilities arrived. For a review of the literature see M. Simms, 'The politics of women and cities: A critical survey', in J. Halligan & C. Paris (eds), *Australian Urban Politics: Critical Perspectives*, Longman Cheshire, Melbourne, 1984, pp. 129–40.

2. See Fay Gale, 'Seeing women in the landscape: Alternative views of the world around us', in J. Goodnow & C. Pateman (eds), *Women, Social Science and Public Policy*, Allen & Unwin, Sydney, 1985. For a summary of recent research see Women and Geography Study Group, *Geography and Gender: An Introduction to Feminist Geography*, Hutchinson, London, 1984, ch. 5.

3. Forty-one per cent said they would use it every day, 69 per cent that they would use it often.

4. For a strong analysis of the effects of class, see C. Allport, 'Women and suburban housing: Postwar planning in Sydney, 1943–61', in J. B. McLoughlin & M. Huxley (eds), *Urban Planning in Australia: Critical Readings*, Longman Cheshire, Melbourne, 1986, ch. 15.

5. Frequency of visiting husband's and wife's parents before and after the move to Green Views (per cent of 1981 sample):

	HIS			HERS		
	Then		*Now*	*Then*		*Now*
Daily	14	} 45	{ 8	17	} 48 49	{ 11
Weekly	31		{ 37	31		{ 38
Monthly	13		12	12		12
At least yearly	16		18	16		18
Never	26		25	24		21
	100		100	100		100

6. Fifty-nine per cent of households in which both husband and wife were Australian-born had at least weekly contact with the parents on one side, as opposed to 54 per cent of those where one spouse was overseas-born. But whereas 27 per cent of the latter households had no contact with parents on either side, this was true of only 4 per cent of households in which both were Australian-born.

7. In 9 cases, his parents had since moved to Green Views or closer; in 5 cases hers had; and 4 of those leaving the estate were moving to get closer to parents (in each case hers) so that they could help care for them.

8. A substantial earlier literature on kin relations is summarized in recent reviews by G. Lee, 'Kinship in the seventies: A decade review of research and theory', *Journal of Marriage and the Family*, vol. 42, November 1980, pp. 923−34. On the relation of distance to contact see G. K. Leigh, 'Kinship interaction over the family life span', *Journal of Marriage and the Family*, vol. 44, February 1982, pp. 187−208.

9. In 21 of the sample households the wife worked and there was a pre-school child. Care was provided as follows: by the child's parent at home or work in (5); other kin (5); local friend (4); other childminder (5); in a creche (2). In 33 households an employed mother had a school-age child and in 17 cases there was no arrangement for after-school care. In the other cases children were with: their parents (6); kin (3); friend (4); unspecified others (2); a child-minder (1). Payment for care was made for only 16 children.

10. Of the 74 families in which the wife was at home, 14 expected relatives to mind pre-school children if the mother went out in the daytime, 32 if she was sick, 39 if they were out socially at night.

11. Thus status and family stage contribute to remaking women's space. See S. Ardener,'Ground rules and social maps for women', in S. Ardener (ed.), *Women and Space*, Croom Helm, London, 1981; and Matrix Book Group, *Making Space: Women in the Man-Made Environment*, Pluto Press, London, 1984.

12. The same theme emerges in David Hickman's current study of a further-out Melbourne suburb.

13. The classic examination of the argument that suburbia is the result of some pre-existing neighbourly instinct or personality is the book by H. Gans, *The Levittowners*, Vintage Books, New York, 1967; there too the patterns were very similar.

14. Comparisons of data collected from different questions in different decades are risky. See R. Wild *Australian Community Studies and Beyond*, Allen & Unwin, Sydney, 1981, on studies of Australian group membership; P. Berger, *Working Class Suburbs*, University of California Press, Berkeley, Calif., 1960, and Gans, *The Levittowners*, discuss the group membership in American suburbia.

15. In 11 per cent the member was the wife, 5 per cent the husband, 16 per cent both, 12 per cent the children, 8 per cent all of them, 3 per cent wife and children, and 3 per cent husband and children.

16. Seventy per cent said this compared with 55 per cent of the families where both spouses were Australian-born.

17. None of the 'empty nest' respondents, and only three of the young childless, had best friends at Green Views, compared with about a fifth in each group with children.

18. C. S. Fischer & S. J. Oliker, 'Friendship, sex and the life cycle', *Working Paper No. 318*, Institute of Urban and Regional De-

velopment, University of California, Berkeley, Calif., 1980 suggest that differences in men's and women's friendships show strongly in some life-cycle stages when there are great differences in opportunities and constraints. Their data on extra-local friendships show young fathers having far more work and outside friendships than young mothers. See also A. Steuve & K. Gerson, 'Personal relations across the life-cycle', in C. S. Fischer *et al.*, *Networks and Places: Social Relations in the Urban Setting*, Free Press, New York, 1977, pp. 79–98, esp. p. 80, for the more general argument that 'people constantly construct and reconstruct their social networks as they move through the life cycle'.

19. E. Litwak & J. Szelenyi, 'Primary group structures and their functions: Kin, neighbours and friends', *American Sociological Review*, vol. 34, no. 4, 1969, pp. 468–81.

20. The figure for our sample would have been higher had childless couples not been excluded for comparability with the American sample. Details of the analysis and the very severe qualifications to interpretation of these data are given in L. Richards, 'Families in a suburb: Network management and its varied results', *La Trobe Working Papers in Sociology*, no. 64, 1983, La Trobe University, Bundoora, Vic.; and L. Richards & J. Salmon, 'There when you need them? Family life stage and social network', *La Trobe Working Papers in sociology*, no. 68, 1984, La Trobe University, Bundoora, Vic.

21. Thirty-two per cent expected 'very much' help from neighbours if the emergency lasted a week, only 22 per cent expected it when it lasted three months. The American data showed a higher proportion—32 per cent—expecting 'very much' from neighbours in a three-month crisis—hardly indicating irrelevance of neighbours. For that crisis, again as Litwak & Szelenyi predicted (*American Sociological Review*, pp. 468–81), it was more common to expect 'very much' help from kin (in Green Views 74 per cent, compared with 73 per cent in the United States).

22. C. S. Fischer, *To Dwell Among Friends: Personal Networks in Town and City*, University of Chicago Press, Chicago, 1982, ch. 11. See also S. H. Croog, *et. al.*, 'Help patterns in severe illnesses', *Journal of Marriage and Family*, vol. 34, no. 1, 1972, pp. 32–41. J. McCaughey shows similar patterns in her case studies, *A Bit of A Struggle*, Longman, Melbourne, 1987.

23. Unlike the original study we recorded the wording of responses to the opening question about each emergency, so we know if specific people were named and if the language indicated assumptions about them.

24. M. Stivens, 'Women and their kin: Kin, class and solidarity in a middle-class suburb of Sydney, Australia', in P. Caplan & J. M. Bujra, *Women United, Women Divided*, Tavistock, London, 1978,

p. 180.

25. Faced with an hour-long emergency, 87 per cent of couples with only pre-school-age children expected very much help, compared with 75 per cent of those with pre-school and school-age children, 61 per cent of those with only school-age children, and 65 per cent of the childless. When crises were longer, the life-stage shape of this curve remained but it was much lower—only 37 per cent of the pre-schooler parents expected very much neighbour aid for a week, only 21 per cent for three months. For details of the analysis see Richards & Salmon, 'There when you need them?'.

26. Richards & Salmon, 'There when you need them?'.

27. The analysis was done with CLUSTAN. For more detailed exploration of the types see L. Richards, 'Shapes in suburbia: Towards a typology of local relationships', *La Trobe Working Papers in Sociology*, no. 67, 1983, La Trobe University, Bundoora, Vic. The items were as follows:

'We are near neighbours. We have kids the same age. We have kids at the same school. We belong to a group or church. We are the same age group. We have a hobby in common. We are the same nationality. Our husbands/wives know each other. We prefer to keep our distance. We exchange greetings but we don't really talk. We help each other with equipment etc. We mix as couples socially. We see each other daytime only. We tell each other jokes. We watch each other's houses. We are often in each other's houses. We talk about very personal things. We knew each other before we came here. We know each other through work. They live much the same way as we do. We respect each other's privacy. We have friends in common. We came here at about the same time. We would stay friends if one family moved away. We met through the children. We have very little in common. We see each other more than once a week. We are acquaintances, rather than friends. The wives do not work. Neither of us have children. They are renting their home'.

28. Of our sample of 150, only 105 named four people they know in Green Views. The remaining 45 cannot be assumed to be so isolated that they know less than four: while this was probably true of a few, in other cases unwillingness to nominate friends, current disputes with them or misinterpretation of the question applied.

10

Not in Your Pocket: The Ideological Backdrop

M: A good neighbour I would like to be friendly with, be able to have a talk to. Oh, perhaps socialize with them occasionally, in a family get-together. I wouldn't like to think I had a neighbour that was continually on my doorstep (I don't think we've got any like that) but someone you can rely on, if you needed help at any time, in case of an emergency or something. Someone that you can trust. People that are good people, I think, that's what you're after. Not sticky-beaks or anything like that.

There is no unanimous definition of a good neighbour at Green Views, but there are clearly two strong threads in the answers. Both in 1978 and in 1981 we asked 'What's your idea of a good neighbour?'[1] Like 'owning your home' and 'good family life', this question was easily answered. People produced instant definitions which sounded very similar. Partly, as in those other areas, this is because the same keywords turn up frequently. But partly it is because of a repeated pattern to answers; most contained two faces. Interviewer comments record our surprise as the split answers recurred (and our difficulties in coding them). 'How's this for a contradiction? She felt it was important to get to know people here— "Neighbours are the only people we do know *really*, but then we hate people who live in your yard". Perhaps I should have coded her differently?'.

Positive attitudes—getting along and helping—dominate (61 per cent of all answers).[2] Next in size (21 per cent) was a group of ambivalent answers combining helping with danger.

These were so commonly offered in the same words that we precoded specifically: 'There when you need them, but not in your pocket'. And finally a small proportion (18 per cent) were entirely negative responses in which a good neighbour was merely not a nuisance.[3]

As with the home ownership material, the number of answers matters, as does the priority given to them. People who gave positive pictures of good neighbours also gave more answers: 'Someone who's there if you need them. Not living in each other's home all the time. You can say hello to them when you go to the letter-box. You borrow a cup of sugar off. That sort of thing. Someone you don't see too much of'. As with home ownership, first responses proved different from later ones. On first response the most common category (37 per cent) was the ambivalent answer. Another 22 per cent gave straight negative responses. This left positive responses in a minority of first answers; most positive answers came in as second or third thoughts, almost like compulsory qualifications.[4] Like 'security' as a reason for home ownership, the two-sided answer seems to work as a ready-made one; if it is produced it is instant. It is also by far the most common single response, offered (as first, second or third answer) by more than half the respondents. And almost all the others balanced a positive and a negative response (or qualified the answer later). The two faces of neighbouring appear in the most reserved and the most antagonistic statements we collected and also in the warmest accounts of local friendship. The balance is expressed not as contradiction but as two faces of the same person.

The same two faces are there in each of the different settings explored in Britain by Abrams. There, too, quotations show a range: some only positive, a few only negative, the majority two-faced. But across this range there is what he called in one setting a 'standard' definition, indicating a 'balance between involvement and distance', 'someone who was there when you needed them but didn't sit around your house all day'.[5] So the two-sided idea of neighbouring, pervasive and 'instant', is possibly, like ideas of home ownership, cross-national. It is also *like* the reasons for home ownership, but *unlike* neighbouring behaviour, extraordinarily uniform across class, life stage and gender.

Life stage, most obvious patterner of neighbour behaviour, is not statistically associated with these answers; each sort of definition occurred in all life stages, and all tended to combine positive and negative aspects. But the life-stage groups did sound different. The young childless were most likely to talk first about helping; they were, after all, unlikely to be at home and if home would be less harassed. Older couples without children at home emphasized 'not a nuisance'; they were less likely to need equipment-lending and more likely to want to avoid problems: 'I've just never gone out of my way. Like, I sort of just know my neighbours' names and that's all. I don't even know the neighbour next door's name. I don't know a thing that's going on around the place'. 'There when you need them but not in your pocket' was most often offered by couples with dependent children, most likely to feel the contradictions, since they were more in need of neighbour contact and more vulnerable to its intrusion.

Self-assessed class showed no patterns; the same phrases occurred in all groups. Intriguingly, ethnic background did show patterns. Those who were born overseas, or whose spouse was, were less likely to stress ability to 'depend on' or 'get along with' neighbours, more likely to talk of occasional help. But they were no more or less likely to give the two-sided definition. The difference between 'his' good neighbour and 'hers' I discuss at the end of the chapter.

Being neighbourly

Turn from values to actions and there are clearer patterns. A strong statistical association appears between life stage and answers to 'What is the most neighbourly thing someone's done for you since you've lived here?'. The association again reflects the difference between young couples without children (whose answers are about expressions of friendship, lending equipment or helping outside) and those with dependent children (much more likely to mention help that is inside the house—with children or in family illness). Obviously, if people do not have children they cannot be helped with them. Less obviously, the most neighbourly experiences of the childless were less privacy-invading and, we might guess, less needed; they were also more likely to be couple experiences rather than favours done for the woman. That the needs of the recipient dominate neighbouring behaviour is underlined by the fact that the most neighbourly things people had done were not significantly related to their own life stage. (You can't help with children if they don't have children.)[6]

Five features of the answers emphasize their ambivalence. First, there is a great deal of neighbouring! People normally both expected and received some assistance from neighbours. Only seven people could either think of no 'neighbourly thing' done for them or nominated that 'they kept to themselves'. All of these were in the two older groups, with children at school or not living at home. Only four people (all older) could think of nothing neighbourly they had done. But the things they thought of were often impressive.

Secondly, these 'neighbourly things' were normally defined as 'little things'. They ranged from contributions like 'bringing in the washing when it's dry because there's a storm coming, particularly when you have a line full of nappies' to major aid in an emergency. A man offered 'brought rubbish bins in to prevent them from being blown away', and his wife put in, 'picked up your mail when you're not at home. Helped you with the shed'. 'No spectacular thing', he said, 'but when it's been seen as necessary, they've done it, and we've done something similar for them'.

Thirdly, most acts cited as '*most* neighbourly' had been either during moving-in or in an emergency. In both contexts they were seen as once-off, context-specific events. 'Hot water and just those neighbourly things—they'd been in a month or so and we didn't have power on, so there's a power lead came across'. We heard no story where neighbours were needed but had not helped: 'One of the neighbours had a bit of an emergency and I just went over and said, "Look, bring the kids over here; I'll watch the kids for you". One of her sons had split his head open. So my husband took her to the doctor's and I took the kids over here'.

This raises a fourth feature of these answers. Especially where there was a common family life stage with young children, such emergency aid was regarded as available almost by right, and that phrase 'without being asked' turned up often, as did 'what anyone would do'. 'They've been good in a few sort of little emergencies', said one man. He added after a pause, 'But it's things that a good neighbour would do anyhow, I would think'.

Fifthly, these often substantial favours were regarded as obviously consistent with a distancing definition of a good neighbour. There are no apparent problems with this bundle of contrasting requirements. A woman who produced, unfinished, the taken for granted two-faced definition went on to illustrate it with considerable aid expected in a family crisis: 'One who doesn't want to live in your pocket, but someone who's there. I mean, we've had examples the last couple of weeks. She was ready to drop everything if you need help, which we did'.

Noting the same contrast between values and action (as a neighbour settled down for a cup of tea with the respondent who had just said she hated such behaviour) Abrams asked: 'Are people under some sort of social pressure to deny that they are effectively attached to and involved with others?'.[7] We found too that people would criticize dropping-in neighbours in the presence of ones who had dropped in. But they did not deny attachment; rather they indicated the ability to negotiate exemptions within the context of knowledge of their dangers. A long informal interview with a woman about to leave Green Views was conducted, at her insistence, in the presence of (and often by!) her neighbour-friend who had dropped in. Both emphatically asserted that neighbouring must be controlled. The respondent's relationships, 'apart from' the visiting friend, were cheerfully described: 'Oh, I say hello to a couple of the other neighbours, but that's all really...I'm not a person that makes a lot of friends. As long as I just know one person in the area I'm happy'. Her visitor declared herself 'much the same', and 'quite happy' with her neighbours: 'They keep to themself and we keep to ours. I don't like people to get too involved with neighbours because you don't want them living in your house and you're practically living in theirs. I like friendliness, you know. How often do we come into each other's houses? Very rarely'. But within these restrictions each had set up a 'one person' exemption that meant they talked daily, went to things together, confided regularly.

A young couple agreed firmly on distancing definitions. His 'good neighbour' was 'There when needed, at their place'. She interjected, 'Don't mind your business'. He added 'trust', then, more cynically, 'Someone you know you can leave the door open and say "go in and help yourself" and still find your television set when you come back from the other room'. But neighbourly things? He said, 'The exchange of children, looking after children', and she: 'Keeping them company. Like the girl across the road, her husband has to go away nearly every week; he's away for two or three nights. So I often go over there, right after she's put the kids to bed'. Whereas the good neighbour definitions are about location—being *there* but not *here*—the stories about neighbourly things are about the ways people work within those definitions.

If the 'good neighbour' has a symbol it is house-watching. The single act most commonly nominated for 'the most neighbourly thing' done for respondents was 'They watched our house while we were away' (25 of the sample of 150) and it was even more commonly given (by 35) as the most neighbourly thing they had done. House-watching is often cited as evidence of local support networks, but I would argue rather that it shows their constraints. It is the ideologically proper neighbour relation. Both halves of the dominant definition are represented. You need a neighbour when you are away; the neighbours can do it because they are there; to help they need not be in your home, let alone pocket. When friendships were not close, it took on considerable significance, symbolizing common values, agreement on the privacy of home, trust with property and information. And reciprocity: to return the favour exactly involves none of the messy arrangements required to repay child-care or assistance with tasks. A woman described her previous 'ideal, ideal' neighbour as 'When we'd go away on holidays, they would notice, and they would offer to come in'. Interaction, ideally, was 'To go in there and have a barbecue lunch occasionally'. (Barbecues appear as the next step from house-watching. The two share the valued features of not requiring going into the home and being easily reciprocated.)

House-watching can become a more intimate interaction, given trust that privacy will not be invaded. But intriguingly such relationships are mostly in the past, like examples of really good mothers.[8] When they were reported they were within a distancing definition. A fine example of controlled access was given by one woman. In a previous location, they had exchanged keys with a neighbour, in case 'one was away and wanted the hot water switched on before they came home'. Meanwhile, they would 'nip in and water the plants' and take mail inside. But the keys were never used when the neighbours were there, and her 'good neighbour' was not 'in and out every day and must know everything that's going on'.

Once the immediate and easily reciprocated assistance with

'getting set up' was over, house-watching became the only common reciprocal act reported between neighbours apart from child-minding. For those who did not have young children it was the currency of neighbouring. A childless professional woman found the idea of 'being a neighbour with someone dropping in all the time for cups of tea or coffee rather obnoxious'. Her husband defined a good neighbour as 'one that minds his own business'. The most neighbourly thing done for them was by a neighbour who 'looked after the house and fed the dogs and cat for us'; their own most neighbourly act was 'virtually the same thing only they didn't have any dogs or cats, so we just kept an eye on their home'.

Can neighbours be friends?

Friends are different. This is highlighted by the tone of surprise when neighbours are described as friends: 'Although he's a neighbour, you could still class him as a friend'. But the difference is awkward to manage; people often felt they should not be making such distinctions, and should not exclude the possibility of negotiating neighbour friendships. We asked 'Can neighbours be good friends?'. Just over half said yes, and only ll per cent gave a flat no. The rest qualified 'yes' with 'possibly' or with conditions like those on 'belonging' discussed in chapters 3 and 4—similar standards, background, age or interests. A woman who said yes added later, 'Sometimes, if they don't live in each other's hair'. This is another body of unpatterned data. Neither class nor life stage affected answers. They were also unrelated to the pattern of 'most neighbourly' acts done for respondents, confirming the impression that needs and opportunities, strongly life stage related, operate beneath general notions of neighbourliness.

Everyone puts stringent requirements on neighbour friends, requirements made neither of a good neighbour nor of a friend. Neighbours should be friendly but are rarely real friends.[9] Friendliness is a simple scale; people make distinctions such as 'friendly but not too friendly'. Terms such as 'real friends' and 'close friends' indicate discrete categories of friendship, and the distinction between being 'friendly' and 'friends' occurs often in the context of neighbouring; the goal was 'not becoming close personal friends', but being friendly. 'Friendly' can mean 'there if needed': 'I don't go out to make friends with a whole lot of people. I sort of do my own thing and I think there's a lot of other people that do the same thing. I could live in this court for four years and very rarely go into anyone else's house. Although I'm friendly with all of them. I could go to any of them, but I don't'.

The exceptions all fall into one of three categories, and each has strict limits to growth. The first is intimate and highly supportive friendships between women 'stuck at home', the second friendships between those involved in the action groups. These are discussed in chapters 11 and 12. The third exception is couple friendships within courts or near-neighbour groups. There were many such cases in our sample area, and they nicely illustrate the distinction between 'friendly' and 'real friends'. This is not to belittle the warmth and pleasure found in these relations. A woman who described her neighbours as 'great', 'terrific neighbours' said: 'We have a lot of parties and all that sort of thing, just in the court. We all get together. And the people over the road from us are moving, but they've bought the block of land that's vacant in the court, and they're going to build on that. They didn't want to move away'. Four other courts held regular social events (usually at the end of the year). One had a social club, begun when a man invited all the ten court families to his birthday. They now collected weekly contributions ($3 a couple) and went out together three or four times a year. The man who was treasurer of this social club said, 'We just go to different places and have a big whale of a time ... it's like the bush'.

The rural community ideal! But it was qualified. Like most street sociability, this was outside the home. A resident of one of the socially organized courts said a good neighbour 'respects your privacy; someone you can have a bit of a yarn to, will keep an eye on your house. It has to be reciprocal. Important to say hello, but we never invite them in for a meal or anything like that'. When social interaction reached inside it was almost always preferred that this be infrequent or restricted to one or two friendships. A woman listed her visiting patterns, pointing to each house in the court (and, intriguingly, identifying the houses she visited as the woman's home): 'I go to hers for about four cups of coffee a day; I've had a few cups of coffee in the few years over at *hers*; I haven't been to theirs—but we'll stand outside for hours and talk in the summer'.

Good neighbours and good friends differ across all these

ideas, in five respects. None are stressed more by people in one class situation, but all are about negotiating inequality. First, as several studies have shown,[10] friendship is about choice and, as many people repeated, 'you can pick your friends but you can't pick your neighbours'. This made 'picked' neighbours very special. In a handful of cases close friends had moved together and the friendship had been solidified by knowledge previously built up and also perhaps by the pleasures of reducing the risk of the wrong neighbours. Vulnerability to undesirable arrivals next door was a common theme.

Secondly, friendship is largely, neighbouring only slightly, about communication. Definitions of a good friend were dominated by answers coded as 'talk, share confidences'—76 in all, mostly first and second answers. But a good neighbour is much more about *not* knowing. In all those definitions of good neighbour the category of 'share confidences' rated only four, and even the non-invasive 'chat to, say hello' only 33. They need to know 'a little bit about your business and so forth, without knowing your personal life inside out'. Such excess of knowledge was associated with lower-class living: 'knowing too much of other people's business, like Coronation Street'.

Thirdly, friends too have to be 'there if you need them' but when said about friends this means that they care constantly. People do not want a neighbour, who is always physically there, to be always caring. They would not say of a friend, as one man did of a good neighbour: 'There when you need them. And probably not there when you don't need them!'. A young man whose family had faced difficult times recalled his own father warning him, 'You think you've got hundreds of friends...but the moment you get into trouble, or any sort of problem, you'll find out just how many friends you've got'. He concluded: 'I think we've got to *know* a lot more people in Green Views, getting into a situation where you've got hundreds of friends and very often, you've only got a few *friends*'.

Fourthly, neighbours have to have 'enough in common' to share the suburban life, including the commitment to privacy: 'Most of us around here are a very similar age. We socialize a bit together and that. I think sometimes you have to keep your distance, though...around here they understand...we don't sort of hang in each other's pockets'. Good neighbours can negotiate such relationships, which gloss over class and ethnic differences. So 'all in the same boat' sets the stage for good neighbouring. But it is not enough for friendship. A real friend, many said, has to have 'lots in common' with you. Friendship is 'a relationship between equals'.[11] Another put it: 'You need a lot in common, including ideas about children. Oh heavens, someone I can talk to, and someone who cares about *me* and knows I care about *them*. And to know that they're there if you're in trouble'.

This is the fifth tension between the two ideas. Friendship is personal, as Allan stresses, in three senses: it is a relationship between individuals, a private relationship and one involving the person 'as he [*sic*] really is'.[12] Ideally, neighbouring is a relationship between households, sometimes even between houses, involving people as presenters and defenders of a family life and life-style. So while it is sad to lose a friend, there is much more at stake if neighbouring goes wrong. You can't *lose* a neighbour.

The problem of control

Four years on there were few open disputes reported to us, but those that were remained unresolved and were gathering growing resentment. Two people were angry at constructions on their fence-line, several at dog owners who persistently failed to control dogs. Those who had appealed to local authorities were nervous about anonymity: 'I didn't mention any names, but anyway the bloke came out and went across the road and apparently said "Oh the neighbour across the road told me that your dog ripped all his garbage bags up". And he didn't like that'. No other means of formal conflict resolution was reported.

Informal control of neighbour nuisances rarely worked. Many instances were reported to us, few were resolved and all appeared cumulative (as in Mandy's court). There was always more than one complaint about a bad neighbour: those who made a noise *also* had old cars around or unfettered dogs. Perhaps they became defined as a nuisance only after more than one violation of standards? Perhaps the norms of neighbouring were so strong that only those impervious to their control violated them? Or perhaps issues (or evidence of lack of common values) that would otherwise be ignored are poured into the simmering cauldron of resentment once one problem has become troublesome? This is especially likely when much is at stake and people are frustrated by having no avenues for resolving conflicts.

Whatever the processes, such cumulative situations produced a concentrated solution perfect for the growth and social uses of stereotypes. The masked differences of class and ethnicity started to matter once the problems were simmering, were thrown in as extra garnish, and came to dominate the flavour of the stew. Mandy said she learned to say 'wog' only after their dog disappeared. Another woman located 'the Indians' as the cause of problems with water drainage. Stereotypes were reaffirmed even when those wielding them were unaffected by the anti-social behaviour: 'We had a young couple living round the corner that were only renting, and they were very hippy-like and they had wild parties and things like that. I just didn't think they suited the place. It's more of a young family area I think'. The woman objecting explained: 'It makes people tense. You're always ringing up and saying, "Will you turn the music down?"'. How frequent were the incidents? 'Oh a couple of times. But I didn't hear them very much round here, but I've got friends that lived right next door, it used to keep them awake.' This recitation is a reaffirmation of the importance of homogeneity. Such Awful Warnings work as a means of informal control, making sense of the sometimes absurd exaggerations of the dangers of having bad neighbours in one's house *all* the time and having *nothing* in common with them.[13]

Attempts to control neighbour nuisances were all frustrated by self-imposed limitations. All those who were offended felt they should not *have* to complain since standards of reasonable behaviour were self-evident and agreed. All saw it as a private problem, so none tried to work with other offended neighbours, even when they complained to each other, and none attempted to find mediating agencies. Grace objected to her neighbours doing 'things that I wouldn't do to them ... I wouldn't like to be smoking anybody's clothes out or building a barbecue to offend anybody on their fence'. She had protested once about the ash, and the neighbour said sorry and put out the fire, but it happened again: 'I don't think I should have to be at them. I mean, they know'. In several cases there was no way the offender could know they had offended! None used a mediator to tell them.[14]

All these simmering issues were about offending actions—noise, smoke, dogs. Controlling the neighbour 'in your pocket' or endangering privacy was far less of a problem—interesting, since these were the problems most widely dreaded. The few examples showed that the appeal to the ideological backdrop always works. In each case, dropping-in neighbours were successfully 'given the hint'. Not one person complained about a neighbour who had remained in their pockets. And the few snoops featuring in our material had been very easily controlled by appeal to common values: 'She started dobbing people in for building things without permits or trucks or cars left in the street or anything. Well now nobody'll have anything to do with her'.

Common values in the same boat

It is not only at Green Views that 'neighbour' means danger, and the danger is both to the private life of family and to social status. The same phrases recur in Australia, Britain and the United States. But whose values are these? Working-class life is supposed to be about belonging. Is the price of social mobility then destruction of community?

Research offers apparently incompatible answers—all old. Classic British studies of mobility from a working-class slum to a new housing estate claimed that 'traditional' community was lost; people found it hard to get to know others in the new estate and there was much more stress on privacy of the home.[15] Studies of 'affluent workers', on the other hand, found that unlike a middle-class sample, they did not keep neighbours at bay; neighbours often took the place of absent kin. The authors concluded the workers were 'neither guided by middle class norms nor aided by middle class social skills'.[16] In the United States Gans explained the 'blandness' of suburban life by 'the transition in which the lower middle class finds itself between the familial life of the working class and the cosmopolitanism of the upper middle class'.[17] The former happened on the street, the latter in meetings and parties; between them lay the private, home-centred life of suburbia.

From another direction, two decades later, feminist critiques of family have picked up the theme of the loss of warm, working-class community. Game and Pringle argue that the Australian working class is 'stuck with' the bourgeois private family dream, compelled to privacy and condemned to suburban isolation.[18] But are ideas of neighbour danger a bourgeois ideology? In each of her Australian samples, Martin found 'the conviction that relations with neighbours are always in danger of getting out of hand and must therefore be kept under continuous scrutiny'. The most caution was heard from the middle-class area, and with it that phrase—neighbours should 'not live in each other's pockets'.[19] Abrams' working-class respondents offered 'someone you could ask for help but didn't live in your pocket', but in each class setting he found people objected to 'popping in'.[20]

The Green Views data argue for a more complex interpretation. Common ideas of neighbour danger stretch across differences in behaviour that clearly matter in people's accounts. So to regard them as mass victims of ideology imposed from above is to ignore those accounts and to miss the variety of ways people work out relationships. The data on crises suggest that the more educated work within the same ideological frameworks but manage their neighbouring differently, tailoring it more closely to the needs of life stage, and being more able to negotiate exemptions that allow active neighbouring when children are young. Those with fewer resources are more ideologically constrained.

But there is no evidence that they have lost a 'community' ideal or that the pervasive ideas of the danger of neighbouring uniformly condemn them to isolation. Yes, all of those who had more interaction with neighbours before the move were in the older, more working-class groups. But there were only a few. Yes, there was a shift in definitions of good neighbours by the time of the reinterview, but it was very slight.[21] Across Green Views the ambivalent ideas of neighbouring predominated, and the accounts of the early years suggest that most people brought their 'knowledge' about neighbouring into the estate with them as knowingly and often as overtly as they brought the contents of the moving van. In all the thousands of words of text there is no sign that those ideas were either formed or substantially changed by their life in Green Views; they were simply *applied* to that life. Unlike people's furniture and curtains, their daily lives and their marriages, all of which were often very clearly altered, the assumptions about neighbouring seemed a constant background to transitions of residence and family life. There was also every reason to suppose (since these people did) that those values were widely supported across the society.

There are certainly messages here about social mobility, but they are not simply about conformity by those striving to arrive. Like the theme of 'the same boat', ideas of a good neighbour were about class. 'People like us' make good neighbours; people who are not 'like us' threaten the image of the area. A bad neighbour is not just the obverse of a good one, but is defined in terms of danger to common values about property maintenance, noise and invasion of privacy, and always illustrated by clearly lower-class behaviour. They 'hit the booze and smash windows' or drive 'screaming' cars, and such things 'make you think of it as a lowly type of suburb'. So these ideas divide and are used to control those who have not been 'successful'.

But like the ideas of 'belonging', these ideas have a real equalizing effect. Barriers to friendship can create good neighbours, so long as behaviour is not visibly lower-class. Migrants are therefore more acceptable than truck-drivers, or those who 'never do anything to the house' and 'drag the whole area down'. In this context the warm response to the migrants who 'don't matter' makes sense. 'I'm quite happy with my neighbours', said one woman. 'We say hello, good morning, nice day, and that's it. Mainly, possibly, because she can't speak Australian. Very nice, quiet people.' So the common values about privacy unify. They also point to a first answer to why loneliness, like class, proved so hard to find.

Space and time

The dangers are about spaces and time, confused in the accounts. In Green Views fences symbolize the ambivalence to 'community'. The family community has no front fences, a provision ensuring problems such as Mandy's with her toddlers. The front displays common values. But the paling fences behind are too tall to look over: 'You have to make your own privacy', said one woman, adding, 'You need high fences at the back!'. The small back area, and the house, are the only spaces available for the private world stressed in the dreams of family life.[22] Accounts of neighbouring problems are full of complaints at how close the houses are and allusions to moving 'out' to buy 'more land'. But the danger of neighbouring is not merely about space. Here, as in Abrams' data, 'physical proximity and distance mattered only if something is made of them.'[23] More often it is about autonomy, which requires controlled good relations. 'Dropping in' and demands for un-reciprocated assistance were linked illogically with unfriend-liness: 'A bad neighbour's always coming in saying "can you do this for me, can you do that for me?" and when you go and ask them, they say no. Someone unsociable. Like you walk out in the street and you look at them and you wave and say hello and they go "Grrr!" and stop inside the house'.

Metaphors make intrusion personal and offensive, referring to private spaces where neighbours should not be. Some are about invasion of the home: 'on your doorstep', 'living in your house' and 'knocking on your door', 'in your home' and 'your yard'. Others are more personal: 'in your hair' and 'your lap', 'under your feet' and 'living your life'. These phrases come easily, ready-made, so taken for granted that, like those offered about owning your home, they can be combined amusingly: 'Not in your pocket all the time, not in your lap'. 'Not in their pocket and them in ours'. Reciprocity is required even of these negatives: 'keep out of their hair and them out of mine'; 'don't spend all the day in your home or you in their home'. The language demands attention. What is it to be in somebody's pocket? Too close, always with them, belonging to them? The recurrence of phrases across countries and time is a strong indication of the resilience of the ideas they carry. The smart modern houses of Green Views have no doorsteps. Who has doorsteps now, or sits on them?

Who has the time? Many of these warnings are about not space but that more precious commodity, time. A man who had 'given the hint' to a neighbour who 'thought it was a great thing to be in and out of each other's houses constantly' explained: 'I like to talk to people; I like to have the odd social drink and the odd get-together, but not on a day-to-day basis ... We're too busy ourselves, trying to get ourselves established'. Being 'too busy' is often mentioned, its context usually the dilemma of dual income employment necessary for the private haven. So what appears as rejection of community turns out to be a theme I turn to in chapters 11 and 12: community was run by women, and the women are now not there. A woman who had taken four years to get to know neighbours explained: 'Everyone's so busy with just life in general. Mainly the working couples; see you've only got the weekends ... And probably just with life in general; it's just going so fast'.

The nostalgia here is not an uncomplicated regret for a slow life. Like the very similar nostalgia in ideas of mothering 'nowadays'[24] it is cheerfully linked with pleasure in the ability to control space, time and social life. If neighbours were friends 'you couldn't sort of invite someone else over because they might—they'd come in at the front door and make it six instead of four'. You also want to control information: 'you can get too knowing with one another'; 'you can be too close. You'd know too much about each other and it would be embarrassing'. A man stressed that talking was not really part of neighbouring: 'If something happens, we don't run over and tell them straight away'. Why not? 'Very little in common, I'd say.' His neighbours had embarrassed them by confiding problems with their marriage: 'We've copped a lot of the who's blaming who'.

If it is achieved, a comfortable relationship can be very stable: 'A person who will mind their own business and let you mind yours. A person who lives their own life and lets you live yours. And there again, will ask you for help in an emergency or you feel you can ask them'. The two-faced definition at its most perfect stands four-square: give and take, and both sides keep your distance. It will be easiest to balance when there is least going on. In these data, very clearly the most comfortable portraits of neighbouring are of uncommitted relationships based on knowledge of controlled segments of family life, and the exteriors of family homes. The result is by no means always isolation, but careful protection of a precious and precarious investment, not only in property but also in the private world of family. The link with upward mobility is unsurprising. The upwardly mobile are achieving the resources to make these investments while committed to the family forms—marriage, children and 'established' family life—that make the investments seem all-important and permanent. And since everyone agrees that neighbour relations are hard to control, those lacking the skills and time for privacy protection and conflict resolution will be more likely to protect their investments by isolation.

Whose community? Hers and his

Neighbouring, then, like home and family, is shaped by the power of ideology. Across the range of real behaviour, from total avoidance to intimate involvement, is stretched the web of assumptions about neighbourhood life in which the dominant notions of privacy and community are interlocked. They give that range a partly masking uniformity (rather as the ubiquitous jogging suit clads a variety of bodies, many ill-suited to jogging). And they pose no problems. Nobody commented on the contradiction between the 'community' ideal and the need to keep community off their doorstep. Those who were lonely never saw the requirement of privacy as the explanation. Within those assumptions, people did their best to create local relationships in terms of their needs and goals, their knowledge of where they were and expected to be chronologically and geographically. Those who had the skills would stretch the constraining social prescriptions—for now, for long enough to make local links sufficient to their needs.

But since women and men were committed in different ways to those goals of family life, it is reasonable to expect that this process of negotiation with ideology will be one in which gender is an important, perhaps the important, factor. If network management is compared to tending a garden, neighbouring is a sociological bonsai. And the principal gardeners will be women.

In the Green Views data gender is statistically associated with few measures of the sets of ideas about the meanings of home, images of the estate, choice of living environment, good family life. Women and men gave family or couple answers; this was *their* dream. And the same, it would seem, is true of ideas of neighbouring. Good neighbour definitions looked almost unaffected by gender. On first offerings, virtually no difference showed, with the exception of one statistically insignificant but intriguing feature. Women and men were equally likely to give both sorts of 'positive' definitions. But men gave fewer in the two-sided category and more straight 'negatives', as though it was easier for them simply to avoid neighbours. Otherwise, at least at this level, the picture was of common sets of ideas from women and men. Moreover, men's and women's definitions remained strikingly alike within each life stage category.

And people themselves sounded as though they saw neighbouring as unpatterned by gender. When we asked for definitions of good neighbours we expected them to describe a neighbour of their own sex; to check, we asked if the respondent was thinking of a woman or a man. To our surprise 85 per cent said 'both', and tapes recorded that most often they had said something like 'they're both the same'. Of course they knew that male and female neighbours did different things; women, for instance, were cited as the source of emergency aid. The answer was firmly telling us that whatever they did, the same rules of relevance applied. This was the case even when the definition offered was specifically about a male or female neighbouring pattern. A woman offered: 'One you can talk to, have a cup of coffee, but not live in each other's house'. Was she thinking of a woman neighbour or a man? 'No, they're both the same.' The few who said they were different were almost all women, and thinking of a woman, and were all among the handful who said neighbours could be good friends.

Couples always agreed on the general rules of neighbouring. In a massive body of data that contains plenty of evidence of marital disputes there is no episode where spouses argued about interpretations of neighbouring, and few where they seemed even to notice differences. Like the conversations about owning your own home, they seemed to access instant, acceptable answers presented as *their* response. When a spouse joins in an interview there is never dissension, and often no awareness that the other is inserting a different meaning:

M: I think a good neighbour is someone who's sociable, someone who's friendly, someone who'll give you a hand occasionally...

W: I'd say the same kind of thing, other than being there if you really needed them.

M: I'd say it's pretty much the same as a good friend, but a good friend is someone more—

W: That knows every little bit about you.

Can neighbours be good friends? They both say 'It wouldn't worry me'. He adds that it can be a problem, 'If you're really going to be really, really friendly with someone, they can be living on your doorstep all the time'. But the symmetry is less complete than it seems. He is talking, it appears, about *her* having someone on *their* doorstep. This exchange occurred half an hour earlier:

W: You don't want somebody in your pocket every minute.

M: That is where you can fall down, if you really got on well with someone—*really* well with someone. I mean if we lived up near Mary, you two'd be sitting on each other's doorstep every day of the week.

W: I wouldn't want to live that close to my girlfriend ...

M: And that, to me, drives you up the wall (laugh).

This is one of several cases where women's best-friend relationships are derided by their husbands, and we have no way of knowing how she responds to his dismissal of her friendship. Perhaps, as Martin guessed of the men in working-class Adelaide, the hostility is 'a ritualistic resolution of the tension between their domestic and his extra-familial roles'.[25] But certainly it is also ideological work, reaffirming the danger of *women's* neighbour friendships. They both feel her next-door relationships are ideal:

W: If I see the girl next door out the front, we'll always say hello and we'll talk; I go in there, say once every couple of weeks to see her and she'll come in here. I'll do something like make a cup of coffee and have a little bit of a talk. That's a friend. We're not in each other's pockets.

M: That's a good neighbour.

It proves to be women, not men, whose experiences cover the range of neighbouring behaviour from total avoidance to highly intimate friendship. Some women gave very distancing definitions of a good neighbour: 'A person who will mind their own business and let you mind yours. A person who lives their own life and lets you live yours'. At the other extreme, they stretched the same description of good neighbour over local links more immediately significant than kin, links that no man described: 'Just somebody to be there, and I think, sometimes, neighbours are more important than family really, because you have to live with your neighbours, so you don't make enemies. But they've got their lives, we've got ours and we all have a good time together, which is quite frequent'. Here 'we' refers to 'a family, I suppose. We're all married'. And 'being there' refers to family too, much more often for women. Asked about the most neighbourly thing she has done, this woman laughs: 'I suppose you could say minding children! Because that really does not sound much, but by Jove, if you want to go somewhere or something crops up—'. Reciprocity is crucial: 'It works both ways. You don't dwell on it, but you know it's there if it's needed'. It is her family that makes the relationship both essential and delicate: 'Because without them, like I say, where do you go? You don't make a habit of it. You don't use it. You don't abuse it. But it's there. And, like I say, we're all in the same boat'.

Women in the same boat: When neighbours are friends

Neighbour friendships are hard work but some women actively sought them, not merely as a default when other friends could not be found but as the desired support. As one woman explained: 'You don't get a friend in a short time'. The goal was 'someone you can talk to and have their confidence' and who was involved with you: 'It's no good having someone sitting there if you feel as though they're looking out the window'. No man, and few women, wanted such close neighbour friendships. The relationship is specifically a woman's, and specifically local: 'Woman, a woman friend. You've got to have someone, yes, and fairly close by'. It is also specifically about life stage, being home with children, and isolated from kin: 'I think a woman sort of understands if you're hassled about your kids and you've got no one to—'. No need to finish the sentence. 'Most women when we moved in here were from another part of the state or interstate—they had no Mum to leave the kids with while they whipped in to the doctors and we were all sort of—or a lot of us—in the same boat.' Not everyone who wants such friendship will find it. They need to locate another person prepared to risk violating the rules about neighbour relationships: 'It did take a while to sort of find that one person in the group that you could feel that you could ring them up at 10 o'clock and say, "Look, can I pop around?" or "How about popping around this afternoon?". And then it would perhaps end up telling them or having a talk about something that might be troubling you'.

Such a relationship will not become a couple friendship: 'You can talk to a woman about anything, but you can't talk to a man about anything can you?'. The men are irrelevant: 'Their husbands are in completely different work—work hasn't brought us together as friends'. They are also likely to be hostile: 'they just think you've got to cope ... Well, Val is supposed to cope, you know, she's the mother. "You're home all day long and you do it, girl." But I know what a problem it is for Val, and I think I try to help her. I've made her a couple of dresses for the kids. She's just someone, she'll ring me up if something's annoying her or she can't manage it and I'll do the same for her'.

A good neighbour? 'Well, she's got to be a friend, you know, someone you can feel you can go and ask them for a cup of sugar whether it be breakfast time—or someone [if] you were running late for school you would ring them up and say, "Look, I'm not going to be home at half past three, do you think you could just watch over her till I get there?" without feeling as though they're saying—someone you've got a bit of confidence in too, trust'. Is that different from having a friend? 'It's very hard, these questions, there is a very fine line, isn't there?'

His needs and hers

The backdrop of these relationships is the trust required for reciprocal child-care. Both women just quoted suggest, as men never do, that when there are young children, neighbours stand in for family. Both assume the context of homogeneity: 'all in the same boat'. Both emphasize that making links is work, and delicate work; there is a fine line. And both take the links very seriously: 'Without them, where do you go?'.

Men would never say such a thing. But men are talking of other needs, though only women seem to see that their needs are different. (Or perhaps only men see only their own needs?) The need for neighbours refers mainly to families, but for men this need is about the family home. For women, whether or not they are in paid work, it is about children, either directly (her responsibility for their nurturing and care) or indirectly (her need for company when young children keep her 'stuck at home'). So it is not surprising that the only people who show no difference between women's and men's ideas of neighbour needs are childless. Once they 'start a family' men's neighbour needs differ sharply from women's in several aspects.

First, women's neighbouring creates a women's sphere, especially (but not only) for those at home with the stresses of first-time motherhood and new needs for company, advice and reassurance. It is not a *separate* sphere, either in the sense that it contains *all* women or in the sense that it is impervious to the world beyond. As I shall show in chapter 11, some women loudly deride and actively avoid this world. Others assume that neighbouring belongs in the women's world, but not that all women seek it or that the constraints on neighbouring should be removed. Rather, their accounts suggest that those ideas are stretched further to allow more company, more advice and reciprocal aid by *some* women's negotiating a temporary easing of the regulations but never an exemption: 'I go over to her place, and she'd come over here, a couple of days. Things are pretty good, you know. It's just that particular thing that annoys me, when you get them at you all the time'. To this woman a good neighbour is 'one that leaves you alone and you're free to sort of say to yourself, "Oh, I'm not going to visit this house for a little while"'. It's a women's world in the sense that 'You never sort of see the menfolk through the day ... you very rarely see the husband'. But men exert power over and even control those women who enter that world.

Though there are men's styles and men's symbols of neighbouring, there is here no men's world of neighbours. When men speak of help it is almost always from men, but it is very much in the context of family weekends and family home tasks. Few men know male neighbours whose wives do not know their wives. So while her daytime neighbouring is often a closed world to him, his is very visible to her. Hers is thus much more vulnerable to misinterpretation through ignorance, and vulnerable anyway, to the low status accorded women's segregated activities.[26]

The second difference is related to this. Women's neighbouring needs will be seen as less legitimate than men's. His are very compatible with the expectations of home-owning bread-winners 'doing the garden' or 'doing things around the house'. Hers are expressed more as a need to get aid in, or even escape from, her duties of nurturing and family administration. But as I showed in chapter 7, a crucial theme in the ideology of family is that nurturing is natural to women. Much of what women 'need' from neighbours is incompatible with strong messages about motherhood. 'Val's supposed to cope, you know, she's the mother'. If coping 'represents the everyday face of ideology',[27] needing neighbours represents its violation. Women's coffee groups broke up in confusion when it was time for the men to come home. And those messages apply equally, or to an even greater extent, to women in paid work.[28]

Thirdly, in the proper path to family life his needs for neighbours will decrease; hers, at least for a while, will increase. The patterning of attitudes to local relationships makes sense in this context. Men who were childless or whose children were grown saw it as important to make local relationships; women were more likely to if they had young children. His practical aid in occasional tasks will become less frequent as they establish themselves. Her needs for company and emergency aid will be greatest at just this stage (when in the proper order of things they start a family). Given the package of ideas about family and time, she is likely to stay at home, so her need will continue to grow at least until she re-enters the workforce, unless work provides support networks or removes the need for them. Once again, women's employment appears not to be the rigid divider: 'A woman's generally at home more and needs company, I think, more than a male, who can make company at, say, work. I think company's very important, if they're there during the day. It doesn't mean, if they're at work, that they're not a good neighbour. It doesn't mean that they're in your house every minute of the day either, every day'.

Fourthly, men's neighbour needs are obviously practical and calculable; hence, compared with women's, much more predictable and controllable and if necessary, avoidable.[29] Ladders and trailers are rarely urgently needed and are available through other means. Women's needs are in unpredictable minor crises, usually requiring an instant response ('Without them, where do you go?'). Women often, men seldom, gave multiple examples for 'most neighbourly things': 'I've had meals sent in or he and the kids have been fed when I broke my arm and when I've had a lot of trouble with my back, it's nothing for her to bring in a casserole'. This woman's own neighbourly acts are as complex. 'I've brought washing in off the line, looked after kids after school when they've been running late—it's very hard to think. Well, like sometimes her car's been going in for a service, could I run her down to the garage?.. and you just do it'.

She highlights a fifth contrast. What men need from neighbours is quite explicitly placed in a different setting from women's needs, and those settings are ideologically loaded. Men's contacts are outside, public, casual, their requests for help are optional and the giving of help unintrusive and usually outside. They describe that stage of settling-in neighbouring as fairly unproblematic: 'You run into someone you know, on the street, and stand and say hello, and talk for a while, or if you need a bit of a hand, to be able to go next door and get someone to come in and give you a hand to move something and vice versa'. The very currency of contact is significant: men make the contact by 'sharing a few cans' 'out front'; women's coffee or tea involves going in when men are not there. The only reports of after-hours good-neighbouring between women that involve company are explicitly during their husbands' absence. When men do define good neighbours in terms of company, it is very occasional company, circumscribed by the insistence on outside settings limiting meetings to chance, even weather!

M: We've got beautiful neighbours at the back (I don't know their surname), great fun and they're really nice friendly people.

I: Do you sort of see them pretty regularly?

M: Oh yes—

W: Oh, no!

M: Well, when you say regularly, he and I are always over the fence talking, but during winter we never saw each other much—we saw each other a couple of weeks ago and he said, 'Oh, you're still alive!'. But it's too bloody cold to come outside; there's nothing to do outside like gardening.

W: We don't know them on a social level.

M: We haven't been out with them. Well, we know them on a social basis because they came into the barbecue and played darts and we got drunk together.

W: But only once.

Not in whose pocket? Gender and danger

The other side of the contrast is between women's and men's notions of danger. Given their different needs, neighbouring obviously poses dangers for women that it does not pose for men. Yet men, for whom the danger is less, were as insistent as women, and often much more aggressive, about the need for distance. Neither women nor men showed any awareness that the problem is not common to both. But the language is different, and the context very different.

Men seem far more concerned about social homogeneity and proof of common values, especially values about property. And there is a clear implication in many statements that his values determine neighbour interaction for the household: 'We don't kind of mix with neighbours', said a husband, explaining, 'You see I cannot stand living on people's doorsteps, and I won't have people living on mine'. A good neighbour is someone 'you can have a good laugh, have a beer with, have a few drinks and that you feel good to be around, you're relaxed; they sort of think like you and you know you've got something in common'. Other neighbours who 'get around looking dirty', he rejected: 'If they're like that, and I've got nothing in common, I don't wish to even talk to them. Not that I'm setting myself up as any better; it's just that I *know* what sort of people they will be, and I've found out that that sort of people usually live on each other's doorsteps. If you get to know them too well they want to come to your house all the time; you've got to go to their house all the time; they're always on your doorstep'.

There are no similar comments from women, and women are less likely to link bad neighbours with class. On the other hand, an intriguing facet of male neighbouring is that it allows the bypassing of class differences. While building a barbecue Keith was approached by 'what's his name', a neighbour with whom he had little in common except the same setting-up stage: 'He's a labourer, a builder's labourer, and he's good with his hands and so on. Quite a nice guy. He just came up to look how I was going and he finished up mixing the cement for me while I did the actual brick work. So that was quite a neighbourly thing—without being asked—quite friendly and quite good'. They have never shared a barbecue, nor has Keith returned assistance, but contact was made—outside— and acceptance won.

By contrast, a woman described their neighbours as 'good'; 'he's Italian, she's Australian and we always get on very well'. But all acts of assistance had been done by the Italian, a mechanic who had removed their rubbish in his truck and fixed their car: 'So they've done a few bits and pieces—him, not sort of her—but they're only still—you know . . . He's different again to what we are, but he's always there'. None of her own neighbourly acts are towards this couple, but she adds, 'I don't see that much of them; they're working'. Women, with their greater need for company, are also more likely to be constrained by class because their neighbouring exposes the house and the behaviour of children, child-rearing habits, and other crucial indicators of suburban status. Only women mentioned competitiveness between neighbours as a danger in interaction, and only women (not surprisingly) mentioned their own standards of decoration or cleanliness as a cause of anxiety when people dropped in. Mandy's comment about the Greeks 'spotlessing' their home fits with her own defiant refusal to fuss about the house, though she knows women who get up at five to clean theirs in case there are visitors.

Again, this is not a simple distinction between women's private worlds and men's public world. For men the danger of neighbours entering the house is about loss of their own private space. 'You're living in such a small area, you have to be—well, you don't *have* to be, but I like to have the privacy of my own home. I don't mind having people come in if they're invited, or if they want to drop around occasionally'. One man's neighbour 'got a bit much', 'popping in every second night' (the phrase belittles, since it almost always refers to women's neighbouring). He defined a good neighbour as 'Someone who's there when you need them—that's about it, besides the social bit' and later balked at the question 'Can neighbours be good friends?'. 'They can, but I wouldn't like it. Too close for comfort. If you had a row with them, it's uncomfortable. I may be social with them once a month, or once every three weeks. That's enough'. His justification for repelling the neighbour neatly presented an ideological package linking neighbouring to family and home: 'The place wasn't your own . . . I built this place for myself and my wife and not for neighbours to come in and out all the time'.

Men, far more likely to talk of 'my home', are also more likely to resist or deride relationships that involve entering the home, and to see privacy as protectable. But then men rarely have to deal with those situations, given the opportunities of meeting and the expectations of family life. Men have much more control over information about the segment of their lives visible here. Women and men talk of having to give 'hints'; only women show concern at the social results: 'It got to the point where I was virtually afraid of going out in my own backyard', said a woman whose neighbour was always 'up over the fence and, "Hello, what are you doing?"'. She anxiously justified her dislike of this: 'They were more or less living on our doorstep. I like to have friends where, when you see them occasionally, you enjoy seeing them. Not to be living in each other's lap. And I started getting very nasty at one stage and I think they got the hint'.

Women usually resisted initiating the process of control. In another case, the husband had insisted she do so: he 'got fed up' with the dogs barking next door. She saw it as her problem, but the costs of bad relations were also hers: 'I'd sooner not fight with anyone. You know, he might come in and do his block and I'd say, "Look, you're not home all day, and if ever there was an emergency, I'd need a neighbour"'. There are many other examples of women being cast as custodians of family privacy, and their dilemma of maintaining both the family's support and their own fine line between privacy and isolation. Another couple went over a much-rehearsed argument. He strained to 'have a go at' the neighbour, she protested: 'I have to sort of restrain him and say, "Well look, you don't want to cause trouble", 'cos he's always wanting to go over and say something about the dog, but it doesn't do any good. They just respond. So I say, "It's probably better just to ignore it and leave them alone"'.

These women's accounts of neighbouring show three different problems of privacy. All clearly relate to ideas of the private home: these are problems not faced by the women struggling for survival in the classic studies of women's networks discussed in chapter 8. All are troubles men do not face or find trivial, and few men even see them as problems for their wives. The first is about privacy of information, having someone 'knowing your business'; the second, the physical invasion of constant visits; the third, loss of control over your life and the threat of being 'used' in situations where reciprocity does not work. All are dodged much more easily at two stages on the family path—before children arrive (women are not there) and after they leave home (women do not need neighbours except for emergencies). And each is incompatible with women's need for neighbours.

Women who are at home during the day are much more likely to have neighbours either 'knowing their business' or trying to find out about it. Men use the phrase but in a different way: a good neighbour is someone who 'minds his own business' and knows just enough: 'They know a little bit about your business and so forth, without knowing your personal life inside out'.

The more personal phrases of physical invasion—'in your hair', 'in your lap'— are used more often by women, and men obviously suffer invasion of space much less. You can lend tools without even seeing each other: 'See, I've got a step-ladder, he hasn't. So I leave my step-ladder up against the side fence . . . if he needs the ladder or the wheelbarrow or the roller, all he has to do is jump the fence and come and get it, 'cos the dogs won't bite him'. Inability to extract oneself from compulsory sociability therefore was more often a woman's problem. One woman says that you want your neighbours to know you but 'not what goes on in your bedroom'. Women's need for 'casual' dropping in is symbolized by the cup of coffee, men's ability to control physical intrusion is symbolized by the barbecue. His good neighbour is: 'One that doesn't bother you. That'll come to you if they want help, but if you want help they're available too. Maybe that you can borrow from or lend to and have in once in a while, maybe over the summer for a barbecue or whatever, but isn't on your doorstep all the time'. (A male neighbour is a summertime thing!)

The need to negotiate exemptions and control them is largely a need of women; the danger of relations getting too close is women's danger. Network management is usually women's work, and hers is much harder than his, since it involves both keeping the balance between friendliness and distance and maintaining the balance of give and take. Between women, reciprocity seems nearer the surface, less easily articulated and far more complex. Women's accounts carry an interesting ambivalence. They feature an apparent anxiety to emphasize the spontaneity of it all ('no trouble', 'never think twice' are common phrases) yet the relationships are painstakingly monitored. A young mother said she had good neighbours:

W: Especially the ones with little kids. They can just run in and say, 'can your [daughter] come over and babysit?' and just try and return it that way. No money changes hands ever, as far as baby-sitting or anything like that. If we're here, we do it for them, and if they're there they do it for us. I would never think twice about ringing someone if I was going to be late and get them to mind the kids.

The accounts also commonly extol flexibility to cover crisis situations where more major help might be needed. The same woman had been required to take her father to hospital: 'I was just able to ring up one of the women and say, "Just grab the kids as they come home and keep them until I get home"'. But behind the spontaneity is the familiar ideological backdrop: her 'good neighbour' is 'someone that doesn't interfere in your business, want to know your business. Someone that you know you can go to for help at any time, and they'll be there ... No one sort of lives in one another's houses, but that you can go to at any time. And vice versa, not just boot on the one foot'.

It is not surprising that women, and only women, appear to work at setting up balanced local relationships in which reciprocity is understood and privacy protected, while urgent needs are catered for:

W:　When you've got your friends, any problem that you've got, you feel free that you can ring them with. And just say, 'Oh look, something's come up—would you mind picking up the kids after school'. An emergency situation or something. You only feel happy to help. I mean, 'cos I don't feel embarrassed to ask. They feel they could ask you the same thing, any little thing.

Reciprocity is far easier in men's neighbouring. Specific tools or tasks with (often literally) concrete results, are easily assessed and the relationship is unproblematic if a similar-sized task or tool is returned or is acknowledged as due.[30] 'I've helped him put his lawn in, sort of thing. I'm sure I'd only have to say something and he'd be only too willing to help me. Which he's offered to do'. Women rely on each other to be there, whatever the need: 'Oh, just helping out when I've been in hospital each time. Not just with minding my daughter but with giving my husband a meal and things like that'. This woman classed her most neighbourly acts as 'the same thing' and gave very different things as examples. What they have in common is that in each case the neighbour does what is necessary. When one neighbour had a baby she 'did the washing and ironing for' the husband, and she had minded another neighbour's son when she worked part-time: 'I didn't get paid for that'.

Yet there are more complaints about reciprocity from men, especially about neighbours being 'free with' their property. Women sometimes cited men's problems in this regard, and always treated these as their problems: 'You see he used to come and borrow my husband's tools and they used to come and borrow each other's tools, and then he got a new mower and my husband didn't have a mower but he wouldn't lend his new mower!'. Women's problems were more likely to be about being 'used' in situations they were unable to control and they complained only of very obvious asymmetry. Most women saw the obligation to help as part of the good neighbour relationship, and the women researchers were sometimes amazed by the tolerance shown. Asked if she felt obligated by neighbour relations, Robyn said cheerfully: 'I think you do; I suppose it's probably what it's all about anyway really. You know, we're always inconvenienced at times and you just don't let the inconvenience bother you'. Her exception was a significant one—she tried desperately to protect her own part-time education from invasion: 'I don't like to have to mind anybody's kids before I go to college. Any other time!'.

Grace's definition of a good neighbour could only be of a woman and defined by a woman: 'Not one that pops in every five seconds. Not a person that seems to ask a lot of you, because I think a lot of people tend to use people and they don't realize, perhaps, they are doing it'. Where men insist on reciprocity and see its absence as very annoying, women find it hard to enforce and its absence a major problem. It is women with young children who are most vulnerable because they already are more likely to have stretched the ideological barriers to neighbour friendship. One young mother emphasized in her definition of good neighbour that 'the caring side of things is important'. But it had trapped her. A neighbour with whom she 'got on well' ('occasionally she'd pop over for coffee or whatever') went into hospital: 'I had the kids for him before and after school, and they came for tea'. Having volunteered, 'because I wanted to, I mean it just happened, I could imagine myself in the same situation' she found herself still minding the children. 'Then I got cross because she started work and she just assumed that I would have them before and after school.'

The story is long, complex and has no happy ending. She is now being paid, and says 'I still feel I'm being used'.

A (male) 'bludger' is obviously misusing neighbourliness and can be assumed to be disapproved. These male bludgers clearly outnumbered the female cup-of-sugar-borrowers described in response to our request for ideas of 'bad neighbour'. Borrowers are the least of women's neighbouring problems. That stereotype of the pesky woman is offered seldom, and as often by men as by women; she is not a threat, just a bit of a joke. She is at least of a varied cast of other neighbour nuisances—neighbours who 'rev cars in the early hours', 'have loud parties' and low standards, 'let their dogs crap all over your lawn' and 'don't bring their bins in'. All are equally scorned by women and men and recalled to confirm what a good neighbour is. Among them, the pesky woman is light relief, a symbol of how we all agree about neighbours:

W: We have a neighbour who I thought only existed in cartoons! She comes over and says, 'Have you got a cup of sugar', or she might come over and say, 'I'm making lamingtons, have you got any cocoa and coconut?'. She came over one day and said, 'I'm cooking a roast dinner. Would you have three potatoes, some pumpkin and a wedge of cabbage?'!

It is important to stress that all these warnings are against too much contact. Not one comment in this context is about the danger of too little. Nobody nominates people who will not participate in coffee mornings as bad neighbours; privacy is a right. The ideological barriers guard against community, not against isolation. Even women very pleased with their present neighbours, and highly active in local contacts, lace their descriptions with warnings about reciprocity and privacy:

W: The best neighbour is one which doesn't live on your doorstep, one that if you don't feel like going in for coffee you can say, 'Not today, I don't want to' and she doesn't get offended. One that isn't always driving you mad talking about the people next door. And one that's there when you need them, so that you can be there when they need you but doesn't make a welter of it...If you're not very careful how friendly you become with your neighbours, and to what extent, you can find that every time you turn round they're under your feet, because they're in such close proximity and you can see too much of them. And it is very convenient to borrow a cup of sugar off your neighbour and if people don't be very careful about this I think that they can make a complete and utter nuisance of your life.

Notes

1. In 1978 we coded and kept write-ins; in 1981, some but not all responses were taped. This set of questions came in the section taped only for group members; so the unstructured material analysed below comes from those tapes, the 1978 and '81 write-ins, and from the vast quantity of other unstructured material on people's ideas of good neighbours. See L. Richards & J. Salmon, 'There when you need them? Family life stage and social network', *La Trobe Working Papers in Sociology*, no 68, 1984, La Trobe University, Bundoora, Vic. The 1981 collection totalled 314 responses; they were precoded on the basis of postcoding of open-ended responses in 1978.

2. For each respondent we coded up to three characteristics of a 'good neighbour'; on average they offered just over two. The total collection (314 responses) is dominated by 'positive' answers (61 per cent—36 per cent in categories about 'getting along' and 25 per cent about 'helping'). The codings combined as 'positive' were 'depend on them when needed', 'helps with occasional tasks' and 'will lend'.

3. 'Doesn't live in your pocket', 'doesn't lower standards', 'not noisy, untidy, nuisance', 'doesn't borrow', 'not competitive', 'not dishonest'.

4. Only 8 per cent gave both first and second answers in the negative or ambivalent categories, while 41 per cent produced positive ones for first and second. Eighty-one per cent of second answers were in one of the two positive groups, and 73 per cent of third answers were. In sharp contrast, both second and third answers produced only a handful (5 per cent and 11 per cent) of the ambivalent 'There when you need them but not in your pocket'. See L. Richards, 'Too close for comfort: Neighbouring in a new estate', *La Trobe Working Papers in Sociology*, no. 70, 1985, La Trobe University, Bundoora, Vic.

5. M. Bulmer (ed.), *Neighbours, the Work of Philip Abrams*, Cambridge University Press, Cambridge, 1986, pp. 53, 65.

6. This is despite a very strong association between most neighbourly things done for and by people. Those who got 'inside' help were most likely to give the same sort of help (69 per cent) followed by those who got 'outside' help (61 per cent)—while no other neighbourly act was reciprocated in the same form by more than half the recipients. This is mainly because people tended to claim for their own most neighbourly acts more helping than they had received! But the effects of life stage were blurred, presumably by the likelihood that, despite people's seeking neighbours in the same life stage, they could not always find them. The younger and older households without children were more likely to give out-

side help.

7. Bulmer, *Neighbours*, p. 51.

8. L. Richards, *Having Families*, rev. edn, Penguin, Ringwood, 1985.

9. Allan draws on Bates, who distinguishes 'real' or 'true' friends from 'the remainder'; see G. A. Allan, *A Sociology of Friendship and Kinship*, Allen & Unwin, London, 1979, p. 40. Suttles distinguishes 'real' from 'everyday' friends; see G. Suttles, 'Friendship as a social institution', in G. McCall (ed.), *Social Relationships*, Aldine, Chicago, 1970. On the limitations of neighbour friendships see Abrams' work, in Bulmer, *Neighbours*. The same distinction between 'friendly' and 'friends' was found by Gans in Levittown and Martin in Adelaide; see H. Gans, *The Levittowners*, Vintage Books, New York, 1967; and J. Martin, 'Extended kinship ties, an Adelaide study', *Australian and New Zealand Journal of Sociology*, vol. 3, no. 1, 1967.

10. See Allan, *A Sociology* for a summary of literature.

11. Allan, *A Sociology*, p. 44.

12. ibid., pp. 38—40.

13. The phrase is Helen Marshall's; her data on childless couples provided insight into their use of Awful Warnings about the burdens of parenthood. See H. Marshall, Not having families: A study of some voluntarily childless couples, PhD thesis, La Trobe University, Bundoora, Vic., 1986.

14. There is a substantial literature on mediation of neighbour disputes.

15. P. Wilmott & M. Young, *Family and Class in a London Suburb*, Nel Mentor, London, 1967; M. Young & P. Willmott, *Family and Kinship in East London*, Penguin, Harmondsworth, 1962.

16. J. Goldthorpe *et al.*, *The Affluent Worker in the Class Structure*, Cambridge University Press, Cambridge, 1969, p. 91. See also Allan, *A Sociology*, ch. 5.

17. Gans, *The Levittowners*, p. 201.

18. A. Game & R. Pringle, 'The making of the Australian family', in A. Burns *et al.* (eds), *The Family in the Modern World*, Allen & Unwin, Sydney, 1983.

19. J. Martin, 'Suburbia, community and network', in A. F. Davies & S. Encel (eds), *Australian Society: A Sociological Introduction*, 2nd edn, Cheshire, Melbourne, 1970, pp. 315—16.

20. Abrams, in Bulmer, *Neighbours*, pp. 49, 51.

21. On first answers almost the same proportion (24 per cent, 1978; 22 per cent, 1981) were negative, but more positive answers were given in 1978 (53 per cent to 41 per cent), fewer 'two-faced' definitions (23 per cent to 37 per cent). Perhaps the off-the-hook answer was learned by some or reinforced in the three years in the estate I can only speculate, since, sadly, the figures could be an artefact of methods: in 1978 we were not 'listening' for the two-

faced answer, and we kept only write-ins, not taped records.

22. The restriction of activity to the fenced back is widely accepted, but also certainly related to class. In a study of four Melbourne suburbs only 32 per cent used the front for any activities, and only 17 per cent in the newer middle-class area where only 2 per cent approved of high front fences. See W. R. Finighan, *Privacy in Suburbia: A Study of Four Melbourne Areas*, CSIRO, Melbourne, 1979.

23. Bulmer, *Neighbours*, p. 52.

24. Richards, *Having Families*, final section passim.

25. Martin, 'Suburbia, community and network', p. 315. Compare C. Williams, *Open Cut*, Allen & Unwin, Sydney, 1983.

26. In this respect Rosaldo's discussion of the dualism of 'spheres' is useful, but I stress the emphasis: they are low status *when* they are seen as women's. M. Rosaldo & L. Lamphere (eds), *Women, Culture and Society*, Stanford University Press, Standford, 1974, ch. 1.

27. H. Graham, 'Coping: Or how mothers are seen and not heard', in S. Friedman, *On the Problem of Men*, Women's Press, London, pp. 104–5.

28. J. Harper & L. Richards, *Mothers and Working Mothers*, rev. edn, Penguin, Ringwood, 1986; B. Wearing, *The Ideology of Motherhood*, Allen & Unwin, Sydney, 1983.

29. D'Abbs found men more likely to pay money for assistance than women, avoiding the necessity to negotiate reciprocity. P. D'Abbs, Give and take: A study of support networks and social strategies, PhD thesis, University of Melbourne, 1983.

30. An aspect of this material that, as Abrams argued, includes altruism as a form of reciprocity. See Bulmer, *Neighbours*.

11

Proper Paths Through Women's Lives: Life Stage and Loneliness

The ideological backdrop of neighbouring, then, works differently for men and women. Men normally move easily within it, rarely constrained by messages about danger as they set about meeting their minimal needs for local relations. Women, equally normally, are enmeshed in the tangle of interlocking ideas with built-in snares; when they most need neighbours there is most danger.

In these accounts few people talk of isolation though many are lonely. Many people told us how isolated *others* were (or must be) at Green Views, and the conditions for such isolation are obvious. But women there rarely speak of social isolation, and only awkwardly, apologetically, of personal loneliness.[1] The ideological backdrop makes neighbouring a part of the parcel of core ideas of family and home; privacy and the proper paths to it. To question the rules of relevance of neighbouring would be to question the whole package.

The paradox of community and isolation is set in that context. This is not to say that all women have privacy imposed on them by all men. Rather, that isolation is imposed on some women by ideology. Privacy appears as a problem for women, not men, but it is not a problem for all women. In previous chapters, none of the neighbouring patterns was explained only by gender and few patterns were even significantly associated with it. Rather, gender, life stage and life chances combined in complex ways, which people often interpreted very differently. And these combinations carried built-in change, since life stage was there in all of them.

The image of suburban loneliness portrays young women trapped at home, not alone but burdened with young children; the suburbs as rows of little boxes whose contents are families. But what little sociology of neighbouring exists has always assumed that people meet 'through the children',[2] and people share the assumption: 'We haven't met all that many people as yet, but I think that will come once we start a family'. Sociology and popular assumptions also agree that in a *new* area it is easy to belong, since common family stage and common experience of mobility overlap to offer opportunity and common need.[3] So why would anyone be lonely?

No family, no community

The childless are unanimous on the subject: people belong only after having families. But they are wrong. Neighbouring begins for most people with the purchase of a home. The transition to home ownership provides the necessary condition; it is a transition many expected and had prepared for. Most wanted it, as a young wife said, 'after living in a flat where everyone kind of kept to their own little doors'.

The childless were most likely to have changed their neighbouring ways on moving. Of those still childless in 1981, three-quarters said in the first survey that they found it easier to talk to neighbours in Green Views than where they lived before (compared with exactly half of the pre-schoolers' parents, and less than half of those with school-age children). Estimates of the time spent with friends before and since the move were the same for the childless, but the proportion spending most or some of their spare time with neighbours was far greater now than before. Parents of pre-schoolers showed a less dramatic increase in the proportion of time spent with neighbours, and for those with school-age children the proportion even dropped marginally.[4]

It was certainly not true that the childless had no local relationships and wanted none. In fact they were found in all types of local relations. But their neighbouring was different in two ways. Most obviously, they were 'never there'. Less obviously, this was the only life stage in which relationships did not vary strongly by gender. They were indeed 'out' of the community; almost all were employed, and under financial pressure: 'You never see them, they all work all the time.

People don't even seem to be there'. They were far more likely than any other group to use house-watching as a symbol of neighbouring. But they also often felt they should do more: 'I don't make a great effort to get to know people in the area simply because, I suppose, we're never here', a young woman said, adding, 'We're probably wrong in the sense that we're not very community-minded'.

Many people wanted more contact. One couple had now separated; he recalled bitterly that 'As a couple with no kids, it was very hard to make lasting relationships with other couples, families that had got children'. Another man longed for a good friend but knew only one couple: 'She's Italian, [they] don't speak very good English'. And they were in the wrong life stage: 'There's not anyone in the same predicament, someone you could mix with at weekends and help with jobs'. Sadly, he concluded, 'We'll probably get our jobs out of the way by the time we meet someone'. They had no kin within reach, and the only 'outside' friends 'would have been nice to visit, only they split up. When you think of the 35-minute drive, that's when you feel lonely'.

Some couples throwing themselves into 'getting set up' found other young people sufficiently established and confident to offer 'young joker' friendships. Others preferred to be absentee home owners. A man explained: 'We don't mix much—just our sort of life style really. We get on well with our neighbours and have a chat with them occasionally'. A few made links through men. When the hotel opened a social club started, and one wife reported that through it her husband 'got to know a few fellas' and she was 'getting to know a few wives'. But she had no other way to meet women.

Almost all the childless couples waited for community 'later on when we have more time'. These strikingly similar accounts have in common the assumption that you gain time, that precious commodity of family life, by having children. Un-packed, this means that the wife does, since she will be at home; her contacts will make friendships for them. Not one of these people mentioned that she may continue paid work, that even if at home she may well lack time. Like the now well-documented ignorance of the loneliness of being at home with a baby,[5] this ignorance of the time schedules of mothers seems almost incredible, given years of media discussion of women's lives. It is paired with ignorance of the likelihood that the husband will have no more time, possibly less, as he picks up the task of fully providing family income. From now on, local networks will be added to her work, just a part of the women's tasks of servicing and maintaining family lives recently likened in a lovely analogy to the onerous, detailed, intricate work of making 'crazy quilts'.[6]

The establishment phase

People were wrong in assuming that community necessarily came with children, but they were not alone in that assumption. Sociologists agree that this 'establishment phase'[7] will be a time when most friendships are initiated, since couples have shifted geographically, children are instrumental in friendship formation, and the 'domain of sociable interaction' will be reduced to 'domestic rather than external' contacts.[8] Certainly for most people, parenthood reduced wider friendships, but the constraints on near ones then applied. Being a home owner had provided only the 'same boat' values; the first birth offered opportunity and necessity for local relationships. But it carried no guarantee.

Who meets people 'through the kids'? The question raises a prior one: *Why* would people meet through kids? All the answers of course are about mothers. The most common is Jane's: mothers are visible when they have young children, collecting them, chasing them.[9] And the young are visible: 'There's a few people that have retired into these houses. You hardly ever see them. They don't get out and about much. The young people, just married and with little kids and that, you see them all the time'.

Moreover, being home with young children makes mothers not only visible but available. It gives them common topics of conversation with other mothers and restricts their movements away from them. This was the complaint of the few women who rejected the 'court life' of suburbia. 'Everybody knows what everybody else is doing ... everybody watches everybody else's ins and outs', said one woman who was leaving; 'I would never live in a court again'. Before their baby was born, her husband's experience had been the same as hers: 'It was different, because she was at work', he said, 'And we were the typical married couple. We would both get home about 5.30 and cook the tea and sit and do whatever we had to do, watch the telly, do the bookwork and go to bed and get up the next day and do that again'. Now they felt that neighbours are 'always prying'. She declared: 'Everybody wanting to borrow tools every five minutes and things like that. The good neighbour thing goes a little bit too far'. The problem was now hers: 'It is all borrow, borrow, and there is a lot of competition in the court, you know, about what have I got and you haven't. You know, I'm mainly talking about women'.

Yet many women yearned for just that sort of interaction. Some of the most unhappy experiences were reported by women who had been at home with young children in the early days of the estate. It was a relief to find later that 'there's lots more babies bouncing around everywhere, so you get to meet people'. In 1978 a young mother had told us she hated Green Views. Three years on she laughed to remember that: 'When that first interview came, I thought it wasn't too good because the baby was only a few months old and I had to rely on the bus, the two buses that came through, and it was a bit hard. . . There were a lot of houses, but not many people'. But when the babies came, 'people were walking their children around and you'd meet them and say hello and that's it'. The phrase nicely encapsulates what many women see as the ease of meeting through children and she makes the point by adding: 'I don't know many people with no children around here. Even down this street, they keep to themselves and that's it'.

And having children makes people look alike. A woman puzzled the contradiction of homogeneity and diversity: 'I think a lot of the houses look much the same, you know, 'cos along here it's all been built by the one mob of builders . . . but everybody leads totally different life styles'. That contradiction is sorted out by parenthood: 'It's only since we've started to have children, I think, that a lot more people have got together. You sort of spend your summer evenings together . . . Before, next-door would go out and over-the-road would go out and we'd sort of go out and that was it'.

So if a woman is at home, starting a family makes her, and other women starting a family, visible, available and alike. But the other mothers have to be there, and so does she, so workforce participation remains the enemy of community. Women who continued paid work made few contacts through children. A young mother who still worked part-time said: 'I don't seem to be in the swing of the community or anything yet or into any community involvement, so it's only sort of pretty superficial at the moment. We only know our immediate neighbours and most of them work'. Women who could not make contacts always considered returning to work: 'It's not exactly fun looking after two children, doing the same thing day in and day out. And it did get to the point where I was very bored and I constantly thought about going back to work. Just being able to get out'. Unable to find child-care, this woman finally achieved a second car so that she could get out, but now intended to use it to return to work: 'I think it might make me a bit more sane. I feel I'm going mad sometimes'.

In many streets there were no other babies: 'I'd go out for a walk from the front to the letter-box and there was such a deathly silence, even if you were hanging out the washing at the back, you didn't hear children. There was no one around, no neighbours around, 'cos you knew they were all at work. Really it was sort of a frightening thing sometimes 'cos you'd sense a noise, I'd sense someone walking up the side of the house or something'. For these women, meeting people became a matter of getting out of the house and the sometimes empty street and this was not always easily done.

Women at home are not restricted to neighbours, of course. Having children also provides meeting places: 'Through the infant welfare centre I've met a lot of local people and our life is sort of Green Views now'. This woman, now very happy, recalled that before the birth of their child there was no chance to meet residents; their social life was where they had previously lived: 'Both of us working full-time and myself on shift work and he does some shift work, it didn't give you the opportunity to meet anybody anyway. But once you have a family, I think you start meeting people and getting involved in community things. I think it makes you feel more at home'. But if getting out is hard for some women, getting *in*, to more organized women's activities, could seem impossible. That could not be achieved by merely being visible, available and alike.

Being at home with children, then, can mean isolation or community. At this stage, since it is women who are at home, gender and life stage are inextricably linked, making sense of what people said when we asked how important it was to get to know people. Gender showed up no differences until it was broken down by life stage. Women and men had given answers clearly patterned on life stage, but they were quite different patterns. When there were pre-school or school-age children, over 40 per cent of men said getting to know people was not important. Only 16 per cent of women with pre-school children said that, though when there were only school-age children the women were as likely as the men to say it was not important. It is women, not men, who feel, as one of Martin's respondents put it, that 'Real friends must be your neighbours, because with little children you have to have somebody close'.[10] But when this is most desired it may be least possible. Life stage is a women's problem.

Women divided

People and sociologists are also wrong in assuming that the effects of children on networks are always positive. Indeed this must stand as one of the sillier contributions of sexism to sociology! It contains a number of astonishing assumptions: that if your child plays with another you will enjoy the company of the mother simply because you have 'the shared interest of and common concern with young children'[11] (the implications for women's unfreedom are enormous); that children do not select playmates and do not reject them; that adult interaction is unfettered by the presence of children. All these assumptions are obviously wrong. Women's accounts and participant observation in women's and mixed groups showed that the constraints of children were always felt and sometimes overwhelming. I want to emphasize six sets of constraints, none of which feature in the literature.

First, stage of young children is crucial, and child stage is more finely calibrated than adult age group.[12] Even small differences in stage of children may mean they interact badly, interfering with or even destroying their mothers' friendships. Robyn, lonely now, said she had 'a very good friend' but with a child younger than hers, 'so I don't see as much of her with the kids, because they're different ages and they don't sort of play too crash hot together'. Moreover, she was still 'back there' with a third pre-school child, ruled by the demands of child-care, constraints on mobility, and the need for other pre-school companions and houses in which they can play without maternal embarrassment. So she was losing links with same-age mothers who had 'moved on' to school-age children and often 'out' to workforce participation.

Thus a mother's opportunities and resources for local links, and her needs and constraints, may be determined not by her age but by the age of her children. As mothers' average age at first birth rises, this will become increasingly significant in the difficult work of managing women's local networks. One of the older women in the groups commented on the new influx of babies and the noise problem in coffee groups. The 'girls that came in later on are girls that have put their babies off until they're 28, 29, 30. So they were only a year or two younger than me anyway'. But the common age of these 'girls' was not a sufficient link; their children set them apart. 'One by one they dropped out', either to return to work or because the mothers of older children 'got very annoyed with all these babies screaming and that. They got very thing about it'. The drop-outs agreed.

W: There was informal coffee sessions going on, but they seemed to be mothers with kids at school and if you went along with a baby you sort of felt out of it. They made you . . . Just their reactions when the baby was crying, you were sort of looking after the baby as well as trying to talk with them. And the fact that their children were at school and they were talking about things that were happening at school, and I guess, in a sense, it was two different worlds.

As children change stage, they move their mothers between those worlds. Women accepted unquestioningly the loss of one friendship group and having to 'start again' with another.

Secondly, families in the same boat may look classless, but young children expose resources and values. Those who came with young children were the most vulnerable. Deprived of the two-income period of setting up, they were still struggling to acquire furnishings and appliances, and their children were in the most obtrusive stage of misbehaviour as the groups started forming. Robyn was one of these people: 'We started off with kids and *they* all started off with two jobs. I mean, we didn't have visitors because we had a black and white television. You *knew* that's why they all went home'. She remembered the early years, women 'raving about what their husbands do and how they've got this and they're *going* to get that'. Most women were unhappy to have meetings in their houses, and one reason (seldom acknowledged) was that 'nobody wanted them to see what anybody had or didn't have'. But there were also 'lots of things about children too. I mean, I could see my bad points in my kids a lot of the time, and you'd look at them and their kid would be killing yours'.

Thirdly, children can close opportunities for meeting just as clearly as they open others up. Especially the 'new mothers', anxious at the behaviour of their offspring, were vulnerable to criticism. One playgroup session became a problem for the organizers: 'When a new mother came no one spoke to them, and the children of one of the mothers were sort of being a bit rough on that new mother's child, which I guess does happen, but they weren't disciplined, they weren't spoken to to stop it'. Organizers battled the problem of mothers' insecurity when children 'played up': 'the children misbehave, so a lot of the mothers won't come back'. The constraint of children affects even the most confident. Jane asked to be left out of the women's group when the draw for office-bearers was on because her young child was so clinging that 'I don't think I could stand it'. Another woman reassured her that 'It could be our children next week', but Jane answered: 'That's not the point, it worries *me*. I can only listen to half the things going on today'.

Fourthly, *all* children disrupt adult activities. Women's groups in the estate faced constant problems with young children. When mothers brought them they were distracted: when child-care was arranged (with great confusion and difficulty) mothers worried and kept checking on children. In either case concern about their children's behaviour often dominated discussion. And women were discouraged from going out to groups by the problems of taking young children: 'If you did have to go out you had to take so much with you, it made me stay home more and more', said a young mother whose two pre-schoolers made her feel 'restricted, cooped up'. She had never tried the organized groups.

A fifth problem follows: children violate privacy. The trouble in Mandy's court began when her daughter wandered in next door. Children are no respecters of private space, time or knowledge, always there when you don't need them, always in your pocket. Caring for children means entering their home, acquiring more information. For those who strongly wish to protect privacy, the 'establishment phase' makes it very vulnerable.

And finally, most obviously, children are incompatible with tidiness, order and even cleanliness, often at a time when the young housewife has just commenced a 'homemaker' life and is anxious to impress both visitors and husband and committing hard-won resources of time and money to consumer durables children can damage ('lounge suites' feature in many discussions). This was the other and more obvious problem with the location of playgroups. For a long time the attempt to arrange public space for playgroups occupied organizers as women withdrew from the groups. Why? Robyn was certain it was 'because they had to have it in their home'. Despite advertising and letter-boxing, the group fell to six or seven.

W: I had a lot of kids here one day and they all brought their lunch and had lunch together, and I let them sit in the lounge room and they made a mess, and I cleaned it up later, like anybody else does. You can't stop them from making a mess! And I think that turned her right off 'cos she just didn't want anybody putting crumbs on her couch, that's the impression I got . . . She didn't mind her child messing my couch before she went home, though! There were a lot like that though. But I suppose if they're home on their own a lot they tend to do a lot of housework because that's all they've got anyway, and you do tend to get really into your housework. I was at one stage, for a while there! I soon got out of that. When he was a baby, when we first came here, there was nothing else to do. So you cleaned windows continually, you did everything all the time. What else could you do? You couldn't go anywhere. You could go for a walk, but there was just enough walks to go on, so you just stayed here and cleaned and cleaned and cleaned.

Together, these factors help make sense of some of the patterns in previous chapters. The useful uniformity of all being in 'the same boat' wore very thin when there were young children, and the mothers of those children were most vulnerable to local status criteria. They were also more likely to be 'middle-class' and moving on, and less likely to be committed to the estate as the end of a housing career. Their need for neighbours as sources of company and reciprocal aid was greater than that of other women, or of men in any life stage. Their opportunity for local contacts was also greater, since they were more likely to be at home and more likely to have the confidence and social skills that came with education. So *some* of these young mothers were in the best possible position to work out local friendships that for now bent the rules within the bounds of acceptable behaviour. But for all, children were also a danger and a constraint, and for those most committed to the estate and its ideological context that constraint could be all-important.

In on the ground floor: The expectations of a new estate

If children are no guarantee of community, neither is a new area. The two interact. Both the opportunities and the constraints of children were more obvious because this was a new area. Certainly in the early years, like other new estates studied, Green Views showed a 'flurry of activity' as people moved in and a flush of 'manifest neighbouring', after which neighbour relations 'dropped off' to 'latent' ones.[13] Certainly moving into a new neighbourhood offered many people a startling experience of community. Most had sought it and expected it, but still many expressed surprise at the amount of neighbouring on arrival. One man reported 'a strange experience', the day after they moved in, of people knocking on the door to welcome them: 'Like, where we lived before, the guy next door to us never, in about eighteen years, never knocked on our door once or never said hello or anything to us. So we were very surprised, kind of shocked'. Gary and his wife had happy memories:

M: We were all in the same boat: everyone was virtually moving into their first house, except one, into his second home. We were all virtually moving into a new home. We all had the same problem with our garden and all the rest of it. We all had to get out there and you had to work at it and you all had to do up your garden. We were all doing the same thing. So we all had, virtually, a common interest. The pre-school was a common interest; schools, there's a common interest. Transport's a common interest, and all the rest of it.

W: Borrowing tools!

M: Borrowing tools, of course, a common interest and things like that. So it was *very* easy. I mean, it would be very hard if it was an established area because there'd be no reason to be able to say ... if you were standing out the front in the summer for five hours, working, and someone brings out a couple of cold cans, I mean, we all just stand around and drink 'em ... we were all doing the same thing and we were all interested in the same things; we were all developing along the same lines.

They remained in the same boat, but this did not encourage interaction when the more obvious stage of 'settling in' was over. Perhaps in the earlier stages it was more obvious that they shared the experience of isolation. A young father said: 'the atmosphere lends itself to belonging, for survival in the area ... I shudder to think what people would do here that didn't get to know other people within the area'. A woman said cheerfully, 'you'd go starkers around here if you didn't get out and mix'.

So it was easy to mix and everyone needed to mix. The need and the common values did not change, yet it became less easy. The stage of the estate and the stage of the families in it created a pattern of 'getting in' followed by relations 'dropping off'. People knew to expect that pattern. At first, estate stage and life stage seemed to have additive effects, each magnifying the other. Meeting 'out front' and offering greetings or aid during the phase of 'doing the garden' offered common opportunities, especially to men in common family circumstances. But often the contacts were merely superficial. One couple told the interviewer how excited they were one day when they discovered that their grass had to be cut. They had no mower.

They decided that they would set out, not knowing anybody, and ask all their neighbours for a mower. They went from house to house, five houses, and at each stop they fell into conversation with the residents. And it was terrific, because they started to talk about, 'Isn't it nice to be here and it's good to know you and how are you'. They got the mower, mowed the lawn, took the mower back and had not seen or spoken to any of those people since. They felt it was 'a oncer'.

For women, too, estate stage and family stage interacted to expose common needs. Several women recalled how easy it was then to work on the assumption that other women shared your needs: 'Everybody wanted to know somebody because they were all just as lonely as each other, the ones who were looking for someone'. Estimates of the time taken for contacts varied, but all agreed it was longer than they expected: 'When we first moved in there wasn't very many people here and everyone was kind of getting their houses to a liveable stage, with lawns and gardens and inside, kind of thing, and I'd say it'd take you twelve months, a couple of years, I'd say, by the time you got to know everybody and got everything ready'. And all agreed that after 'the first flush' it was different: 'We were in right at the beginning, in the first stages, and if you're on the first stages of anything, you always feel as though you belong. It's when you come in after something is more settled that you have troubles perhaps integrating'.

But people also made it clear that they themselves put constraints on neighbouring from the start. Gary and his wife had been in Green Views nearly five years: 'And I don't think we've got to know them that much better than we did three years ago'. People they knew through the kindergarten had lost touch: 'Most of them have got their families; they've all got families and kids now. Before, we probably had more freedom. We were probably more social'. His neighbour accepted the same process: 'As time's gone on, naturally, everybody becomes a little bit more involved in their own problems and you don't seem to have as much time'.

The explanations sound simple, but jar with the facts. Nobody had time in those early days and neighbouring did not take time: it was done during tasks. The isolation remains, as does the need for company. But the barriers have been placed around the established homes once neighbours know enough of each other. Perhaps too because now there is more to know: at the start everyone had sheets in the windows; now you can tell who still has no lounge suite. Looked at this way, the early neighbouring is a fact-gathering exercise. Sharing the excitement and the tasks of moving in, neighbours gather sufficient information to know if these are people like them, rather as dogs gather knowledge in intimate but controlled enquiry. From then, the assertion that everyone is in the same boat serves as an assurance of common values. So long as they are not visibly different, people can relate on the basis of this assurance. But the rules of relevance of such relationships will strictly contain them to the segments of lives visible in the suburban setting.

Of course the 'dropping off' of relations is inevitable, not regretted (at least openly), and happens, as Gary says, 'naturally': 'By the time you get home at night time, especially in winter, you don't feel like going out anywhere, and the weekend comes and you don't feel like staying around the house! . . . I don't think the longer you live here is going to make all that much difference really'. As the figures in earlier chapters showed, he was right. Family and settling-in transitions combine with attitudes to work and leisure, family and home-haven to ensure what for most men was a sought and satisfactory steadying of local relations. Many referred to the 'stage' or 'phase' of getting set up, as in 'We've gone through that phase'. It was only women (and only some of them) who regretted its end. Grace explained how quickly this stage was over: 'We were all putting in our lawns and straightening out and levelling off things and doing a little bit of concrete work ... But of course, once those jobs were done, it was sort of finished; they didn't sort of need each other to help'. It would be too simple to assume she means there is no help needed. Rather the visible jobs are done, the 'same boat' jobs symbolic of moving in. 'That goes, because everything's established'. But the relationships established will not be community, since community involves knowledge and understanding of people and not merely of the segments of their lives in which they are residents.

The second-home owners had less need for help. The interaction of family stage and estate stage for the 'young ones' was not mirrored in the experience of older families. Less likely to find neighbours their age, they also had fewer problems with becoming established and therefore fewer opportunities to meet over the outside tasks that confirmed commitment to privacy and to the proper paths of family life. From the beginning they had more to protect—the status knowledge that is in 'established' homes. Because their children were at school there was no need to set up the sort of relationships that would work for sharing child-care and emergencies, so far less need to gather knowledge about others. They neither needed to stretch the strands of ideology to allow close neighbour relations nor were given as many opportunities to do so. And since they were more likely to be staying, the danger of any explorations of local links was greater.

As the wheel turns: None of the neighbours bother me

As couples move past the family-centred stage, existing neighbour relations may be adapted. But those who move house when children are older lose previous local relationships and have least chance, need or excuse to replace them. In Green Views they clearly had the least neighbour involvement. Most wanted it that way; in most cases they indicated that freedom from family-centredness allowed them to insist on always-valued privacy. (Been there, done that.)

W: I was involved in several committees when the children went to the other school ... and I went through a stage when I was stuck at home with a young family and that was my social outlet...I used to attend all the Mother's Club functions and I thoroughly enjoyed it. I had a very good time doing it, but once I had done it and I got my licence and I got my own car and I got a job, I had been that scene and I was not interested in it.

The result is in many cases a comfortable chosen anonymity. 'I don't know the girls that live around here except to wave to', said one woman. 'Who belongs to who, I get all mixed up. Who runs in and out the houses, I never know which one belongs to which house.' This was as she wished: 'None of the neighbours bother me. And it's not as though I'm not neigh-bourly, because I just don't have time to. Most of the ladies around here are the same, I think'. They were in the same stage: 'You see the young ones with their children, bustling off somewhere'. As a young mother at home she had made and managed neighbour relations: 'You had someone who would do these things for you, who would pick up your child from school, because you had to go somewhere else that day, and you'd pick them up when you got home. That's the kind of thing that *should* go on in a community'. But equally, people *should* move on. In the map of proper paths this includes workforce participation, and she had clear priorities, shaped by the time- and energy-consuming tasks of everyday woman's life: 'We've made our whole life our work ... I don't have time to sort of make friends or you know pop in and out of people's homes ... with working and looking after this house and running the kids to their sports and playing sport myself and shopping'.

Couples with school-age children seemed to have changed their neighbouring little on arriving at Green Views. Over two-thirds had had very little or no contact with neighbours before, and here had as little. Less than half found it easier to talk to neighbours than before the move. The interplay of class with life stage reappears here: those who did least neighbouring were parents of school children and were also those more likely to call themselves working-class and more likely not to be moving on. Awareness of class differences may have isolated some of the upwardly mobile.

This awareness worked to isolate some people who felt they did not belong. A woman separated from her husband since they moved to Green Views had minimal contact with neighbours and indicated that this had always been her preference. Before, she had lived where 'the houses were more spread out', on acre blocks, but even there had found 'a few of those to be the same way, wanting to know everything, all of your business'. Still, that was different: 'It's not the same as suburban living . . . coming every day and having cups of tea. They were there when you needed them'. In Green Views she had no interest in neighbours as friends and actively sought control over her own private space: 'I usually like to stay very quiet when I'm home. I don't want neighbours coming in for cups of tea and all that sort of thing you see. I just like my friends that I can go and visit and they can come and visit me'. The threat of neighbourly cups of tea was so strong that she used the phrase half a dozen times in a few minutes of discussion. Her idea of a good neighbour firmly combined the two poles of support and distance. And these were realized wonderfully in 'next-doors': 'They'll do little things for me but not sort of come in for cups—see they're two bachelors! That's why. And they're very, very nice people. And they don't sort of come inside all the time and want cups of tea. And I've got my privacy still'.

She is one of the two women, both with full-time jobs and school-age children, for whom home is a haven from work: 'You see, your home is like a retreat. You've got enough hustle and bustle out there. And when you come home, you like to know that you can have a little bit of time by yourself, and it's no fun when you've got people coming and going for cups of tea and talking, because normally, neighbours I've found, neighbours gossip'. The new neighbours knocking on the door are not a welcome surprise to her, but 'the beginning of the end'.

But what of those who did not welcome isolation? In the experience even of a few years many people passing through the young child-bearing stages found that as children grew they lost the early local links. Those who came with older children or after children had left home often remained lonely.

A retired man and his wife had strikingly different attitudes to the estate. He was splendidly happy in his 'retreat'. She was pleased for him, but explained: 'You see, it's a young area, which I didn't bargain on. I just thought I'd be seeing people walking around and past your window, and I never see a soul walk past my windows all day'. She amended that: 'except a few joggers and things like that'. It was a 'big jump' to come here. But her husband loved it: 'So I put up with it, but personally speaking, I wouldn't stay here if I was by myself'.

A woman whose loneliness puzzled her said, 'I don't know why I haven't joined anything really; probably because I don't know anyone'. She had lost touch with former friends and not made new ones. Why not? 'I've been very active up until we moved here. I was doing jazz ballet, I was doing netball, swimming and fitness classes, and I'm doing nothing at the moment. I'm doing absolutely nothing. It does get me down a bit. But when we first moved in, with the expense of everything, I couldn't afford to do it, and the time involved because I was trying to get extra work at the time too, and therefore you just couldn't fit it in. And I just haven't really got around to doing it again. And I really must'. But she will not. They are selling up, leaving a now patterned life which she finds hard to understand:

W: Like this morning, for instance, I got up this morning and took the children to school. And because I didn't go to the market, I came home, read my paper and then went to bed for an hour. And after, I thought, look at me, I'm in perfect health. There's nothing wrong with me, and here I am laying in bed. And really because I was lost, I felt utterly lost. And isn't that ridiculous! Now I mean why did I go to bed (laugh)? And as I said, I'm in perfect health. There's nothing wrong with me. I think, too, my children being so much older, you know, I found I'm a bit lost. I really needed a younger one around. But I don't really want one now (laugh). But I think if only my children were a bit younger. I mean, I really need, perhaps I need an extra job or something during the day. Isn't it awful! I hadn't even— I've noticed a funny thing, the more housework I have to catch up on—but if there's not much to do, like say if there's only dishes in the sink that need washing, a couple of beds to make, I just can't make a move. That sounds ridiculous, you know, I mean it'd only take half an hour. Maybe I'm in fear of—once I've got done what I have to do, I've got nothing to do, nothing to worry about doing.

Her puzzle emphasizes a feature of women's lives rarely mentioned in the literature. Given the dominant ideas of family life and women's places, women are bound to the wheel of the life cycle as men are not. Men's statements about life stage carry implications of choice: 'I belong here because I hang my hat up here', said one. He did not want to 'get involved, because I've got to a stage of life where I don't want to be involved in anything that will take up more energy than necessary'. But for older women, just as the period of young family-raising exposes them to the dangers of local relationships and justifies their need for these, so too the inevitable passing of that stage leaves them with neither the acceptable need nor the opportunity. Some, like Jane, anticipated, planned for and skilfully used these changes, welcoming the new segmentation of their lives and networks. Others were left stranded. Some obvious factors mattered enormously. Those who could negotiate a return to work were much more likely to be able to remake their networks competently, and those who had been involved in groups were more likely to retain some contacts. But the break with local life could be brutal for women dependent on child-related activities and lacking the resources and skills to remake their lives.

W: With everyone going back to work it's not that easy. Often our children do things together. That's really the way you seem to make friends ... Most of the girls I know are working, doing something. They are either doing nursing or teaching. A couple of friends work at Safeways because they got jobs up there; it's convenient. It may not perhaps be what they were doing before but the hours suit and there is no worry about getting to work or being away from the children very far, and the hours are a bit more flexible up there. But I think most people do go back if they can.

The literature has tended to ignore the period of relations 'dropping off'. When this period is recognized it is explained in terms of problems of creating neighbourliness in 'new communities',[14] rather than the interaction of gender and life stage. They interact inevitably, whatever a person's resources or skills; in this the experience of all women is common, so long as they remain committed to the expected paths of family life. As couples pass through those stages, life stage and gender impact in turn on their experience, rather as the powerful water jets and pummelling brushes take turns to batter the cars being drawn irrevocably through a mechanical car-wash. The battering is less alarming because it is predictable. But the occupants watching from inside, however different their driving skills, are relatively powerless to change the order of things, though relatively confident that the family vehicle will emerge shining and undamaged.

Nobody's lonely

W: Well, in this area they're mostly Australians. I say "hello" but I don't really know anybody. I suppose I'm too busy! That doesn't sound too good, does it. I don't know really. Everybody *works* here. This is one of the problems, I think. You know, everybody here *works* ... I'm not really lonely for people. I've got my Mum, and I have a fairly busy life otherwise, you know. I've got aunts to visit and a sister to visit, and friends outside of Green Views. Green Views is not, I mean I don't feel that I'm trapped here, or anything like that. I don't think you need to be.

There are many things going on here. There are no problems, but no opportunities; she does not need contacts, and nobody needs to be lonely. Everyone belongs. Anyone can tap into the family community. If people are lonely it is their own fault. Loneliness, like inequality, was hard to locate and obscured by ideology.

There is of course some truth in the assertion that 'it's your fault'. The management of local social networks is, for at least some people, a very active process over which they have considerable control, and so is the planning of at least the early family stages. For *some* the result will be considerable local interaction, but for others it appears to be isolation. Why? People say it depends on personality; to some extent they are undoubtedly right. But other dividers intrude for women, and they were not acknowledged as women's problems. Women were the bearers of ideology and most vulnerable to the barriers it set.

Gans concluded from his years of living there that in Levittown, 'if there is a "malaise", it is female but not suburban'.[15] In Green Views, there is certainly a malaise, if widespread loneliness can be so described. Certainly it is female (though this is not to underestimate the loneliness of many men). It is not suburban in the sense that the popular critics of suburbia would have it. There is no uniform isolation, uniform neurosis or uniform unhappiness of women in Green Views. Many are not there, or when they are want only privacy. But isolation is suburban in two ways. It occurs in the context of physical distance from previous networks, and it is set in that 'suburban' ideology of private family life which makes sense of the contradictory experiences described, and obscures the social causes, even the existence, of women's loneliness. What Friedan called the 'problem that has no name'[16] is not only still nameless in Green Views; it is denied.

'It's your own fault if you're lonely' is asserted by women who used to be, women who are and women who have never been lonely, as well as by men. Making friends 'wouldn't take long if you didn't want it to take long, because I think everybody's so nice, you could make friends just walking up the street if you wanted to. But as I said, I never had the time for anything like that, because I worked'. They also say Green Views is a family community. Very few people say *they* are lonely, or lonelier now than they were before the move. Everyone belongs in one sense or another; they are all in the same boat. Everyone who is prepared to say they are lonely agrees it is their own fault.

To say it is your fault if you do not find friends is rather like saying it is your fault if you do not get pregnant when you are trying to. There is all that opportunity going for you—a whole system working for you. But under examination the system is far from a guarantee of success: look at all the things you have to get right! So too local friendships require perfect timing, the right conditions. While most women can get pregnant if they try and some do without trying, some however much they try will be unable to. Isolation in this regard is rather like infertility; it is cruel and pointless to say 'Well, most can'. The odds against any egg are astronomical.

The odds against any woman finding community in this 'family community' by accident are also astronomical. Certainly there is a social system apparently working for her. In the new community are gathered people like her in life chances and life stage. Professional and self-appointed facilitators assist with contacts, transport, encouragement. The messages are all about meeting: we have the same goals, we are the same sort of people, have 'a lot in common', are all in families, all home owners, all getting set up, have the same needs, are getting established. It is in this context that people say 'It's their fault if they're lonely'. But each of these messages is false; they are wishes, dreams, not statements of fact. The combination of social probabilities with ideological filters makes a formidable obstacle course through which a search for friendship must run. And the lonelier a woman is, the more formidable the obstacles, since loneliness will erode competence.

'All in the same boat' not only masks inequality but enforces the anonymity of all but the visible segment of residents' home-owner lives. Those who feel unable to compete or are open to criticism shrink from exposing their houses and their children to scrutiny. So class works for loneliness, ethnic difference works for loneliness, and if she or her neighbours are 'different' or feel it, her chances are immediately restricted.

'Everyone belongs' masks those who do not. Certainly the new community maximizes the chances of finding people in the same life stage, but it cannot guarantee this. Children divide. Near neighbours are likely to be same-age adults but not guaranteed to have same-stage children. And if they are and do, they are unlikely to be at home.

'The family community' masks the fact that 'nobody's home', by far the most common phrase when people talk of loneliness. In the early stages those at home with children were bitterly lonely because nobody was there. Our tapes recorded many of those recitations of court maps that make sense if the hand-waving is visualized; women were redrawing the picture they had drawn every morning: 'She's working, she's working, she's home now but you don't see her'.

'Community' itself masks the power of ideological constraints on neighbouring. When the babies came, for many women opportunity came too: common problems and things to talk about. But women cannot be close if they are 'too close for comfort'. Caution and constraint apply even to these most longed-for relations. They should be held outside (but children are inside). Women 'go up the wall', but have to go outside their walls to talk safely to a neighbour. And if they do make close friendships locally they threaten the dream they are there to create—the private world of family, marriage and home. Community is inimical to privacy. That dream, the whole reason for being there, may have other meanings for their husbands: *our* dream of security, autonomy, privacy, hides *his* goals and his relationships to work. Those may not be the women's, but must determine women's relationships at home.

And that moment of opportunity, home with the children, is so brief (like the chance of pregnancy!) that women seeking friendships have to move fast. Most women will not stay at home until their last child goes to school. So 'they're going back' is a frequent comment, and the overlapping slices of time have to be sufficient to get to know someone well enough to be able to depend on them. Women can of course get to know others well enough to set up an agreement that they are there when needed. Many such comfortable neighbouring relationships occur in these data. But few friendships.

Why then does everyone say there is no need to be isolated? 'It's your fault if you can't cope', is the same sort of cruelty when said to young mothers, the same process of 'blaming the victim'. Empirically, it is usually not her fault, but the message is ideological: mothers naturally mother. Here, similarly, ideology masks a real lack of opportunity and real social problems. The pregnancy analogy tells us more about the process. Why do people (falsely) insist that getting pregnant is easy? The answer, I suggest, is because of clear ideological messages about the ever-present dangers of getting pregnant. Unmarried girls are brought up learning how to avoid pregnancy while achieving their dreams. Similarly, the ideology of the family community is all about avoiding the omnipresent dangers of invasion of space, knowledge and time, while creating the dream of family life.

Negotiating close neighbour relationships in that context is rather like maintaining a passionate *and* safely celibate affair. It can be done, but usually is not. In the 'family community' it would be as unwise to assume that all families have adequate social supports let alone community as it is to assume they all suffer suburban isolation. Most will be able to ask for help in an emergency, but nobody will know if there are ongoing troubles. Partly this is because most do not want it known. Privacy is what the majority (most men and many women) wanted. And it is what almost all thought they should want.

Those who achieved intimate local friendships usually did so away from near neighbours by forcing themselves, sometimes almost literally, to 'join things': 'It is a case of having to, otherwise there is nothing. There is no social life in Green Views, there are no recreation facilities, it is designed so that you don't become too isolated in the street designs, no front fences, but you could very easily make the four walls of your house your front fence and it is a case of having to go outside the home to get involved'.

The final chapter is the story of the groups they formed. But it is not a story of easy community, rather of the dividers dominating each aspect of life at Green Views exposed in a public arena. For the women and men active in the groups, community was not guaranteed; conflict often was, and friendships seldom resulted from sometimes years of gruelling hard work. Throughout the stories of the groups class differences divided, the life stage wheel still inexorably turned, and gender determined experience.

Notes

1. Late in the project I wrote in the RA newsletter, which was distributed to every house in Green Views, asking for people who felt lonely there to contact us and tell us about it. There was not one reply.

2. For a discussion of this issue see Abrams' review in M. Bulmer (ed.), *Neighbours: the Work of Philip Abrams*, Cambridge University Press, Cambridge, 1986, p. 42.

3. L. Carey & R. Mapes, *The Sociology of Planning: A Study of Social Activity on New Housing Estates*, Batsford Press, London, 1972. See also L. Kilmartin & D. Thorns, *Cities Unlimited*, Allen & Unwin, Sydney, 1978, ch. 9. Studies of local groups have almost all been done by men and of men's groups. We were aware from the start that we counteracted this imbalance by not moving in the predominantly men's groups—the sporting clubs and the 'social club' at the pub were the outstanding ones. But this focus was determined by the history of the groups—we went where the first groups developed—as well as by our own gender.

4. Before, only 14 per cent of the childless spent most or some spare time with neighbours, now 55 per cent did. For those with only preschool-age children the increase was from 21 per cent to 51 per cent; for those with both pre-schoolers and school-age children it was from 15 per cent to 40 per cent. For those with school-age children it went from 31 per cent to 29 per cent.

5. L. Richards, *Having Families*, rev. edn, Penguin, Ringwood, 1985; A. Oakley, *Becoming a Mother*, Martin Robertson, London, 1979.

6. The analogy is drawn in L. Balbo, 'Crazy quilts: Rethinking the welfare state debate from a woman's pont of view', in A. S. Sassoon (ed.), *Women and the State: The Shifting Boundaries of Public and Private*, Hutchinson, London, 1987, pp. 45−71.

7. R. Rapoport & R. N. Rapoport (eds), *Working Couples*, London, Routledge & Kegan Paul, 1975.

8. See Bulmer, *Neighbours*, for a review of the literature; for different settings see P. Willmott & M. Young, *Family and Class in a London Suburb*, Nel Mentor, London, 1967; S. Edgell, *Middle-Class Couples*, London, Allen & Unwin, 1980.

9. Two Australian studies indicate the importance of visibility; see J. Martin, 'Suburbia, community and network', in A. F. Davies & S. Encel (eds), *Australian Society: A Sociological Introduction*, 2nd edn, Cheshire, Melbourne, 1970; and L. Bryson & F. Thompson, *An Australian Newtown: Life and Leadership in a New Housing Suburb*, Penguin, Ringwood, 1972.

10. Martin, 'Suburbia, community and network', p. 337.

11. Abrams in Bulmer, *Neighbours*.

12. The distinction between adult age, family life stage and child

stage is extremely important and little explored. More recent work on life stage is sensitive to 'events' such as first and last child starting school, and demographers have distinguished up to twenty-four family stages by child stage. See C. Young, *The Family Life Cycle*, Australian Family Formation Project, monograph no. 6., Australian National University, Canberra, 1977. But the normal failure of age, life stage and child developmental stage to overlap similarly in groups of any size has hardly been explored; with the stratified shifts in age of women at first birth more variety is to be expected.

13. Bulmer, *Neighbours*, p. 42; see also C. S. Fischer, *To Dwell Among Friends: Personal Networks in Town and City*, University of Chicago Press, Chicago, 1982.

14. For example Abrams' analysis of the 'falling off' of relations (the same phrase recurs) because of 'gossip and borrowing', in Bulmer, *Neighbours*.

15. H. Gans, *The Levittowners*, Vintage Books, New York, 1967, p. 226.

16. *The Feminine Mystique*.

12

'A Terrible Lot of Lamingtons': Gender at Home

'Getting in' in Green Views meant two very different things: getting into the formal groups and getting into social friendships. People frequently assumed the two were always related. They were wrong. Group membership might provide contacts but it offered friendship only temporarily and to few. And it exposed the sharp dividing lines under the ideological veils of uniform community—real, hard differences of class, life stage and gender, each having real, hard social results, and each meshed with the others. It also exposed the ways that women's paid work shapes relationships. Like the estate, the groups rapidly produced class divisions which tangled with life-stage divisions and with the effects of gender. Like the estate, they created different social worlds for women at home.

Becoming 'involved' was approved, perhaps the only acceptable way to be close to neighbours, and the only way of finding friendships with non-neighbours. Superficially, it looks a guaranteed method: everybody can join. In all our records of group activity there is none of a person's being turned away from group meetings. Most groups were constantly seeking new members to take on tasks and executive positions. All groups at some time put on the committee anyone who volunteered. People had only to find, or create, the group, and go to the meeting. So the question recurs, why would anyone be lonely?

Both Robyn and her husband, lacking educational or financial resources, managed to start groups. Ken took complaints to the Labor member of parliament, who suggested a residents' action group and supplied advice, duplicating facilities and even models of a constitution. The developer, DVP, provided a room for the first meeting. It was attended by four representatives of DVP, all the local councillors, the MP and about 60 of some 300 residents then in the estate—more than any meeting would attract for some years. Ken thought it was 'pretty pathetic': 'I've never been on a committee before but I thought that was woeful. All these people are complaining!'. He was elected president of the Residents' Action Group (RA) and presided over a period of demands for 'the kinder and street lighting and all that sort of stuff'. A group broke away to concentrate on the Preschool, and the association changed character. In his view, 'The ones that went on later— excuse me for saying this—were the glory hunters'. Seeking what? 'Power. All the little memos that they used to send around to the houses ... We just had "The Green Views Residents' Action Group" and that was it. On their ones, they'd put: "Forwarded through John" or "Forwarded through Bill" and try and big-note themselves all the time. It was pathetic, you know, I couldn't handle it any more so I gave it the flick.' Robyn too 'sort of lost interest' in the RA: 'It seemed to get more like, "I'm this and I'm that; I do this and I do that"'. First her husband, and later she, took on the presidency of the Preschool group, which had started with a women's friendship base from the playgroup where Robyn had begun group activity.

W: I said to the Health Centre Sister, 'I want a playgroup; is there anything going on here?'. She said, 'No. If you want to start one, here's a lady's name, she's interested. Off you go'. I thought, 'Oh great!' but I understood she didn't have the time, so I thought 'Oh well, I'll go round there shake, shake! and knock on this lady's door. And I went round there, and she was very friendly and asked me in and we got to know each other. She had a lot of friends around there with children who were at home, which there wasn't around here then.

Ironically, having no one at all may have helped her, as it did Jane. Another who joined soon after had a strikingly similar account of the courage first approaches took.

W: There was no one living here for company ... There was a sign in the milk bar and I thought, 'Oh well, here we go', so off I went and knocked on this lady's door.

Robyn thinks many were deterred by other women. Delivering pamphlets, she met a woman who 'raced out of her house and said, 'Hi! Hi! Hi! Isn't it lonely at home!' sort of. She was almost desperate. And I said, 'Look, come around'. My address was on the thing, but she never did.

That court, she said, had 'a lot of women who tend to rubbish someone else who gets out and does something . . . Some people think there's something wrong with you if you want to be involved in community groups. Like people might think that you're not coping at home 'cos you have to get out'. Ideas of family and privacy link with ideas of class: 'I think there's a lot of class kind of thing too—only the low, stupid people get involved in community things 'cos the government should give things to you anyway, and you shouldn't have to be helped because you don't need to because . . . we've got money and we live here and somebody else should do it'.

Who rows the boat? Class and group formation

At the annual general meeting of the RA, at which Ken 'gave it the flick', it acquired Susan, who later became president. She had been in the estate a week and was working in sales full-time, but was 'curious about the area that I was going to live in, what it had to offer'. So 'getting in' was done through a contact, a neighbour who was a 'professional' (a nurse) so 'quite comfortable going out and mixing with people'. They went together to the meeting. 'I wouldn't have had the courage, I think, to go along by myself'. The nurse, also later a group office-bearer, said exactly the same thing in a separate interview. But the meeting needed no courage: 'I found them very ordinary people'. Ordinary? 'Workers, tradesmen, housewives, no special qualifications, apart from perhaps one girl who was definitely career orientated; she had a very important job in the company she worked for . . . She was the only one who had any degree of confidence and knowledge of procedure.' Not only qualifications, but also office-bearers were lacking; the breakaway groups and a series of disputes had added to the disorder. Bill had been approached to act as chairman because he was 'a mature gentleman'. Volunteers were called for the committee, everyone who volunteered got on, and Susan became secretary because she had the most legible handwriting.

This was the start of a phase in which the association was very energetically run by a few people to whom both qualifications and procedure mattered. Venue mattered too, as did format. It was always held in (public) DVP rooms. Few had previous experience of running groups, but they borrowed books, and a complex agenda faced each meeting. In that first year as secretary, Susan sent out 27 letters in one month. All business was allocated to sub-committees. There was little social activity outside the meetings; a social sub-committee folded within the first few months. Her classification of members divided them into the 'community-conscious' and the 'newcomers' or 'casuals'. The casuals were: 'housewives, they simply wanted to meet people, they didn't appear to be terribly well educated—lonely. They were there, I'd say, for social reasons, because they indicated that they didn't understand, comprehend or want to be terribly involved in the documentation or the procedure aspects'. The community-conscious she described as having 'a rather stable environment', far better organized, 'professional people'. There were two other women, one 'educated—potentially professional, but at home because of family', the other 'the only person who I'd say would have been not on the same level because she was at home'.

Three other RA members produced the label 'professionals' and then backed down on it. The woman at home was more cautious in describing the group: 'I was going to say "professional" people, but they weren't. There was a mixture of people—electrician, tradesman, teacher'. But the RA acquired a reputation summarized by Keith—'they're extroverts and they're pushy and they're all professionals and so on'.

M: I think you *do* find that a lot of these people are professionals, particularly the males. I don't know that they're so much pushy but I think you'll find that most of the males are in fairly high-pressure jobs and I think they're almost looking to continue it after hours because maybe watching TV's not for them and they'd prefer to be under a little bit of pressure than not. And that may be why you don't get that sort of person that doesn't do that type of job. Mainly they're happy to take it fairly easy at work and then shuffle off and go home and watch TV and get up in the morning and go back again! I don't know, but people that I've known on the estate who are sort of in the manual field—qualified people, tradesmen and so on, butchers, plumbers, this sort of thing—don't seem to be prepared to come out and do things. Maybe they get tireder physically . . . Oh, Bill was a tradesman. I might be generalizing too much there. And Kenneth's a tradesman. But—

He went on to list male RA members: 'He's at a managerial level', 'a computer consultant', 'a teacher', 'a systems analyst' (whose wife was 'a receptionist/typist or secretary'). Another man had 'a sort of manual job, no, I think he's in computers'; another was 'an accountant by profession, a general manager of a credit corporation'; another 'works in a bank'. 'So looking at them, you're looking at a lot of white-collar people.' At another time he said: 'You've sort of got—without saying different *classes* of people, that's what I mean. Different variants of niceness!'.

So men's jobs determined the new face of the RA, though they were a mixed lot, and for most of these years at least three women were active. Keith's list left out two wives of the professional men (his own and another teacher currently out of the workforce) though it was they who did the most professional work for the RA—editing the newsletter, working within the welfare bureaucracy, designing and completing a community services directory for the area. Like him, Susan felt that being in the workforce was what mattered: 'We were all pretty well professional people, dealing for eight hours of the day in a professional environment. You get used to going to different departments and going to different people, talking to them, researching. There's not the fear—you do it as part and parcel of your job or as a result of your confidence, which comes from your educational standard'. Thus the RA was seen as a men's group, and one that represented neither the variety of life chances at Green Views nor the range of life stage. There were few who were not 'established'; Susan ran through the list, describing in each case a 'lovely house'. And there were few who were not moving on. These were people briefly committed to the estate but concerned to contribute:

M: We were basically saying that we would stay put for at least five years ... We chose to come here quite deliberately; we thought that Green Views had more to offer than most new estates. So that when you do decide to come to a place, I think that you're more or less obliged to do something about building it the way that you want it to be ... And Green Views is going to be what the people here are going to make it, not what DVP have promised it will be.

They spent time and effort on a vast array of issues and earned hostility. One man described them as 'two bob millionaires on a little bloody ego trip'. Several people told us a member was pursuing his (always his) own interests through the power the group gave. When the Council moved play equipment after a neighbour protested at the children's noise, a furious resident was certain 'three people from the Action Group' living by the park to which it was moved, had 'wanted some play facilities for their kids and that's a fact'. The complainant reverted to the trucks issue:

M: They sent round this dirty great screed; you know, 'Why should we have trucks parked in the estate, etc. etc.'. They picked on this one guy ... In point of fact, three of the peanuts on the committee drive bloody semi-trailers and park them across intersections. Two of them have caused bloody near fatal accidents on this estate, but their trucks are never touched. That's been checked too.

The president who followed Bill worked to reduce the image of the committee as 'stirrers', stressing they were not 'trendy conservationists' but 'concerned about just the normal things that concern the suburban person'. He saw the name as unfortunate—'I don't think that the key word should be action'—and succeeded in having it changed. But the group had certainly never been radical.

Life-stage groups

In contrast, the breakaway groups, the Preschool group and the school Interim Parents' Association (IPA) were about life stage, not class. There is no mention of occupation, his or hers, in descriptions of active members. The children provided both the need and the stimulus, restricting parents, especially mothers, from other ways of making friendships. But most of all they provided ideological justification. Joining these groups did not breach the rules of relevance about neighbouring, or violate family duty, since they were for family. Years down the track Robyn checked off her activities: 'The playgroup was for the kids, the baby-sitting club was—well, to get rid of the kids! The kinder was for the kids. I'm not on anything at the school at the moment 'cos I don't think I can handle that just yet. My husband is—on the Council. Little Athletics is for the kids'.

Children provided the reason for women to go out to meetings, and in particular to go out at night, leaving husbands child-minding. This was not always undisputed. In most cases there was some tension, and in two, curfews were imposed by husbands controlling transport. (For some men the RA offered the same freedom from family. Keith saw this, from the man's side: 'Maybe that sort of person doesn't want to go home to the family and they'd prefer to say, "No, no, too busy, I've got to go out to work", and do some work in the community. Because I know that some of these people at least are under a lot of pressure to stay home'. He cited one man: 'He gets to work before 7 in the morning and gets home at 6 or 7 at night and then off he goes to the Residents' Association, that doesn't go down too well!'.)

But just as children linked neighbours awkwardly and temporarily, so too did they bring parents into the life-stage groups in an apparent community of interest that by no means guaranteed communion. It was transient; a brief interlude. When children left Preschool, many links were dropped. And the common interest covered but did not remove inequalities. For many it brought friendship, but for others it meant resentment and conflict. People assumed, especially of women (as one man said) that 'they were all about the same age so they got on all right together; they knew each other pretty well'. They were often wrong.

Both the life-stage groups, the Preschool and IPA, had two sharply distinguished phases: fund-raising before the facilities were obtained, and fund-raising after. In the first phase there were constant tensions. As with the RA, the venue mattered, but these groups met more often in people's homes and 'didn't have the same air of formality and they weren't often as well run and didn't stick strictly to business'. Anxiety about the home as a status symbol dominated. The founders of the Preschool group all had new homes, although 'some of them weren't very elaborate, some didn't even have very much furniture'. Since the 'done thing' was to serve supper, competition became a major issue, especially for the women. Thus, in ways that mattered enormously to women, 'space defines the people in it' and 'people define space'.[1] A few of 'the older ones' were in 'their second house', Gary said, but 'the bulk of people were all in the same position: we all had mortgages and all the rest of those great burdens'.

The first Preschool committee was of 'pioneer' couples, living close, childless or with young babies, who threw themselves into raising vast quantities of money from their own extremely limited resources. All remembered that period with nostalgia; it involved a lot of social occasions for couples: 'We did it because we liked it, we did it because we enjoyed it'. None of the other accounts of group work contain such enjoyment. But it was not easy. There was resentment that 'we had to raise so much, and it was just a matter of it coming out of our own pocket'. The second phase was easier because 'there was a kinder and people'. But then resentment grew towards the people benefiting from the fund-raising and not supporting it. Family is its theme music: 'I just don't think they want to get involved or come to things that are there to raise money. They just want to send their children and get them out of their hair'. Critical parents appeared once the Preschool opened up, protesting because waiting lists were already full or objecting to details of administration. The men were especially vocal about these.

M: The bulk of them, to me, are self-opinionated, arrogant Bs. They want everything for themselves and they're not prepared to get off and do anything to help. They want for them, number one, and blow the rest of you...All those rotten, apathetic morons who came to the annual meetings and opened their big mouths and made comments.

The IPA group was always seen as different, and rapidly acquired a stereotype. Just as the RA was never only 'professionals', so the IPA was never only women. But in all these comments it is seen as a women's group; its women dominated, it did women's work and its organization and interaction were regarded as women's. One of the men in it declared: 'I'm not running them down because they're housewives, but they were housewives who wanted the best school for young Johnny'. It was 'a mother's club without the school', he said: 'They don't like Penelope's hands. She's wearing a horrible coat again. And if nobody tells her about her acne I'm not going to speak to her!'.

The groups were compared in the language of gender. 'There was very little bitchiness', Susan said of the RA. There was a lot, everyone agreed, in the IPA, and everyone saw this as a women's problem. Women had started the group, increasingly desperate at the continued delay of the school, angry at years of transporting children to the tiny, overcrowded country school down the dangerous highway. Symbolically, they began with their own resources, planning a programme 'where seven girls got round to everybody's home for dinner once a month', and started with one providing '*everything* for the seven of us, three-course meal, wine and everything, one lunch time. And we each put in a dollar and we got our first seven dollars'. It was formalized at a meeting at which some 20 parents, including many men, joined. The man who chaired the meeting recalled that, 'I suppose because of their children—it sounds pretty sexist—the women were more vocal, more forceful'.

This was not a simple split between groups of women and men, rather between women's and men's styles of interaction and priorities and between women's and men's work. 'The women in the IPA were more the dominators', said a man; 'They were pushy'. The first year featured personality clashes, scape-goating and open conflict; close friendships emerged and ended. In the second, more men joined, some knowing each other from the RA; and in the third Ken and another man were pulled in to 'try and do something'. Their condition was that they did no fund-raising, since that would 'over-commit' them. But he recalled: 'We made another couple of thousand dollars'. The men were listened to more, one said, 'because they were less emotional'.

Attitudes and behaviour reinforced each other. The 'casuals' in the early RA were indeed women at home, committed to motherhood. The bureaucratic work on 'community issues' was indeed different from fund-raising. Fund-raising *was* women's work. It was done by women; women, and often only women, wanted to do it, and women consistently avoided other group activities. 'Women are good at being the workers', said one, who was an active fund-raiser. 'Give them a job to do and I think most women can do it. But I don't think they can always run a meeting, or run the committee ... Most women, most housewives (and that's all Green Views mainly consists of), some of them can't be bothered being chairperson. I know when it was time for elections, like, "Oh no! Oh Jesus!"—you know the attitude.'[2]

In the unfolding battle over the primary school the interplay of ideology and its structural setting gave a dramatic inevitability to the conclusion. A public meeting was called to discuss alternative designs for the school. Suddenly a choice was forced. The proposal was to build not the architect-designed 'permanent' structure promised and expected since the estate opened four years earlier, but a cheaper alternative, now Education Department policy. This would have a permanent 'core' and portable light-construction classrooms—less convenient, less comfortable, more vulnerable to being removed if numbers dropped and, crucially, associated with lower-class areas. The RA had followed this development with anxiety and fought to hold the authorities to the promised permanent structure, which contained community facilities and would unquestionably look better. The officials in attendance at the meeting threatened unspecified delays if Green Views insisted on its permanent school. That threat was too much for many women: the RA lost. 'People voted contrary to what they said they would', the chairman asserted. Why? 'Most of the men voted no and most of the mothers [*sic*] voted yes.' The RA, he explained, had not expected this, being 'very much a male-dominated situation, with no design or anything else except that we are not involved in most of the things that get these housewives into fund-raising'.

Women's work: A sociology of fund-raising

The RA did nothing overtly to discourage women. But nor did it undertake fund-raising: after amending its constitution so that the Parks, Sports and Recreation Sub-Committee could raise money for the Football Club, it passed on to the club the $48 earned and in this period never raised funds again. Susan explained: 'You've got to have people who can devote the time. Someone has got to go out there and physically organize things, usually in working hours ... You can't be ringing up a business house and asking for a gift at 10 o'clock at night, and that's when most of us had our free time'. In the RA 'the men had a fair bit of influence', said one, 'It was sort of like going to the club rather than going down to the pub for a beer'. The IPA 'was fund-raising, and that's all they wanted to do', Susan said. 'It was more social to them. There was no hard work.'

No hard work?! Over the years we were in the estate, the labour of fund-raising and the small rewards for it were constant themes. Those in the groups concerned with the needs of young children were regularly required to produce, create, organize, donate, sell, solicit, contribute, bake, sew, persuade, promote, perform, attend, purchase. The pressure was unremitting because the goals were unspecified: 'You can raise a lot of funds by having a bigger, better fair and maybe twice as many lamington drives or twice as many fund-raisings and dinner dances'. And for the parents (usually the women) in the groups there were constant rounds of cake stalls, raffles and social gatherings within the limited range that can make money for the organizers: wine and cheese nights, fashion parades and the ubiquitous 'party plan' events in private homes: 'They get sick of going to Tupperware parties and jewellery parties and things like that, but the one where we had a clothing party, that the lady came along [to] and sold her clothes, people seemed very interested in that.' But 'still, you go, don't you' even to Tupperware. And buy? 'Not all the time, I don't think you can', but later the same woman says, 'I think you do, that you should'.[3] A social gathering such as a fashion parade means unacknowledged work: 'It's so easy to provide a little basket supper and we all make a few cakes and a few sandwiches'. Long hours are spent debating the details of task allocation, who will bring what, which of the range of often highly-priced, unnecessary items will be demonstrated and sold under the flags of friendship and community to make profits for an outside company and a small contribution for the group organizing the event.

One Preschool meeting recorded that a Tupperware party had raised about $50. There had been 25 people present and about $370 worth of goods had been purchased by the women. Tickets for the pancake night were then discussed; the price was set at $5 for members and $6.50 for non-members, including spouses of committee members. After an uproar the price for spouses was reduced, but with warnings that there would be resentment that committee members paid less. People kept saying, 'Well, we probably pay more anyway, by the time we bring something'. The discussion moved to a raffle and cake stall, two women protesting: 'Not at the shopping centre, it's too cold' and 'The woman in the cake shop got shirty last time'. Expense for a mat cover was dodged by one woman volunteering her mother-in-law's labour: 'She's a dressmaker, it will take her a couple of minutes'.

But this was the expected women's labour—not recognized

as work but labour for love, not 'hard work' in the hard, real world. Whereas the RA was in the 'public' sphere, dealing with 'real' issues by bureaucratic means, the fund-raisers were working out of private homes for family and community, making real money, but with their domestic labour. Listing those who contributed in the early years, Bill realized he had forgotten one woman: 'She's the kind of person who didn't speak out very often, but she'd still be there to help when it was needed. She'd always be there to man [!] the cake stall or whatever. That sort of thing, the sort of things that people don't think about; somebody standing out in the cold for three hours, selling rotten old cakes. You need all those sort of people'.

The fund-raising always included and needed men but they were often invisible, a nicely ironic balance to the 'thereness' of women in public life. 'You need manpower like to help with setting things up'; men had contacts, 'like getting donations of things for a raffle, say, or paper to have stuff printed on'. But 'the women are the workers, like they'll be the ones that'll do a cake stall'. So a good division of labour was important. 'I would have liked to see more men on', said one IPA member, 'You had to sort of ask your husbands'. Meanwhile, men on these groups saw themselves as getting 'the dirty jobs': 'those women had it all worked out' laughed one, grumbling about the heavy trestles that they 'couldn't let' the women lift. People outside the fund-raising groups rarely mentioned the projects initiated and carried out by men—a car trial, compost drives and many of the social events. At an IPA meeting organizing a school fun day, men volunteered to operate the drink machine, hire equipment, get a spit, provide meat, collect bread (if it could be ordered by one of the women), get bags for the bag race and sports equipment from work; then one was 'dobbed in' to be Santa. In all this discussion the women had been involved only with collecting items. Ken was asked if he would see the principal, and said, 'I work'; a woman then volunteered to do so.

Fund-raising, the new industry of the suburbs, deserves serious attention as a form of volunteer work. Like all such work it is undertaken in the name of families, largely carried out by women, has low status, limited rewards and serves to mask the inadequacies of welfare provisions.[4] 'I think mainly the people who join the committees are the people who want to help out in the community', said one man. 'You know, these fund-raising committees, they want to fill in the gap where the Education Department or the government falls short.' To have sufficient preschool-age children needing a pre-school is merely a necessary, never a sufficient condition for getting one. To be promised it by the developer merely makes it more likely that should it be approved land will be allocated. To have sufficient fund-raising power to put up thousands of dollars urgently is the next requirement: 'We pulled out all stops. They raised about $4000 in less than a year. So we worked hard, and that was a whole lot of raffles that we all put our own money into. There was a whole lot of progressive dinners that we all cooked up and had them all at our place'.

It took a few years before there were regular protests that, as Jane concluded ruefully, 'Yes, you do all the work and you spend all the money'. Our records show the first flood of protests in 1980 at a Preschool meeting:

Robyn said that it was always the same few who were expected to be involved and it was expensive . . . This sparked off a long and animated discussion of the other mothers who were not supporting the kinder. The topic kept re-emerging when discussing the cake stalls proposed for July and the working bee. Jane and others talked about how the non-committee mums avoid them at the kinder . . . One said she has 'nearly had her head eaten off' when she has suggested that the fees would have to be raised if mothers didn't support the kindergarten's fund-raising activities . . . Women accused the uninvolved of being 'lazy': 'Surely they can throw a 30c cake into the oven'. It was a clear 'us' and 'them' situation . . . One suggested they have a roster for the mothers to do morning teas and for the husbands to do the working bees. They also talked about how the children could be encouraged to coerce the mothers to be involved, e.g. wash the towels; it appears that the children see it as an 'honour' to wash the kinder towels.

The available structures of fund-raising offer few options in which the fund-raisers themselves do not have to contribute money and sometimes substantial labour and time. Companies organized to sell through fund-raising groups rely on the publicity, transport and marketing effort of the volunteers. Having donated these, members usually ended up purchasing much of the seemingly endless stream of packaged lamingtons, sweets, sponge cakes and chocolates that flowed from profit-making companies into the estate. A lamington drive required that lamingtons be ordered, pre-paid, delivered and distributed, and sold urgently while the cakes were fresh. Everyone was eating lamingtons that week. Moreover, the value of women's labour was kept as low as possible, since problems of coercing people to spend money meant that profits were minimized: 'They were selling sponges and what have you for 50 cents. They were donated, of course, but the product involved in making them was well in excess of that'. She did not cost the labour. Having baked all night for the cake stall, donating ingredients and labour, a member would end up purchasing something another woman had baked.[5]

The resentment was justified merely on the grounds of economic exploitation. But it was also about the ways fund-raising endangered and misused privacy. Personal taste and decorating skill were exposed by events in private homes, and personal friendship and loyalty misused to make profits. Two episodes from the life of the IPA illustrate the tensions and conflicts surrounding the 'social' activity of fund-raising. They also illustrate the problems people—and sociology—meet in taking seriously the conditions of women's daily lives. Both were widely treated as absurd, but both nearly destroyed the group. The first occurred merely three months from the group's formation. In a discussion about raffle prizes, a woman suggested that her husband could donate a light fitting, duly described. Another commented under her breath: 'I wouldn't put it in my dunny!'. (Different versions of this remark occurred later, including, 'I would put it in my toilet'.) After the meeting, one woman summarized: 'There was a big blow-up and everything went all out of proportion. And then everybody [said], "I can't take any more of this", etc.'. The office-bearers resigned, emergency meetings were held, but somehow they survived the end of the year. 'At the Christmas Fair, all this was going on and everybody was bitching between one another ... Everybody was, "Oh, oh, oh" over the light fitting.' The group re-formed, but only to face another battle—raffles. The new president was a 'good worker', but a woman of deep religious beliefs who approved neither of gambling nor drinking. Raffles were the first issue: 'Everybody else didn't have anything against raffles, bar the one who was sitting at the head of the table!' A wine and cheese night was held 'behind her back, and she didn't like that. And because all that was going on, the secretary felt that she couldn't take any more and she resigned'.

In both cases, women not directly involved in the issues had resigned, and the phrase is the same—'can't take any more'. Of what? 'Pressure' is the common word, and the adjectives used are from stereotypes of women's behaviour—'bitchy', 'catty'. The intense personal squabbling was extremely distressing to many. The president was finally forced to resign, and the group 'fell in a heap' again. Re-formed, it was more successful, 'because a lot of the women disappeared and we seemed to have had more men', explained a woman. Men took the jobs of president and secretary. That helped, she said, 'The less women, the less talking, I suppose!'. The main interest now was in keeping control of funds raised; should the committee fold, these would go to the Education Department. There was little social interaction beyond committee meetings, but at last the school was built.

Why should light fittings and raffles cause such painful conflict? Analysed as work, the fund-raising process offers answers, but this is my analysis, not one offered by participants in the groups. The light fitting was a prize for a raffle; donated prizes required contacts, usually through husbands. To refuse it meant foregoing the chance for a raffle, and to deride it meant impugning the husband's work status and the taste of the wife offering it. A raffle was the least costly of fund-raising events for members, both in terms of money and time, and one of the few means of fund-raising of which it was not painfully true that the people who did all the work also spent the money. So prizes for raffles were much desired, and opposition to raffles rankled. Traders in the shopping centre, local business houses, and husbands with contacts were all pressured for raffle prizes. Party-plan events were held at which the committee members spent their own money to gain a single 'free' item that could be raffled. Termed a hostess gift, this was 'donated' by the company to reward the woman who had provided the ideological and physical setting for such a sales exercise—her home, her labour as hostess and usually the refreshments.

His groups and hers

The IPA disbanded when the school opened. A meeting was held to form a School Council, the advisory and policy-making body most of whose members would be elected from the parents. For those involved in the groups it was the turning point in the estate's short history. At this dramatic moment the actors who came out of the large cast of the earlier groups into the spotlights at front stage were men, and the most obvious were the husbands of the women who had baked cakes, sold lamingtons and run raffles.

The School Council as formed had three women members: two representatives of the teachers, and one young English-woman who put herself forward and got on as president of the parents' group. Among the 'oldtimers', as far as we could gather, no woman proposed to stand and no man even considered a woman standing. Keith summarized the process of selection:

M: Diane was at this stage running the canteen. She wasn't on the School Council, but she's been replaced by her husband. [She continued to run the canteen.] He went on the School Council. There was me, the incumbent treasurer who couldn't get out—no, I didn't want to get out. [Joanne was now the vital link of the RA to the coffee mornings and Mothers' Club.] Dick was there, he was always pretty reluctant, or he seemed to be, he only came on because no one else would do it. [His wife was the one who was always there to 'man' the cake stall.] He took on the secretary's job because no one wanted to be secretary. Kenneth came on because this might have been back into his line: he'd gone off the Interim Parents, but when we got back to the School Council he came back as president. [Robyn had another baby and had dropped out of the kinder group but was in the school Mothers' Club.] I don't think we could find enough people to be on it. And because Dick was on it: he got Ken to come on it, 'Look mate, friend, buddy, we need extra people'.

As the language indicates, it was men who were needed. The women assumed this too. It seemed obvious that Diane's husband, not she, should go on the council, so obvious that Keith could reproduce dialogue:

M: He had never done anything before, because she was doing so much, I suppose; he was home looking after the kids. And she had her hands pretty full during the day with the canteen, and so on, so she said, 'Look, I'm not going to this sort of thing', so he said, 'Well, I'll go in your place'.

'This sort of thing' was policy work. It drew two other husbands whose wives had been very active in the IPA and two men who had been in it themselves. There was criticism from at least one man because there were 'too many people from the IPA on it, too many fund-raisers'. The representative of the parents' group was Grace, one of the few women whose husband was not now on the council. [Hers was involved in the Football Club, for which she carried the load of catering on Saturdays.]

The school still required active fund-raising, and everyone assumed the women would do that: 'The Mothers' Club always raises money for the school, so we needed that'. For some time, in anticipation, a debate had run in the coffee mornings and IPA over the naming of the fund-raising support group and its timing: 'Mothers' Club' or 'Parents and Friends'?; daytime or night? The women at home wanted the traditional daytime mothers' club. Joanne commented they 'pushed their way and got it; it all used to be discussed at coffee morning every week'. Robyn had voted for 'Mothers' Club', 'because I couldn't really see any men coming along to assist us'. It became the first of many issues on which they would clash with the new headmaster, who thought it obvious that in an estate where 'nobody's home' in the day, meetings must be held at night. In a compromise, two groups formed—with non-sexist names—but as one woman explained, 'When you say "Parents and Friends" if you're talking to somebody, you go back and say that it's like a mothers' club'. The husband of one of them referred archly to 'all those little old ladies—well, little young ladies, in the Mothers' Club'.

Fund-raising continued, as did the style of meetings. The evening group had more men; in a compost drive on football Grand Final Day three men lugged 560 bags of compost around the estate. The Mothers' Club needed office-bearers, 'no one wanted to take on anything, and Diane was asked would she like to be president'. Everyone else was 'volunteered' for the committee. But the women agreed it was more pleasant than the IPA: 'It's female, see, there's no men ... we understand what we want. We're fund-raising'. The new solidarity was intriguing. Could it be that everyone was wrong in assuming the prior conflict occurred because this was a group of women, or was it because they were now doing only women's work?

A new confidence was demonstrated when the headmaster refused to let the children take home raffle tickets to sell; urged the women instead to run cake stalls and fairs. Now that the school was established, raffles represented to the women release from the earlier phase when there was no wider contributing audience to reach: 'An Easter egg raffle, or a Christmas hamper raffle, you're sending the tickets home to every child in the school, to sell ten tickets'. The Council (largely married to the Mothers' Club) at first supported the headmaster. Grace had to: 'let them know what the ladies thought about it, how strongly they felt about having a raffle. Because these ladies represent the mothers who were helping to do everything at the school. They're involved, not only as a day group, reading, canteen, the same mothers, and they're the ones who are doing all the work'.

In this material there are strong assertions of 'fact' about gender and group performance that move between descriptions of experience in the real world and ideological assumptions. They come as often from women as men and are confirmed by both, questioned by neither. Women and men acted on these assumptions and remade the ideology as they went along.[6]

Men were said to have, were expected to have, and in our observation *did* have greater authority, especially in groups containing men. The old ideas were weak enough to allow women leadership, but too strong to allow them authority. Those women who took on the presidency of the RA (Susan), the Preschool group (Robyn) and IPA were constantly under criticism. Once RA president, Susan became the object of intense speculation about her family life and especially her ability as a mother. In her court: 'There was potentially eleven men and eleven women who could comment on me while I was there, living within eye distance. The men were free of criticism outside of the committee because what involvement they chose to pursue was tolerated. The women, that was a different kettle of fish'. The woman she called a 'potential professional' was not subjected to such criticism: 'She got involved with playgroups, women's groups, groups that the women saw as being in keeping with the female role'.

Robyn recalled: 'I had commented to me, when I ended up being president, that I shouldn't have done it because I was a woman, and that a man was better'. She thought the comment unfair, although, 'I *realized* men have got a better hold over women at a meeting ... They just feel that women aren't as good as them at standing up to be president, and the name "president" sounds more like a man's job anyway'. But the criticism came more from women: 'It's funny, it's as though the men had said their bit about how the guys should be there, and then they became more supportive. But some of the women were really smart all the time: "Who does she think she is?". Maybe they wanted to be there, but didn't have the courage or something'. One of the women described this presidency as 'the blind leading the blind'.

Men were expected to, and did, have a different style of leadership: 'Kenneth was a perfect president because everything was cut and dried and he knew exactly what he wanted to put in the meeting, he never let anyone be off the track—or they did sometimes but he could always jokingly get everyone back, you know, "Excuse me ladies you can have your chit-chat afterwards", and everyone would just turn round and listen'. This is a *woman* speaking, and no offence is taken at the quoted evidence.[7] Another Preschool committee woman said: 'You need a very strong person and someone that can, even if it is your best friend sitting beside you at the table, pull them into line and be able to go out of the meeting and have it all forgotten. That's where our committee fell down, you know, too many people got too easily offended'. Is that something women do? 'Women do it all the time.'

Men were expected to have, were seen as having, and in our observation did have a different style of interaction—more rational, efficient, formal, and less emotional. Women's groups commonly were described, by women and men, as cliquey and bitchy, men's groups never were. 'They tend to become very catty, as women can', said a male on the Preschool group. 'I don't doubt as men can too', he added dubiously, but men clearly did not. In our records the RA only once sought women. Needing a secretary who could take minutes, Bill asked, 'There must be some lady on the estate?'.[8] But the 'women's groups' needed and sought men, not only for putting up the trestle tables but also for restoring order. Everyone agreed on this.

When the time came to form a committee to earn the necessary money for a second preschool, several of the 'old-timers' went along to help. Change was evident: *this* time the discussion turned early to the pressures of fund-raising and the need to avoid over-using the committee members. But the gendered patterns of authority were unchanged. The male local councillor chairing the meeting said simply 'nominate yourself'.

Finally ten, all women, gave their names in. [The councillor] then startled everyone by saying 'We need some men!'. He gave a jolly little spiel about how if you got on, you could haul your mates along to help in working bees, and he proceeded to pick out men! He bullied two blokes out of the audience, neither of whom seemed at all keen, and a third volunteered from the back row. I turned to Susan ... my expression must have shown some of my surprise at this ploy and Susan (absolutely straight, no suggestion of irony) said, 'Oh yes, you have to have men'. When I looked surprised she said, 'They give stability'. I swear she was not joking.

There are other phrases here that suggest women see their own groups as unstable, transient, sometime things without structure, open to whim and personal interference. And perhaps that they see *women* as being typically this way. But there are also signs that they see women's groups as potentially a source of strength, especially when no men are there to spark conflicts.[9] A woman who had played a considerable part in the fund-raising groups described how she became 'stronger'. At first 'I'd be sort of waiting for someone else to say something, "Well here goes"'. The fear was of 'being made a fool of'. To avoid that: 'You have to be strong, very—not vocal (just talking all the time) but very determined, you know, and strong; know what you're talking about and check up on all the facts before you stand up'. Susan was like that, this woman said, and she linked the male skills to women's workforce participation. The right sort of work gave women confidence: 'They're in PR work all day long and very good at it'.

W: Most other women put their priorities: family, and then your committee and then whatever. But those type of women I would say would have their families organized [so] that they looked after themselves, and they're very good at organizing their priorities, where most women get muddled up. You know, they get in a mess at home and the housework hasn't been done because they're on the phone all day talking with somebody about a problem in Green Views ... With that school vote, that time was very bad ... I'd be on the phone and the baby would be screaming, you know, she'd be stuck in a cupboard, and if you've got someone like the MP, you can't say, 'Excuse me for a moment', too many times, you've just sort of got to grin and bear it. You've got to be a particular kind of person to handle a situation like that or be running a committee that's involved in hassles, fighting.

These are real differences, for all that they are social constructs. 'Arguments about gender are plagued by an assumption that what is biological or "natural" is somehow more real than what is social', and since sex roles are social, 'if you poked a finger at them it would go right through'.[10] The women in the IPA were not simply playing 'sex roles' they were acting within and recreating sets of ideas about family, home and local relationships in which gender was always the strongest, but never the only thread. A division into male and female, public and private worlds would cut through every group process at Green Views.[11] Rather, the group processes were all about people's *conviction* that families and family work and family homes are private worlds and women 'man' them. Convictions that the private world is a separate women's world drag women back into the forms of work and behaviour so labelled. This set of ideas, like the related sets about good family life and home ownership, contains much truth but profoundly distorts it.

Private and less than private

The myth of two spheres is exposed by group activity. Men were active in all groups except the Mothers' Club *because* of their commitment to family and in at least some cases to partnership in marriage. They were involved in groups and, through domestic discussion, drawn into even the informal women's networks in which they could not participate. There was little that was private about those groups except their association with women, family issues and homes; to label them part of the private world on that basis is mere tautology, ignoring the big money they raised and their real political results. But nor were they seen as part of the public world of work; they confronted it, battled with it and attempted to use it, in awkward relationships mediated by husbands.

There is little that is private about the sphere these groups operate in. It intrudes on the precious privacy of family *from* outside surveillance, leaking information about marriages, resources and homes. It intrudes on the time and peacefulness of family life, taking adults, especially women who would otherwise have been at home, out into a political arena where other skills are learned and other contacts made. It is not a homogeneous sphere, and by no means mainly women's. But its concerns are family and local. Some of these groups are clearly more *domestic* than others, groups in which the concerns of family justify and dominate activities and which are driven by the work of women. Those women bring with them personal styles and political tactics that are seen as women's ways, not because they are private or peaceful, nurturing or caring, but because they are seen as inefficient, irrational and impractical, and always dominated by the needs of children and changed by the moving life-cycle. This non-private sphere in turn affects the worlds of families, making them less private.

The group activity in important ways exposes the private world, already embattled. It not only leaks information, but uncovers the dividers of class and life stage. And while it exposes gender differences, it makes workforce participation a clear divider, and so divides women. Those who work are more likely to be in the groups defined as 'political', linked much more clearly to the world of work. Those in the life-stage groups are labelled by them—all those 'little young ladies'—and located by them in ideology, more vulnerable to the 'old' ideas regretting workforce participation, less able to negotiate with ideological proscriptions. So the life-stage groups contained women; to the extent that they offered support networks these were networks in support of tradition. But they were constantly fighting inevitable life-cycle change, losing members and support, building cumulative resentment at having to do all the work and spend all the money while women who earned money left the estate during the day (as the planners had always meant them to).

The groups occupy a zone best described by Harman's term the 'non-residential domestic sphere'.[12] Within this, women dramatically affected the real future of Green Views. But both women and men reinterpreted crucial power disputes and battles for the status of the estate as bitchiness or the concerns of 'little young ladies', in which women's activities could not be seriously considered as 'work', 'political' or 'professional'. This non-residential domestic arena freed women from few of the limitations of the private world and gave access to no clean 'public' sphere. Nor could it guarantee friendship and community. Certainly those involved in the groups met people through them. But what resulted was often anomalous closeness, an awkward, constrained intimacy. Such relationships have been termed 'intimate secondary relationships' in recent work welcoming the new forms of belonging they represent: limited knowledge, controllable but intense personal involvement in public settings for public purposes. Such relationships may in some cases 'permit newcomers to experience warm relationships yet make commitments to friendships slowly'. They also may 'encourage a feeling of belonging, thus adding to community integration as well as to personal satisfaction'.[13] But in Green Views they rarely did, for men or women, and they divided women as normal neighbouring could not.

Loneliness and local groups

To assess the relationships women gained through groups is no simple job: indeed it emphasizes the importance of not generalizing about women's worlds or women's groups. They were not equally involved, not equally contained by these convictions about women's work. Occupational position intrudes, alongside class and life stage, to confuse the division by gender. And women are divided from other women by workforce participation.

Women in paid work were much more able to control the effects of the groups. They evaded the traditional ideas of family and home if their employment was justified in terms of both. That justification would be supported by the networks formed at work, outside the estate. If a woman goes 'out' to work her relationship to the streets in which nobody's home can be unproblematic.

W: You don't talk much with the neighbours, first because you're too busy in the house—most of the people work, husband and wife work, the kids go to school, come back home and they have to do whatever they have to do in the home and there's no time to do a bit of social life around the neighbourhood.

If women wish to avoid local groups, work is the perfect excuse to remain 'out', living the private family life for which they are working, and possibly negotiating less intrusive and more supportive near-neighbour relations. For those very few employed women who sought involvement in the groups, being at work helped in gaining the confidence to 'get in', and in dodging the conflict and sometimes seething resentments of those at home and the expense and difficulties of the fund-raising activity.

But the women at home, likely to be isolated by the apparent emptiness of the suburb, were unlikely to get companionship from the local groups. Problems of courage and competence to get out and get in were women's problems; no man said he had to go along with a friend. And they were worst for those without recent work experience. The pressure to contribute was felt by most women at home, but by contributing they were not guaranteed friendships. Those who do not join, said one man, 'stand out like a dog's back leg'. Yet it was women at home who said of other women that you do not have to be lonely.

W: We wouldn't have got to know the people we know if we hadn't of been involved, and that's what happens to a lot of people on the estate. People say, 'there isn't anything to do', and 'I don't see a soul all day'. I mean, I've made that statement meself, and you'll never get to know anybody if you don't go out there and meet them.

But those who do 'go out' are unlikely to gain community. Mapping group members' nominations of those they knew best, we found few close networks of group members, though most of the neighbourhood clusters of nominations across our sample had group members within them. Those in groups were nominated more often, probably for complex reasons: more likely to be 'outgoing', they also had cause to contact neighbours.[14] Gary recalled: 'You'd find that if someone volunteered to do something, they'd rope in a person who was close'. But friendship is different from being known. There is no question that for some women the groups brought friendships of the 'family lifer' type. They did this for few men, but then few wanted them to. And there is also no question that for women the groups provided only temporary community. Those at home who had the confidence and made the contacts could find, given luck, others in the same life-stage boat. Some of these friendships lasted but they had strict limits. Like all local relationships they were constrained by the ideology of the private family, and curtailed by the temporary links of the life-stage boat as children's stages changed. But further constraints applied to attempts to make friendships through groups.

First, part of the irony of isolation was that those most genuinely convinced that 'it's your own fault if you're lonely' closed opportunities for others. If strong groups of friends did form they tended to deter others from joining: 'Nothing nasty about it, but when they sat down, they always sat together'. Several women placed people, without prompting, into 'old ones' or 'newcomers'. 'If there's a wine-and-cheese on, we all say "Are you going? Are you going?" . . . Maybe we're frightened of meeting new people!'. Two commented that they would have hated to come to Green Views later, to experience the sort of closure of groups they themselves operated: 'It was easier for the first ones here because they *had* to go out and find people'. Everyone asserted all were welcome: 'But you have new ones come, it's very hard to get them in without them getting themselves in. They have to push themselves into a conversation'. The cliques defeated their purpose; while they held their members, their apparent closure to newcomers critically limited the resources available: 'Those raffles that they run or the cake stalls they've run, it's been the same—the executive and their friends'. Joanne, now settled in another area, found women's groups 'a very, very closed shop'. She felt the stranger now: 'Because they've all been here for ever and now I'm the new person. I know what it's like, watching new people come into Green Views and me being the one with all the knowledge and the familiarity and stuff'.

Secondly, the groups catered only to those who enjoyed committee activity. A woman who said she had 'just gradually worked into everything' acknowledged: 'but not everybody's like me. I mean there's lots of people on this estate that'll just sit in their houses and never go anywhere. Or they're at work. I find an awful lot are at work'. Many people remained unaware of the groups or, like one man moving out, knew nothing about them and disliked what they represented: 'I think the Fence around it sort of makes you feel that they want you in— everybody's in together and I think there's a committee'.

Thirdly, groups tended to limit, rather than open up, other social opportunities. While they were historically linked, it was more often by schism or division than co-operation. There was never an open network incorporating all groups: 'Everyone seems to be getting into their little nooks', said a woman leaving after three years. It was as false a description of Green Views as 'nobody's home' but equally revealing: 'I think people are starting to settle into their little thing, whatever they're going to be interested in'.

Fourthly, 'getting involved' in the groups became very time consuming for those who were 'workers'. As Jane said, a woman might as well go to work. Lack of time meant the risk of isolation from other parts of the network. The resentment about the small and dwindling numbers attending meetings is spiced by stories of having to 'volunteer' for office. As the early enthusiasm died the demand for membership became louder: 'The Youth Club's crying out for help and the Tennis Club needs members and the action group's nearly finished because it has no members and the Kinder Committee is now trying to get another kinder committee going—like everything's new and everyone's after people'. This woman, like many others, saw this as a stage to be gone through: 'I got sick of committees. I find Green Views hasn't satisfied our needs and I know a lot of other people feel the same'.

Fifthly, to succeed in the groups, people had not only to raise the courage to get in, but also maintain the courage to be visible, meet people, be 'pushy', even to risk, rather than foster, local relationships: 'Some people are born leaders; you need a committee who can push and know where to push in the right places, and I think there's people who are definitely into that'. This may not make you friends—'neighbours hide' was something several people said. But there were constant complaints about those who would not 'put themselves out', a phrase which in this context seems almost a sociological pun, carrying the double meaning of going out of your way and exposing your *self* to public scrutiny. Those most notable through the groups were those with the confidence and competence not to need them. A woman commented: 'Jane was a big coercer! A good worker anyway. More front than Myers'. A man praised her: 'If there were ever raffle tickets or anything to sell, Jane was the lass, and she would do it wonderfully at morning coffee, playgroups, whatever, everybody and anybody got sold raffle tickets'. (Both statements use past tense, offering almost an obituary now that she has returned to the paid workforce.)

Finally, the seemingly unavoidable clashes and conflicts of the groups created miserable experiences for many who sought friendships. 'Once bitten, twice shy', said a woman who had resigned from the IPA. She would not join the Mothers' Club. 'It'll be the same back-biting, bitching and tacky conversation'.

Another who had left said sadly that she had thought the IPA would be a 'group of nice ladies'.

Yet almost all the women we talked with were convinced that 'you get on a committee without really trying'. A young English migrant had found 'everybody's been so nice and just kind of *want* you there'. Those who belong are, in Mandy's words: 'The people who want to belong—really. They have to make an effort themselves, I think, to belong'. She cited a woman who had left: 'They said that people weren't friendly, but I'd hardly even met them'. But the other side of the question 'Who doesn't belong?' recalls the processes of division.

W: The ones that don't want to! Oh gee, I haven't really met any people who don't belong except of course the ones over the road. Because they live in the area, but they only exist in it; they're not involved in it. It's like they're this single little thing sitting in a bubble or something, and they're the only thing there. Because I don't know how you can live somewhere and feel like you belong somewhere if you don't involve yourself there. I don't understand how people can drive in and out and go to their home, that one home, and then go out again, without ever associating with anything around them.

As the dust of the farmland was replaced by green lawns, the dust of the group conflicts settled and the groups moved into a new stage in which most appeared closed to newcomers, and many of the 'old-timers' got little out of them socially. Looking back over the conflicts, both women and men saw a history of involvement, disillusion and routinization of what originally seemed spontaneous and emotionally rewarding.[15] The case of one woman who had most strongly opposed the president of the IPA, and subsequently resigned, typifies these conflicts. Many people called her 'a worker', everyone agreed that she had been outspoken, but there was considerable sympathy: the workers were the ones under pressure. Grace, who had also resigned, said, 'It sort of does put you off when they're sort of squabbling'. Especially given the costs: 'It was us turning up to *our* little thing and trying to raise a little bit of money that way. Lamington drives, fine. We were the ones going out, trying to get orders, there was nobody else'. As though it explained things (and perhaps it did) she added, of the woman who had led the attack, that she '*had* sold a terrible lot of lamingtons'.

But Grace, committed to staying home, had made all her friendships through the groups: 'Those that have got their children off to school are both working—there's not a lot home. And those that are home are the ones that are involved'. Yet so many women at home were lonely, and the puzzle was that they seemed to want isolation. 'Some are quite happy to stay in their house and not move out of their world'.

Notes

1. S. Ardener, 'Ground rules and social maps for women', in S. Ardener (ed.), *Women and Space*, Croom Helm, London, 1981, p. 12.

2. Pauline Hunt has described such a setting as one where 'the situation itself breeds traditionalism', *Gender and Class Consciousness*, Macmillan, London, 1980, quoted in R. W. Connell, *Gender and Power*, Allen & Unwin, Sydney, 1987, p. 243.

3. The sociology of 'party plan' selling is a serious area for investigation of women's work. See M. Brigden & S. Young, 'Home economics', *New Socialist*, December 1986, pp. 16–17.

4. Feminist literature has strongly made the point that domestic labour is not seen as work, but the finer distinctions of volunteer labour require more attention. See C. V. Baldock, 'Volunteer work as work', in C. V. Baldock & B. Cass (eds), *Women, Social Welfare and the State*, Allen & Unwin, Sydney, 1983, pp. 279–97. See also J. Finch & D. Groves, *A Labour of Love: Women, Work and Caring*, Routledge & Kegan Paul, London, 1983.

5. The financial logic of such efforts has not escaped those who are exploited by them, but in Green Views at least there was no rejection of the method of fund-raising. I suspect this is partly because of two beliefs: that women *want* to demonstrate their support and skills and that doing so promotes group cohesion, even if the cakes are ludicrously cheap, and that they will not merely donate money. I learnt recently of a Californian school committee which some years ago introduced the idea of a 'notional cake', that is, a financial donation for those who had no time to make a cake or no inclination to see their labour so devalued.

6. Too few studies have stressed the ways in which such a situation, in Finch's words, 'makes perfect sense' to women; J. Finch, *Married to the Job: Wives' Incorporation in Men's Work*, Allen & Unwin, London, 1983, p. 168. See K. Dempsey, 'Gender relations: Examination of social closure by men against women', *La Trobe Working Papers in Sociology*, no. 75, 1986, La Trobe University, Bundoora, Vic., for an account of gender relations that 'make sense' in a similar way in a country town.

7. Some of this text recalls valuable aspects of Rosaldo's account of the messiness of women's lives, associated with physical processes that are wet and warm (not cut and dried!) and to do with life and death. While raffles and chandeliers are hardly matters of life and death, the undoubted messy structure of women's groups and intimacy of knowledge and gossip has a lot to do with wet and warmth. See M. Rosaldo & L. Lamphere (eds), *Women, Culture and Society*, Stanford University Press, Stanford, 1974.

8. This was one of the few times when the presence of a female

researcher seemed to affect response—another woman grinned at Jan and observed that the secretary did not have to be a woman.

9. Jessie Bernard has explored some of the ambivalence of groups in women's 'sphere'; J. Bernard, *The Female World*, Free Press, New York, 1981, chs 5—6.

10. Connell, *Gender and Power*, p. x.

11. For different reasons that framework failed to work on the study of women in a country town by Kerry James; see 'Public or private: Participation by women in a country town', in M. Bowman (ed.), *Beyond the City*, Longman Cheshire, Melbourne, 1981. The two settings offer complementary critiques of the model. She stresses the evidence of 'entrepreneurial behaviour' by middle-class wives linking relations of class and status to which they have access, and significantly participating in the placement of their families in 'the public face of the town' (p. 111) indicating the 'social processes in our society which link the two domains so closely that the identification of men with one and women with the other cannot be admitted' (p. 104). But there too 'the ideology of separate spheres' retains its power, masking these women's status-related activities. The groups within Green Views offer no such access to wider systems of class and status and the present focus can give no indication of women's part in their husbands' 'public' lives, but certainly there is no reason to suppose they have none.

12. E. J. Harman, 'Capitalism, patriarchy and the city', in C. V. Baldock & B. Cass (eds), *Women, Social Welfare and the State*, Allen & Unwin, Sydney, 1983, p. 120. In the introduction to the revised edition of *Mothers and Working Mothers* I used the term 'no-man's land' for the extra-familial family-linked activities of women , but while it conveys something of the war-zone experience of these groups it misleads by confirming the myth that there are no men there. J. Harper & L. Richards, *Mothers and Working Mothers*, rev. edn, Penguin, Ringwood, 1986.

13. P. Wireman, *Urban Neighbourhoods, Networks and Families*, D. C. Heath, Lexington, Mass., 1984, pp. 8—9.

14. Up to 1979 the Residents' Association, Preschool Association and Interim Parents' Association were the only formal groups in the estate, and to the end of 1980, 49 households had at some time been involved in at least one. Our random sample in 1978 picked up 35 of these. We asked in that interview for the four people in Green Views the respondent 'knew best'. These data are obviously limited—by exclusion of 14 group member households, and restriction to four 'known', and by the fact that the survey interviewed only one member of each household (not necessarily the group member) but they give some insight into the social setting of group membership.

15. See C. Bell & H. Newby, *Community Studies*, Allen & Unwin, London, 1971, for a discussion of this Weberian concept in this context. I am not suggesting here that there was a simple inevitable slide from communion to routinization: it is important that most groups never had communion and the loss of enthusiasm had many causes. One may be a process of whittling away of membership. As those women who can, because of ideological and life-stage position, move into the workforce they leave a very non-random selection of women at home defending an embattled version of traditional family ideology, and committed to the survival of their own groups. The processes recall what in a very different context I called a 'residual group', a group formed by erosion of membership and highly committed to maintaining both the ideology it stands for and its image as viable and significant. See L. Richards, 'Displaced politics', in J. Jupp (ed.), *Racism in Australia*, Allen & Unwin, Sydney, 1986.

Bibliography

Abercrombie, N. *et al. The Dominant Ideology Thesis*. Allen & Unwin, London, 1984.

Allan, G. A. *A Sociology of Friendship and Kinship*. Allen & Unwin, London, 1979.

Allport, C. 'The princess in the castle: Women in the new social order housing', in Women and Labour Publications Collective. *All Her Labours: Embroidering the Framework*. Hale & Iremonger, Sydney, 1984.

Allport, C. 'Women and suburban housing: Postwar planning in Sydney, 1943−61,' in J. B. McLoughlin & M. Huxley (eds), *Urban Planning in Australia: Critical Readings*. Longman Cheshire, Melbourne, 1986.

Ardener, S. 'Ground rules and social maps for women', in S. Ardener (ed.), *Women and Space*. Croom Helm, London, 1981.

Balbo, L. 'Crazy quilts: Rethinking the welfare state debate from a woman's point of view', in A. S. Sassoon (ed.), *Women and the State: The Shifting Boundaries of Public and Private*. Hutchinson, London, 1987.

Baldock, C. V. & Cass, B. (eds). *Women, Social Welfare and the State*. Allen & Unwin, Sydney, 1983.

Barrett, M. *Women's Oppression Today*. Verso, London, 1980.

Barrett, M. & McIntosh, M. *The Anti-Social Family*. Verso, London, 1982.

Bell, C. 'On housing classes'. *Australian and New Zealand Journal of Sociology*, vol. 13, no. 1, 1977, pp. 36−40.

Bell, C. & Newby, H. *Community Studies*. Allen & Unwin, London, 1971.

Bernard, J. *The Female World*. Free Press, NY, 1981.

Berger, B. & Berger, P. *The War Over the Family: Capturing the Middle Ground*. Penguin, Harmondsworth, 1983.

Berger, P. *Working Class Suburb*. University of California Press, Berkeley, Calif., 1960.

Berger, P. L. & Kellner, H. 'Marriage and the construction of reality', in H. P. Drietzel (ed.), *Recent Sociology No. 2: Patterns of Communicative Behaviour*. Macmillan, New York, 1970.

Bernades, J. '"Family ideology": Identification and exploration'. *Sociological Review*, vol. 33, 1985, pp. 275–94.

Bernard, J. *The Female World*. Free Press, New York, 1981.

Boyd, R. *The Australian Ugliness*. Penguin, Ringwood, 1968.

Brigden, M. & Young, S. 'Home economics'. *New Socialist*, December 1986, pp. 16–17.

Broom, L. F. *et al.* (eds). 'Social stratification in Australia', in J. A. Jackson (ed.). *Social Stratification*. Cambridge University Press, Cambridge, 1968.

Bryson, L. 'The Australian patriarchal family', in L. Bryson & S. Encel (eds), *Australian Society*. 4th edn, Cheshire, Melbourne, 1984.

Bryson, L. 'Gender divisions and power relationships in the Australian family', in P. Collins (ed.), *Family and Economy in Modern Society*. Macmillan, Houndmills, Hants, 1985.

Bryson, L. & Mowbray, M. 'Who cares? Social security, family policy and women'. *International Social Security Review*, no. 2, 1986, pp. 183–200.

Bryson, L. & Thompson, F. *An Australian Newtown: Life and Leadership in a New Housing Suburb*. Penguin, Ringwood, 1972.

Bryson, L. & Wearing, B. 'Australian community studies—a feminist critique'. *Australian and New Zealand Journal of Sociology*, vol. 21, pp. 349–66.

Bulmer, M. (ed.). *Neighbours: the Work of Philip Abrams*. Cambridge University Press, Cambridge, 1986.

Burgess, E. W. *et al. The Family from Institution to Companionship*. 3rd edn, Van Nostrand Reinhold, New York, 1963.

Burke, T., Hancock, L. & Newton, P. *A Roof Over Their Heads: Housing Issues and Families in Australia*. Institute of Family Studies, Melbourne, 1984.

Burns, A. 'Why do women continue to marry?', in N. Grieve & A. Burns (eds) *Australian Women: New Feminist Perspectives*. Oxford University Press, Melbourne, 1986.

Burns, A., Bottomley, G. & Jools, P. (eds). *The Family in the Modern World*. Allen & Unwin, Sydney, 1983.

Burton, C. *Subordination*. Allen & Unwin, Sydney, 1985.

Busfield, J. & Paddon, M. *Thinking about Children*. Cambridge University Press, Cambridge, 1977.

Campbell, F. & Kriegler, R. 'Illusion and disillusion: The ideology of community in an industrial town', in M. Bowman, (ed.), *Beyond the City*. Longman Cheshire, Melbourne, 1981.

Carey, L. & Mapes, R. *The Sociology of Planning: A Study of Social Activity on New Housing Estates*. Batsford Press, London, 1972.

Cass, B. 'Housing and the family'. *SWRC Reprints*, Social Welfare Research Centre, Kensington, Vic., 1980.

Cass, B. & Radi, H. 'Family, fertility and the labour market', in N. Grieve & P. Grimshaw (eds), *Australian Women: Feminist Perspectives*. Oxford University Press, Melbourne, 1981.

Castells, M. *The Urban Question*. Edward Arnold, London, 1977.

Clark, S. D. *The Suburban Society*. University of Toronto Press, Toronto, 1966.

Commonwealth of Australia. *Cost of Housing*. Report of the Committee of Inquiry into Housing Costs, Australian Government Publishing Service, Canberra, 1978.

Connell, R. W. 'The concept of role and what to do with it'. *Australian and New Zealand Journal of Sociology*, vol. 15, 1979, pp. 7–17.

Connell, R. W. *Gender and Power*. Allen & Unwin, Sydney, 1987.

Connell, R. W. *Ruling Class, Ruling Culture*. Cambridge University Press, Cambridge, 1977.

Crompton, R. & Mann, M. (eds). *Gender and Stratification*. Polity Press, Cambridge, 1986

Croog, S. H. *et al*. 'Help patterns in severe illnesses'. *Journal of Marriage and the Family*, vol. 34, no. 1, 1972, pp. 32–41.

D'Abbs, P. 'Family support networks and public responsibility', in *XXth International CFR Seminar on Social Change and Family Policies*. Institute of Family Studies, Melbourne, 1984.

D'Abbs, P. Give and take: A study of support networks and social strategies. PhD thesis, University of Melbourne, 1983.

D'Abbs, P. *Social Support Networks: A Critical Review of Models and Findings*. AIFS monograph, Australian Institute of Family Studies, Melbourne, 1982.

Dalley, G. *Ideologies of Caring*. Macmillan, London, 1988.

Davidoff, L., Esperence, J. & Newby, H. 'Landscape with figures: Home and community in English society', in J. Mitchell & A. Oakley (eds), *The Rights and Wrongs of Women*. Penguin, Harmondsworth, 1976.

Davies, A. F. *Images of Class*. Sydney University Press, Sydney, 1967.

Day, A. *We Can Manage*. AIFS monograph, Australian Institute of Family Studies, Melbourne, 1985.

Day, A. & Harley, A. 'I hope something comes of all this'. *La Trobe Working Papers in Sociology*, no. 72, 1985, La Trobe University, Bundoora, Vic.

Delamont, S. *The Sociology of Women*. Allen & Unwin, London, 1980.

Dempsey, K. 'Gender relations: Examination of social closure by men against women'. *La Trobe Working Papers in Sociology*, no. 75, 1986, La Trobe University, Bundoora, Vic.

Donzelot, J. *The Policing of Families*. Pantheon, London, 1979.

Duncan, J. 'From container of women to status symbol: The impact of social structure on the meaning of the house', in J. Duncan (ed.) *Housing and Identity: Cross-Cultural Perspectives*. Croom Helm, London, 1981.

Duncan, J. (ed.). *Housing and Identity: Cross-Cultural Perspectives*. Croom Helm, London, 1981.

Duncan, N. 'Home ownership and social theory', in J. Duncan (ed.), *Housing and Identity: Cross-Cultural Perspectives*. Croom Helm, London, 1981.

Edgell, S. *Middle-Class Couples*. Allen & Unwin, London, 1980.

Eipper, C. 'Class processes: Key issues for analysis'. *Australian and New Zealand Journal of Sociology*, vol. 18, no. 2, 1982, pp. 214–27.

Eisenstein, H. *Contemporary Feminist Thought*. George Allen & Unwin, London, 1984.

Elshtain, J. B. *Public Man, Private Woman: Women in Social and Political Thought*. Princeton University Press, Princeton, NJ, 1981.

Finch, J. *Married to the Job: Wives' Incorporation into Men's Work*. Allen & Unwin, London, 1983.

Finch, J. 'The vignette technique in survey research'. *Sociology*, vol. 21, 1987, pp. 105–14.

Finch, J. *Family Obligations and Social Change*, Polity Press, Cambridge, 1989.

Finch, J. & Groves, D. 'Community care and the family: A case for Equal opportunities', in C. Ungeson, *Women and Social Policy*. Macmillan, London, 1985, pp. 218–41.

Finch, J. & Groves, D. (eds). *A Labour of Love: Women, Work and Caring*. Routledge & Kegan Paul, London, 1983.

Finighan, W. R. *Privacy in Suburbia: A Study in Four Melbourne Areas*. CSIRO, Melbourne, 1979.

Fischer, C. S. *To Dwell Among Friends: Personal Networks in Town and City*. University of Chicago Press, Chicago, 1982.

Fischer, C. S. & Oliker, S. 'Friendship, sex and the life cycle'. *Working Paper No. 318*. Institute of Urban and Regional Development, University of California, Berkeley, Calif., 1980.

Foucault, M. *The History of Sexuality*. Allen Lane, London, 1979.

Frankenberg, R. *Communities in Britain*. Penguin, Harmondsworth, 1966.

Frankenberg, R. 'In the production of their lives, men (?)...sex and gender in British community studies', in D. Barker & S. Allen (eds), *Sexual Divisions and Society*. Tavistock, London, 1976.

Gale, F. 'Seeing women in the landscape: Alternative views of the world around us', in J. Goodnow & C. Pateman (eds), *Women, Social Science and Public Policy*. Allen & Unwin, Sydney, 1985.

Gamarnikow, E. *et al.* (eds). *The Public and the Private*. Heinemann, London, 1983.

Game, A. & Pringle, R. 'Beyond *Gender at Work*: Secretaries', in N. Grieve & A. Burns (eds), *Australian Women: New Feminist Perspectives*. Oxford University Press, Melbourne, 1986.

Game, A. & Pringle, R. *Gender at Work*. Allen & Unwin, Sydney, 1983.

Game, A. & Pringle, R. 'The making of the Australian family', in A. Burns, G. Bottomley & P. Jools (eds), *The Family in the Modern World*. Allen & Unwin, Sydney, 1983.

Gans, H. *The Levittowners*. Vintage Books, New York, 1967.

Gerson, K. 'What do women want from men?'. *American Behavioural Scientist*, vol. 29, 1986, pp. 619–34.

Glaser, B. & Strauss, A. *The Discovery of Grounded Theory*. Aldine Publishing Co., Chicago, 1965.

Glezer, H. 'Antecedents and correlates of marriage and family attitudes in young Australian men and women'. *XXth International CFR Seminar on Social Change and Family Policies*. Institute of Family Studies, Melbourne, 1984.

Glezer, H. Changes in marriage and sex role attitudes among young married women: 1971–1982. Paper to the Australian Family Research Conference, Canberra, 1983.

Goldthorpe, J. *et al.* *The Affluent Worker in the Class Structure*. Cambridge University Press, Cambridge, 1969.

Graham, H. 'Do her answers fit his questions? Women and the survey method', in E. Gamarnikow *et al.* (eds), *The Public and The Private*. Heinemann, London, 1983.

Grieve, N. & Burns, A. (eds). *Australian Women: New Feminist Perspectives*. Oxford University Press, Melbourne, 1986.

Grieve, N. & Grimshaw, P. (eds). *Australian Women: New Feminist Perspectives*. Oxford University Press, Melbourne, 1981.

Hall, S. *Culture, Media, Language*. Hutchinson, London, 1980.

Hall, S. 'Ideology in the modern world'. *La Trobe Working Papers in Sociology*, no. 65, 1983, La Trobe University, Bundoora, Vic.

Hallman, H. W. *Neighbourhoods: Their Place in Urban Life*. Sage, Beverley Hills, Calif., 1984.

Harman, E. J. 'Capitalism, patriarchy and the city', in C. V. Baldock & B. Cass (eds), *Women, Social Welfare and the State*. Allen & Unwin, Sydney, 1983, pp. 104–29.

Harper, J. *Fathers at Home*. Penguin, Ringwood, 1980.

Harper, J. & Richards, L. *Mothers and Working Mothers*. Rev. edn. Penguin, Ringwood, 1986.

Hayden, D. *Redesigning the American Dream: The Future of Housing, Work and Family Life*. W. W. Norton & Co., New York, 1984.

Haywood, D. 'The great Australian dream reconsidered'. *Housing Studies*, vol. 1, 1986, p. 213.

Hernes, H. M. 'Women and the welfare state: The transition from private to public dependence', in A. S. Sassoon (ed.), *Women and* the State: The Shifting Boundaries of Public and Private*. Hutchinson, London, 1987.

Holmes, A. *Housing and Young Families in East London*. Routledge & Kegan Paul, London, 1985.

Howe, A. L. 'Family support of the aged: Some evidence and interpretation'. *Australian Journal of Social Issues*, vol. 14, no. 4, 1979, pp. 259−73.

Ineichen, B. 'Home ownership and manual workers' lifestyles'. *Sociological Review*, vol. 20, 1972, pp. 391−412.

James, B. 'Public' and 'private' divisions in a single-industry town. Paper to the Sociological Association of Australia and New Zealand, Brisbane, 1985.

James, K. 'The home: A public or private place? Class, status and the actions of women'. *Australian and New Zealand Journal of Sociology*, vol. 15, no. 1, 1979, pp. 36−42.

Jupp, J. *Racism in Australia*. Allen & Unwin, Sydney, 1985.

Kemeny, J. *The Great Australian Nightmare*. Georgian House, Melbourne, 1983.

Kemeny, J. *The Myth of Home Ownership*. Routledge & Kegan Paul, London, 1981.

Kendig, H. & Mugford, S. *Ageing and Families: A Social Networks Perspective*. Allen & Unwin, Sydney, 1986.

Kilmartin, L. & Thorns, D. *Cities Unlimited*. Allen & Unwin, Sydney, 1978.

Kilmartin, L., Thorns, D. & Burke, T. *Social Theory and the Australian City*. Allen & Unwin, Sydney, 1985.

Kingston, B. *My Wife, My Daughter and Poor Mary-Ann*. Nelson, Melbourne, 1975.

Kirkby-Jones, W. B. Housing Australians—an industry overview. Paper to the Housing Industry Association, Sydney, 1981.

Kondos, A. 'The hidden faces of power: A sociological analysis of housing legislation in Australia', in R. Tomasic, *Legislation and Society in Australia*. Law in Society Seminar, Illinois, 1979.

Kriegler, R. *Working for the Company*. Oxford University Press, Melbourne, 1980.

LaRossa, R. 'Fatherhood and social change'. *Family Relations*, vol. 37, 1988, pp. 451−7.

LaRossa, R. & Wolf, J. H. 'On qualitative family research'. *Journal of Marriage and the Family*, vol. 47, 1985, pp. 531−41.

Lasch, C. *Haven in a Heartless World*. Basic Books, New York, 1979.

Lee, G. 'Kinship in the seventies: A decade review of research and theory'. *Journal of Marriage and the Family*, vol. 42, November 1980, pp. 923−34.

Leigh, G. K. 'Kinship interaction over the family life span'. *Journal of Marriage and the Family*, vol. 44, February 1982, pp. 197−208.

Lewis, R. 'Some changes in men's values, meanings, roles and attitudes toward marriage and the family in the USA', in *XXth International CFR Seminar on Social Change and Family Policies*. Institute of Family Studies, Melbourne, 1984.

Litwak, G. & Szelenyi, J. 'Primary group structures and their functions: Kin, neighbours and friends'. *American Sociological Review*, vol. 34, no. 4, 1969, pp. 468–81.

Lofland, L. 'The "thereness" of women: A selective review of urban sociology', in M. Millman & R. M. Kanter (eds), *Another Voice*. Anchor Books, New York, 1975.

McCaughey, J. *A Bit of a Struggle*. Longman, Melbourne, 1987.

McDonald, P. Can the family survive? AIFS discussion paper no. 11, Institute of Family Studies, Melbourne, 1984.

McDonald, P. 'The baby boom generation as reproducers'. *Australian Family Research Conference*. Institute of Family Studies, Melbourne, 1983.

McDonald, P. 'Families in the future: The pursuit of personal autonomy'. *Family Matters*, no. 22, 1988, pp. 40–7.

McDowell, L. 'Towards an understanding of the gender division of urban space'. *Environment and Planning D: Society and Space*, vol. 1, 1983, pp. 59–72.

McLoughlin, J. B. & Huxley, M. (eds). *Urban Planning in Australia: Critical Readings*. Longman Cheshire, Melbourne, 1986.

Marshall, H. Not having families: A study of some voluntarily childless couples. PhD thesis, La Trobe University, Bundoora, Vic., 1986.

Martin, J. 'Extended kinship ties, an Adelaide study'. *Australian and New Zealand Journal of Sociology,* vol. 3, no. 1, 1967, pp. 44–63.

Martin, J. 'Suburbia, community and network', in A. F. Davies & S. Encel (eds), *Australian Society: A Sociological Introduction*. 2nd edn, Cheshire, Melbourne, 1970.

Matrix Book Group, *Making Space: Women and the Man Made Environment*. Pluto Press, London, 1984.

Matthews, J. *Good and Mad Women*. Allen & Unwin, Sydney, 1984.

Miles, M. & Huberman, M. *Qualitative Data Analysis*. Sage, Beverley Hills, Calif., 1983.

Morgan, D. *Social Theory and the Family*. Routledge & Kegan Paul, London, 1975.

Nisbet, R. A. *The Sociological Tradition*. Basic Books, London, 1966.

Oakley, A. *Becoming a Mother*. Martin Robertson, London, 1979.

Oakley, A. *The Sociology of Housework*. Martin Robertson, London, 1974.

O'Donnell, C. *The Basis of the Bargain*. Allen & Unwin, Sydney, 1984.

Pahl, R. R. *Divisions of Labour*. Blackwell, Oxford, 1984.

Parsons, T. 'Age and sex in the social structure of the United States'.

American Sociological Review, vol. 7, 1942, pp. 604−16.

Perin, C. *Everything in Its Place: Social Order and Land Use in America*. Princeton University Press, Princeton, NJ, 1977.

Rakoff, R. M. 'Ideology in everyday life: The meaning of the house'. *Politics and Society*, vol. 7, 1977, pp. 85−104.

Rapoport, R. & R. N. (eds), *Working Couples*. Routledge & Kegan Paul, London, 1975.

Rapp, R. 'Family and class in contemporary America: Notes towards an understanding of ideology', in B. Thorne & M. Yalom (eds), *Rethinking the Family: Some Feminist Questions*. Longman, New York, 1982.

Ravetz, A. 'The home of woman: A view from the interior'. *Built Environment*, vol. 10, pp. 8−17, 19.

Rehak, P. H. Stoking up dreams: Some aspects of post-war housing in the suburbs of Melbourne. PhD thesis, Monash University, Clayton, Vic., 1988.

Reiger, K. *The Disenchantment of the Home*. Oxford University Press, Melbourne, 1985.

Rex, J. 'The sociology of a zone of transition', in R. Pahl (ed.), *Readings in Urban Sociology*. Pergamon Press, Oxford, 1969.

Richards, L. 'And they all have pretty children...'. *La Trobe Working Papers in Sociology*, no. 77, 1986, La Trobe University, Bundoora, Vic.

Richards, L. 'Australian family studies'. *Contemporary Sociology*, vol. 14, 1985.

Richards, L. 'Families in a suburb: Network management and its varied results'. *La Trobe Working Papers in Sociology*, no. 64, 1983, La Trobe University, Bundoora, Vic.

Richards, L. 'Family and home ownership in Australia: The nexus of ideologies', in M. Sussman, K. Boh & G. Sgritta (eds), *Strategies in Marriage, Family and Work: International Perspectives*. (Special issue of *Marriage and Family Review*, forthcoming 1989.)

Richards, L. *Having Families*. Rev. edn, Penguin, Ringwood, 1985.

Richards, L. Ideology at home? Family and home ownership in the Australian context. Paper to the National Council on Family Relations, Atlanta, Georgia, 1987.

Richards, L. 'The impossible dream', in D. Davis (ed.), *Living Together*. Centre for Continuing Education, Canberra, 1980.

Richards, L. 'It means a family life: Home ownership and family values in an Australian estate'. *La Trobe Working Papers in Sociology*, no. 76, 1987, La Trobe University, Bundoora, Vic.

Richards, L. 'Mothers'. *Australian Society*, vol. 3, 1984, pp. 40−1.

Richards, L. 'No man's land', in J. Harper & L. Richards, *Mothers and Working Mothers*, rev. edn. Penguin, Ringwood, 1986, intro.

Richards, L. 'Shapes in suburbia: Towards a typology of local relationships.' *La Trobe Working Papers in Sociology*, no. 67, 1983, La

Trobe University, Bundoora, Vic.

Richards, L. 'Too close for comfort: Neighbouring in a new estate'. *La Trobe Working Papers in Sociology*, no. 70, 1985, La Trobe University, Bundoora, Vic.

Richards, L. & Richards, T. The impact of computer techniques on qualitative data analysis. Paper to the Social Science Research Conference, Brisbane, August 1988.

Richards, L. & Richards, T. 'Qualitative data analysis: Can computers do it?'. *Australian and New Zealand Journal of Sociology*, vol. 23, 1987, pp. 23–35.

Richards, L. & Richards, T. Qualitative data: Computer means to analysis goals. Paper to the Sociological Association of Australia and New Zealand, Sydney, 1987.

Richards, T. & Richards, L. 'NUDIST: A system for qualitative data analysis'. *ACS Bulletin*, October 1988, pp. 5–9.

Richards, T. & Richards, L. *User Manual for NUDIST: A Text Analysis Program for the Social Sciences*. 2nd edn, Replee, Melbourne, 1987.

Richards, L. & Salmon, J. 'There when you need them? Family life stage and social network'. *La Trobe Working Papers in Sociology*, no. 68, 1984, La Trobe University, Bundoora, Vic.

Rosaldo, M. & Lamphere, L. (eds). *Women, Culture and Society*. Stanford University Press, Stanford, 1974.

Rosow, I. 'Home ownership motives'. *American Sociological Review*, vol. 13, 1948, pp. 751–6.

Rothblatt, D., Garr, D. & Sprague, J. *The Suburban Environment and Women*. Holt, Reinhart & Winston, New York, 1979.

Rubin, L. *Worlds of Pain: Life in the Working Class Family*. Basic Books, New York, 1976.

Russell, G. *The Changing Role of Fathers?* University of Queensland Press, St Lucia, Qld, 1983.

Saegert, S. 'Masculine cities and feminine suburbs: Polarised ideas, contradictory realities'. *Signs*, vol. 5, Spring 1980, pp. s.96–s.111.

Salmon, J. & Richards, L. The Green Views project. Unpubl. Report, Department of Sociology, La Trobe University, Bundoora, Vic. 1980.

Sandercock, L. *Cities for Sale: Property, Politics and Urban Planning in Australia*. Melbourne University Press, Melbourne, 1975.

Sassoon, A. S. (ed.). *Women and the State: The Shifting Boundaries of Public and Private*. Hutchinson, London, 1987.

Scutt, J. *Even in the Best of Homes: Violence in the Family*. Allen & Unwin, Melbourne. 1983.

Seeley, J. R. *et al. Crestwood Heights*. University of Toronto Press, Toronto, 1956.

Simms, M. 'The politics of women and cities: A critical survey', in J. Halligan & C. Paris (eds), *Australian Urban Politics: Critical Per-*

spectives, Longman Cheshire, Melbourne, 1984, pp. 129—40.

Stacey, M. 'The division of labour or overcoming the two Adams', in P. Abrams *et al.* (eds), *Practice and Progress: British Sociology 1950—1980*. Allen & Unwin, London, 1981.

Stacey, M. *Tradition and Change: A Study of Banbury*. Oxford University Press, London, 1960.

Stacey, M. & Price, M. *Women, Power and Politics*. Tavistock, London, 1981.

Stacey, M. *et al. Power, Persistence and Change*. Routledge & Kegan Paul, London, 1975.

Stack, C. *All Our Kin: Strategies for Survival in a Black Community*. Harper & Row, New York, 1974.

Steuve, A. & Gerson, K. 'Personal relations across the life-cycle', in C. S. Fischer *et al., Networks and Places: Social Relations in the Urban Setting*. Free Press, New York, 1977.

Stivens, M. 'Women and their kin: Kin, class and solidarity in a middle-class suburb of Sydney, Australia', in P. Caplan & J. M. Bujra, *Women United, Women Divided*. Tavistock, London, 1978.

Stolk, Y. & Penman, R. *Not the Marrying Kind*. Penguin, Ringwood, 1984.

Strauss, A. *Qualitative Analysis for Social Scientists*. Cambridge University Press, Cambridge, 1987.

Stretton, H. 'Housing—an investment for all', in J. B. McLoughlin & M. Huxley (eds), *Urban Planning in Australia: Critical Readings*. Longman Cheshire, Melbourne, 1986.

Stretton, H. *Ideas for Australian Cities*. Georgian House, Melbourne, 1975.

Suttles, G. 'Friendship as a social institution', in G. McCall (ed.), *Social Relationships*. Aldine, Chicago, 1970.

Thompson, E. P. *The Making of the English Working Class*. Penguin, Harmondsworth, 1968.

Thorne, B. & Yalom, M. (eds). *Rethinking the Family: Some Feminist Questions*. Longman, New York, 1982.

Thorns, D. *Suburbia*. MacGibbon & Kee, London, 1972.

Ward, T. 'Comment on Jim Kemeny's "Home ownership and finance capital"'. *Journal of Australian Political Economy*, no. 3, 1978.

Watson, S. *Accommodating Inequality: Gender and Housing*. Allen & Unwin, Sydney, 1988.

Wearing, B. Beyond the ideology of motherhood: Leisure as resistance. Paper to the annual conference of the Sociological Association of Australia and New Zealand, Canberra, 1988.

Wearing, B. *The Ideology of Motherhood*. Allen & Unwin, Sydney, 1983.

Werthman, C., Mandel, J. S. & Dienstfrey, T. *Planning and the Purchase Decision: Why People Buy in Planned Communities*. University of California Institute of Urban and Regional Development, Berkeley, Calif., 1965.

Wild, R. *Australian Community Studies and Beyond*. Allen & Unwin, Sydney, 1981.

Williams, C. *Open Cut*. Allen & Unwin, Sydney, 1983.

Williams, P. 'The politics of property: Home ownership in Australia', in J. Halligan & C. Paris (eds), *Australian Urban Politics: Critical Perspectives*, Longman Cheshire, Melbourne, 1984.

Wilmott, P. & Young, M. *Family and Class in a London Suburb*. Nel Mentor, London, 1967.

Wireman, P. *Urban Neighbourhoods, Networks and Families*. D. C. Heath, Lexington, Mass., 1984.

Women and Geography Study Group. *Geography and Gender: An Introduction to Feminist Geography*. Hutchinson, London, 1984.

Yeatman, A. 'Gender and the differentiation of social life into public and domestic domains'. *Social Analysis*, no. 15, 1984, pp. 32–49.

Young, C. *The Family Life Cycle*. Australian Family Formation Project, monograph no. 6, Australian National University, Canberra, 1986.

Young, M. & Wilmott, P. *Family and Kinship in East London*. Penguin, Harmondsworth, 1962.

Index